1972

h

THE AGE OF JOHNSON

THE AGE OF JOHNSON

Essays Presented to
Chauncey Brewster Tinker

Edited by Frederick W. Hilles

Introduction by Wilmarth S. Lewis

NEW HAVEN AND LONDON: YALE UNIVERSITY PRESS

Copyright 1949 by Yale University Press.
Second printing, August 1964.
Printed in the United States of America by
The Carl Purington Rollins Printing-Office of the
Yale University Press, New Haven, Connecticut.

CONTENTS

PART IV. OTHER ASPECTS OF THE AGE

FOREWORD

THIS book was presented to Mr. Tinker at a festive occasion on Shrove Tuesday in 1949. He had at that time retired from teaching but was still Keeper of Rare Books in the Yale University Library, a position that he continued to hold for the rest of his life. He died in his eighty-seventh year on 17 March 1963, after surviving some of those who had contributed essays in his honor.

The book has become something of a collector's item. Long out of print, it is now reissued without any textual changes and is dedicated to the memory of one of the great teachers of the twentieth century.

F. W. H.

New Haven, Connecticut
February 1964

FOREWORD

INTRODUCTION

Wilmarth Sheldon Lewis

THIS book was projected several years ago. It was then hoped to have it ready to present to Mr. Tinker on his retirement from teaching in June, 1945. Professor Hilles was to have been, as he has now become, the editor of the undertaking, but the war intervened.

To give the book a unity that *Festschriften* sometimes lack, it was confined to "The Age of Johnson." Although Mr. Tinker's own published work ranges from Beowulf to Housman, with, especially of late years, notable contributions to the study of the nineteenth-century poets, it is perhaps as an "eighteenth-century man" that his influence has been strongest. What would happen to the teaching of the Age of Johnson in this country if all his students were removed from our college and university faculties?

Except for Dean Simonds and myself, the contributors are former members of Professor Tinker's course, "The Age of Johnson," in the Yale Graduate School. Most of them elected Mr. Tinker as the supervisor of their doctoral dissertations and virtually all of them have, as the saying goes, "remained in the eighteenth century." Some years ago the leading article in *The Times Literary Supplement* spoke of "the Yale School of Eighteenth-century Scholars." The author of it mentioned Mr. Tinker, but he was also thinking of Mr. Tinker's colleagues, Wilbur Cross and Professor Nettleton, whose work on Sterne, Fielding, and Sheridan is part of the solid structure of eighteenth-century research and criticism. Nor should we forget, in a review of Yale's pioneer contributions to eighteenth-century studies, the work of Lounsbury, Beers, and Phelps. When "The Age of Johnson" appeared in the University's Courses of Study pamphlet the ground for it had been well prepared.

In the last century scholars, with a few notable exceptions, regarded the eighteenth century as a poor relation of its elder sisters. Then, in 1922, appeared *Young Boswell* and *Nature's Simple Plan*. The eighteenth century, or one should say more specifically, the second half of the eighteenth century, became not only respectable but exciting. Bliss was it in that dawn to be alive. We all had the feeling that we were gallant persons rescuing a beautiful young lady guarded by a dragon named Macaulay.

Although I had not the privilege of taking the graduate "Age of Johnson," various of its former members have told me what happened in it—Mr. Tinker himself has told me. It was limited to about six students a year and was divided into two sections that met fortnightly. At these two-hour sessions each student read aloud a ten-minute paper—exactly ten minutes—on a subject that he had been given. The subjects were almost anything dealing with the literary life of the eighteenth century. Frequently Mr. Tinker gave a student a MS from his own library to edit or lent him a book that suggested a bibliographical problem. Mr. A read his paper, probably with considerable nervousness, and when it was over it was called to his attention whether or not he had failed to make full use of his ten minutes or had exceeded his allotted time. If Mr. A in his paper on, let us say, Lady Diana Beauclerk, failed to indicate the significance of her gypsies and chubby innocents in the eighteenth-century scene, he probably was not chided for it, but if he mispronounced any word or used a careless expression or phrase, that was quickly brought to his attention. Stated thus the course sounds pedestrian and unimaginative. Exactly the opposite was the case.

If one were to choose a single word to describe Mr. Tinker's teaching, I think the word would be exciting. This word fits his teaching whether he taught in his own library or in the ancient fastness of A-1 Osborn Hall, where in the undergraduate "Age of Johnson" he lectured twice a week to two hundred and more. He came to every class that he ever taught with the trepidation and nervousness of a great actor. Suppose he should fail? This apprehension gave to his teaching a high voltage of electrical current that stimulated even the most lumpish of his auditors.

For many years he taught two sections of Freshman English, of about thirty students each. The course was largely his handiwork. The first term was given over to Shakespeare: in my year we began with *Henry IV, Part I,* and then read *Romeo and Juliet, Much Ado About Nothing, King Lear,* and *The Tempest.* The second term we read Carlyle, Ruskin, and Tennyson—a selection of authors that did not go uncriticized by some of Mr. Tinker's colleagues. But the fact of the matter is that Mr. Tinker could have taught Mother Goose or the telephone book and produced an electric effect upon his auditors.

My first class with Mr. Tinker was also my first class at Yale College. On the top floor of Phelps Hall I found sitting in a chair on the platform a young man dressed in what seemed to me then, and I have no doubt that I was correct, the height of fashion. He sat there motionless, bent over a book, while we took our seats and waited for the class to begin. When the Chapel clock struck the half hour he pushed back his chair with a loud scrape, went to the door, and banged it shut. Returning, he began briskly, "Shakespeare has dated this play for us in the first speech. Did anybody notice what it was?" I had spent enough time on the preparation of the assignment to know it by heart. I recalled

> those blessed feet
> Which fourteen hundred years ago were nail'd
> For our advantage on the bitter cross,

but I hadn't the courage to raise my hand and say so. Neither had anyone else, and Mr. Tinker had to read the passage himself. From then on we were caught up in a rush of excitement. Now, after thirty-five years, I can feel the pulse and beat of that first hour and I can recall more things "Tink" taught us on subsequent days than were taught me by all my other instructors put together.

When I was in college there was a certain hangdog, apologetic air about many of the classrooms at Yale. Above the proscenium in Lampson Lyceum was the line

Non Studiis Sed Vitae Discimus.

That was a suitable motto for the place: at Yale life was the thing and not scholarship. The main business of the undergraduates was outside the classrooms, for outside one practiced the art of getting on with his fellow-men. But Mr. Tinker took a different view of what was important at Yale. In his view a classroom was a place where young men were stirred up, where they were taught to think, and where they were shown the beauty and significance of English literature. He made large demands upon his students and he saw to it that they were fulfilled. He was a "hard" teacher, a disciplinarian. If you did not put in two hours of intensive preparation for each class you would not do well in it and you wanted to do well in it. The undergraduates respected "Tink" since they could not fool him; he pounced upon any slackness or dereliction with wonderful swiftness, and they liked it. The minute pains he took with every lecture or recitation was, they sensed, flattering. He was "a character"; but he conveyed to them, beneath a frequently sharp and injured manner, a warm and affectionate interest. It is impossible for his thousands of students to picture Yale without him.

Mr. Tinker's bibliography is a remarkably long one. Few people have any conception of how much he has written. He takes a modest view of it. He says, "I shall be remembered for my students." The students he has in mind are his former graduate students. He is very proud of them. "These," he will say with a familiar wave of the hand, "are my jewels."

Books of this sort tend to have a valedictory air, but, happily, it is absent here. Mr. Tinker is as active as ever he was, in his library, and in the Rare Book Room. To him enter now a group of his former students with this book, the modest return for what he has given them. They have come from their teaching posts in California and Florida, Oregon, England, Georgia, Canada, and many other places far from New Haven. They hand him their present with some apprehension. Will he like it? Will he think it well done? They regard the judge once more with terror, gratitude, and affection. What an alarming and delightful friendship it has been! That it may last forever is the wish of all who have known "The Age of Johnson"!

PART I

THE CLUB

JOHNSON'S VILE MELANCHOLY

Katharine C. Balderston

IT is only in our time that the seriousness of Dr. Johnson's life-
long struggle against deep-rooted psychic maladjustment has
been adequately recognized. Boswell, of course, knew of his
"vile melancholy, inherited from his father," and that Johnson
considered that it had made him "mad half his life—at least not
sober"; [1] but he uneasily protests against Johnson's confounding
this melancholy with madness.[2] The eighteenth century was just
emerging from the demoniacal superstition concerning madness,
and held firmly, among its otherwise conflicting views on the subject, only to the theory that it was physical in origin. The modern
conception of the functional disorders of the mind and their intimate connection with "insanity" was to receive its first impulse
from Pinel and Mesmer after Johnson's death, and was, of course,
not fully formulated until the time of Kraepelin and Freud.[3] Boswell, then, in defending Johnson against his own conviction of
near-madness, was speaking according to the view of his own age.
Even as late as 1887 the acute G. B. Hill thought that Boswell himself had exaggerated Johnson's constitutional melancholy.[4] Recent
critics, and in particular W. B. C. Watkins,[5] equipped with the
insights of modern psychiatry, have read the evidence more profoundly and have convincingly demonstrated the dark and painful
struggle of Johnson's inner life against pathological fears of death
and a sense of mortal sin. These later studies have also confirmed
in detail Walter Raleigh's observation, made in 1907, in his significant Leslie Stephen lecture on Johnson, that the peculiar impres-
siveness of Johnson's observations on life springs in large part from
their having been drawn from his own painful experience. But

1. Boswell, *Life of Johnson,* ed. G. B. Hill, revised and enlarged ed. by L. F. Powell
(Oxford, 1934), V, 215.
2. *Ibid.,* III, 175–176.
3. *Cf.* Gregory Zilboorg, *A History of Medical Psychology* (1941), chaps. vii–xi.
4. *Life,* II, 262, n. 2.
5. *Perilous Balance* (Princeton University Press, 1939), §§ 2, 3, 4.

neither Raleigh nor Watkins, nor any other modern critic, knew as much about the personal tragedy of Johnson's inner life, the cause of it, or the extent of his triumph over it as I believe may now be inferred from the evidence at hand.

This evidence, all relating to Johnson's fear of insanity and to his behavior during the recurrent crises of his melancholia (which is mostly to be found in the pages of Mrs. Thrale's diary, and the footnotes thereto),[6] has not hitherto been formally assembled and examined. It is scattered, dark, and difficult to interpret, which may account for the fact that it has been overlooked by the two important studies [7] of Johnson made since the publication of the diary. Moreover, the weight of the evidence is cumulative; no one item, taken by itself, could be viewed as significant. One further obstacle confronts the lay critic who attempts to interpret the evidence —that it belongs to the field of the clinical psychologist. Previous attempts, however, of professional psychiatrists [8] with one exception [9] have lacked sufficient knowledge and insight to reach conclusions which can satisfy any close student of Johnson's life and works. They have necessarily lacked also the particular information with which this article is to deal. I shall therefore present that information, and conclude with a layman's opinion as to how the

6. *Thraliana,* ed. Balderston (Oxford, 1942), pp. 203 and n. 2, 205 and n. 6, 384 and n. 4, 386, n. 2, 415, n. 4, 423, 625 and n. 4, 728 and n. 1.

7. J. W. Krutch, *Samuel Johnson* (1944) and B. H. Bronson, *Johnson Agonistes* (1946). C. E. Vulliamy's *Ursa Major* (1947) does make use of the facts in *Thraliana* but so wrongheadedly that I disregard it.

8. R. M. Ladell, "The Neurosis of Dr. Samuel Johnson," *British Journal of Medical Psychology* (1929), IX, Pt. IV, 314–323; Edward Hitschmann, "Samuel Johnson's Character, a Psychoanalytic Interpretation," *Psychoanalytic Review* (1945), XXXV, 207–218.

9. W. Russell Brain, "A Post-mortem on Dr. Johnson," *London Hospital Gazette* (1934), XXXVII, 225–230, 288–289. Dr. Brain, after pointing out the long-recognized fact that Johnson's odd physical habits were produced by a *tic,* or compulsion neurosis, examines his melancholia and comes to the conclusion that it, too, was a result of a psychic compulsion neurosis. He suggests three possible psychiatric explanations of the basic cause: a Freudian one—that Johnson was the victim of an Oedipus complex; an Adlerian one— that he suffered from an inferiority complex caused by his physical and social handicaps, which thwarted his ambition and his obvious intellectual superiority; and a Jungian one, of an unresolved conflict between his uncompromising rationalism and his strong, uncontrolled, and misunderstood emotional drives. Brain cautiously (and I believe quite rightly) refuses to commit himself, since all three theories have much evidence to support them. He seems to me to have recognized the complexity of Johnson's case as no one else has, though his study is extremely brief. My attention was directed to this article as well as to those cited in the previous footnote, by Mr. Herman Liebert.

facts may be interpreted as a factor in Johnson's complex neurotic difficulties. My analysis makes no pretense at a final clinical diagnosis; but I am sure that no such final clinical diagnosis can be made without taking into account the evidence I shall here present.

Before presenting this evidence to the reader, I should remind him that in her published account of Johnson Mrs. Thrale-Piozzi revealed nothing that Boswell himself could fairly have taken exception to (although G. B. Hill thought that he alluded to her and Hawkins in that passage of the *Life* [10] where he accuses "some" of Johnson's friends of giving credit to his groundless fear of insanity from a desire to depreciate him). The passage from her *Anecdotes of Johnson* shows her solicitous, as was Boswell, to indicate that his fear of insanity was only a "disease of the imagination":

Mr. Johnson's health had been always extremely bad since I first knew him, and his over-anxious care to retain without blemish the perfect sanity of his mind, contributed much to disturb it. He had studied medicine diligently in all its branches; but had given particular attention to the diseases of the imagination, which he watched in himself with a solicitude destructive of his own peace, and intolerable to those he trusted. Dr. Lawrence told him one day, that if he would come and beat him once a week he would bear it; but to hear his complaints was more than *man* could support. 'Twas therefore that he tried, I suppose, and in eighteen years contrived to weary the patience of a *woman*.[11]

This cumulative evidence, hinting at an untold chapter in Johnson's life, and in his relations to Mrs. Thrale, should be considered in the order of the dates attached to the separate items. First, there is an object which I know only by its description in the catalogue [12] of the sale of Mrs. Piozzi's library, which took place in Manchester after her death, in 1823. It was a padlock, to which was attached a label reading: "Johnson's padlock, committed to my care in 1768." Next, there is an entry of Johnson's in his pocket diary for 1771,[13] cast in Latin (as Johnson often did with matters of weight or privacy), "De pedicis et manicis insana cogitatio," which can be

10. *Life*, I, 66 and n. 2.

11. *Johnsonian Miscellanies*, ed. Hill, I, 199–200.

12. Preserved in the Rylands Library collection, listed as English MS 613. The item in the catalogue is No. 649.

13. Belonging to the Isham collection.

translated only as "insane thought about foot-fetters and manacles."
Third, there is the curious letter written in French by Johnson to
Mrs. Thrale while staying at Streatham in 1773, during the last illness of Mrs. Thrale's mother, and Mrs. Thrale's no less curious reply
to it, both of which were first published (Mrs. Thrale's only in part)
by J. D. Wright, in the *Rylands Library Bulletin*.[14] They were
cautiously commented on by Wright, who was frankly bewildered
by them, and also by J. L. Clifford, in his admirable biography of
Mrs. Piozzi, and by Watkins.[15] None of these critics could understand them, since, taken alone, they tell an unintelligible tale. Since
they are important in this story, and are relatively inaccessible in
print, I give them here entire. Johnson writes:[16]

Madame Trés Honorée
   Puisque, pendant que je me trouve chez vous, il faut passer, tous les jours,
plusieures heures dans une solitude profonde, dites moi, Si vous voulez que
je vogue[17] a plein abandon, ou que je me contienne dans des bornes pre-
scrite. S'il vous plait, ma tres chere maîtresse, que je sois lassè a hazard. La
chose est faite. Vous vous souvenez de la sagesse de nôtre ami, *Si je ferai &c.*
Mais, si ce n'est trop d'esperer que je puisse être digne, comme auparavant,
des soins et de la protection d'une ame si aimable par sa doceur, et si venerable
par son elevation, accordez moi, par un petit ecrit, la connoissance de ce que
m'est permis, et que m'est interdit. Et s'il vous semble mieux que je demeure
dans un certain lieu, je vous supplie de m'epargner la necessité de me con-
traindre, en m'ôtant le pouvoir de sortir d'ou vou[s] voulez que je sois. Ce
que vous ne coûtera que la peine de tourner le clef dans la porte, deux fois
par jour. Il faut agir tout a fait en Maîtresse, afin que vôtre jugement et
vôtre vigilance viennent a secours de ma faiblesse.
   Pour ce que regarde la table, j'espere tout de vôtre sagesse et je crains tout
de vôtre douceur. Tournez, Madame tres honorèe vos pensèes de ce côte la.
Il n'y a pour vous rien de difficile; vous pourrez inventer une regime prati-
quable sans bruit, et efficace sans peril.
   Est ce trop de demander d'une ame belle qu'est la vôtre, que, maîtresse des
autres, elle devienne maîtresse de soy-même, et qu'elle triomphe de cette in-
constance, qui a fait si souvent, qu'elle a negligèe l'execution de ses propres

14. "Some Unpublished Letters to and from Dr. Johnson," *The Bulletin of the John
Rylands Library* (1932), XVI, Pt. I, 33–34, 61–65. Johnson's letter will appear in R. W.
Chapman's forthcoming edition of the letters as No. 307.1. The full text of Mrs. Thrale's
letter appears in *Thraliana*, p. 384, n. 4.
   15. *Hester Lynch Piozzi (Mrs. Thrale)* (Oxford, Clarendon Press, 1941), pp. 102–103.
Watkins, *op. cit.*, p. 92.
   16. The uncertain French accents and sentence divisions are preserved as written.
   17. *Sic.* "Vague" is obviously intended.

lois, qu'elle a oubliée tant de promesses, et qu'elle m'a condamnè a tant de solicitations reiterèes que la resouvenance me fait horreur. Il faut ou accorder, ou refuser; il faut se souvenir de ce qu'on accorde. Je souhaite, ma patronne, que vôtre autoritè me soit toûjours sensible, et que vous me tiennez dans l'esclavage que vou[s] sçavez si bien rendre heureuse

Permettez moi l'honneur d'être
Madame
Vôtre très obeissant serviteur.

To this amazing epistle, sent, it must be remembered, to a hostess under the same roof, and probably written in French for the sake of guarding it from the curiosity of a servant, Mrs. Thrale replied:

What Care can I promise my dear Mr. Johnson that I have not already taken? What Tenderness that he had not already experienced? yet it is a very gloomy reflexion that so much of bad prevails in our best enjoyments, and embitters the purest friendship. You were saying but on Sunday that of all the unhappy you was the happiest, in consequence of my Attention to your Complaint; and to day I have been reproached by you for neglect, and by myself for exciting that generous Confidence which prompts you to repose all Care on me, and tempts you to neglect yourself, and brood in secret upon an Idea hateful in itself, but which your kind partiality to me has unhappily rendered pleasing.—If it be possible shake off these uneasy Weights, heavier to the Mind by far than Fetters to the body. Let not your fancy dwell thus upon Confinement and severity.—I am sorry you are obliged to be so much alone; I foresaw some ill Consequences of your being here while my Mother was dying thus; yet could not resist the temptation of having you near me, but if you find this irksome and dangerous Idea fasten upon your fancy, leave me to struggle with the loss of one Friend, and let me not put to hazard what I esteem beyond kingdoms, and value beyond the possession of them.—If we go on together your Confinement will be as strict as possible except when Company comes in, which I shall more willingly endure on your Account. Dissipation is to you a glorious Medicine, and I believe Mr. Boswell will be at last your best Physician. For the rest you really are well enough now if you will keep so; and not suffer the noblest of human minds to be tortured with fantastic notions which rob it of all its Quiet.—I will detain you no longer, so farewell and be good; and do not quarrel with your Governess for not using the Rod enough. H.L.T.

These letters require a fuller analysis than the limits of this article allow. Their exact meaning cannot, of course, be recovered at this late date. But it is clear that the tone of Dr. Johnson's letter is abnormal—both in respect to his usual sturdy independence of mind and conduct and in respect to any normal standard of human intercourse. His dependence on her is supine, his subjection to her all but servile. He seems to crave this subjection as to a superior being, seeking and ensuing a "slavery" which she, and apparently she only, can "render happy." His one fear is that she will not make her rule severe enough; his one rebuke that she has subjected him, by her inconstancy in her office, to reiterated supplications whose remembrance horrifies him. It is a pathological document, the product of a sick mind. In her reply, tactful, tender, and respectful as it is, she shows that she fully recognizes the abnormality and danger of his state of mind. She shows also a clear recognition of the fact that his "kind partiality" to her is a grave complicating factor in the obsession which is driving him to "confinement and severity," since her administration of the discipline renders the idea pleasing to him, when he should be aroused to combat it. Mrs. Thrale's dilemma was clearly a painful and delicate one, torn as she must have been between her disinterested devotion to him, her common-sensical recognition of the dangers involved, the paramount need not to expose his condition by seeking counsel elsewhere, and the perhaps unrecognized flattery to her undeniable vanity which this extraordinary relationship must have given her. Clearly, too, both letters show that the situation here depicted was not an isolated or unique one. Johnson begs that he be considered worthy of her protection "comme auparavant," rebukes her for displaying inconstancy "si souvent," and is anguished by the recollection of his "solicitations reiterèes." She in turn has *foreseen* the trouble which might arise in bringing him to Streatham at a time when her mother's illness forced her to neglect him. Is it possible to avoid the conclusion that these letters of 1773 reveal only an episode of a long case history of which the padlock entrusted to her in 1768 and the enigmatic entry in Johnson's notebook for 1771 were earlier witnesses?

But the evidence for this abnormal aspect of Johnson's life does not stop here. There are confirmatory, and it seems to me conclusive, allusions to it in Mrs. Thrale's diary. These allusions are cryptic, oblique, and widely scattered, but their very intrusion, against

Mrs. Thrale's conscious intention to keep the whole matter secret, is a testimony to their importance and their truth.

A study of these allusions shows that Mrs. Thrale had been Johnson's confidante in his painful secret since 1768, but that she regarded his confidence as too sacred a trust to betray even in her private journal. Until Johnson's death she had thought herself the sole possessor of the knowledge that Johnson feared insanity; but when she read Thomas Tyers' account of him in the *Gentleman's Magazine* for December, 1784 (where that fear is alluded to), she wrote: "Poor Johnson! I see they will leave *nothing untold* that I laboured so long to keep secret; & I was so very delicate in trying to conceal his fancied Insanity, that I retained no Proofs of it—or hardly any [18]—nor ever mentioned it in these Books, lest by dying first *they* might be printed and the Secret (for such I thought it) discovered." [19] Her profession to have made no allusions to it in the diary was made in good faith, although, as I have already indicated, the pressure of the secret was too great to allow her feminine vanity to conceal it completely. The first oblique but unmistakable comment [20] appears in her diary for May, 1779, where it appears as a casual instance of men's general proclivity to find themselves, at some period of their lives, under the dominion of a woman:

Our stern Philosopher Johnson trusted me about the Years 1767 or 1768—I know not which just now—with a Secret far dearer to him than his Life: such however is his nobleness, & such his partiality, that I sincerely believe he has never since that Day regretted his Confidence, or ever looked with less kind Affection on her who had him in her Power.—Uniformly great is the Mind of that incomparable Mortal; & well does he contradict the Maxim of Rochefoucault, that no Man is a Hero to his Valet de Chambre.—Johnson is more a Hero to me than to any one—& I have been more to him for Intimacy, than ever was any Man's Valet de Chambre. [21]

In December of this same year she wrote: "How many Times has this great, this formidable Doctor Johnson kissed my hand, ay & my

18. This exception evidently allowed for her preservation of the padlock (which she kept until her death) and possibly also of Dr. Johnson's letter.

19. *Thraliana*, p. 625.

20. Earlier but less demonstrable allusions occur, I believe, on pp. 203 and 205.

21. *Thraliana*, pp. 384–385.

foot too upon his knees! Strange Connections there are in this odd World! his with me is mere *Interest* tho';—he loves Miss Reynolds better." And to this astonishing passage she added an explanatory gloss (I doubt not after Johnson's death, when the dissemination of his "secret" had weakened her sense of responsibility for conceal-ment): "a dreadful & little suspected Reason for *ours,* God knows —but the Fetters & Padlocks will tell Posterity the Truth." [22] One cannot escape the ominous refrain of the fetters and padlocks in this unrecorded chapter of Johnson's life.

But there is yet a darker hint of Johnson's pathological condition in the diary, in the same entry where she first alludes to his con-fiding his secret to her, and again disguised in general terms, and given its pointed application by a marginal gloss which I assume, as in the case of the one cited above, to have been added after John-son's death. She writes: "And yet says Johnson a Woman has *such* power between the Ages of twenty five and forty five, that She may tye a Man to a post and whip him if She will." The marginal com-ment on this is: "This he knew of him self was *literally* and *strictly* true I am sure." [23] At this point one is bound to inquire whether Mrs. Thrale's role, beyond that of jailer and turnkey, was not also that of beater; and whether her allusion in the letter ("do not quarrel with your Governess for not using the Rod enough") was literal rather than figurative.

The evidence is now stated and the delicate and difficult task of interpretation at hand. A thoroughgoing interpretation would necessitate a complete re-examination of Johnson's private life and emotional history—a study which I believe is very much needed but which the space limits of this article forbid. I can only assert that such study as I have made of that history, in the light of the evidence here assembled, leads me to believe that the root of his neurotic difficulties, his torturing melancholy, and his despairing sense of guilt was not his indolence and love of food and drink (as Watkins would have us believe) [24] but a strong amorous na-ture severely repressed after his wife's death. Also, a study of all

22. *Ibid.*, p. 415 and n. 4.
23. *Ibid.*, p. 386 and n. 2.
24. *Op. cit.*, "The Castle of Indolence."

Johnson's pronouncements on and descriptions of melancholy and madness [25] shows conclusively that his conception of madness involved only one type—the type that I believe he discovered incipiently in himself—that which arose from obsessive indulgence in culpable fantasy, which aroused melancholy despair in the victim, and finally impaired or destroyed his sense of reality. The only point at which I should expect to find shocked disagreement concerns the type of fantasy which Johnson himself found so compulsive and which, from his inability to conquer its dominion, drove him so close to despair, since he believed that the mind was its own master and morally responsible for the sinful ideas which it contemplated.[26] I am convinced that the weight of evidence indicates that these fantasies were erotic in their nature. With Boswell, I would deny that his sense of guilt arose from "such little venial trifles as pouring milk into his tea on Good-Friday." [27]

Certainly the peculiarities of his conduct in relation to Mrs. Thrale, reviewed in this article, must have sprung from erotic maladjustment. It takes no Freudian to point this out. At the crises of his illness it seems inescapably evident that his compulsive fantasy assumed a masochistic form, in which the impulse to self-abasement and pain predominated. The fetters, the padlocks, and the whippings, which must be inflicted by the beloved object, are phenomena fairly commonplace in the records of sex pathology. The quoted letter has all the stigmata of the masochist's state of mind as described by Krafft-Ebing:

"a peculiar perversion of the psychical *vita sexualis* in which the individual affected, in sexual feeling and thought, is controlled by the idea of being completely and unconditionally subject to the will of a person of the opposite sex, of being treated by this person as by a master, humiliated and abused. This idea is colored by sexual feeling; the masochist lives in fancies in which he creates situations of this kind, and he often attempts to realize them.[28]

If the reader is shocked into repudiating the inferences I have drawn, out of tenderness for Johnson's memory and reverence

25. See especially *Ramblers* 85 and 89; *Idler* 32; *Rasselas*, chaps. xli–xliii; *The Vision of Theodore; Life*, III, 175–176; IV, 208.
26. See especially *Rambler* 8.
27. *Life*, IV, 397.
28. *Psychopathia Sexualis*, tr. Rebman (Chicago, Login Brothers, 1908), p. 115.

for his character, let me remind him that there is no slightest shred
of evidence that Johnson, in the extremities of his dependence,
ever gave Mrs. Thrale cause for offense. He must have acted
throughout with uniform probity and dignity, which aroused her
admiration rather than her repugnance. It will be remembered that
she said in this connection, "Johnson is more a Hero to me than to
any one." And we may justly infer that this was because of, and
not in spite of, those services to him which were more intimate
than those of a valet de chambre. It seems certain to me that Mrs.
Thrale, although complacently assured of Johnson's devotion to
her and alarmed at the abnormality of his obsession, had not the
slightest awareness of the erotic pathology underlying his "hateful
idea" and her own role of "governess." She never thought of Johnson's attachment to her in any other light than that of "kind
partiality," and in her moods of resentment she thought of his
dependence as "mere Interest . . . he loves Miss Reynolds better."
Her ministrations were only those of a person who could help to
distract and allay his morbid fears of insanity—and whose efforts
to do so for eighteen years at last wore out her patience.

I am not so sure of the extent of Johnson's own comprehension
of his malady, but I believe that he could have been only partially
aware, if at all, of its hidden implications. The medical science
of Johnson's own day did not, of course, as yet recognize the malady
or the symptoms. The clearest clue to Johnson's own understanding
of his case which is available to us (in lieu of those two destroyed
quarto volumes whose loss, as he told Boswell, would have made
him go mad) [29] is the following important pronouncement of
Johnson, which, moreover, confirms, out of his own mouth, the
inferences I have drawn from the other evidence for this unsus-
pected phase of his life. It is that "serious Conversation on melancholy and madness" which he and Boswell held at Ashbourne, in
1777:

He [Johnson] said Gaubius's saying to me that a man was not mad when he
was conscious of an excessive disorder in his imagination, was not just, for
that a man often has consciousness of his situation when mad; nay, almost
in every case had it. Said he: "A man indulges his imagination while it is

29. *Life,* IV, 405–406.

pleasing, till at length it overpowers his reason." This I have experienced frequently in a certain degree. He said, "A Madman loves to be with people whom he fears; not as a dog fears the lash, but of whom he stands in awe." This I almost ever experience . . . I was glad to hear it philosophically mentioned by Dr. Johnson. He said, "Madmen are all sensual in the lower stages of the distemper. But when they are very ill, pleasure is too weak for them, and they seek pain." [30]

This passage, read many times before, struck me with astonishment when I first read it in the light of the facts assembled in this article. It is, as are all Johnson's comments on "madness," clearly a commentary on his own case, though Boswell, like the generations of his readers, was far from suspecting it. The significant point is that he here adds an all-revealing coda to his other comments on the inception and progress of diseased imagination—that climactic stage of "seeking pain." Behind this remark we may see the shadow of the padlocks, the fetters, and the whipping post—compulsions which were explicable to him only as evidences of madness and which he judged unsparingly as such. And as for the role of Mrs. Thrale—I infer that she is the being whom the "madman" loves to be with, because of the awe in which he holds her. She was at once, I surmise, the unrecognized erotic object from whose ministrations his maladjusted libido sought relief and at the same time, to his conscious mind, the revered woman, object of his awed respect and adoration, who by her very virtue could in some mysterious fashion check his abnormalities and exorcise his devils. I doubt not that unless Dr. Johnson had thus misinterpreted and rationalized his obsession, his stern moral rectitude would have prevented his seeking her help. I have sought no psychiatrist's opinion as to whether such a self-deception is plausible, or to be paralleled in the annals of psychiatric case histories. But from what I know of the ingenuity of the unconscious mind in general, and of Dr. Johnson's particular moral and emotional complexity, it seems to me a defensible hypothesis. Perhaps it is not too rash to hazard the further guess that Johnson's well-known exaggerated devotion to a succes-

30. *Private Papers of James Boswell from Malahide Castle in the Collection of Lt. Col. Ralph H. Isham*. Prepared for the press by Geoffrey Scott and Frederick A. Pottle, in 19 volumes (New York, privately printed, 1928–36), XIII, 41. I cite this version rather than the parallel one in *Life*, III, 175–176, since it contains some matter omitted in the later version.

sion of high-minded and virtuous women—Molly Aston, Hill Boothby, and his wife in particular—as well as to Mrs. Thrale, had its obscure root in this psychic need.

If my inferences come anywhere near the truth, they seem to me to explain, as nothing advanced by Johnson's biographers has been able to explain, the violence of his repudiation of Mrs. Thrale when she married Piozzi. Neither the loss of his creature comforts, nor the disruption of the only domestic happiness he had ever known, nor his doubtless sincere conviction of her rash imprudence and failure in her duty to her children, nor even the wound she inflicted on that half-paternal, half-romantic love of her which his biographers have recognized quite explains his irrational and unjust behavior at that juncture. He acted like a man wounded to the quick, who could find relief only by stamping on her memory. And he acted also like a man in a panic, and so I believe he was. What greater blow to his ego could he have had than to be deserted by the woman to whom he had abjectly exposed his uttermost weakness? And what greater blow to his security than to discover that the object of his idolatry, whose supposed superiority to the temptations of the flesh had been his own bulwark, was a mere mortal with clay feet? Like Othello's, his relief must be to loathe her.

JAMES BOSWELL, JOURNALIST

Frederick A. Pottle

JAMES BOSWELL has been known as biographer for more than 150 years, but it is only in the last twenty that we have acquired the means of knowing him as journalist. It is too soon to say what rank will be assigned to his journal as an independent work of art, but one conclusion is already clearly indicated. Any investigation of the development of the method displayed in the *Life of Johnson* will end as a study of the journal. Without depreciating the superior reputation which the *Life* will probably always hold and will probably always deserve, it is still necessary to say that Boswell's primary literary achievement is to be sought elsewhere. The *Life of Johnson* is, in a very real sense, a development of his journal.

If a man who has read a good many of the great English biographies sets himself to answer the question: "What is it that gives the *Life of Johnson* its unique distinction as literature?" I can imagine him in the end returning only one answer: "The conversations." This is not to say that the handling of other portions of the work is not competent and often brilliant; it is merely to say that other biographers seem to have handled everything else about as well as Boswell. Some things perhaps even better. The construction of the *Life,* for example, is remarkably inartificial.[1] Boswell adopts a mechanically chronological scheme, which, with the year 1740, settles down to an annual review, each section baldly headed by the year and Johnson's age in that year. Within this loose and accommodating framework are inserted, with relatively few editorial exclusions, all Johnson's letters that Boswell could come at, excepting the letters to Mrs. Piozzi, which, as a group, were probably inaccessible to him for reasons of copyright, and which he would in

---

1. I first heard this observation made many years ago by Colonel Isham, the owner of the Boswell Papers, at a time when I myself was unfamiliar with the journals. I wish also to record general indebtedness to Geoffrey Scott's brilliant study, *The Making of the Life of Johnson* (the 6th volume of the *Boswell Papers*).

any case have been unwilling to request leave to reprint.[2] To put the matter in the mildest way, the inclusion of this largely unselected mass of correspondence represented a biographer's easiest choice. In the last year of Johnson's life, just before the death, Boswell interrupts the thread of his narrative to insert "specimens of various sorts of imitations of Johnson's style," which come at that point for no better reason than that he had promised (in a part of the book already printed) to get them in somewhere, had so far found no really appropriate place, and now had to do it by force. And nearly all readers, I think, will agree that Johnson's opinions on Boswell's legal cases would better have gone in an appendix.

The *Life of Johnson* is almost continuously entertaining, but so are many other biographies. It becomes unique only in paragraphs headed by sentences like, "My next meeting with Johnson was on Friday the 1st of July," followed by dramatic conversation. And those portions of the *Life* are junks of Boswell's journal, sometimes so little changed that the original leaves of the journal served as printer's copy.

Even when this is granted, it is too often assumed that Johnson (or to be more precise, the intention to write a life of Johnson) was the force which created and formed the journal. There can no longer be any doubt that Boswell was driven to the keeping of a journal not by a desire to store materials for a life of Johnson but by a conviction that he had not lived his own life fully till he had recorded it; and it is also clear that he had demonstrated mastery of all the essential techniques of the journal several months before he met Johnson. He began keeping some kind of diary at least as early as the autumn of 1758, about the time of his eighteenth birthday. We are not yet in possession of all his early records, but enough

2. Mrs. Piozzi published the letters in March, 1788; the printing of Boswell's book began in January, 1790. Her volumes had no second edition, but the first edition may well have been in print as late as the time of the appearance of the *Life* (May, 1791). Boswell had about 340 of Johnson's letters already, and to have included in addition the more than 300 to Mrs. Piozzi would have made it impossible for him to keep his work to the two large volumes he had fixed as a limit. He could certainly have improved the *Life* by substituting some of the letters to Mrs. Piozzi for some that he did print; and I find it hard to believe that Strahan and Cadell, who had purchased the copyright, would have refused a reasonable request. But he had decided to be severe on Mrs. Piozzi, and consequently could not ask the favor.

has been recovered to indicate that they were fragmentary and, with one possible exception, unambitious.[3] On September 4, 1762 (the meeting with Johnson occurred on May 16, 1763), he began writing an elaborate continuous journal, which he continued without any gaps at least to January 30, 1765.[4] It was carefully written on quarto sheets, the entire manuscript running to nearly two thousand pages. At the outset it suffers in comparison with the later journals by not being a really private record (he was showing it to at least two friends), and by a self-conscious air which shows that he is thinking too much of literary models and is writing for literary effect. But it contains, almost fully exploited, every feature of the journal with which the Johnsonian conversations have familiarized us. Boswell's powers as a writer developed surprisingly little after his twenty-second year. The superiority of the later journal is not so much due to increased literary skill as to the fact that Boswell himself became a more interesting man as he grew older.

To specify. One of the unique features of the Johnsonian conversations in the *Life* is the vivid individuation of the speakers by swift and economical descriptive touches which have something of the character of stage directions. Here are pre-Johnsonian specimens: [5]

MR. SHAW, A RETIRED ATTORNEY, "precise, starch'd and proud. Wears a dark brown Coat, a buff vest and black bretches; has a lank iron countenance; wears a weather-beaten scratch Wig; sits erect upon his chair, and sings *Tarry Woo* with the English accent." [6]

3. On December 16, 1758 (*Letters of James Boswell*, ed. C. B. Tinker [1924], I, 6), Boswell reported to his friend Temple that he had accompanied his father on the Northern Circuit, and "at the particular desire of my friend Mr. Love," had kept "an exact journal," which had been sent to Love "in sheets, every post." This journal, which has not been recovered, may possibly have been of a finished and elaborate nature. The recovered fragments earlier than the autumn of 1762 (May 5–16, 1761, August 14–October 21, 1761, November 12, 1761–April 7, 1762, June 9–? July 30, 1762) are either what I have called elsewhere condensed journal, or rough and cryptic notes containing a good deal of shorthand cipher.

4. The entries for August 5, 1763–May 24, 1764, are missing, having been lost in Boswell's lifetime (*Boswell Papers*, VII, 125; *The Hypochondriack*, ed. Margery Bailey [1928], II, 262). Boswell's foliation indicates that the missing portion covered over 500 pages. Since there are no gaps in what has survived, it is safe to infer that the missing portion also was continuous.

5. "Pre-Johnsonian" in the sense that they were written before Boswell met Johnson in the flesh. He was already familiar with Johnson's writings.

6. *Boswell Papers*, I, 60 (September 15, 1762).

DR. COULTHARD, "an Apothecary, a true-looking Englishman with a round-cut head and leather bretches, a jolly dog who sung us a Song that the Boy sings, who sweeps Drury-lane Stage, before the candles are lighted." [7]

MISS MAXWELL, "an honest-hearted, merry, jocular girl, of size somewhat corpulent but has a very agreable countenance and can walk and dance with all imaginable cleverness." [8]

MR. RALPH CARRE, "who has been upwards of twenty years an Attorney in London, a round man with a Bob-wig, and his coat buttoned, of manners plain and somewhat vulgar. . . . He spoke too much and too minutely, took too much snuff and raised too often a kind of alehouse laugh." [9]

For conversation, the crucial pre-Johnsonian example in the Journal is the following, which I have greatly abridged:

THURSDAY 4 NOVEMBER [1762] . . . Erskine and I went and waited on David Hume. We found him in his house in James's Court, in a good room newly fitted up hung round with Strange's prints. He was sitting at his ease reading Homer. He told us that Mr. Mallet was just going to publish his life of the Duke of Marlborough, a pretty large work in two Quarto Volumes, which would throw great light on the transactions of that period; That Mr. Mallet had the best opportunities of intelligence. He had all the Marlborough papers. Lord Chesterfield carried him to the hague, where he learnt all that they knew there, and he went to Paris where he learnt what were, at the period in which Marlborough lived, the great court secrets; but might now be known to every body. Mr. Hume hoped he would be free without respect to parties; "And indeed," said he, "this is an advantageous time, as the distinction between Whig and Tory is allmost abolished. Altho' Mr. Mallett's writings possess only mediocrity, yet they discover taste and the art of Composition. Therefore," said he, "I imagine this will be a good Work." Mr. Mallet has written bad Tragedies because he is deficient in the pathetic, and hence it is doubted if he is the Author of *William and Margaret*. Mr. Hume said he knew people who had seen it before Mallet was born. Erskine gave another proof, viz that he has written *Edwin and Emma*, a Ballad in the same stile, not near so good. . . . *Fingal* is not much heard of at present. The English were exceedingly fond of it at first but hearing that it was Scotch, they became jealous and silent. Doctor Blair's *Dissertation* will awaken attention to it. It is a fine piece of criticism; but it were to be wished that he had kept it a little lower than Homer. For it might be a very excellent Poem and yet fall short of *the Iliad*. Macpherson, the Translator, is a most curious fellow. He is full of highland Prejudices. He hates a Republic and he does not like Kings.

7. *Ibid.,* I, 92 (October 11, 1762).
8. *Ibid.,* I, 89 (October 7, 1762).
9. *Ibid.,* I, 105 (October 17, 1762).

He would have all the Nation divided into Clans, and these Clans to be all-ways fighting. He has got a dislike to study and cannot settle to read a quarter of an hour. Lord Bute does not know what to do with him. He was offered a Professorship but that he refused, alledging that a studious life was the dullest of any. He would not go into the Church, altho' he was sure of being a Bishop tomorrow; and, except he could be brought in upon a particular good footing, he would not accept a commission in the Army. As he is a Scotchman, Lord Bute does not chuse to put him upon the list of Pensioners, and therefore generously gives him two hundred a year out of his own pocket. Mr. Samuel Johnson has got a Pension of £300 a year. Indeed his Dictionary was a kind of a national Work so he has a kind of claim to the Patronage of the state. His stile is particular and pedantic. He is a man of enthusiasm and antiquated notions, a keen Jacobite yet hates the Scotch. Holds the Episcopal Hierarchy in supreme veneration and said he would stand before a battery of cannon to have the Convocation restored to it's full powers. He holds Mr. Hume in ab-horrence and left a company one night upon his coming in. Garrick told Mr. Hume that Johnson past one Evening behind the Scenes in the Green room. He said he had been well entertained. Mr. Garrick therefore hoped to see him often. "No, David," said he, "I will never come back. For the white bubbies and the silk stockings of your Actresses excite my Genitals." . . . I asked Mr. Hume to write more. He said he had done enough and was allmost ashamed to see his own bulk on a Shelf. We payed him a few compliments in pleasant mirth. Thus did an hour and a half of our Existence move along. We were very happy.[10]

It will be objected that there is a prime difference between this record, almost entirely in *oratio obliqua,* and the dramatically cast conversations of the *Life:*

REYNOLDS. "A printer's devil, Sir! Why, I thought a printer's devil was a crea-ture with a black face and in rags." JOHNSON. "Yes, Sir. But I suppose, he had her face washed and put clean clothes on her. (Then looking very serious, and very earnest.) And she did not disgrace him;—the woman had a bottom of good sense." [11]

There is undoubtedly a superiority in the method of dramatic cast-ing which cannot be exaggerated, but the method was not one which Boswell worked out at the time he was writing the *Life;* it was not even one which he hit upon after he met Johnson. It occurs very early in his records, but oddly enough was at first a

10. *Ibid.,* I, 126–129.
11. *Life,* IV, 99 (April 20, 1781).

feature of his rough notes and "papers apart" [12] rather than of his elaborately finished journals. Down to (I think) the London journal of 1772 he seems to have felt that in a finished style of writing conversation had better either be reported indirectly in words which preserved "the heads and the very words of a great part" of what had been said (his own comment on the record of Hume's conversation quoted above), or given directly with appropriate narrative tags: "Said he," etc. But in the hasty and provisional style of writing which he employed for jotting down notes of conversation to be journalized later, he was likely to use the method of dramatic casting. The first extended example which I recall in the notes is a long dialogue (in French) between himself and the charming young Dutch widow Mme. Geelvinck. It was recorded at Utrecht on February 9, 1764, nine months after he met Johnson. But there is among the Isham Papers an unpublished "paper apart" containing some brilliantly finished dramatic dialogue which must have been written about April 14, 1763. It is headed "History of Erskine and Boswell's Letters" and records the comments of various of Boswell's acquaintances on his recent publication of the breezy and impudent correspondence between himself and the Honorable Andrew Erskine. I quote the section devoted to Lord Eglinton's remarks, with no editorial interference except to complete and regularize the punctuation:

LORD EGLINT. "How do you do, Jamie? Why, Jamie, you have been playing the very devil, you & Erskine. You have been publishing private letters between you." B. "My Lord, is it not something very terrible"? EGLINT. "Upon my soul, Jamie, I would not take the direction of you upon any account for as much as I like you, except you would agree to give over that damned publishing. Lady N— [13] would as soon have a Raven in her house as an Author. By G—, I heard it asserted today in a public assembly that you had done it for money. Your father would give you none, and Erskine's Regt. was going to be broke. I wonder realy at Erskine, for he seems to be a douse, sagacious fellow." B. "Poor fellow! My Lord, I've led him into the scrape. I've perswaded him." EGLINT. "He cannot be very sensible if you have perswaded

12. Boswell's own term for an isolated paper in which some portion of his autobiographical record was written up in considerable detail in advance of the posting of the journal. Such "papers apart" were seldom incorporated in the journal.

13. The Countess of Northumberland, whose patronage Boswell was at the time soliciting.

him. You must get it supprest or put in an advertisement in the papers denying it. By the Lord, it's a thing Dean Swift would not do. To publish a collection of letters upon nothing. Nor Madam Sevigné either." B. "My Lord, hers
are very fine." EGLINT. "Yes, a few at the beginning; but when you read on,
you think her a d—nd tiresom Bitch."

After 1772 this style occurs not infrequently in the fully written
journals when a conversation of any length is recorded, though
the more general method is still to use indirect discourse or direct
discourse with narrative tags. What happened in the revision of
Johnsonian passages for the *Tour* and the *Life* was that Boswell
greatly extended the use of the dramatic method. Since he had
always, even when reporting in the third person, used "the very
words of a great part" of what had been said, the revision generally
required nothing more radical than the change of pronouns and
tenses and the substitution of "JOHNSON" for "Mr. Johnson said" or
"Said he." A more delicate and crucial kind of revision consisted in
the occasional insertion into the dialogue of brief but telling stage
directions: " 'No, Sir, (said Gwyn,) I am putting the church *in* the
way, that the people may not *go out of the way.'* JOHNSON. (with a
hearty loud laugh of approbation,) 'Speak no more. Rest your
colloquial fame upon this.' " [14] But it is possible to adduce many
specimens of even this device from the original records.[15]

14. *Life,* II, 440 (March 19, 1776). In the journal (*Boswell Papers,* XI, 171–172) the
order is less effective, and no mention is made of the laugh.

15. For proof that Boswell in the preparation of the *Life* was on the alert for opportunities for this kind of dramatic heightening, see G. B. Hill in *Johnson Club Papers* (1899),
pp. 79–80. Hill shows that some of the stage directions were added as late as the revises.
For an example of stage directions in the original journal, see the delicious conversation on
the uses of dried orange peel (*Boswell Papers,* X, 171; *Life,* II, 330–331). The stage directions are altered in the revision, but there are two of them in the journal as against one in
the *Life.*

In this survey of the development of Boswell's use of dramatic casting I have simplified
in order to be clear. The first example of dramatic casting that I can find occurs in a dialogue
between Boswell and Lord Marchmont near the beginning of the journal (October 18,
1762: *Boswell Papers,* I, 106). One short speech of Lord Marchmont's is introduced by
the tag "LORD" instead of by "Said he." The next example in the journal is the conversations with Rousseau (December 3–15, 1764: *Boswell Papers,* IV, 55–117). But the dialogue
here, though more fully written than in the corresponding rough notes, has not been
brought up to the usual style of the finished journal. In his notes for the period and often
later, Boswell writes dialogue continuously without the names of the speakers; in the fully
written journal he almost never fails to assign each remark clearly to the person who made
it. The dialogues with Rousseau, besides being in places condensed to the point of obscurity, omit the speakers' names. I have no doubt that Boswell regarded this portion of

It would be interesting to know whether it was on Edmond Malone's advice that Boswell decided to use the method of dramatic casting more freely in his published Johnsoniana than in his private records. Such advice would come very appropriately from a professional student of the drama. Certain it is that Malone collaborated with Boswell in the revision of the original MS of the Hebridean Journal, the first installment of his Johnsonian biography; certain it is that much of the revision of that journal by which indirect discourse was changed to direct discourse or to dialogue is in Malone's hand. But it seems to me quite as possible that in this matter Malone was merely helping Boswell carry through a pattern he had already decided upon. What effect Malone's unrecorded oral advice may have had we shall never know, but Malone's *hand* does not appear in the manuscript until a portion of copy corresponding to 77 pages of the first edition had been completed. In those 77 pages there is much dramatic casting. We should not overlook a remark of Boswell's entered in the journal almost five years earlier: "I told Erskine I was to write Dr. Johnson's life in Scenes." [16]

his record as provisional, and that if he had polished it in 1764 he would have chosen the device of narrative tags rather than that of direct casting. The notes in London, 1766 (*Boswell Papers,* VII, 67–84), contain extended passages of dialogue dramatically cast (generally with no indication of who is speaking), and the interview with Pitt which they contain comes very close to the style of the fully written journal. But there is always something about these notes that indicates that Boswell regarded them as a provisional record. They are on pieces of paper of varying sizes; the writing is hasty; they omit and abbreviate words; they were enclosed by Boswell in a wrapper endorsed "Mems. From Paris, and so forth." And so on, down to the London Journal of 1772, where dramatically cast conversation appears abundantly in a record which has clearly received Boswell's final touches. It is entered neatly and in a large hand in a bound notebook; words (except as noted below) are not omitted or abbreviated; speakers are carefully labeled. That Boswell was conscious of a departure in method is indicated by the sentence introducing the first conversation: "I shall give what past, as much as I can, in the way of dialogue" (*Boswell Papers,* IX, 20).

It remains to add that an inexperienced investigator of Boswell's MSS, by making too much of defects of punctuation, might conclude that none of the conversation in his journal is really "finished." On the whole he punctuates the journal fully and fairly consistently, but he was always, even when preparing for the press, very cavalier in the use of marks of quotation. Generally he omits them altogether; when he does employ them, he is likely to indicate the beginning of a speech but not the end. Nor does he often write the names of speakers in full in dialogue dramatically cast, his usual style being *"Johns."* and *"Bos."* But these are not indications of provisional recording. The pointing of the dialogues in a journal like that of 1772, whatever its defects, is up to the standards of his best manuscript style. In abbreviating the names of speakers he follows the usual typographical style of the printed plays of the period.

16. *Boswell Papers,* XIV, 132 (October 12, 1780).

It is possible that the word "scenes" had its full technical sense and meant "in the style of a play." At any rate, Malone's intervention can have amounted to no more than counsel to make fuller use of a device abundantly illustrated in the original journal before him. The greater part of the conversation recorded on the page of the manuscript in which his hand first appears was already dramatically cast.

I have often been moved to wonder what literary models may be reflected in Boswell's dramatic journalizing. Hardly other private journals. Of the journals known to us, none, I think, is dramatic in his sense; besides, how many private journals were accessible to him? Court memoirs possibly: he could not have known Lord Hervey's *Memoirs,* which apart from its strongly satirical motivation, is a startlingly Boswellian handling of history,[17] but Hervey may have followed a tradition which my limited reading does not enable me to recognize. Printed plays certainly: Boswell was from an early age an enthusiastic lover of the drama. The device of printing conversation as dialogue with the names of the speakers rather than tags like "Said he" can come ultimately from no other source. But no amount of reading of the printed plays of the eighteenth century would have helped Boswell or anybody else to that minuteness of graphic depiction which he himself happily compares to a Flemish picture. It was not, I think, until the end of the nineteenth century that playwrights began to provide their readers with extended and minute stage directions.

An influence, or at least a relationship, which I wish someone would consider more thoughtfully than I can is that of the great English novelists Sterne and Fielding. Boswell read *Tristram Shandy* and met Sterne personally at an impressionable age (his twentieth year), and for some months after that meeting his own writing was heavily tinged with Shandyism.[18] The direct stylistic influence fortunately soon waned, but who better than Sterne could

17. See especially that astonishing dramatic sketch, "The Death of Lord Hervey, or, A Morning at Court," II, 585–596 of Romney Sedgwick's edition (1931). It even contains a few of the little stage directions describing characteristic gestures which Boswell uses to such good effect: "QUEEN [striking her hand upon her knee]," etc.

18. See F. A. Pottle, "Bozzy and Yorick," *Blackwood's Magazine,* CCXVII (March, 1925), 297–313.

have revealed to him the power of dialogue and the virtue of gesture? Sterne's characters are whimsical and very un-Boswellian, but his method is basically realistic: no one ever came closer to the actual idiom of conversational English; no nondramatic writer has ever maintained so perfectly the illusion of actual speech. If Boswell's own dating is to be trusted, he came to *Tom Jones* a year after his introduction to *Tristram Shandy* but still well before the inception of the journal. Some time in 1761 he heard Love, the player, read the novel—it was Love who had previously urged him to keep a journal—and was greatly impressed. He admits that when he himself read it aloud twenty years later he admired it less,[19] but I take this simply to mean that he could not duplicate the effect of Love's telling impersonation of the speakers. At any rate, whenever Fielding is mentioned by him elsewhere, it is always with the highest approbation and, more significantly, with the discriminating comment of a craftsman who acknowledges a master in his own line. His quiet but firm dissent in the *Life* from Johnson's preference of Richardson is characteristic: "Fielding's characters, though they do not expand themselves so widely in dissertation [as Richardson's], are as just pictures of human nature, and I will venture to say, have more striking features, and nicer touches of the pencil." [20] If filial piety had not held his hand, he might well have gone on to say that in the area in which he was comparing the two novelists—of course not on all counts—he considered Fielding as much the superior of Johnson as he was of Richardson. That this really was his opinion is made clear by his notes: "Read out paper of Rambler on holy thursday [April 1, 1779] . . . Said Johns cd not give real scenes of life so clean as Fielding; allways with bulk of sentiment like earth, not clean lines as in Cov Gard." [21] To find Johnson accused of muddy draftsmanship by Boswell is surprising, but the judgment is acute. Johnson's attempts at realistic portrayal in the *Rambler* (for example, the two papers on Misella) are

19. *Boswell Papers*, XV, 91 (June 29, 1782).

20. *Life*, II, 48 (March 26, 1768).

21. *Boswell Papers*, XIII, 214; "Cov Gard." is Fielding's *Covent Garden Journal*. A good specimen of the kind of essay Boswell has in mind is No. 33, nearly all in conversation: the linen draper's clerk from London masquerading as a profane beau at an inn in Somersetshire. He talks, in fact, very much like Lord Eglinton in the bit from Boswell already quoted.

blurred by interwoven moralizing; Fielding draws with swift, clean lines. And so does Boswell. In the characterizations and conversations of Fielding I find much that could have helped a young man who "wanted a Subject": who "was sure that he had genius, and was not deficient in easiness of expression; but was at a loss for something to say." [22] As a matter of fact, bond unknown to him had been given and he had already found his subject. It was his journal, that unrecognized, nameless work of art which an irresistible impulse was forcing him to create.

22. *Boswell Papers,* I, 101 (October 14, 1762). Boswell's description of himself to Lord Kames.

BOSWELL'S PORTRAIT OF BURKE

Thomas W. Copeland

I

IN the period when Boswell's artistic powers were regarded as almost purely mechanical, one could give a simple account of the lesser figures in the *Life of Johnson*. They were men who, being close to Johnson, had come within the range of Boswell's recording lens. As it was a most efficient lens, they were recorded vividly. Apparently all equally vividly. This being so, a modern reader might consider Boswell's book as not only a picture of Johnson but a kind of group picture of his whole circle. When we reach the last page, as Macaulay said, ". . . the clubroom is before us, and the table on which stands the omelet for Nugent, and the lemons for Johnson. There are assembled those heads which live forever on the canvas of Reynolds. There are the spectacles of Burke and the tall thin form of Langton, the courtly sneer of Beauclerk and the beaming smile of Garrick, Gibbon tapping his snuff box and Sir Joshua with his trumpet in his ear."

This is an attractive description of what Boswell achieved, but we hardly need Macaulay's overstatements to make us suspect that it is not wholly reliable. To tell the truth, the details of Nugent's omelet, Burke's spectacles, and Sir Joshua's ear trumpet did not come from the *Life of Johnson;* in order to represent that work as being equally graphic in all of its parts, Macaulay had to import them from elsewhere. If we pause to consider the question raised by the passage, we may actually prefer the exact opposite of Macaulay's easy assumption. The *lack* of uniformity on Boswell's canvas is one of its notable characteristics. Certain of the lesser figures, such as Goldsmith and Garrick, are, to be sure, almost always picturesque. But what of other figures no less important, such as Burke and Reynolds? It was not an accident that these two had to be supplied with their "properties" of spectacles and ear trumpet; Boswell never sharpened either figure with a single physical detail.

The twentieth century has been willing to recognize that Boswell was an artist, and of a somewhat temperamental sort. There is nothing surprising in the fact that he had different manners of treating different subjects, or that he responded more eagerly to some of his material than to other. Those who have analyzed his portrait of Johnson have accustomed us to look for such variations. Certain traits of the older man interested Boswell, either because they were traits his own nature needed—such as strength of will or moral clarity—or on the other hand because they corresponded to parts of his own nature he wished to understand—such as a disposition to melancholia. In treating such traits, Boswell's art never failed him. But other aspects of Johnson, such as his softer, more playful moods, seem to have meant less to Boswell emotionally, and we find them better recorded by other writers than they are in the *Life*.

Analysis of the artistic success of "Boswell's Johnson," and also of "Boswell's Boswell," has been carried out with the greatest subtlety. We may ask, however, whether comparable analysis of Boswell's emotional and artistic relationships to his other most important characters has not been neglected. What psychological or other factors are involved in the success of the portrait of Goldsmith? Why do Garrick and Gibbon, in different ways, lend themselves so well to Boswell's art, and appear (when they do appear) in such sharp outlines? On the other hand, why does the luminous canvas so often fade into dark, blurred patches when he tries to record the features of Burke or Reynolds?

Probably most readers would agree that of the larger portraits in Boswell's group picture, Burke's is the dullest and most bituminous. Boswell himself allows us to see the extent of its artistic failure. He regularly describes the original as a man of exceptional brilliance. He quotes Johnson again and again in praise of Burke's powers, or admitting that Burke is his greatest rival as a talker. But actually, in Boswell's book, Burke appears very seldom; when he does appear, he usually says very little; the image we get of him is cloudy and unimpressive. Why Johnson should speak of so dim an apparition as "the first man everywhere," or "the only man whose common conversation corresponds to the fame which he has in the world," is distinctly puzzling to the reader.

II

Coleridge once compared Burke and Johnson as talkers, and offered his own account of the disparity of their reputations:

Dr. Johnson's fame now rests principally upon Boswell. It is impossible not to be amused by such a book. But his *bow-wow* manner must have had a good deal to do with the effect produced,—for no one, I suppose, will set Johnson before Burke,—and Burke was a great and universal talker;—yet now we hear nothing of this except by some chance remarks in Boswell. The fact is, Burke, like all men of genius who love to talk at all, was very discursive and continuous; hence he is not reported; he seldom said the sharp short things that Johnson almost always did, which produce a more decided effect at the moment, and which are so much more easy to carry off.

A modern reader might startle at Coleridge's saying "no one, I suppose, will set Johnson before Burke." Probably for the reason suggested—that Boswell preserved his fame—Johnson would be given the supremacy either as a talker or a mind, by a large percentage of modern readers. We know from Boswell's "chance remarks" and from some other sources that their contemporaries thought the two rivals almost perfectly matched.

Coleridge is doubtless right, however, in assuming that they had different styles of talk, and that it was a much easier task to "carry off" what Johnson said. The dramatic explosions of wit, wisdom, and rudeness which Boswell recorded by the hundred, a great many other people who knew Johnson could report with some success; they were already formed for circulation as anecdote. The Doctor *coined* his talk. Burke, if we can judge at all by his parliamentary eloquence, was at the opposite extreme in style. His virtues Johnson summed up as "copiousness and fertility of allusion; a power of diversifying his matter by placing it in various relations." He spoke very rapidly, and with a marked Irish accent. Boswell himself commented on the trouble Burke must have given the parliamentary reporters: "Dempster described Cavendish taking down while Burke foamed like Niagara. 'Ay,' said I, 'Cavendish bottling up.'" Perhaps Boswell had had his own experiences of the inefficiencies of that kind of bottling.

From comments, if not reports, one can guess a few more of the

qualities Burke's talk must have had. It was, like Johnson's, gladi-
atorial. One should not be deceived by the evidence that Burke
sometimes showed a greater humility than Johnson, as in saying
that it was enough for him to have "rung the bell to him"; he was
the most persistent as well as the most experienced debater among
the Doctor's acquaintances. Indeed, if one can have an opinion at
this distance, there is a likelihood that in pure power of argument
he was Johnson's superior. Johnson's strokes were more violent,
but violence in an argument is not always the sign of victory. "Burke
keeps to Johnson," someone said in Boswell's presence. "Yes," was
the reply, "like a man fishing salmon with a single hair: lets him
flounce, then draws." Burke was a mental athlete par excellence;
he was in addition about twenty years younger than Johnson; perhaps too his public life of strain and shock was a better conditioning
than Johnson's more self-indulgent existence. The older man sometimes groaned when he thought of the eternal readiness of his opponent: ". . . the pulse beat higher in Burke's tongue," he said, "at
two o'clock in the morning than in that of any other man at nine at
night."

Though he was energetic and persuasive, Burke never took "good
talk" as seriously as Johnson did, or strove to give so high a finish to
his colloquial style. Burke was always in a hurry. The magnitude
of his mind gave one kind of distinction to any of his extended
utterances, but "distinction" in the sense of a carefully managed
art of expression he flouted on principle. He was much more likely
to go to the opposite extreme. Johnson's strictures on the low
quality of Burke's wit were amply provoked by his habits of punning, playing with ideas, fooling, and *letting himself down* in ways
most able speakers avoid. Johnson must have felt that in wit, an
important attribute of good talk, his rival was putting himself out
of the competition.

The eighteenth century valued one element in conversation far
more than we usually value it today. This was the element of sheer
information. A talker was admired for being ready to inform his
hearers extempore on a variety of subjects; as the phrase was, he
"diffused knowledge" through his conversation. Here, as in the
aptitude for debate, we can believe that Burke had a slight advan-

tage over Johnson; his printed *Works* range over a wider variety of subjects, and his active involvement in every department of affairs was even more astonishing; he was in turn political leader, historian, philosopher, journalist, and practicing critic. It is not surprising that men like Malone and Reynolds, who among the Johnsonian circle were perhaps most soberly bent on self-improvement, were the ones who in comparing Johnson and Burke inclined toward the latter.

Neither is it surprising, however, if the range of his information, like his "copiousness and fertility of allusion," like the style of his debating, or the lack of style of his wit, succeeded in making Burke rather exceptionally difficult to record.

III

Boswell tells us that he was a law student at Glasgow when he first "contemplated the character of Mr. Burke . . . and viewed him like a planet in the heavens." The two men did not actually become acquainted till they met at the table of Sir Joshua Reynolds about twelve years later. If we can judge from Boswell's enthusiastic record, the first meeting was an auspicious one; it certainly had one kind of animation. Burke was in a very unexalted mood for a planet in the heavens: punning and disporting himself carelessly. Boswell was delighted with the tone of things and tried, with fair success, to make his own puns as outrageous as Burke's.

Their acquaintance, nonetheless, did not develop at once. Indeed Boswell in the *Life of Johnson* appeared to forget this first meeting altogether. Referring to their *second* meeting, the following year —on the night of his own election to the Literary Club—he spoke of "Mr. Edmund Burke, whom I then saw for the first time. . . ." The phrase is doubly inaccurate, for besides the meeting at Sir Joshua's, Boswell had before this seen Burke in the House of Commons, and recorded—again with enthusiasm—his impressions of him:

It was a great feast to me, who had never heard him before. It was astonishing how all kinds of figures of speech crowded upon him. He was like a man in an orchard where boughs loaded with fruit hung around him, and he pulled apples as fast as he pleased and pelted the ministry. It seemed to me, however, that his oratory rather tended to distinguish himself than to assist his cause. There was amusement instead of persuasion. It was like the exhibition of a favorite actor. But I would have been exceedingly happy to be him.

Perhaps one reason the acquaintance did not progress more rapidly was that although Boswell was much impressed by Burke and eager to cultivate his friendship, Burke was not able to feel equally serious about Boswell. He granted that Boswell was entirely good-natured, but insisted that that was no more credit to a man than having a strong constitution; when Johnson proposed Boswell for the Club, Burke doubted that he was "fit for it." Once he was elected, Burke, like the other members, enjoyed his company fully, but he may never have changed his opinion of Boswell's intellectual capacities.

On Boswell's side there was also a serious shortcoming in their relationship, if we consider it as potentially an ideal one. Boswell needed celebrities. Nothing is clearer after reading the journal than the degree to which he distrusted his own moral and psychological strength and struggled to appropriate the strength of famous and powerful people. If the word tufthunter, which has sometimes been applied to him, means a person who has only frivolous or external reasons for seeking out the great, it is unfair to apply the term to Boswell, for his pursuit of strength in the men about him was anything but frivolous; it had the seriousness of an instinctive drive. But Boswell did stalk the great, for serious reasons if not for light ones; there was an unpleasant rigidity about his manner of approaching any man who carried a Name.

One of the uses to which Boswell put his Names when he had them was that of serving as models of rectitude, or of worldly poise and easiness, for the incessant self-judgments of the journal. Burke was admirably qualified for such a use. Boswell adopted him as a kind of symbol of happiness of a public kind. "I was in such a frame as to think myself an Edmund Burke," he would write, ". . . a man who united pleasantry in conversation with abilities in business, and powers as an orator." Or, "I was in fine cheerful spirits tonight, spoke a good deal, fancied myself like Burke, and drank moderately of claret." On a less exuberant day: "But it is absurd to hope for continual happiness in this life. Few men, if any, enjoy it. I have a kind of belief that Edmund Burke does. He has so much knowledge, so much animation, and the consciousness of so much fame." But if self-assurance returned: ". . . fancied myself like Burke."

This purely private manner of using a friendship may have had psychological dangers of its own, but it was scarcely so embarrassing to the relations of the two men as Boswell's open efforts to win Burke's political patronage. Burke, in spite of Boswell's idealized image of him, was never in so comfortable a political situation that he had many favors to bestow; and though he found Boswell a congenial companion, he may have doubted that he was a public servant worth a strenuous recommendation. Boswell indeed was diffident of his own claims. The first letter he wrote to Burke explained awkwardly that he would have written at an earlier date but Burke's party had seemed about to come into power and he did not wish to look like a place-hunter. Whether accidentally or not, Burke seems never to have answered this letter. Boswell wrote two more letters within the next year; the one which survives was to inform Burke of the political situation in Edinburgh, which was hostile to a bill Burke was championing. Burke's reply was light and mocking, making a joke of the whole matter and speaking of a happy meeting he had had with Johnson in London when *no* political matters were discussed. As far as we know, Boswell did not write again till three years later, at a time when Burke's party had finally come to power. This letter was a lightly disguised request for a place. Boswell said he could move to London, as he had long thought of doing, if he could only increase his income by £600 a year. Did Burke have any ideas on that subject? "When I was last in London," said Boswell, "you asked me on one of our pleasant evenings over your homebrewed, 'how I *could* live in Edinburgh?' I answered 'Like a cat in an air-pump.'" Burke responded to the request as well as he knew how, by writing a letter recommending that Boswell be given a vacant post as judge advocate in Scotland. The letter, though Boswell later spoke of it as precious to him because Burke's praise was so high, did not secure the post.

In his various attempts to draw closer to Burke, Boswell was hampered by the fact that he was a Tory and Burke a Whig; he made heroic but rather obvious efforts to minimize the difficulty. In the early days when Burke championed the Americans Boswell also sympathized with them and emphasized it in dealing with Burke. Much later, when Burke was campaigning against the French Revolution, Boswell insisted his old friend was at last on the Tory side, so that again they were in agreement. A conversation Boswell recorded in 1790 summarizes pretty well the extent of their harmony:

BURKE. "This revolution in France would almost make me adopt your Tory principles." I. "Nay, you are one of us. We will not part with you." BURKE. "You have the art of reconciling contradictions beyond any man I know." I. "Yes, I was a Tory and an American." BURKE. "You were not always an American." (This was an unjust suspicion of time serving on my part.) . . . He (indelicately, I thought) mentioned Mr. Hastings. I could not but say "I am on the other side there, I know not how." He was Irishly savage a little, but full and flowing.

It was on the question of Warren Hastings and India that Boswell was most embarrassed by his opposition to Burke's party. At a time when he was being unusually serious about political matters, and was planning to run for Parliament himself, Boswell had brought out a pamphlet attacking Fox's India Bill. For years after that time he thought Burke must have been nursing this knowledge as a bitter grievance. "I was sorry to perceive Burke shy of me," he wrote, four years later, "but my loyal zeal against the India Bill was a *lethalis arundo* in his side." It was at least the kind of *lethalis arundo* to which men in politics become very much accustomed; Burke had probably forgotten it entirely.

In the later years of the journal, and in their later correspondence, we see a curious change come over Boswell's attitude toward Burke. Instead of admiring him and enjoying his company as he had in earlier years, Boswell repeatedly shows discomfort and embarrassment when in Burke's presence. How much Burke provoked this by alteration in his own manner, it is impossible to say; there is no convincing evidence that he treated Boswell otherwise than as he always had. But laments and accusations concerning his "coldness" constantly recur, and Boswell's own behavior becomes that of a man thoroughly ill at ease. When in 1784 Burke went to Glasgow to be installed in the honorary post of Lord Rector of the University, he may have been a very little late in informing Boswell of his arrival in Scotland. Boswell's manner of responding to the "slight" was extraordinary. He immediately went to Glasgow, where he appeared at Burke's inn before breakfast on the day of the installation. He did not want to speak to Burke personally until he had prepared the ground with a letter, and wrote suggesting that Burke must be offended with him for his "Tory zeal." To insure his forgiveness, Boswell pointed out that it was Easter week! ". . . if in this cursed strife you 'have ought against me,' and will not be fully reconciled with me even in *this week,* pray tell me frankly." Burke's servant happened to recognize Boswell on the stairs and asked him if he wished to see Burke at once. Boswell declined but asked the servant to take his letter to Burke. Burke (a little puzzled, perhaps) immediately came into the parlor where Boswell was waiting nervously; they "embraced complacently." Boswell again said something about his fears of an estrangement. Said Burke, "What has made you go so mad of late? As to quarreling with you, that cannot happen; for as you observe as to Langton . . ." "In short," the journal breaks off, "he conveyed a compliment that my pleasantry was such that one would be a loser by quarreling with me." Burke explained his delay: "As to telling you when I came to Scotland, I did not know myself till we were dismissed. *Deus nobis haec otia.*" He invited Boswell to breakfast at once.

Boswell's uneasiness on this occasion may be chargeable to a state of nervousness over his political "career" at the time; it is altogether probable that the coldness and anxiety were all on one side. There was, however, an occasion two years later on which Boswell probably did really irritate Burke. The journal says: "I imprudently touched on a calumny against Mr. Burke, in order to be enabled to refute it. We parted on sad terms. I was very uneasy. . . ." Boswell again preferred to discuss their difference in letters, of which *five* passed between them before the matter was settled amicably.

If Burke's annoyance with Boswell ever actually went beyond such a temporary flurry, it may well have been because of Boswell's eagerness to chronicle small matters. Burke as a man in politics was under constant attack by paid slanderers in the newspapers; there was no aspect of his life, public or private, which they did not exploit or distort. His settled principle of defense was to reply to nothing that was said of him, but to take care that as few facts as possible were certainly known. He had excellent reasons for fearing Boswell's notebooks. Charles Fox, whose political position was far more secure than Burke's, was supposed to have made it a rule not to talk in Johnson's presence, because the conversations were known to be recorded. Boswell, as the entry in the journal itself tells us, knew that he was imprudent in questioning Burke. He was also warned by Malone against the special dangers of his "habit of recording"; it was the "cause of B——'s coldness," said Malone, who quoted B—— as saying, it "throws a restraint on convivial ease and negligence."

The assumption that the two men were estranged is treated as a certainty in the later years of the journal. In 1787 when Boswell sat with Burke and Mrs. Burke at the playhouse, the occasion was noted only with sadness: "I sat in Mrs. Burke's box, where was Edmund. It was awkward and uneasy to be cold with people with whom I had once been on the easiest footing." The next year when he met Burke's brother Richard: "Dick Burke was too rough and wild in his manner today, and I could perceive either liked me worse than his brother did, or had less art to conceal his dislike—on account of politics." When Edmund at about this time agreed to dine at Boswell's home, the nervous host sent him two separate letters reminding him of the engagement. Burke came, of course, and "seemed quite easy and polite," but did not succeed in disarming everybody. This time it was Mrs. Boswell who had the suspicions. According to the journal: "She said he must be a very perfect politician who could conceal the resentment which he must entertain against me for having so keenly opposed his party, but that she believed he would show it whenever he had the opportunity."

Poor Burke's efforts to show good will were finally so little trusted that it was a matter for comment and astonishment if he did *not* produce a feeling of discomfort. In the latter part of 1790 Boswell described a social occasion to Malone: "Burke was admirable company, all that day . . . easy with me as in *days of old*. I do upon my honor *admire* and *love* him. Would that he had never seen Lord Rockingham but had 'ever walked in a perfect way.' "

But such confidence was only temporary. Three months later Boswell was again working himself up over another supposed misunderstanding; he did *not,* he assured Burke in a letter, write the epigram which had appeared over his name in the *Oracle;* he was as indignant with the author of it as Burke himself could be! Burke replied the next day that he had never seen the epigram but was sure Boswell would do nothing discreditable.

Two months later the *Life of Johnson* was published.

IV

The portrait of Burke which appears in the *Life of Johnson* has two or three noticeable peculiarities.

For some reason at which we can only guess, Burke is frequently introduced or discussed or quoted without his name being mentioned. Boswell speaks of "an eminent friend of ours," or "an eminent public character," or "one of the most luminous minds of the present age," or makes use of an initial or a blank, and the context permits us to infer that Burke is meant. In one or two cases we can convince ourselves that the passage might have offended or embarrassed Burke—which justifies the anonymity for those cases. But usually what is said seems innocuous. We wonder why it was more necessary to disguise Burke than, say, Reynolds or any other subordinate figure.

If the average reader of the *Life* will review those impressions of Burke which he is able to recall, he may be surprised to find how many of them come from Johnson rather than from Boswell—how often Boswell's only contribution is quoting the words of the Doctor. "Yes, Sir; if a man were to go by chance at the same time with Burke under a shed to shun a shower, he would say—'this is an extraordinary man.' If Burke should go into a stable to see his horse dressed, the hostler would say—'we have had an extraordinary man here.' " Or, "Burke's talk is the ebullition of his mind; he does not talk from a desire of distinction, but because his mind is full."

Or, "I can live very well with Burke; I love his knowledge, his diffusion, and affluence of conversation; but I would not talk to him of the Rockingham party." Or, "Yes, Burke *is* an extraordinary man. His stream of mind is perpetual."

By the side of such vivid sketches and tributes, Boswell's own efforts at drawing Burke are strangely ineffective. As has been said, they are not usually in dramatic form, which means that they are not in Boswell's best mode. They are likely, rather, to be complimentary phrases used in introductions: "Mr. Burke . . . whose splendid talents . . . ," "Mr. Burke, whose orderly and amiable domestic habits . . . ," "Mr. Burke, who while he is equal to the greatest things, can adorn the least. . . ." Such fulsome expressions do not create any living image for a reader.

One naturally asks why Boswell fell so much below himself when he had to deal with Burke. It is hardly for the purely external reason that in a *Life of Johnson* other figures than Johnson had to be subordinated; Burke is not so much subordinated as badly blurred. But on the other hand, we would be going too far if we asserted that Boswell's art was essentially unsympathetic to Burke; a dozen vivid passages in the journal contradict such an idea. It is safer to assume that the special failure of Boswell in the *Life* is a problem of that particular work, and a problem which is not yet solved.

There is, however, one last remark to be made upon the portrait in the *Life*. It is almost, but not quite, uniform in its lack of vigor. We have said that Boswell seldom presented Burke talking, and this is generally true; but there is one day which is a complete exception. In his record for April 3, 1778, Boswell presents Burke talking fluently. It is the day on which Boswell made his most ambitious effort to preserve a conversation at the Club; most readers will recall it by the fact that various speakers are distinguished by arbitrary letters—E. for Burke, R. for Sheridan, P. for Reynolds, and so on. Considered purely as a piece of dramatic recording, the entry for April 3, 1778, is perhaps the greatest tour de force in the *Life of Johnson;* Boswell presents no less than *eight* people taking part in a general conversation.

Burke, who in the rest of the biography seldom speaks at all, and almost never makes two speeches consecutively, here speaks seventeen times on one day. His treatment of the topic closest to his own interests—the question of the value of a speech in Parliament if it does not change a vote—is probably our best surviving sample of his conversational power. He also talks at length on emigration, comments learnedly on the Irish and Dutch languages, and makes enough attempts at wit to show us the range of his talent there. The degree to which he leads the talk is also notable; of the seven main topics discussed, four are introduced by Burke, and a fifth brought up when Sheridan draws Burke out with a flattering question.

It is a scene which helps to restore to proportion our group picture of the Johnsonian circle.

GOLDSMITH, THE GOOD-NATURED MAN
Edward L. McAdam, Jr.

HIS heart was soft even to weakness: he was so generous that he quite forgot to be just." So Macaulay characterized Goldsmith, who indeed described himself in much the same way in a letter to his brother Henry: "I had contracted the habits and notions of a Philosopher, while I was exposing myself to the insidious approaches of cunning; and often, by being even from my narrow finances charitable to excess, I forgot the rules of justice, and placd myself in the very situation of the wretch who thank'd my bounty." One finds a similar statement in Sir William Honeywood's condemnation of his nephew, the Good-Natured Man: "I saw, with regret, those splendid errors, that still took name from some neighbouring duty; your charity, that was but injustice; your benevolence, that was but weakness; and your friendship, but credulity."

If further evidence is needed to show that Goldsmith was perfectly aware of his own failings, one may adduce the character of the Man in Black, which Goldsmith's sister said was a self-portrait.

The dilemma in which Goldsmith found himself was, I believe, basic, and one from which he never escaped either in his life or in his writings. Naturally generous, he was at the same time insecure. He was short, plain, disfigured by smallpox, awkward socially. His habitual stammering may be taken as the result of his unsureness, not its cause. Certainly a person of average good looks who had attended universities in three countries and traveled in half a dozen might be expected to acquire some ease of manners. His lack of physical attractiveness, his stammering, and his clumsy manners may furnish an answer to why there was no great love affair in Goldsmith's life. He knew a good deal about prostitutes; the lively description of how the Chinese Philosopher is entertained by the London whores is too good to be second hand or pure imagination, and in the *Life of Nash* he remarks that there are in the neighborhood of any university "girls who with some beauty, some coquetry, and little fortune, lie upon the watch for every raw amorous youth." It will be remembered that Marlow lost his shyness in the presence of such girls: is it too much to suggest that Goldsmith found a satisfying sense of dominance in pleasures which he was able to purchase?

His desire to shine in society, and his love of giving extravagant dinner parties, may also be interpreted as a wish to dominate, to play the part of a wealthy host. One of his biographers shrewdly suggests that Goldsmith was a bore rather than a fool in company —he wished to monopolize the conversation at whatever cost. What it did cost in terms of defeat and ridicule is amply set forth by Boswell. The result, however, merely emphasized his difficulty.

A corollary to his social behavior is his extravagant dress. His "bloom-coloured coat" was an obvious device to draw attention to himself, and at the same time a compensation for his lack of physical attractiveness.

Even his charitable actions—though it is unpleasant to suggest this—may have had some basis in a desire to dominate. To relieve distress was a pleasure if done in person, however unworthy the object. To contribute anonymously to a subscription for a hospital might not be quite so satisfactory. Even at an early age, however, Goldsmith had qualms about the justice of his behavior. Whether the Fiddleback story is true or not, the self-justification is as obvious as the artistry: the poor mother to whom he gave half a crown had "eight little clean Children" and a husband arrested for debt. The children's cleanliness showed that the mother was not a shiftless creature, and their number may have been meant to indicate that nature, not extravagance, was the cause of the husband's poverty.

Let us revert for a moment to Goldsmith's letter quoted above: "I had contracted the habits and notions of a Philosopher, while I was exposing myself to the insidious approaches of cunning . . ." This is self-justification, and partly self-deception, but it has a basis in truth. The "insidious approaches of cunning" I consider a reference to crooked gamblers. That Goldsmith gambled for the sheer nervous excitement involved is probable, especially since he shows so plainly in the *Life of Nash* how impossible it is to give any other justification for the vice. The philosophy which afforded no protection against dishonesty may be called sensationalism. His briefest statement of this, often repeated, occurs in Letter VI of *The Citizen of the World:*

I know you reply, that the refined pleasure of growing every day wiser, is a sufficient recompense for every inconvenience. I know you will talk of the vulgar satisfaction of soliciting happiness from sensual enjoyment only; and probably enlarge upon the exquisite raptures of sentimental bliss. Yet, believe me, friend, you are deceived; all our pleasures, though seemingly never so remote from sense, derive their origin from some one of the senses. The most exquisite demonstration in mathematics, or the most pleasing disquisition in metaphysics, if it does not ultimately tend to increase some sensual satisfaction, is delightful only to fools, or to men who have by long habit contracted a false idea of pleasure; and he who separates sensual and sentimental enjoyments, seeking happiness from mind alone, is in fact as wretched as the naked inhabitant of the forest, who places all happiness in the first, regardless of the latter.

There is no religion in this philosophy—indeed, he allows the Chinese Philosopher to ridicule the dogma of the Trinity—but I am unable to discover that religion played any part in Goldsmith's life, though he respected his father's and Henry's profession and had once thought of it for himself. This sensationalism I conceive to be merely a rationalization of his own desires, though it also has a curious and probably indirect relationship to Mandeville's "private vices, public benefits." Although Goldsmith inveighed against "luxury" in *The Traveller* and *The Deserted Village,* and Boswell reports a similar attitude, this had not always been his opinion. But where Mandeville ironically commends luxury as the nurse of civilization, only to show that it is wholly destructive of individual virtue, Goldsmith in *The Citizen of the World* defends it because, like sensation, it increases "happiness," as civilization advances: "The more various our artificial necessities, the wider is our circle of pleasure; for all pleasures consist in obviating necessities as they rise: luxury, therefore, as it increases our wants, increases our capacity for happiness." Furthermore, "to luxury we owe not only the greatest part of our knowledge, but even of our virtues." Mandeville would have been shocked, I suspect, at the way Goldsmith manipulated these arguments. As an example of the sort of virtue that occurs only in civilized communities, Goldsmith mentions the subscription for the relief of the French prisoners of war, which is a type of public charity which he himself refers to vanity. Mandeville defines virtue so narrowly as to make it unattainable by human beings; Goldsmith's definition is so vague and so generous as to have little relation to any philosophy or religion except his own sensationalism.

As might be expected from this attitude toward luxury, Goldsmith was unsympathetic toward "Nature's simple plan":

Observe the brown savage of Thibet, to whom the fruits of the spreading pomegranate supply food, and its branches an habitation. Such a character has few vices, I grant, but those he has are of the most hideous nature: rapine and cruelty are scarcely crimes in his eye; neither pity nor tenderness, which ennoble every virtue, have any place in his heart; he hates his enemies, and kills those he subdues.

We may now inquire how Goldsmith put his theories into practice. From the earliest events of his manhood to the last weeks of his life he was torn between his easy, pleasure-loving nature and the necessity to support himself. He knew perfectly well that he ought to have his eye on the main chance, and in his advice to others, particularly his brother Maurice and his nephew William, he was as practical as any businessman, but neither in his life nor in his writings was he able to arrive at any satisfactory solution between the demands of practicality and those of the heart.

In the study of the Man in Black, for example, the ironic solution is in fact no solution at all: "In short, I now find the truest way of finding esteem, even from the indigent, is—to give away nothing, and thus have much in our power to give." Aside from the fact that the Man's description of himself is not true, it merely points up Goldsmith's difficulty: how can one be both practical and generous at the same time? The best answer that Goldsmith can suggest is an heiress: the Man in Black was "upon treaty of marriage with a rich widow," and Honeywood was rescued by the beautiful and wealthy Miss Richland. Exigencies of plot made this impossible for Dr. Primrose, but he was able to recoup his follies and live happily ever after when his daughter married the wealthy Sir William Thornhill. Given enough money, one can be generous.

Or perhaps frugality was the answer. In one of Goldsmith's fables, Asem, another good-natured man, is reconciled to the world as it is by finding that a world entirely free from vice is not only devoid of civilization but also of virtue itself. Avoiding the fundamental problem, Asem returned to society and found that in a few years "frugality" solved all of his difficulties.

Frugality Goldsmith himself never achieved, though he continued to recommend it as a virtue, to be carefully distinguished from avarice. In *The Bee* he urged the writing of success stories to inspire the young:

Instead, therefore, of romances, which praise young men of spirit, who go through a variety of adventures, and at last conclude a life of dissipation, folly and extravagance, in riches and matrimony, there should be some men of wit employed to compose books that might equally interest the passions of our youth, where such an one might be praised for having resisted allurements when young, and how he, at last, became lord-mayor; how he was married to a lady of great sense, fortune, and beauty: to be as explicit as possible, the old story of Whittington, were his cat left out, might be more serviceable to the tender mind, than either Tom Jones, Joseph Andrews, or an hundred others, where frugality is the only good quality the hero is not possessed of.

Goldsmith himself wrote for money, made money, and was an excellent judge of the commercial value of his own writings. When Bishop White asked him in 1770 why he did not write a pamphlet on the decay of the peasantry, he replied, "It is not worth my while. A good poem will bring me a hundred guineas but the pamphlet would bring me nothing." This was the initial sum Goldsmith received for *The Deserted Village* in that year, which may be compared with the 15 guineas Johnson was paid for *The Vanity of Human Wishes* and the 200 guineas for which Johnson, in 1777, agreed to write *The Lives of the Poets*. Johnson considered himself a good businessman in his relations with the publishers, but the evidence available indicates that Goldsmith's earnings in the seventeen years of his literary career were far larger than Johnson's, whose career lasted almost three times as long. But, whereas Johnson's stern moral character enabled him to be generous without dissipation, Goldsmith was never able to attain this ideal.

Furthermore, however uncongenial to Goldsmith was this virtue of frugality, it was equally lacking in popular appeal. Possibly with this in mind he took up the common cry against luxury in his Advertisement to *The Vicar of Wakefield:* "In this age of opulence and refinement, whom can such a character [the Vicar] please?" The novel itself is not a tract against luxury but primarily a humorous idealization of Goldsmith's early life—his relationships with his father and perhaps his brother Henry, and his travels on the Continent. This idealization of the past continued in *The Traveller,* though Goldsmith makes it clear that he has not given up his notions on sensationalism: in Switzerland, where there is no luxurious nobility to make the peasants envious, nevertheless

> If few their wants, their pleasures are but few;
> For every want that stimulates the breast
> Becomes a source of pleasure when redrest.

And "Their morals, like their pleasures, are but low." (This sounds like his earlier antiprimitivism.) Although commerce has left Italy and only a contented peasantry remains, still "sensual bliss is all the nation knows." In both of these countries the absence of luxury has not brought the benefits to the peasantry which might have been expected. When he turns to France Goldsmith glows with the recollection of his youthful pleasures "beside the murmuring Loire," but brings himself up sharply with the patriotic observation that the French are an idle and frivolous nation. Industrious Holland is at first more attractive, but soon shows the expected vices of craft, fraud—and dullness. And finally England displays a mixture of virtues and vices which appear to be inextricable: liberty produces "the lords of human kind" but also "Keeps man from man, and breaks the social tie"; this in turn strengthens "the bonds of wealth and law," with the ultimate prospect that all the populace will lie in "one sink of level avarice." From this horrid prospect Goldsmith flies in nostalgia to the deserted village. It is not a solution of a problem but merely an emotional retreat.

In *The Deserted Village* Goldsmith turns on luxury with wrath and vigor. He has forgotten all of his arguments in its favor and now attributes to it all the inequities and hardships of the enclosure movement and the English laws against Irish trade. His wrath may be in part contrived: the success of *The Traveller* may have induced him to carry the theme to an extreme. But it is even more, I think, the final expression of Goldsmith's insecurity in London, which at times reached the edge of despair. He was returning to the good things of his childhood and adolescence, as he chose to remember them: the warmth of village life, his love of his father, and "dear lovely bowers of innocence." In contrast to this we may remember the letter to his uncle, written seventeen years earlier: "I was dispised by most, and hateful to myself. Poverty, hopeless poverty, was my lot, and melancholly was beginning to make me her own." No, he was not anxious to return to Sweet Auburn, because it had no geographical existence. Indeed, two months after *The Deserted Village* appeared, he was off to Paris on a gay trip with the Horneck girls.

Less than four years later, Goldsmith was dying, his mind not at ease, as his doctor reported. But he exists for us still as the good-natured man whom he portrayed so often, always seeking a security which he did not find and pleasure which could not wholly satisfy him, justifying and then condemning the luxury which he loved —a weak man who never gave up, a great artist who, even displaying his own weaknesses, contributed far more than did Garrick to the gaiety of nations.

SIR JOSHUA'S PROSE

Frederick W. Hilles

O N a May afternoon in 1776 Sir William Forbes was host to a distinguished company at his villa near London. One of his guests, Sir Joshua Reynolds, remarked that beauty could not be discriminated. George Colman, disagreeing, suggested that there was a difference between languishing beauty and lively beauty, and when Boswell pointed out that " 'twas of stile Sir Joshua had talked," Colman stuck to his guns, saying that styles too could be distinguished by their excellence. "Tell me then," challenged Reynolds, "the distinctive quality of Addison's style." [1]

On a July afternoon in 1807 Sir Harry Englefield entertained a similar group at his home in London. The conversation turned on English prose, "and after much had been said, it was allowed by all present that Sir Joshua Reynolds, in His Lectures, wrote with more purity & simplicity than any other modern writer, & might for the excellence of His style in that respect be compared with Addison;— having clearness, ease, and no affectation." [2]

Much has been written of the *Discourses,* but to the best of my knowledge the question of style has been passed over, or dismissed with a few vague adjectives. And yet that question calls forth others more specific. Is Sir Joshua's prose Addisonian, as Sir Harry's friends imply? Reynolds himself said he was of Johnson's "school." Is his prose Johnsonian? Herbert Read classifies him as a traditionalist. What are the characteristics of the traditional style as revealed in his writings?

As a stylist Sir Joshua must be judged by his *Discourses* and the three letters to *The Idler* which antedate them. With a few negligible exceptions he allowed nothing else of his to be published in his lifetime. We have no way of knowing what alterations he would have made before printing his journals, his jeux d'esprit, and his

---

1. *Boswell Papers*, XI, 278.
2. *The Farington Diary*, ed. James Greig (London: Hutchinson & Co., 1924), IV, 173.

admirable biographical sketches. Nor can our study include his personal letters, if we are to understand the comments which critics have made of his prose style. Here, for example, is a sentence from a letter which Reynolds wrote to Burke, describing Rotterdam:

> But the Keys are magnificent, rows of fine houses, high at least and fine in their half a mile long perfectly in a strait line with a Row of Elms between the houses and the ships which lye close to the Quey so that the branches touch the masts whilst on the other side the Canal the shiping have for their background the rows of Trees with houses appearing between them.[3]

Not, admittedly, a typical sentence, but surely one which is in marked contrast to his published writings. As he himself said in another letter, "I am forced to write in a great hurry, and have little time for polishing my style." [4]

Fortunately, to limit ourselves to the *Discourses* and *Idlers* is not a serious restriction. The letters to *The Idler* were printed in 1759, when the author was thirty-six years old, a successful painter but still relatively unknown. The final discourse was printed in 1791, a year before Sir Joshua's death, at a time when he was generally regarded as the greatest living painter. There is a gap of thirty-two years between his first and last publication. If his style changed as he matured, an examination of the *Idlers* and *Discourses* should reveal the fact.

But examination reveals little difference between the early and the late writings. This is an excerpt from *Idler* No. 79:

> It is very difficult to determine the exact degree of enthusiasm that the arts of Painting and Poetry may admit. There may perhaps be too great an indulgence, as well as too great a restraint of imagination; and if the one produces incoherent monsters, the other produces what is full as bad, lifeless insipidity. An intimate knowledge of the passions, and good sense, but not common sense, must at last determine its limits. It has been thought, and I believe with reason, that Michael Angelo sometimes transgressed those limits; and I think I have seen figures by him, of which it was very difficult to determine, whether they were in the highest degree sublime or extremely ridiculous. Such faults may be said to be the ebullitions of Genius; but at least he had this merit, that he never was insipid; and whatever passion his works may excite, they will always escape contempt.

3. From the original in my possession.
4. *Letters of . . . Reynolds,* ed. Hilles (Cambridge University Press, 1929), p. 20.

The same topic is discussed in the fifteenth discourse:

That Michael Angelo was capricious in his inventions, cannot be denied; and this may make some circumspection necessary in studying his works; for though they appear to become him, an imitation of them is always dangerous, and will prove sometimes ridiculous. "Within that circle none durst walk but he." To me, I confess, his caprice does not lower the estimation of his genius, even though it is sometimes I acknowledge, carried to the extreme: and however those eccentrick excursions are considered, we must at the same time recollect, that those faults, if they are faults, are such as never could occur to a mean and vulgar mind; that they flowed from the same source which produced his greatest beauties, and were therefore such as none but himself was capable of committing: they were the powerful impulses of a mind unused to subjection of any kind, and too high to be controled by cold criticism.

The first passage was written while George II was on the throne; the second after Washington had become President of the United States. Clearly the excerpt from the last discourse with its quotation from Dryden, with the sentence lengths skillfully varied, with its easy progression from beginning to end of the paragraph, is the more polished bit of writing. Sir Joshua is confident; Mr. Reynolds, author of the three letters to *The Idler,* is less sure of himself. Yet I for one should find it very difficult to distinguish from internal evidence between what Reynolds wrote in 1759 and what he wrote in 1769 or 1779.

In general we may apply to his style what Johnson said of the man; it is the same all the year round. Here and there a purple passage is to be found, such as the one Northcote heard Reynolds read to Burke.[5] And the concluding paragraphs of the final discourse reveal an emotion in the speaker which is not characteristic. Here and there, too, we meet with clumsy writing, like the phrase which a contemporary reviewer extracted from the eighth discourse: "by recommending the attention of the artist to an acquaintance with the passions." But I consider unjustified such sweeping statements as that by Horace Walpole, ordinarily an acute critic in such matters. He reported that the twelfth discourse "was observed to be much more incorrect in the style than any of his former." [6] To me

5. James Northcote, *Life of . . . Reynolds* (London, 1818), II, 316.

6. *Anecdotes of Painting in England,* ed. F. W. Hilles and P. B. Daghlian (Yale University Press, 1937), p. 69.

the twelfth seems no more "incorrect" than those which were written earlier or later. I should characterize it as a polished piece of writing, typical of what is to be found in the other discourses.

Without further ado, then, I shall present two extracts as characteristic of their author. One is from the first discourse, the other from the last, although I am not concerned with the time when either was written. I have selected them almost, as the phrase goes, at random. They are long enough for the development of a thought, short enough to be used in an essay of this length. A careful scrutiny of these selections should make clear to us how Reynolds put words and sentences together. The blind man judging the shape of an elephant by feeling its trunk? I reply with the Latin tag popular in the eighteenth century: *ex pede Herculem*. From the first discourse:

I would chiefly recommend, that an implicit obedience to the *Rules of Art,* as established by the practice of the great MASTERS, should be exacted from the *young* Students. That those models, which have passed through the approbation of ages, should be considered by them as perfect and infallible guides; as subjects for their imitation, not their criticism.

I am confident, that this is the only efficacious method of making a progress in the Arts; and that he who sets out with doubting, will find life finished before he becomes master of the rudiments. For it may be laid down as a maxim, that he who begins by presuming on his own sense, has ended his studies as soon as he has commenced them. Every opportunity, therefore, should be taken to discountenance that false and vulgar opinion, that rules are the fetters of genius; they are fetters only to men of no genius; as that armour, which upon the strong is an ornament and a defence, upon the weak and mis-shapen becomes a load, and cripples the body which it was made to protect.

How much liberty may be taken to break through those rules, and, as the Poet expresses it,

        To snatch a grace beyond the reach of art,

may be a subsequent consideration, when the pupils become masters themselves. It is then, when their genius has received its utmost improvement, that rules may possibly be dispensed with. But let us not destroy the scaffold, until we have raised the building.

From the fifteenth discourse:

In reviewing my Discourses, it is no small satisfaction to be assured that I have, in no part of them, lent my assistance to foster *newly-hatched unfledged*

opinions, or endeavoured to support paradoxes, however tempting may have
been their novelty; or however ingenious I might, for the minute, fancy them
to be; nor shall I, I hope, any where be found to have imposed on the minds
of young Students declamation for argument, a smooth period for a sound
precept. I have pursued a plain and *honest method;* I have taken up the art
simply as I found it exemplified in the practice of the most approved Painters.
That approbation which the world has uniformly given, I have endeavoured
to justify by such proofs as questions of this kind will admit; by the analogy
which Painting holds with the sister Arts, and consequently by the common
congeniality which they all bear to our nature. And though in what has been
done no new discovery is pretended, I may still flatter myself, that from the
discoveries which others have made by their own intuitive good sense and
native rectitude of judgement, I have succeeded in establishing the rules and
principles of our Art on a more firm and lasting foundation than that on
which they had formerly been placed.

I assume everyone will agree that these passages are highly characteristic of Sir Joshua's thinking. The reverence for the past, the
abhorrence of ingenious and novel opinions, the emphasis on good
sense and judgment, ideas which Sir Joshua held in common with
Burke and Goldsmith and Johnson, underlie all that he wrote. But
our concern is with manner rather than matter, and here too the
passages seem to me highly characteristic of the author.

The first thing to be noticed is that although twenty-two years
elapsed between the writing of the two passages, the tone and
rhythms are the same. The author has plenty of time. The sentences
are long, and there is a marked tendency to wordiness. And yet,
owing to careful balance, the sentences do not get out of hand. It
is not a diffuse style. A certain crispness and control are secured
through antithesis, and the varied rhythms of the individual sentence form part of a more sustained rhythm.

In a belated obituary we are told that "there was a polish in the ex-
terior of Sir Joshua, illustrative of the Gentleman and the Scholar."
The extracts reveal this polish. In the one he quotes Pope; in the
other he has italicized the two phrases from *Hamlet.* The earlier
selection contains the elaborate armor simile and concludes with a
metaphor. These "decorations," as Sir Joshua would have termed
them, are functional. Together with other elements, they retard the
tempo and support the prevailing tone, which is dignified, deliberate, urbane.

There is a smooth, easy-flowing quality to the phrasing, partly due to initial connectives, partly to syntax. To show how each sentence or each paragraph moves into the next would be tedious. Two examples from the second selection should suffice. The "nor shall I . . . be found to have imposed" is a dominant seventh which is resolved in "I have pursued," and this sentence in turn, ending with "the most *approved* Painters," is followed by the most obvious inversion in either selection: "That *approbation* which the world has uniformly given, I have endeavoured to justify. . . ." Here the object of the sentence, placed out of its normal position, binds the sentence more closely to what precedes it. Throughout these selections there is a high degree of coherence.

The style is smooth; it is also emphatic. And the emphasis is achieved in various ways. Never going to the extremes of Johnsonese, Sir Joshua gains emphasis through parallelism. When Old Masters are called "perfect" and "infallible" guides, the second adjective is redundant. "False" and "vulgar" differ in meaning but, when yoked together as here, result in nothing more than an added weight to the thought. The same is true, as Polonius might have admitted, of *"new-hatch'd unfledg'd."* Significantly Reynolds has amplified the other Shakespearean phrase, writing "plain and *honest"* instead of *"honest."*

More conspicuous is parallelism when coupled with anaphora, "however tempting . . . however ingenious," or when there are three elements in each member, "intuitive good sense . . . native rectitude of judgement." It is possible to distinguish between "intuitive" and "native" or between "good sense" and "rectitude of judgement," but in this passage each phrase seems to mean no more than "innate right thinking." Repetition of the idea deepens the impression.

Needless to say, when a parallel structure is used to bring out opposites, emphasis is increased. Early in the second selection Reynolds contrasts "a smooth period" with "a sound precept." Here three elements in each member are linked by alliteration and the two members contrasted in meaning. But the phrase is the more noticeable because it in turn is in apposition to what precedes it. The result is a double antithesis, two parallelisms forming a third:

"declamation" rather than "argument," "a smooth period" rather than "a sound precept."

There is no doubt that diction also plays its part in making the style emphatic. Sir Joshua, like all educated writers of his time, preferred words of Latin rather than Anglo-Saxon ancestry, the long word rather than the short. It is because of this and because of his tendency to write impressive-sounding phrases, that his style has been dubbed "presidential." For example, "those models, which have been passed through the approbation of ages," might be in simpler language "models tested by time." Again "helped to promote" would be less pompous than "lent my assistance to foster," and we have already noticed "rectitude of judgement," a phrase which sounds Johnsonian and which had been used by Burke.

Frequently it is not the long word itself but the way in which it is used that colors the passage. Like Johnson, Reynolds naturally thinks in abstractions. Hence he speaks of "that *approbation* which *the world* has *uniformly* given." And often an abstract quality is made subject of a sentence. "Their genius has received its utmost improvement," he writes. "Novelty" is "tempting," "discovery" is "pretended," "art" is "exemplified." In this connection a study of a sentence near the end of the first selection is rewarding. The subject, a compound clause of twenty-six words, can for our purpose be reduced to "How much liberty may be taken." The simple predicate is "may be a subsequent consideration." Colloquially we might say, "you may think about breaking the rules later."

The passive voice seems to dominate throughout. Rules are "established" by masters, obedience "should be exacted" by teachers, models "should be considered" by students, opportunity "should be taken" by all, armour "was made" by unspecified artisans, liberty "may be taken" and rules "dispensed with" by artists. Reynolds is "assured" by [we suppose] his friends and will not "be found [by anyone] to have imposed" on the minds of novices. We learn further that "in what has been done [by me] no new discovery is pretended" [by me]. Among other effects such writing re-enforces generalization.

Related to this, I believe, is the normal unemphatic use of the expletive "it" or "there." Almost any page written by Reynolds will provide an example. Midway in the first selection we read, "it may be laid down as a maxim, that . . ." Remove these words, and the sentence is a somewhat Johnsonian aphorism, "He who begins by presuming . . ." The aphorism itself is general: the reference is to anyone who behaves in this way. But when the words which we have removed are restored, the generality is heightened. It may be laid down by whom? The subject is impersonal.

In the text, immediately before the example just cited, we read: "He who sets out with doubting, will find life finished before he becomes master of the rudiments." Where Johnson and Reynolds begin a phrase with "he who," Addison and Steele commonly write "a man who." Now "man" in this context is not particularized, but an added abstraction creeps in when the indefinite "he" is substituted for the generalized noun.

So much for analysis. Only by descending to particularities can we give meaning to those adjectives which have been applied to Sir Joshua's style: clear, easy, unaffected, perspicuous, elegant, nervous. Doubtless if other passages were subjected to the same sort of treatment, some alteration of the lights and shadows would occur, but the general impression would remain the same. Sir Joshua was an artist. The dignity which he advocated in painting he achieved in writing.

Many of the characteristics noted in our analysis are to be found in Johnson's prose. It would be surprising if this were not so. The two men were contemporaries, they were close friends, they were both generalizers. In his penetrating study of Johnson W. K. Wimsatt writes:

What he said about the dignity of generality has its most obvious reflection in the fact that his own writing may, as we have said, be characterized as exceptionally general and abstract. Johnson, the last great neoclassicist, the reactionary, was the one who most seriously attempted to put into artistic practice the neoclassic uniformitarian ideal. . . . In his elaborate system of parallelism and antithesis, in the "philosophic" pomp of his diction, he devised a way of lending to the abstract an emphasis, a particularity and thickness. . . . By limiting himself faithfully to the abstract, he achieved more with it than did any other neoclassicist.[7]

7. *The Prose Style of Samuel Johnson* (Yale University Press, 1941), p. 96.

Here the key word is in the first sentence. Johnson's writing is *exceptionally* general. We have seen that Sir Joshua, a later neoclassicist, a less positive reactionary, adopted the Johnsonian devices, and that his writing is emphatically abstract. The difference between the two styles is one of degree.

Johnson was called Sir Joshua's "oracle." Reynolds confessed that Johnson taught him "to think justly." With this in mind a reading of the sixth discourse is illuminating. There Sir Joshua develops his theory that "genius is the child of imitation."

It is by being conversant with the inventions of others, that we learn to invent; as by reading the thoughts of others we learn to think. . . . He, who borrows an idea from an antient, or even from a modern artist not his contemporary, and so accommodates it to his own work, that it makes a part of it, with no seam or joining appearing, can hardly be charged with plagiarism. . . . Borrowing or stealing with such art and caution, will have a right to the same lenity as was used by the Lacedemonians; who did not punish theft, but the want of artifice to conceal it.

Edgar Wind has shown that in his painting Reynolds practiced what he preached, borrowing an expression or an attitude from one master or another. Can we detect the same tendency in his writing?

Throughout his *Discourses* we come across Johnsonian echoes. We find phrases like "that slow progression of things, which naturally makes elegance and refinement the last effect of opulence and power"; sentences like "At that age it is natural for them to be more captivated with what is brilliant, than what is solid, and to prefer splendid negligence to painful and humiliating exactness"; paragraphs like "These instructions I have ventured to offer from my own experience; but as they deviate widely from received opinions, I offer them with diffidence; and when better are suggested, shall retract them without regret." And we have already noticed Sir Joshua's fondness for the Johnsonian aphorism. Here are a few culled from the *Discourses:* "Nothing can come of nothing: he who has laid up no materials, can produce no combinations." "But let no man be seduced to idleness by specious promises. Excellence is never granted to man, but as the reward of labour." "What has pleased, and continues to please, is likely to please again."

We know that Reynolds deliberately copied from Johnson. An amusing piece of evidence has recently come to light. In my possession, thanks to the generosity of Colonel Isham, are manuscript notes made by Reynolds in 1783 when reading *The Lives of the Poets*. Among other sentences copied from the *Life of Cowley* is the following: "His known wealth was so great that he might have borrowed without loss of credit." In his next discourse, while defending Raphael from the charge of plagiarism, Reynolds writes: "I have given examples from those pictures only of Raffaelle which we have among us, though many other instances might be produced of this great Painter's not disdaining assistance: indeed his known wealth was so great, that he might borrow where he pleased without loss of credit." Surely this is a bit of whimsy, to pilfer a sentence of Johnson's when discussing Raphael's "thefts."

Reynolds was profoundly influenced by Johnson and acknowledged his indebtedness. Nevertheless, no one has accused him of writing Johnsonese. His style is what Saintsbury called characteristic. Herbert Read, as was said earlier, terms it traditional. And it is not difficult to account for this.

Buffon's famous dictum is to the point. How did Sir Joshua's friends characterize him? Johnson: "The most invulnerable man I know; the man with whom if you should quarrel, you should find the most difficulty how to abuse." Burke: "his native humility, modesty, and candour, never forsook him, even on surprise or provocation; nor was the least degree of arrogance or assumption visible to the most scrutinizing eye, in any part of his conduct or discourse." His temper, according to Malone, was modest and equable, according to Boswell equal and placid, according to Barnard mild, according to Mrs. Thrale peaceful. His manners, according to Goldsmith, were gentle, complying, and bland.

Such a man would instinctively shy away from the overemphatic, would avoid all extremes, would strive to appear normal. "Peculiar marks," he wrote, "I hold to be, generally, if not always, defects; however difficult it may be wholly to escape them." Hence he expresses himself in a style which admits of no eccentricities, no mannerisms. I have tried without success to discover the distinctive quality of his style. It is that of the cultured gentleman of his day.

A few months before Reynolds became author, Horace Walpole in an unpublished letter [8] to Dalrymple remarked: "a good style (in writing) has grown almost as common as a good print." This good style, everyone knows, derived from Addison, and there are passages in the *Spectator,* particularly when the pleasures of the imagination are discussed, which Reynolds might have written. I should say that Sir Joshua's style is basically Addisonian with Johnsonian overtones. It is the middle style, "exact without apparent elaboration . . . elegant but not ostentatious."

This type of writing has recently been examined by James Sutherland, who puts his finger on its principal defect:

A prose based upon good manners will have many virtues; it will be essentially social, it will aim at giving pleasure and avoiding offence. But it will often lack one quality which to many modern readers must seem indispensable: it will not, of itself, be exciting. When, as with Addison, the writer 'thinks justly but thinks faintly,' there will not be sufficient urgency in either matter or manner to hold the attention for long.[9]

This criticism might be applied to Sir Joshua's writing. And yet—

In April, 1801, Francis Horner, an original founder of the *Edinburgh Review,* wrote in his journal:

next to the writings of Bacon, there is no book which has more powerfully impelled me to resolve these sentiments than the "Discourses" of Sir Joshua Reynolds. He is one of the first men of genius who have condescended to inform the world of the steps by which greatness is attained; the unaffected good sense and clearness with which he describes the terrestrial and human attributes of that which is usually called inspiration, and the confidence with which he asserts the omnipotence of human labour, have the effect of familiarising his reader with the idea that genius is an acquisition rather than a gift; while with all this there is blended so naturally and so eloquently the most elevated and passionate admiration of excellence, and of all the productions of true genius, that upon the whole there is no book of a more *inflammatory* effect.[10]

With this rhapsody in mind listen to the words of La Bruyère which Reynolds copied into a commonplace book shortly before his *Idlers*

8. In Mr. Lewis' unrivaled collection at Farmington.
9. *Essays on the Eighteenth Century Presented to D. Nichol Smith* (Oxford, Clarendon Press, 1945), p. 97.
10. *Memoirs and Correspondence,* ed. Leonard Horner (Boston, 1853), I, 153.

were written: "Quand une lecture vous élève l'esprit, et qu'elle vous inspire des sentiments nobles et corageux, ne cherchez pas une autre règle pour juger de l'ouvrage, il est bon, et fait de main d'ouvrier."

GARRICK'S LAST COMMAND
PERFORMANCE

Mary E. Knapp

EARLY in 1777, the year after Garrick had made his triumphant final appearance at Drury Lane, he was summoned by George III to read at Court. No subject ever received royal command with more ardent gratification. Johnson misunderstood Garrick's very nature when he pronounced on his retirement: "He should never play any more, but be entirely the gentleman and not partly the player." It is highly ironical that one of the three young gentlemen boarded and taught at Edial should shortly be proclaimed the chief mimic of the British stage. During the rest of his life Garrick retaliated for the restraint which he felt in Johnson's company by mimicry in his absence, and if we could now applaud until the spirit of Garrick reappeared, we might pass by Archer, Abel Drugger, Ranger, and Don Felix to see him imitate "the manner of his old master with ludicrous exaggeration; repeating, with pauses and half-whistlings interjected,

> *'Os homini sublime dedit,—caelumque tueri*
> *Jussit,—et erectos ad sidera—tollere vultus';*

looking downwards all the time, and, while pronouncing the four last words, absolutely touching the ground with a kind of contorted gesticulation." [1] Garrick could be nothing but the player; by a gesture or facial expression he could transform a street or a room of a tavern into a stage. In the drawing rooms of Paris in 1764 he acted scenes from *Macbeth, Hamlet,* and *King Lear* to brilliant audiences spellbound in admiration. In the royal audience he expected the same fervor and the same eager response.

George III, unlike his grandfather, had a fondness for the theater.

---

1. With this and Boswell's other well-known descriptions of Garrick's impersonating Johnson and with the unauthenticated but persistent anecdote of his sitting for Fielding's portrait, compare *Boswell Papers,* IX, 265, where, under May 9, 1772, Boswell records that Garrick "gave us Fielding, Johnson, TETTIE, etc. . . ."

As a boy he had taken part in private theatricals at Leicester House, playing Portius in *Cato* and speaking an occasional prologue, forthwith published in the *Gentleman's Magazine*. He often appeared in the royal box at Drury Lane, and in his conversation with Johnson in 1767 he made a flattering reference to the universality of Garrick's acting. He frequently commanded performances; for example, it was "by command" that Garrick returned to the stage on November 14, 1765, after two years' absence. On this occasion he directed his prologue to the royal box, comparing himself to a veteran recalled to the service and concluding with a fervid declaration of loyalty.[2]

One of the pieces standing highest in royal favor was Garrick's "dramatick satire," *Lethe,* which he had written in 1740, in the earliest days of his career, for the benefit of Henry Giffard, the manager of the Goodman's Fields Theater.[3] Like all Garrick's ventures at Goodman's Fields, *Lethe* was at once successful. For the first performance Johnson wrote the prologue, Garrick the epilogue, and the piece was presented by an excellent cast, including the singer John Beard, later to be manager of Covent Garden on the death of Rich, his eccentric father-in-law; Macklin, famous for his Shylock; Henry Woodward, the Mercutio of the century; Mrs. Clive, who had already established herself as a great comic actress, especially happy in the characters which Fielding had written for her; and James Raftor, Mrs. Clive's brother, who "told a story better than anyone" and made Horace Walpole laugh for two hours.

Few other afterpieces were so constantly demanded by decade after decade of theatergoers and none other was supported by a longer succession of great actors and actresses. Under Garrick's management it was performed 154 times at Drury Lane. It became part of the repertoire of Covent Garden, the Haymarket, and the provincial theaters, and in 1751 it began its long history on the American stage.[4] To present *Lethe* was to insure the success of the

2. The *London Chronicle,* December 7–10, 1765.

3. For Dr. Taylor's "pleasant anecdote" of Johnson's triumph over Garrick and "old Giffard," see Boswell, *Life,* I, 168–169.

4. A playbill from the *New York Mercury* announces *Lethe* as the afterpiece to *The Stratagem* to be performed at the theater in John Street, December 7, 1764. (See plate opposite p. 114, George C. D. Odell, *Annals of the New York Stage.*)

evening's entertainment. It was chosen as the afterpiece to benefit performances such as that of *Comus* for Mrs. Elizabeth Foster, April 5, 1750. Johnson's letter to the *General Advertiser,* urging the public to attend, closed with the notice: "There will be a new prologue on the occasion, written by the authour of Irene, and spoken by Mr. Garrick; and, by particular desire, there will be added to the Masque a dramatick satire, called Lethe, in which Mr. Garrick will perform." The following December *Lethe* was given as an afterpiece to *The Stratagem* for the benefit of one of Farquhar's daughters "in great distress."

The popularity of *Lethe* was due to the sprightliness of the dialogue and to the amusing characters, unrelated except through absurdity, by which the actors not so much satirized as merely reflected current fashions and follies. The episodic structure of the play and the opportunity it afforded for a rapid series of impersonations—the off-stage acting in which Garrick delighted—made it particularly suitable for the command reading at Court. In choosing *Lethe* he was confident that he would please the royal audience.

During the thirty-seven years from 1740 to 1777 Garrick occasionally revised *Lethe* by adding or omitting characters to adapt the satire to the times. Many of these characters did not appear in print; some of them are known only through newspaper notices and playbills; others, such as those added in 1772 and 1777, are extant in unpublished manuscripts in the Huntington and Folger Libraries. The various stages of the text, from the primitive version of 1740 through the perfected edition of 1757 to the degenerate revision of 1777, present a complicated and baffling evolution. For the general pattern Garrick borrowed Vanbrugh's *Aesop,* a translation of Boursault's *Les Fables d'Ésope,* first performed at Drury Lane in 1696. Here, as in *Lethe,* Aesop is represented as the adviser and censurer of mankind, pointing his wisdom with fables in verse. Garrick discarded Vanbrugh's rather silly plot, which emphasizes Aesop's relationship to King Midas, but retained the flexible scheme of introducing absurd, quarrelsome characters as a means of light social satire.

The first version of *Lethe*—the manuscript is in the Huntington Library—is very slight and hardly more than a sketch of the play as it was eventually published in 1749. It provides one of the earliest indications of the friendship between Garrick and Fielding and of their connection as dramatists, for Garrick borrowed two characters, Miss Lucy and Mr. Thomas, acted by Mrs. Clive and her brother, from Fielding's successful ballad opera, *The Virgin Unmask'd,* a farce which had had a long run every season since 1735 and was then being played at Drury Lane. Miss Lucy was given a song recounting the trivialities of a Fine Lady's day from the morning dressing table to the midnight ridotto—"Such, such is the Life of a Belle." [5] She quarreled with Mr. Thomas in Garrick's epilogue, a little acting piece designed for Mrs. Clive, and bantered the critics in the pit and the footmen in the upper gallery. After 1741 Fielding's characters disappear from the cast.

More important in the development of *Lethe* than either Vanbrugh or Fielding was James Miller, who in 1739 had written a sprightly dramatic fable called *An Hospital for Fools,* which should have been received with "universal applause," for not only is it lively and amusing but it was presented by actors such as Macklin, Woodward, and Mrs. Clive. Miller used as a basis for his fable a similar but slighter satire by "knowing Walsh," from which he borrowed the device of transporting a crowd of fools to the underworld to be examined by Aesculapius. He pilfered whole speeches from Walsh and animated them to fit into his play. He added four remarkably vivacious songs for Mrs. Clive, Dr. Arne writing the music. But *An Hospital for Fools* through no lack of merit in itself was damned by Miller's enemies and as a "rioted" play was withdrawn after the first night.

Garrick knew that Miller's piece should have taken the house from pit to gallery. Like his own plays, prologues, and songs, it commented on current fashions in dress, manners, and amusements. With its ridicule of operas and oratorios, its assortment of knaves and dunces, its concluding song to prove that if folly is incurable fools give each other endless entertainment—all this presented by caricature and impersonation—it was a play made to Garrick's

5. "The Life of a Belle," one of Garrick's best songs, was set to music by Carey and printed as Plate XLVIII of *The Agreeable Amusement,* a collection of popular songs and ballads. With the piece appears the companion song, "The Life of a Beau," which Mrs. Clive sang in a performance of Miller's *The Man of Taste,* Drury Lane, May 13, 1738.

hand. Sometime between 1741 and 1749 *An Hospital for Fools,* dialogue, characters, and cast, transmigrated to *Lethe,* thus beginning an unexpectedly long posthumous career. Garrick preferred Vanbrugh's Aesop to Miller's Aesculapius; he rewrote and again enlivened the speeches; he introduced songs for Beard and added characters which are personalities as well as types, but in spirit and substance *Lethe* remains Miller's play. It is true that Garrick gave the satire a characteristic twist; for example, in the part of the Fine Gentleman, played by Woodward, he ridiculed the beaux who loitered behind the scenes until the play began and then braved the missiles of the upper gallery to appear on the stage, interrupting the actors to whom they paid no attention. On the other hand, he took the boisterous, rattlebrained Fine Lady, Mrs. Riot, almost bodily from the daughter in *An Hospital for Fools.* Both parts were written for Mrs. Clive to parody Italian opera, as she had also done in Fielding's Miss Lucy, a character who bears not a little resemblance to Mrs. Riot, all three being but an expression of Mrs. Clive's personality.[6]

The most important alteration in the text of *Lethe* was the addition of Lord Chalkstone, first announced in the playbills for March 27, 1756, as a "new modern character," to be played by Garrick, and, as it proved, one of his most popular parts. Chalkstone, who even at this remove is still an entertaining old rake, at once took a place among Garrick's comic characters with Sir John Brute. For the part Garrick appeared in a long black greatcoat heavily trimmed with fur, worn over a red topcoat; his white wig was topped with a high-brimmed hat set far back on his forehead to emphasize his features; he dangled an eyeglass on a ribbon and carried a cane on which he leaned clumsily. In the Theater Collection at Harvard there is a small, brightly colored print showing these details. The same costume appears in the elaborate drawing by Gabriel Smith, *Mr. Garrick in the Character of Lord Chalkstone.* Quite apart from

---

6. Tate Wilkinson (*Memoirs,* III, 41–42) gives a vivid account of the importance which Mrs. Clive attached to the character, Mrs. Riot, and of her anger when Garrick presumed to have the playbills of *Lethe* printed with only his part mentioned: "Madame Clive at noon came to the theatre and furiously rung the alarm bell: for her name being omitted was an offence she construed so heinous, that nothing but vengeance, and blood! blood! Iago was the word!"

the history of *Lethe* and Garrick's acting, Chalkstone is of some interest in being a vivid reflection of the times. The five satirical stanzas at the bottom of Smith's plate end:

> Chalkstone! thy Rank thou truly knowst,
>   The Nobleman I see!
> And, Heav'n be prais'd! our Isle can boast,
>   Of many a Lord like Thee.

But Garrick, who dearly loved many a lord, loved Chalkstone.

His entrance was heralded by his friend and admirer, Bowman: "There's a Spirit! Mr. *Aesop*—There's a great Man!—See how superior he is to his Infirmities; such a Soul ought to have a better Body." Ogling the audience through his eyeglass, he made humorous critical comments on their vices and foibles—on the rage for gaming: "Though my Body's impaired—my Head is as good as ever it was; and as a Proof of this, I'll lay you a hundred Guineas"; on duelling: "I have been run through the Body myself, but no Matter for that"; on landscape gardening:

Ay, *Styx*—why 'tis as strait as *Fleet-ditch*—You should have given it a Serpentine Sweep, and slope the Banks of it—The Place, indeed, has very fine *Capabilities;* but you should clear the Wood to the Left, and clump the Trees upon the Right: In short, the Whole wants Variety, Extent, Contrast, and Inequality—[*Going towards the Orchestra, stops suddenly, and looks into the Pit*] Upon my Word, here's a very fine *Hah-hah!* and a most curious Collection of Ever-Greens and Flow'ring-Shrubs—[7]

It was satire with no purpose beyond entertainment. Chalkstone, the forerunner of Lord Ogleby in *The Clandestine Marriage,* is Garrick's most characteristic creation. On January 23, 1766, after a performance of *Zara* and *Lethe* "by command," Hopkins, the Drury Lane prompter, recorded with fervor in his diary: "Mr. Garrick played Lusignan and Lord Chalkstone.—It is almost impossible to express how finely he played both characters." [8]

By 1777 *Lethe* was fraught with memories of Garrick's entire

7. 5th edition (1757). For this quotation and a detailed discussion of *Lethe* see Elizabeth P. Stein, *David Garrick, Dramatist* (Mod. Lang. Assn., N.Y., 1938) pp. 25–34.

8. *Drury Lane Calendar,* ed. Dougald MacMillan (Oxford, 1938), p. 117. On this occasion Rousseau, under the conduct of Hume, sat in Garrick's box. Their Majesties, says Hume, stared at Jean Jacques rather than at the play (Burton, *Life and Correspondence of David Hume* [1846], II, 309).

theatrical life. Even before he made his "first" appearance at Goodman's Fields he had acted two characters of *Lethe,* when Giffard's company was on tour in Ipswich. For the command reading he could resume the Poet, the Drunken Man, and the Frenchman— parts which he sacrificed to play Chalkstone; Chalkstone himself he had given to Tom King, who first acted the part on April 24, 1769, when Mrs. Clive made her final appearance, playing the Fine Lady and speaking an epilogue written for her by Horace Walpole. To play the Fine Lady was to play Mrs. Clive, and it was equally impossible to play the Fine Gentleman without recalling Woodward's mannerisms.[9]

Using the edition of 1757 as a basis, Garrick retained all the familiar characters and added others, including William Fribble, restored from the unpublished acting version of 1772, now in the Huntington Library. The new characters, some of whom, like the noisy Mrs. Carbine, are merely repetitions, were provided with a rather wooden dialogue, and by their number alone disrupted such unity as the piece could boast. In order to comment on the absurdities of the headdress then in fashion and to ridicule the towering feathers first worn by his friend the Duchess of Devonshire, Garrick created a Lady Featherby, who visits Aesop to discuss the innovation. She declares, somewhat out of part: "If our Grandmothers had worn feathers as we do now, they wou'd have been lock'd up in Bedlam," and then points out to Aesop an example of the kind of headdress Chalkstone had discovered in the pit of Drury Lane: "You see on my Head here are several Objects of Trees, Temples, Churches, Canals, Obelisks, &c. These very Objects shall all be *Illuminated* at our next Ball." [10] Whatever the pertinency of the criticism, Lady Featherby is but a dull counterpart of Mrs. Riot.

9. There are extant two lifelike Chelsea figurines showing the very attitude as well as the dress of Mrs. Clive as the Fine Lady and Woodward as the Fine Gentleman in *Lethe.* (Plate opposite p. 40, Mrs. Clement Parsons, *Garrick and His Circle* [1906].) The artist Charles Mosley made a careful engraving of Mrs. Clive as Fine Lady, the plate, which the *Dictionary of National Biography* describes as one of Mosley's best, being now in the British Museum.

10. Quoted by permission of the directors of the Folger Library. The absurdities of headdress in the 1770's called forth much amusing comment. The frontispiece of Bell's *British Theatre* (1776–81), Vol. II, is a print of Garrick in the ridiculous costume in which he last appeared as Sir John Brute in *The Provok'd Wife*. Weighed down with a great structure of feathers, ribbons, and flowers, he is shown toying with a fan and simpering, "So! how d'ye

Unhappily it occurred to Garrick that a parallel could be drawn between his relationship to George III and that of Aesop to King Midas, and therefore in the final revision of *Lethe* he reverted to Vanbrugh's play in both tone and method, closely following him in using fables to reprimand the guilty and admonish dunces. One of the fables, *The Leopard and the Fox* (originally *The Lion and the Fox,* for in Garrick's fables one animal is quite as appropriate as another), he had written in 1748, inspired perhaps by the success of the *Fables* of his friend Edward Moore. Although Garrick scribbled his verse hastily wherever he had a minute's chance—in coaches, in church, in inns, in the greenroom during the intervals of rehearsals, so that the Duke of Gloucester's singularly inept remark to Gibbon would have been quite fitting to him—yet he was careful never to lose a stray couplet; he had copies of all he had ever written and frugally revived lines or, as in the present instance, entire poems.

Through all his thirty-five years on the stage Garrick had been in constant demand as a writer and speaker of prologues, and even Johnson, who was in general contemptuous of Garrick's verse, declared that he had written more good prologues than had Dryden. But in an unlucky moment Garrick abandoned the heroic couplet in which most of his good prologues are written and, following the irregular stanza which Vanbrugh had used in *Aesop,* he wrote for the last command performance a prologue in the form of a fable.[11] After three tortuous and limping introductory stanzas in which he described himself as tongue-tied with joy—

> To Honour call'd, when the full heart
> Beats all its feelings to impart
> And to its gratitude give way,
> The tongue refuses to obey;
> For, needed most, we seldom find
> The key that should unlock the mind—,

he compared himself to Aesop obeying the summons of Midas and

---

like my Shapes now." See, too, Garrick's epilogue to Mrs. Cowley's *The Runaway* (1776), and his prologue to Sheridan's *A Trip to Scarborough* (1777).

11. There are at least two copies of the "New Occasional Prologue," one in the Folger Library, introducing the final revision of *Lethe,* and the other in the Theater Collection at Harvard. It is quoted here from an unidentified newspaper clipping in the Yale Library.

produced his fable of the mimic blackbird and the royal eagle. Such was the imitative skill of the humble blackbird that he attracted great audiences of the "feather'd throng":

> Some mount and perch upon the trees,
> Which represent the galleries,
> The bushes, boxes; and the pit, the ground,

and loud they clapped their wings in approbation. But at last the blackbird growing old gave up his mimic art and to private shades repaired:

> The eagle saw with piercing sight,
> What the old Blackbird would delight,
> Perhaps might yield some sport;
> So sent for him to Court.

But the royal audience, unlike ordinary playhouse birds, did not applaud, and the play—the Fine Gentleman, Mrs. Riot, Chalkstone, Lady Featherby all—was received in equal silence. Northcote described the scene to Hazlitt: "Garrick complained that when he went to read before the court, not a look or a murmur testified approbation; there was a profound stillness—every one only watched to see what the King thought. It was like reading to a set of wax-work figures: he who had been accustomed to the applause of thousands, could not bear this assembly of mutes." [12] The new characters, the flattering prologue had been in vain. How different this reception from that of the French drawing rooms! Garrick withdrew humiliated to seek the sympathy of his friends.

The first account we have of the command reading is anything but sympathetic and comes from the pen of Horace Walpole. In a letter dated February 27, 1777, he tells Mason that Garrick is so jealous of the attention being paid to the French actor, Caillaud, that he "would be glad of an Act of Parliament that should prohibit there ever being a good actor again in any country or century."

But this is not all; he has solicited King George to solicit him to read a play. The piece was quite new, *Lethe*, which their Majesties have not seen above ten times every year for the last ten years. He added three new characters equally novel, as a Lady Featherby, because the Queen dislikes feathers. The piece was introduced by a prologue *en fable;* a blackbird grown grey-haired,

12. Hazlitt, *Conversations of James Northcote*, ed. Edmund Gosse (1894), p. 216.

as blackbirds are wont to do, had retired from the world, but was called out again by the eagle. Mr. Hare asked Garrick if his Majesty looked very like an eagle? The audience was composed of King, Queen, Princess Royal, Duchess of Argyll, Lady Egremont, Lady Charlotte Finch; the Prince of Wales was not present; and all went off perfectly ill, with no exclamations of applause and two or three formal compliments at the end. Bayes is dying of chagrin, and swears he will read no more.[13]

The comments of his friends were ruthless when the prologue and the failure of the performance were discussed by a party at Dr. Burney's on Thursday morning, March 20, following the reading. Fanny Burney, yet untaught in the ways of royalty, reported the conversation to Mr. Crisp, who for his part had not been pleased with Garrick's treatment of his tragedy, *Virginia*.

"There is not," said Dr. Johnson, "much of the spirit of *fabulosity* in this Fable; for the *call* of an eagle never yet had much tendency to restore the voice of a *blackbird!* 'Tis true that the fabulists frequently make the *wolves* converse with the *lambs;* but, when the conversation is over, the *lambs* are sure to be eaten! And so the *eagle* may entertain the *blackbird;* but the entertainment always ends in a feast for the *eagle.*"

"They say," cried Mrs. Thrale, "that Garrick was extremely hurt at the coolness of the King's applause, and did not find his reception such as he expected."

"He has been so long accustomed," said Mr. Seward, "to the thundering approbation of the Theatre, that a mere *'Very well,'* must necessarily and naturally disappoint him."

"Sir," said Dr. Johnson, "he should not, in a Royal apartment, expect the hallowing and clamour of the One Shilling Gallery. The King, I doubt not, gave him as much applause as was rationally his due; and, indeed, great and uncommon as is the merit of Mr. Garrick, no man will be bold enough to assert he has not had his just proportion both of fame and of profit. He has long reigned the unequalled favourite of the public; and therefore nobody will mourn his hard fate, if the King and the Royal Family were not transported into rapture, upon hearing him read *Lethe.* Yet Mr. Garrick will complain to his friends, and his friends will lament the King's want of feeling and taste;—and then Mr. Garrick will kindly *excuse* the King. He will say that His Majesty might be thinking of something else; that the affairs of America might occur to him; or some subject of more importance than *Lethe;* but, though he will say this himself, he will not forgive his friends, if they do not contradict him!" [14]

13. Walpole, *Letters,* ed. Mrs. Paget Toynbee (Oxford, Clarendon Press, 1903–5), X, 21.
14. *Dr. Johnson & Fanny Burney,* ed. C. B. Tinker (London, 1912), pp. 7–8.

One of Garrick's most amiable characteristics was his childlike eagerness to please, and he had more than usual sensitivity about the opinion of his friends. For many months after his unapplauded last appearance he consoled himself by reading them *The Mimic Blackbird* and by sending copies of the fable about in his letters, as he frequently sent his occasional verse, sometimes receiving answers in kind, but always the applause which was as essential to his versifying as to his acting. On June 3 he read the fable to Mrs. Thrale, who did not have to feign admiration, for she records: "Mr. & Mrs. Garrick have been here, so I have heard the Eagle & the Blackbird, & a very pretty Thing it is I think . . . ," [15] the "so" being significant. He read it to Hannah More and later sent her a copy, she, in return, writing him a flattering critical analysis of the poem, pointing out its "beauties" stanza by stanza. "Who pepper'd the highest was surest to please." More surprising is a letter from Gibbon, written in Paris August 14, begging Garrick to "send us, without a moment's delay, your elegant fable." He had given Madame Necker an "impartial" account of *The Mimic Blackbird*, "and, though a good subject, I will venture to say that she is as capable of tasting its beauties as any monarch in Christendom" [16] —a comment the more gratifying as it was true.

Many years later when Fanny Burney, then a lady in waiting, was required to read Colman's *Polly Honeycombe* to the Queen, she sympathized with Garrick: "Easily can I now conceive the disappointment and mortification of poor Mr. Garrick when he read *Lethe* to a Royal Audience. Its tameness must have tamed even him." But she observes sadly—and the knowledge would have saved Garrick much humiliation—"Such is the settled etiquette." [17]

15. James L. Clifford, *Hester Lynch Piozzi (Mrs. Thrale)*, p. 153.
16. *The Private Correspondence of David Garrick* (1831–32), II, 256.
17. *Diary & Letters of Madame D'Arblay*, ed. A. Dobson (1904–5), IV, 360–361.

GIBBON'S PARADISE LOST

Lewis P. Curtis

I

IF Gibbon had happened otherwise, the world would have lacked two works of supreme art—a history and a man. The marvelously ordered structure of the *Decline and Fall of the Roman Empire,* the urbanity of the immortal style, no less than the author's poised affability and self-control, would have been something quite different. Had Gibbon been a French philosopher—too many critics have tried to make him such—he would have bent history to serve the cause of reform in eighteenth-century Europe. He would have been distressingly, if wittily, earnest. Unfortunately for those who would understand the purpose because they enjoy the content of his history, Gibbon chose to remain, like his book, a work of art. He preferred to let his readers draw their own conclusions about what he was trying to say in the *Decline and Fall.* Besides, he was an English gentleman and, for all his devotion to "Fanny Lausanne," an English squire and landowner, a captain of militia, a member of Parliament, and even a placeman. In the good times of the eighteenth century English squires had not the Frenchman's need to reform government. They were, under the king, already in sufficient control. And they much preferred enjoying to reforming and facts to theory. Like Warburton's Moses, if they often neglected to declare their moral or political creed, they never intended to imply that they wanted either. They took these things for granted, or, rather, almost for granted. In their letters or speeches in the House of Commons they talked facts but most frequently they weighed and tested facts in terms of received maxims. They were not without ideals, however casually, except in times of crisis, they expressed them.

In this respect Gibbon resembled his class. He held to maxims and principles common to Whigs (and who was not a Whig?) in the reign of George III. He was not at pains to make these maxims at all times consistent. "The fact is," Black has written, "Gibbon was not a philosopher in the strict sense of the word. He has nothing to say of the ultimate meaning of the events he describes, nor is there any 'schematic tendency' in his history comparable to that which dominates his thorough-paced contemporaries." [1] And even if Coleridge could go so far astray as to declare that Gibbon "had no philosophy" (a different matter from being no philosopher), he was overlooking the all-too-English casualness, not to say reticence, which Gibbon maintained throughout his history. Even D. M. Low, the most learned of Gibbon's biographers, betrays his own deception when he tells us that Gibbon, after all, "has nothing to prove."

Nothing to prove; granted—in the French sense of the word; the *Decline and Fall* is not systematic history. But Gibbon lived in the eighteenth century, not in the twentieth when too many historians write history for history's sake, and some historians appear to write biology instead of history. He lived in an age that believed unquestioningly in rules and principles. After Bolingbroke's advice Gibbon narrated as historian and as philosopher mindful of rules and principles he often hinted. The hints (they are Gibbon's asides) repay attention. It does, then, seem worth while asking once more what Gibbon in his history was trying to do.

Obviously he was trying to write universal history, the history of the world (that is, of all that merited knowing about the history of the world) from the age of the Antonines to the fall of Constantinople over a thousand years later—"the greatest, perhaps, and most awful scene in the history of mankind." [2] He was building that bridge which Carlyle saw swinging gorgeously from one peak of civilization in ancient Rome to the next enlightened peak in the Renaissance. Yet all the time, in spite of the rise and fall of thrones, dominions, princes, barbarians, and fanatical Christians, in spite of Gibbon's apparent excursions from end to end of the empire, his narrative seems not to budge. It is transfixed in immobility. "In the pages of the *Decline and Fall*," as Carl Becker has so subtly described the core of the history,

1. J. B. Black, *The Art of History* (London, 1926), p. 158.
2. Edward Gibbon, *The Decline and Fall of the Roman Empire* (The Modern Library), II, 1457. Hereafter cited as *DF*.

we seem to be taking a long journey, but all the time we remain in one place: we sit with Gibbon in the ruins of the Capitol. It is from the ruins of the Capitol that we perceive, as from a great distance, a thousand years filled with dim shapes of men moving blindly, performing strangely, in an unreal and shadowy world. We do not enter the Middle Ages. . . . *The Decline and Fall* is a history, yes; but something more than a history, a memorial oration: Gibbon is commemorating the death of ancient civilization; he has described, for the "instruction of future ages," the "triumph of barbarism and religion." [3]

This illusion of immobility has a demonstrable cause. Gibbon was writing history *en philosophe*. To write history philosophically in the eighteenth century meant writing with both a specific method and a general purpose. The method (it passed for scientific) prompted the historian to avoid providential explanations of man's past and to trace historical results back to their strictly secondary causes. The general purpose—the specific purpose might vary in a Montesquieu, a Hume, or a Voltaire—was instruction: instruction not about mere happenings nor yet about mere Romans or Englishmen. The philosopher-historian held to a broader aim. At once a cosmopolitan and a humanist, he sought mankind and offered his histories as instruction about the constant and universal principles of human nature. "To the eyes of a philosopher," wrote the young Gibbon, "events are the least interesting part of history. It is the knowledge of man, morality and politics he finds there that elevates it in his mind." [4] The philosopher-historian, he thought, should look for "system, connection, sequence," [5] adhere to impartiality, "one of the fundamental laws of history," [6] reach up to "simple ideas," seize and combine "first principles," [7] refuse to sacrifice the "unfolding of the true counsels and characters of men" for "the smooth and specious surface of events," [8] and never permit "history, which undertakes to record the transactions of the past, for the instruction of future ages," to condescend "to plead the cause of

3. Carl Becker, *The Heavenly City of the Eighteenth-century Philosophers* (Yale University Press, 1932), pp. 117–118.

4. Edward Gibbon, *Miscellaneous Works* (London, 1814), III, 126. Hereafter cited as *MW*.

5. *MW.*, IV, 63.

6. *DF.*, I, 501.

7. *MW.*, IV, 58.

8. *DF.*, II, 1181.

tyrants, or to justify the maxims of persecution." [9] Thus armed with the philosophical method and inspired with so high a purpose, Gibbon set out to find evidence of human nature in the wreckage of Rome.

"The same effects must be produced by the same passions." [10] To Gibbon it was obvious that from the sameness of human nature must flow, as if mechanically, the morality, the politics, indeed the history and the spirit of an age. In such light the historian considered himself as no less a scientist of the moral than Newton was of the physical order of things.

Order of things. How that phrase "order of things" echoes in the memory. Have we not read it a thousand times? Bolingbroke justified certain rules of life and conduct "because they are conformable to the invariable nature of things." [11] "Taste," said Sir Joshua, "is fixed and established in the nature of things." [12] To Burke "the principles that guide us in public and in private, as they are not of our devising but moulded into the nature and essence of things, will endure with the sun and moon." [13] The humanist has a scale of values. The humanist historian weighs dead men in the scale of the natural order. That order is not only natural, it is moral and it is inescapable. Therefore when once the historian has marshaled his evidence and satisfied himself as to his style he has only to trace the effect, for good or for ill, stemming from causes, and causes, moreover, essentially ones of choice and, behind choice, of the passions or prudence that impel choice. Here then in philosophic history, for all to read, lay the knowledge of how to discern futurity in the past. The present was only the past in translation.

The reason for the immobility of the *Decline and Fall* is plain. Gibbon sat all the while in the ruins of the Capitol, weighing the diverse characters of his dramatis personae in the scales of the natural and moral order, until at the end of his labors he rose, satisfied that he had described the triumph of barbarism and religion; or,

9. *DF.*, I, 453–454.

10. *DF.*, II, 1354.

11. Henry St. John, Viscount Bolingbroke, *Letters on the Study and Use of History* (1735) in *Works* (Philadelphia, 1841), II, 193.

12. Sir Joshua Reynolds, *Discourses* (The World's Classics), p. 109.

13. Edmund Burke, *Correspondence*, ed. Fitzwilliam and Bourke (London, 1844), I, 332–333. Burke to ?Bishop Markham, 1771.

to change the metaphor, he stood, like some eighteenth-century philosopher in his laboratory, surrounded by retorts, analyzing the elements of human character and always testing his solutions in terms of inexorable and universal law. No wonder the history does not move. Like Hume and Voltaire, Gibbon ignored the genius of the Middle Ages because the civilization of that era failed to conform to the Hellenic standards in which he had educated himself and with which, like Pope, he identified the moral order. That is why Gibbon had to be the censor of Romans, the censor of mankind. The historian, he wrote in his *Vindication* of the first volume, owed "to himself, to the present age, and to posterity, a just and perfect delineation of all that may be praised, of all that may be excused, and of all that may be censured." [14] The moral approach is foremost, whatever Gibbon, a better geographer by far than Montesquieu, might add of physical causes. He was, to be sure, strangely muddled as to why the Roman Empire declined and fell. Possibly he never gave more than passing thought to the question before he began to write his history. Luxury and despotism, a long peace and uniform government, tyrants, the army, the barbarians, the loss of honor and independence, immoderate greatness, the civil wars of Constantine, Christianity and superstition, the calamities of Italy, the suicidal conquests of Justinian—the causes are almost endless and they advance in geometric progression. But extending across his vast canvas like the figures on Bernini's colonnade Gibbon's characters, his emperors and their consorts, his kings, soldiers, chieftains, bishops, anchorites, prophets, and eunuchs stand for what he thought them—leaders, with opportunity to bring happiness to their kind, who for the most part acted, if nothing worse, unwisely.

Here in these heroes lies Gibbon's real determinant. "In human life, the most important scenes will depend on the character of a single actor." [15] By compassing the death of Mohammed "the lance of an Arab might have changed the history of the world." [16] Through Charles Martel's victory at Poitiers "was Christendom delivered by the genius and fortune of one man." [17] Gibbon's theory

14. *MW.*, IV, 631.
15. *DF.*, II, 1261; I, 900.
16. *DF.*, II, 675.
17. *DF.*, II, 801.

of causation was dramatic. It was also personal and it included not
only the leaders of a society but the followers who looked to the
leaders for example. In effect Gibbon equated happiness and the
prevalence of right principles. "Honour, as well as virtue," he wrote,
"was the principle of the republic; the ambitious citizens laboured
to deserve the solemn glories of a triumph; and the ardour of the
Roman youth was kindled into active emulation." [18] Again, "if all
the barbarian conquerors had been annihilated in the same hour,
their total destruction would not have restored the empire of the
West: and if Rome still survived, she survived the loss of freedom,
of virtue, and of honour" [19]—in short, Rome still survived the informing principles of the Republic. Truly, as Bolingbroke insisted,
"history is philosophy teaching by examples," [20] and by philosophy
Bolingbroke meant the true principles of morals and politics. Gibbon assented to this maxim by exploiting it on every page of the
Decline and Fall. Always he is observing how his characters choose,
what influences of education or of passion drive them to their choice;
always he is balancing their virtues against their vices and judging
characters in terms of character. Gibbon had no doubts about "the
two great sources of knowledge, nature and antiquity." [21] Yes,
history was philosophy teaching by examples, and sometimes history was examples teaching philosophy. But whom were philosophy and examples to teach? "The experience of past faults . . . is
seldom profitable to the successive generations of mankind." [22]
Gibbon's opinion of the multitude is notorious.

There remained the proper pupils of philosophy, the leisured
class. Especially in England, where the leisured class consumed
much of its leisure in the duties of a governing class, Gibbon might
hope to bequeath a book of wisdom for the guidance of statesmen
and philosophers. True, he seldom addressed himself to those who
searched history for the principles of sea power or of political economy. Yet in so far as the teaching of character, the necessity of virtue
and wisdom in the restraint of one's power, the indispensability

18. *DF.*, II, 91.
19. *DF.*, I, 1255.
20. Bolingbroke, *Works*, II, 177, 191.
21. *MW.*, III, 19.
22. *DF.*, II, 206.

of freedom, of emulation and liberal education to the making of a human being are of moment to society—in so far as the manners and institutions that had promoted happiness and letters in the past could be shown to conform to those of Georgian England—Gibbon brought practical truths to the members of his class. He never confessed this aristocratic purpose—that would have been unlike him. But since almost everyone in England believed that the governing class must study history,[23] Gibbon's silence on this point is unimportant beside the cumulative evidence within his book. The *Decline and Fall* is a memorial oration. It is, to boot, a sad, stupendous warning to the governing class. Here in the desolation of a thousand years of history lies proof of the destiny of states that depart from the maxims alike of the Roman Republic and of England's Glorious Revolution. Gibbon, soaked in the values of his order, taught its members what they already accepted. His entire history revolves around a formula, around three words, the contents of their social conscience. These words are virtue, wisdom, and power.

II

The governing class agreed upon fundamentals. Its members enjoyed that will to action which springs from the inner unity and agreement of the more responsible minds. They possessed a central conviction, a conviction almost banal had it not provided the warp of English history until forgotten in the nineteenth century. The governing class believed in the supremacy of the moral will. Nor laws nor institutions (and so thought Gibbon) [24] might avail to build the good society unless those laws and institutions were informed with the principles of freedom, virtue, and wisdom. Agreed upon this fundamental concept and occupied with politics, speculation, tattle, or fetes, the members of the class never bothered to transmit to posterity the constitution of their ideals. Like Gibbon they were content with scattered maxims. But they drafted the clauses of this philosophy in letter after letter, and in speeches or formal studies the thinkers of the class (and they were many) pro-

23. Dorothy Koch, "English Theories Concerning the Nature and Use of History, 1735–1791." Unpublished dissertation, Yale, 1946.
24. *DF.*, I, 693.

vided copious evidence of a philosophy of character, of character and leadership. Most of these men and women were bent upon changing society. They were not radicals. They were robust conservatives. Enormously they enjoyed their constitution in church and state, their rents and acres, their unrivaled civilization, founded as it was on commerce and on poise. Neither Walpole's maxim, *quieta non movere,* nor Henry Fox's "I give you so much, and you shall give me in return, and so we'll defy the world and sing Tol de rol" are typical of their sentiments. Conservatives, they yet were meliorists. They revered right and meant by the good life the things that are—minus the things that ought not to be. Their idealistic yearnings they expressed in a phrase, virtue and wisdom. It is the sacred maxim of the eighteenth century—as old as Plato, as young as Winston Churchill. It lies still unnoticed in countless books of the time. Capable of universal application, the words virtue and wisdom—with power added—denoted a philosophy of leadership and social obligation. They were accepted, they were soberly expounded, because they embodied truths already revealed by philosophers and theologians and proved, apparently, by history itself. Power, virtue, and wisdom were a deduction from the invariable constitution of things, even from the Providence of God.

Like Vincent de Beauvais in the thirteenth century the governing class looked into the mirror of nature for guidance. The class was not surprised, it was merely startled, it was profoundly awed to see itself reflected. Indeed the entire social pyramid, of which the governing class represented the apex, appeared to be a replica of the hierarchy of nature—some essences great, some less, all in their several ranks composing equilibrium and therefore order. Thus Gibbon believed that "the distinction of ranks and *persons* is the firmest basis of a mixed and limited government," [25] and venerated the natural aristocracy of the noble, wise, and virtuous. He may have had his doubts about God's Providence. He had none about the vitalizing power of a wise and virtuous aristocracy. The aged emperor Gordianus, for example, he thought to be "a last and valuable remains of the happy age of the Antonines, whose virtues he revived in his own conduct."

25. *DF.,* II, 349.

The family of Gordianus was one of the most illustrious of the Roman senate.
. . . The birth and noble alliances of the Gordians had intimately connected
them with the most illustrious houses of Rome. Their fortune had created
many dependents in that assembly, their merit had acquired many friends.
Their mild administration opened the flattering prospect of the restoration
not only of the civil but even of the republican government. . . . The capital
of the empire acknowledged, with transport, the authority of the two Gordians and the senate, and the example of Rome was followed by the rest of
Italy.[26]

Such was the natural response of Romans to their firm and
moderate masters, and such the nature of even a provincial synod,
where "the multitude was governed by the wisdom and eloquence
of the few." [27] How "wise or fortunate," Gibbon reflected, "is the
prince who connects his own reputation with the honour and interest of a perpetual order of men." [28] How happy Justinian (had he
been wiser), how happy in the hero Belisarius. How useful heroes
themselves—Moses, Cyrus, Alfred, Gustavus Vasa, Henry IV of
France; "the first place in the temple of fame"—so runs Gibbon's
manuscript note in his own copy of the *Decline and Fall*—"is due
and is assigned to the successful heroes who had struggled with ad-
versity; who, after signalizing their valour in the deliverance of
their country, have displayed their wisdom and virtue in foundation or government of a flourishing state." [29] Burke, as usual, gave
the classic utterance to the concept of a natural aristocracy: "A true
natural aristocracy is not a separate interest in the state, or separable
from it. . . . It is formed out of a class of legitimate presumptions
which, taken as generalities, must be admitted for actual truths. To
be bred in a place of estimation; to see nothing low and sordid . . .
to have leisure to read . . . to be habituated in armies to command
and to obey . . . to be a professor of high science, or of liberal and
ingenuous art. . . ." Who does not know the marvelous, sagacious
lines? Surely Gibbon at Lausanne, if he read this passage, must
have lifted his eyes more than once from Burke's page to his own
portrait by Reynolds. Gibbon may have read on and seen his own

26. *DF.*, I, 152–155.
27. *DF.*, I, 422.
28. *DF.*, II, 323.
29. Edward Gibbon, *The History of the Decline and Fall of the Roman Empire*, ed.
J. B. Bury (London, 1900), I, xxxvi.

conclusion: "These are the circumstances of men that form what I should call a *natural* aristocracy, without which there is no nation." [30]

The order of Nature justified social subordination, and men (even as lions) know the true prince. But what of the princes themselves: how are they, the heroes, the governors, to learn their duties both as private persons and, for it is of greater moment, as statesmen? The eighteenth century pointed to the example of God's providential attributes, to his "power, light, virtue, wisdom and goodness." [31] "For that," Hooker had said so long ago, "which moveth God to work is goodness, and that which ordereth his work is wisdom, and that which perfecteth his work is power." [32] No man has invented a shrewder maxim of government, either of self-government or of the government of men. The political history of the world is no more than a record of the use or abuse of this formula. Connoting the mind of God, so much of the definition as human imperfection might comprehend ought to, yes, must, said the eighteenth century, inform the conscience of the governing class.

Gibbon often mocked or deplored vagaries of religious perception; yet throughout his life he adhered implicitly to what was, in fact, a religious concept of society and government. Take, for example, the providential attributes. "Omnipotence . . . ," said Gibbon, "is guided by infinite wisdom and goodness." [33] Mark well that verb "is guided," for the verb knits the three attributes indissolubly together. God, had he chosen to make a standard for action out of his infinite power alone, might have ruled as perfect evil.

> Pow'r unattended, terror would inspire,
> Aw'd must we gaze, and comfortless admire.
> But when fair Wisdom joins in the design,
> The beauty of the whole results divine! [34]

30. Edmund Burke, *Works* (Boston, 1884), IV, 174–175.
31. Sir Walter Raleigh's list as quoted in Johnson's *Dictionary, s.v. attribute.*
32. Richard Hooker, *Of the Laws of Ecclesiastical Polity,* Bk. V, chap. lvi, 5, in "Works" (Oxford, 1850), I, 623.
33. *DF.,* I, 685.
34. Samuel Boyse, *Deity: A Poem* (London, 1739), p. 27.

Thus the Deity with infinite justice had restrained his power by wisdom and goodness.

On earth, then, as it is in heaven. As with God's good Providence so it ought to be with governors and constitutions.

Neither Gibbon's noblest Romans nor his English associates thought of finding in power the source of their standards. Power to them was a means, not an end. They were not yet romantics. Their education had taught them to distinguish public duty from the objectives of a heated imagination. They abhorred enthusiasm as they detested tryants. They believed in what Babbitt used to call the inner check. So Gibbon's heroic apostate, the Emperor Julian, tried to stem his power by imitating "the moral attributes of the Deity." [35] And if the prince failed voluntarily to limit the exercise of power, Gibbon saw that Nature could do it for him. "The exercise of boundless despotism is happily checked by the laws of nature and necessity. In proportion to his wisdom and virtue, the master of an empire is confined to the path of his sacred and laborious duty. In proportion to his vice and folly, he drops the sceptre too weighty for his hands; and the motions of the royal image are ruled by the imperceptible thread of some minister or favourite." [36] The *aristoi* had possibly created God in the image of their ideal selves. They would not have been surprised to hear God declare in the words of Catherine the Great, *Je suis aristocrat, c'est mon métier.* "There is," said Burke, "no qualification for government but virtue and wisdom, actual or presumptive." [37]

And if princes and magistrates must learn to temper authority with wisdom and virtue, how still more necessary it became to build this principle of checks and balances into the constitutions of mankind. Gibbon was wholly abreast the age of Montesquieu, Blackstone, and the Founding Fathers in America when he confessed admiration for "a martial nobility and stubborn commons, possessed of arms, tenacious of property, and collected into constitutional assemblies" and concluded such to be "the only balance capa-

35. *DF.*, I, 798, 745.
36. *DF.*, II, 863.
37. Burke, *Works*, III, 297.

ble of preserving a free constitution against enterprises of an aspiring prince." [38] Gibbon, the Whig, distrusted princes. He deplored a society in which any one aggressive force so topped the others as to destroy the balance of interests. His model constitution was the English, as adjusted in 1689. He saw its prototype in the Roman Republic: "The temperate struggles of the patricians and plebeians had finally established the firm and equal balance of the constitution, which united the freedom of popular assemblies with the authority and wisdom of a senate and the executive powers of a regal magistrate." [39] And elsewhere he completed this confession of Whig faith by adding: "The choice of the people is the best and purest title to reign over them." [40] In constitutional checks and balances, coupled with the indispensable spirit of public virtue, Gibbon found the key to ordered liberty.

Every page of the *Decline and Fall* exhales the spirit of freedom. Freedom is the source of public virtue,[41] is "the happy parent of taste and science," [42] "the source of every generous and rational sentiment." [43] Freedom, to this precursor of Mill, spurs the spirit of emulation, that "most powerful spring of the efforts and improvements of mankind." [44] For proof Gibbon pointed to Athenians and Arabs. Conversely, the want of freedom inspired fear, and fear, in turn, "the dark and implacable genius of superstition," [45] which brought death to the Roman Empire and much, if not all, of its woe. The rise of Christianity and the fall of the Empire, as G. M. Young suggests, appeared to Gibbon to be "parallel effects of a general collapse of the intellect under the pressure of a world-tyranny," the Church.[46] The right institutions, moreover the right spirit, had gradually faded even from the memory. Once, indeed, an emperor (the abject Honorius) tried to convene a partly free, representative body. The annual assembly of Arles consisted

38. *DF.*, I, 53.
39. *DF.*, II, 91.
40. *DF.*, II, 216.
41. *DF.*, I, 9.
42. *DF.*, I, 52.
43. *DF.*, II, 9.
44. *DF.*, II, 878.
45. *DF.*, I, 258; II, 6.
46. G. M. Young, *Gibbon* (London, 1932), p. 96.

of all that was respectable in Gaul—the Pretorian prefect, the seven provincial governors, the magistrates, and perhaps the bishops of about sixty cities, besides a competent

number of the most honourable and opulent *possessors* of land, who might justly be considered as the representatives of their country. They were empowered to interpret and communicate the laws of their sovereign; to expose the grievances and wishes of their constituents; to moderate the excessive or unequal weight of taxes; and to deliberate on every subject of local and national importance that could tend to the restoration of the peace and prosperity of the seven provinces. If such an institution, which gave the people an interest in their own government, had been universally established by Trajan or the Antonines, the seeds of public wisdom and virtue might have been cherished and propagated in the empire of Rome.

Checks and balances would have secured both the monarch and the community. But the remedy was partial, the application tardy. The lamp of liberty burned low. Had these matters been otherwise the Roman Empire, "under the mild and generous influence" of freedom, "might have remained invincible and immortal." [47]

How vast is Gibbon's self-assurance, how sublime his conclusion that a society which elects to guide its power with wisdom and virtue may live forever. Certainly Gibbon underestimated the effect of techniques in shaping a society, and in his constant emphasis upon the necessity for character in leaders he overlooked the role of personality. Still, his concept of society as the product of conscience or the want of conscience has use, especially when what Gibbon thought should be the contents of that conscience is understood. Obviously he preferred the cardinal virtues to the more passive Christian precepts of piety and humility. His early Christians inspired him with enormous mirth—sometimes with bitterness. But all his esteem went out to Julian, the physical hero of his tale, to the Apostate, whose virtues Gibbon used as the measure of all heroes. The list is long: firmness (how often George III stressed firmness), moderation, justice and clemency, prudence, intrepidity, affability, flexibility of mind, love of fame and country, humanity. The list of "manly virtues" is long, it is pagan, and therefore to an eighteenth-century gentleman the list was incomplete.

47. *DF.*, I, 1149.

Yet the gentleman would have understood these virtues. They were symbols of something absolute and universal and they lifted him to a place where in his imagination he associated with the great, heroic, wise, and virtuous dead. If he had hearkened to historians, poets, tutors, priests, parents as well as to writers on education, on painting, and the English constitution, he had learned that the end of life is virtue and wisdom. If not overwhelmed or stifled by such concentrated evidence respecting the cultural unity of the civilization which he enjoyed, he might hope to share in the justice of Aristides and in the intrepidity of Regulus. He might by his example bequeath a name renowned for public virtue both to his family and to his countrymen. He would be remembered when people spoke of "the wisdom of our ancestors." Humble before this ideal and in conduct more disciplined than his forebears, he strove to be imposing. Outward dignity of manners, of language, even of possessions, should, he thought, reflect the inner gravity of his mind and social conscience. English might be his tailored park, Roman must be his porticoes. These should fulfill a moral purpose. Theirs was the function to excite the moral imagination to revere the wisdom and virtue of a public servant.

In such way the English gentleman developed character and leadership; and in the end his education was a moral education which, as Whitehead says, is impossible without habitual visions of greatness.

III

Gibbon never wrote the history of the Roman Republic. Had he realized his youthful ambition to trace the history of Rome from Romulus to Augustus,[48] his critics might perhaps have paid as much attention to the positive side of his teaching that Porson saw as to his destructive opinions on Christianity. Mr. Low might have qualified his conclusion that "Gibbon was neither a propagandist nor a preacher," and Becker assuredly would not have turned the whole purport of the *Decline and Fall* upside down by stating that it was Gibbon who "made the direct frontal attack on the Christian

48. *Le Journal de Gibbon à Lausanne,* ed. Georges Bonnard (Lausanne, 1945), December 7, 1763, p. 169.

centuries." Gibbon was neither revolutionary nor republican. But for him the Republic disclosed a golden age because it embodied those pragmatic values by which he judged succeeding centuries. To it he delighted to return from time to time, when fatigued by the constant aspect of "a declining monarchy," there once again to breathe its "pure and invigorating air." [49] Following the banishment of the kings, "the republic reposed on the firm basis which had been founded by their wisdom and virtue." [50] Imperceptibly at first, decline set in with the Empire. Yet the spirit and the image of the Republic, if not the constitutional checks and balances, lingered into the second century. Under Trajan and the Antonines "the firm edifice of Roman power" (an absolute monarchy in the guise of a commonwealth) "was raised and preserved by the wisdom of ages." [51] It was preserved by the dead hand of the past.

Nonetheless Gibbon made of the second century the high tableland of happiness. It was not perfect, since the forms and not the substance of a free constitution, the image and not the reality of liberty, masked a most un-English despotism. But if not perfect, the second century was good, so good in fact that Gibbon chose it for his starting point. And in the following précis of the century he set forth the complete statement of his faith, his philosophy, and the thesis which he defended from beginning to end of his history. It is the most pregnant passage Gibbon ever wrote.

If a man were called to fix the period in the history of the world, during which the condition of the human race was most happy and prosperous, he would, without hesitation, name that which elapsed from the death of Domitian to the accession of Commodus. The vast extent of the Roman empire was governed by absolute power, under the guidance of virtue and wisdom. The armies were restrained by the firm but gentle hand of four successive emperors, whose characters and authority commanded involuntary respect. The forms of the civil administration were carefully preserved by Nerva, Trajan, Hadrian, and the Antonines, who delighted in the image of liberty, and were pleased with considering themselves as the accountable ministers of the laws. Such princes deserved the honour of restoring the republic had the Romans of their days been capable of enjoying a rational freedom.[52]

49. *DF.*, II, 323.
50. *DF.*, II, 594.
51. *DF.*, I, 25.
52. *DF.*, I, 70.

Here is Gibbon's starting point, here the ski jump of humanity. But if humanity swept downward to disaster, the portly Gibbon, as he retraced the descending track from this moment in Chapter III, picked his way laboriously among the thorns and rocks of intolerance, folly, passion, and ignorance, until with Petrarch he began to mount the steepy heights that led ultimately upward to the eighteenth century.

Along the slow course of his story Gibbon chants a dirge no less melancholy than the litanies of the "barefooted fryars" to whom he listened that gloomy, immortal night in 1764, as he sat musing amid the ruins of the Capitol.[53] It is the death of the heroic spirit that he mourns, and one after another Gibbon passes, like a medieval preacher, like Lydgate and Sidney and Spenser, like the historical painters of his age, along the endless line of his emperors and leaders, pointing in his book to their mostly fatal example. None of these, assuredly not Julian, is the real hero of his piece. The hero is the potential character of man. About this character Gibbon wrote the mightiest epic of the century.

Suppose a great epic in prose, an epic that would let Gibbon try his strength with his masters, Homer and Herodotus. Long ago, in 1762, he had likened the rules of heroic poetry to those of history.[54] He approved, apparently, the introduction of a chorus into epics, because the chorus served as "a perpetual moral commentary upon the drama, enforcing every virtuous sentiment, rectifying every vicious one; and pointing out the important lessons which may be drawn from the catastrophe."[55] What else are the reflections, moral and political, with which Gibbon embellishes the *Decline and Fall?* What else the philosophic hints?[56]

Suppose then an epic history, and the subject matter, as Fielding said of his "heroic, historical, prosaic poem," *Tom Jones,* "nothing more than human nature." Suppose this humanistic aim to be, what Xenophon failed[57] and Fielding succeeded in achieving, exhibition of man in terms not of the incredible but of the probable. The spirit

53. *The Autobiographies of Edward Gibbon,* ed. John Murray (London, 1896), p. 405.
54. *MW.,* IV, 125.
55. *MW.,* IV, 127.
56. See *DF.,* II, 1218 n. 42.
57. *MW.,* III, 131.

of the eighteenth century, of Pope and Marlborough, of Thomson, Newcastle, Adam Smith, and Boswell, had little sympathy with those who sought to invent new epic fables. "Epic poetry," said Walpole, "is the art of being as long as possible in telling an uninteresting story; and an epic poem is a mixture of history without truth, and of romance without imagination. . . . Epic poetry . . . is not suited to an improved and polished state of things." [58] Decidedly. But there might be a prose epic, a tragic, epic history, a study, like *Paradise Lost,* in the degeneration of human character. No need to betray enthusiasm, to preach or declaim, to copy the dogmatists of d'Holbach's circle. The times were good. And Gibbon wrote for his amusement. Still, he might, in passing, reflect upon the counsels and characters of men and mayhap warn the governing class to take away the things that ought not to be.

The last volume of the *Decline and Fall* appeared in 1788. For the next four years Gibbon, among his white acacias at Lausanne, watched with ever consuming alarm the uncoiling of the "monster," democracy, in France. "That country," he wrote in September, 1789, "is now in a state of *dissolution."* The French—the year was 1791—"have only exchanged despotism for anarchy." "If they had been content with a liberal translation of our system . . . they might have raised a solid fabric, on the only true foundation, the natural aristocracy of a great country." "I am as high an aristocrate as Burke himself." "What a strange wild world do we live in!" —"this total subversion of all rank, order, and government, could be productive only of a popular monster, which after devouring every thing else, must finally devour itself." "The hopes of the wise and good"—he writes after the declaration of war—"are now fixed on the success of England," on "England, the sole great refuge of mankind against the opposite mischiefs of despotism and democracy"—"I . . . rejoice that you are now armed . . . against the new barbarians, who labour to confound the order and happiness of society." "At this momentous crisis we should enlist our whole force of virtue, ability, and spirit." With humanists today Gibbon

58. Horace Walpole, *Letters,* ed. Toynbee, XII, 273–274. Walpole to Mason, June 25, 1782.

stood appalled before the flooding tides of passion, ignorance, and tyranny.

He failed, of course. He failed to teach the revolutionaries who were to carry beyond France the total subversion he so dreaded. Yet he had, in a sense, taught Englishmen because he taught them what they knew before. To that end, as well as in the hope of fame, he had spared no pains to make his vision comprehensive, his style luminous, his knowledge encyclopedic, and his statements exact. He had adhered to "the great law of impartiality." Gibbon had been impartial in defense of aristocratic principles.

THOMAS PERCY, SCHOLAR

Irving L. Churchill

THE Reverend Thomas Percy, M.A., became a member of the Club early in the year 1768, about four years after its establishment. With at least two of its members, Johnson and Goldsmith, he had been on terms of personal friendship for approximately ten years. Johnson, for example, had stayed with Percy for nearly two months at his rectory in Easton Mauduit, Northamptonshire, in the summer of 1764; and Percy had seen something of both men on his occasional visits to London. Since shortly after the publication of his *Reliques of Ancient English Poetry* in 1765 he had enjoyed the patronage of the Earl of Northumberland, as his domestic chaplain and private secretary, and in that capacity was pleasantly established in London for a substantial part of each year.

It is easy to imagine, I think, that Percy not only was flattered by his election to the Club but regarded it as an appropriate recognition of his qualities as a friend and as a literary man and scholar. For in 1768, at the age of almost forty, Percy possessed a substantial reputation as a scholar and editor. He had published seven works within six years, beginning in 1761, in fields as diverse as Runic poetry and the Song of Solomon. His most important publication, *The Reliques,* had gone through two London editions and one in Dublin. His now largely forgotten version of a Chinese novel, *Hau Kiou Choaan,* had appeared in French, German, and Dutch translations. His circle of acquaintances included a number of scholars of the time—such men as Thomas Warton at Oxford and Richard Farmer at Cambridge—with whom he maintained an active correspondence and a mutual interchange of information and of books on literary and antiquarian matters.

Since Joseph Ritson's criticisms in the 1780's, however, of Percy's treatment of the textual sources of some of the ballads in the *Reliques,* and particularly since the publication of the Folio MS in 1867–68 by Hales and Furnivall, it has been generally agreed that, whatever virtues of energy and enthusiasm Percy may have possessed, he certainly had no conception of the methods·or the obligations of the scholar. But in the light of information rather recently made available, notably *The Correspondence of Thomas Percy and Richard Farmer,* it appears that the scholarly qualities of the man deserve a reappraisal.

In the heyday of his editorial and publishing activities—that is, in the early 1760's in his quiet Northamptonshire parsonage—he was in close contact with many of that group of eighteenth-century scholars who were emphasizing the necessity of getting back to first editions and of making careful collations in order to establish accurate texts. They were often of mutual assistance to one another, and Percy gave and received aid on terms of complete equality with the best of them. Indeed, he was a worthy associate of these men whom he regarded as his personal friends, and they acknowledged him as a fellow worker.

One of Percy's projects in these years was an edition of Surrey's poems, the idea for which seems to have occurred to him because of his acquisition of a copy of the 1559 edition of *Tottel's Miscellany.* "What encourages me to undertake it anew," he wrote to Thomas Warton on November 28, 1762, "is the having in my possession a very ancient Copy printed in 1559: which is much more correct than those more commonly known in 1565, 1567, 1585 etc: I shall also collate an old Copy in the public Library at Cambridge, dated 1574." He had already shared the news of his copy with Richard Farmer (June 5, 1762), telling him that it was "seven year [s] older than any Copy I ever heard of before," and expressing interest in Farmer's report of a copy as early as 1557. This latter proved to be the property of Edward Capell, from whom Percy eventually borrowed it (Letter to Farmer, February 1, 1766).

In his proposed edition of Surrey's poems, to which he later decided to add the poems of Wyatt, Percy was undertaking the same kind of task that Tyrwhitt performed for Chaucer and Malone for Shakespeare. Through the years, as his correspondence with Farmer reveals, he searched assiduously for the earliest editions of *Tottel's Miscellany,* and established his own text only after careful collation of several editions, including what he supposed to be the earliest one. He also sought for stray poems of both authors, in an attempt to make his own text complete, and was the first modern editor to discover Wyatt's *Psalmes* and Surrey's *Aeneid* and *Ecclesiastes*.

With the energy characteristic of Percy, he undertook to prepare an edition of the works of the Duke of Buckingham at the same time that he was working on Surrey. A letter to Farmer (October 9, 1763) presents a rather typical example of his editorial methods and illustrates again the importance which he attached to the collation of early editions:

I have now got together all the editions of the Rehearsal: the 2ᵈ and 3ᵈ which I so long wanted, are now in my Escritoire: I only want one play of Ned Howard's, viz. *The 6 Days adventures* 4ᵗᵒ 1671. to compleat my Key, the last sheet of which alone remains unprinted, to revise it and a few other afterthoughts.—For the life, I have made some additions to my materials by the favour of Dʳ Birch, and Lord Royston, consisting of extracts from scarce books, and some original Letters of the Duke, never published. Mʳ Tonson has also procured me one or two scarce tracts relating to him, which before I was not possest of.

Even in the preparation of the *Reliques* Percy devoted an enormous amount of his own time and energy to collating texts, and what he could not do for himself he often asked his friends to do for him. He borrowed numerous volumes of songs and ballads from their private libraries and, when they were university men, from the libraries of the universities with which they were connected; he borrowed or bought other volumes from the London booksellers. Very often he dispatched transcripts of ballads to his friends to be collated with manuscripts in the libraries to which they had access. Among those who gave him generous aid of this sort were Thomas Astle at the British Museum, Warton at the Bodleian Library and the Ashmolean Museum at Oxford, and Farmer and Edward Blakeway at Cambridge, where they made use of the extensive Pepysian Collection at Magdalene College. Quite typical of the thoroughness which he exacted of himself as well as of his collaborators is this request Percy made of Farmer in a letter of September 9, 1762: "Lastly be so kind as to collate the inclosed song with the original in the Pepys Library, and send me all the References &c that are in Pepys's Ist Volume of Old Ballads Folio, it is said that a more ancient Copy of this song is preserved in the Bodleyan Library. Please to transcribe the account." On another occasion (January 30, 1763), when Percy felt that he was making unreasonable demands upon Farmer's time, he suggested that the latter "throw off some part of the load upon that idle fellow Blakeway. He has no pupil-drudgery to call him off from the more noble persuit of ascertaining the Dates, and settling the readings of *half-penny ballads.*"

The care which Percy exercised in "ascertaining the Dates" and otherwise establishing background information, as he worked on each of his successive books, was in every respect equal to that which he devoted to collation of texts. With the zeal of a true scholar he would turn over half a dozen volumes, if necessary, to write one footnote; or he would write half a dozen letters to scholar friends who might be expected to have desired information at their finger-tips. To cite but a few instances, when he decided to include the "Turnament of Tottenham" in the *Reliques* he asked Farmer to examine the works of the early bibliographers Leland, Bale, etc., in an attempt to discover the date of the supposed author Gilbert Pilkington; when he began to work on that portion of the *Reliques* devoted to songs and ballads illustrating Shakespeare he asked Farmer (Letter of December 31, 1763) to send him all the volumes of Warburton's and Theobald's *Shakespeare,* Meres' *Palladis Tamia,* and all of Farmer's own early quartos, to supplement Percy's own First and Second Folios; he devoted large portions of two letters to Farmer in December, 1763, and February, 1764, to a discussion of the authorship of "The Passionate Shepherd to His Love" and "The Answer," weighing the conflicting authorities one against another, asking Farmer's help in establishing the dates of these authorities, and finally reaching the decision with which modern editors concur—that Marlowe and Raleigh, respectively, were the authors.

The thoroughness of Percy's methods in conducting his investigations extended to the preparation of his works for publication. An examination of his *Hau Kiou Choaan,* or his volumes on Runic poetry, as well as his *Reliques,* reveals that he was generally scrupulous in citing titles and exact page references to the volumes he had consulted. His one serious criticism of Farmer's *Essay on the Learning of Shakespeare* was its deficiency in this respect. In his letter of congratulations to the author (January 15, 1767), after passing along Johnson's "unreserved applause," he adds: "If I might venture to hint at anything I could have wished further: it would have been only that you had given us . . . the full title and date of some of the curious old Tracts you quote." Percy proceeded to indicate some two dozen points in the *Essay* where he felt the need of fuller explanations or of more precise bibliographical data. Farmer accepted Percy's suggestions and added notes to his second edition on most of the items that Percy had enumerated.

There are other instances of Percy's assistance in the scholarly enterprises of his friends. Though one gains the impression that on the whole he asked for and received aid much more often than he gave it, this situation was in large measure due to his less favorable location with respect to large libraries. When Thomas Astle sent him a sale catalogue of old plays, he was quick to recognize the significance of the 1597 quarto of *Richard II* for his friend Edward Capell's Shakespearean research. With obvious satisfaction he passed the news on to Farmer (Letter of May 10, 1762): "I have been so happy as to be instrumental in procuring him a Copy of Shakespear's *Richard II* earlier than he had ever heard of." Percy was always intensely interested in the projects of his friends and thoroughly enjoyed sending them bits of pertinent information which he had gleaned from his wide reading in many rare and curious volumes. And he showed undisguised pleasure when they used his contributions in their books, as they sometimes did. Five notes, for instance, in the Appendix in Volume VIII of Johnson's *Shakespeare* are Percy's. Even in his last years, when his own projects had been laid aside and most of the friends of his middle age were dead, he followed eagerly and with an alert and critical mind the researches of Edmond Malone. The correspondence of these two men frequently contains observations and bits of information from Percy, and appreciative acknowledgments from Malone. But the most notable example of this sort of assistance was in the second edition of Warton's *Observations on the Faerie Queene,* where, wrote Percy to Farmer (September 9, 1762), "Mr Warton has done me the honour to insert in his new Edition, a few crude Remarks which I occasionally made in my Letters to him." Among these insertions was an entire letter in which Percy had argued that Chaucer's "Sir Thopas" is a parody on the old metrical romances. Richard Hurd in his *Letters on Chivalry* (1762) is credited with being the first to take this view, but the facts with respect to the printing and publication of Warton's book indicate that Percy had arrived at this opinion independently at least a year before Hurd's book was published.

This last incident provides another example of Percy's interesting pioneer accomplishments in the scholarship of his day. His achievements of this sort were sometimes the result of persistent search and inquiry, sometimes merely of good luck, but at other times can be justly ascribed only to the breadth of his scholarship and his critical insight. His discovery of Wyatt's *Psalmes* and of Surrey's *Aeneid* and *Ecclesiastes* has already been mentioned. He also perceived that there was a connection between Surrey's work and that of Petrarch. In a very interesting letter to Farmer (February 28, 1764) he writes: "Pray have you any friend that understands Italian, that could be prevailed on to compare *Surrey's Poems* with *Petrarch's Sonnets,* I have discovered that many of the former are verbal Translations from the latter: I do not sufficiently understand Italian to persue this research accurately, and yet it ought to be done.—I will send both Petrarch and Surrey, if you can get them to be collated for me." In his *Reliques* he published for the first time a rondeau attributed to Chaucer, which Farmer had discovered in the Pepysian Collection and which most modern editors accept as genuinely Chaucerian. In the realm of etymology he first proposed an explanation of the word "pit" in its theatrical usage, as derived from the old playhouse in Drury Lane called The Cockpit, and although Malone disputed this interpretation, it is confirmed in the *Oxford English Dictionary.*

Not the least important of Percy's qualities as a scholar was his healthy skepticism. Much as he depended upon his friends for the specialized information they could give him, he retained his critical independence in matters involving judgment and interpretation. He differed with his friend Capell as well as with Matthew Prior in assigning the date of the "Nut-brown Maid." He doubted the correctness of Warton's opinion that "The Boy and the Mantle" was derived from "Le Court Mantel," and even though Farmer's opinion supported Warton's, Percy nevertheless presented his own view of the matter in the *Reliques*. He questioned the accuracy of Farmer's statement that Sir Anthony Denny survived Surrey by four years, and asked to know the source of Farmer's information. He warned Farmer against accepting too readily the idea that "the Gargantua alluded to by Laneham, and Meres, is the *Gargantua* of Rablais," and added the shrewd surmise, "I rather suspect it to be some vulgar old book of Chivalry, whence Rablais borrowed the name of his giant."

Such is the portrait of Percy the scholar as he appeared to his friends and fellow workers in the field of scholarship: a man whom Johnson could justly praise for his "minute accuracy of enquiry." He was tireless and painstaking in his investigations, generous in the assistance he gave to others, discerning and independent and frequently original in his critical judgments. He appreciated the values of scholarship, possessed a scholar's conscience, and habitually employed sound scholarly methods.

Why then, it may be asked, was he so unscholarly in the treatment of some of his ballad texts? To answer that question adequately, as it deserves, would lengthen this essay unreasonably. The essence of the matter, however, is that in common with most of his generation he regarded folk ballads as trivial compositions hardly worth the attention of a serious scholar. Wisely or unwisely, and only under great pressure from his friend Shenstone, he deliberately chose to sacrifice textual accuracy in some cases for readability. There is little doubt that if his editions of Surrey and Buckingham had been published in the 1760's or 1770's, as he had hoped—instead of unfortunately never reaching the stage of publication—Percy's reputation as an editor and scholar would stand much higher than it does today and would reflect more accurately his real stature as a scholar.

CHARLES BURNEY, CRITIC

Benjamin C. Nangle

MADAME D'ARBLAY was in her eightieth year when she set herself with filial piety to studying the manuscript of her father's history of his life, and extracting from "the minute amplitude of this vast mass of matter" such material as she deemed proper for submission to the public eye. The results were not altogether fortunate. Too often the Memorialist seems more concerned with her own sensibilities and moral reflections than with her father's career. But she does give numerous facts and near facts concerning the various Burneys, often even abandoning, for the purpose of recording them, the remarkable prose which she invented for the execution of her task.

She tells us, for instance, that in 1791

a fresh, yet voluntary occupation, drove his newly restored leisure away, and opened a course of bookish and critical toil, that soon seized upon every spare moment. This was constituting himself a member amongst the Monthly Reviewers, under the editorship of the worthy Mr. Griffith.

Of the articles which were Dr. Burney's, no list has been found; and probably none was kept.

This tantalizing series of statements is accurate in three respects. Dr. Burney did review for the *Monthly,* his association with it was voluntary, and he did perform conscientiously his duties as a reviewer. But the Memorialist was in ignorance of certain facts, had with the passage of years doubtless forgotten others, and probably dismissed still more as not offering "any interest for the general reader." Actually, four Burneys—if we include Fanny's contribution of a single paragraph—expressed their critical opinions in the influential columns of the *Monthly*. The history of their reviewing activities still awaits its narrator.

It begins, not in 1791, but in the spring of 1783. Even for the Burneys the opening of 1783 was an exciting time. The second volume of the great *History of Music* had been published in 1782, as had *Cecilia,* Fanny's second novel. The history had established Dr. Burney as the foremost scholar in his field, and the novel his daughter as the most discussed novelist of the time. "Next to the balloon," as Mrs. Barbauld wrote, "Miss Burney is the object of public curiosity." James was commanding H.M.S. *Bristol,* fifty guns, against the French in the Indian Ocean. Charles the younger, having secured his degree at Aberdeen, was serving as classical master in William Rose's school at Chiswick, and making love to Rose's daughter, whom he married on June 24, 1783.

Professionally as well as romantically, young Charles's association with the school at Chiswick was happy and fruitful. Dr. Rose was a learned and eminent man, with a fund of energy which must have excited the admiration even of a Burney. Translator of Sallust, prominent dissenting clergyman, famous schoolmaster, friend (Scot and Dissenter though he was) of Dr. Johnson, he still found time to be the most prolific contributor to *The Monthly Review.* In effect, he was almost co-editor with Griffiths; back in 1749 he had written the first article in the first number; he had married Mrs. Griffiths' sister, and throughout the years had remained Griffiths' closest colleague and most trusted adviser. In view of these facts, it is not surprising that *The Monthly Review* for April, 1783, contained a scholarly disquisition contributed by Dr. Rose's promising young classical master and prospective son-in-law.

This, and not Fanny's unidentified article by Charles Burney the elder in 1791, constitutes the first appearance of a Burney in the *Monthly,* and marks the beginning of a period of over thirty years in which nearly every number of the review contained contributions from some member of the family. Although Fanny was ignorant of the fact, authorship of articles in the *Monthly* was being recorded in Griffiths' copy, which now reposes in Bodley's Library. By referring to it, we can add several thousand pages to the Burney canons.

Of all this mass of material the reviews written by Dr. Burney the elder undoubtedly offer, to adopt Madame d'Arblay's phrase, the most interest to the general reader. Charles the younger owed his place on Griffiths' staff to his proficiency in the highly technical field of classical scholarship; and throughout his long career as a

Monthly Reviewer he used the periodical as a medium for the publication of articles which today would appear in the learned journals of classical research. As his reputation increased he satisfied increasingly Griffiths' implacable demand that his writers on technical and scholarly subjects be competent scholars in the field with which they were dealing. It is salutary for us to remember Parr's ranking of the three great Grecians in England—Porson, Parr, and Burney—and reflect that all three were reviewers for Griffiths.

For the general reader James Burney's contributions are somewhat too specialized. But they carry authority. James had been invalided home in 1785, afflicted with some obscure liver complaint induced by the climate of India. Although his health was soon restored he never again succeeded, in spite of oft-repeated appeals to the Admiralty and even a memorial to the King, in securing assignment to active duty. Eventually he accepted the fact that he was never again to see active service, and devoted himself to his great history of voyages and explorations in the South Seas. Beginning in June of 1795 he reviewed for the *Monthly* most of the numerous books which were appearing in connection with voyages of exploration and discovery. Few men in England were better qualified by training and experience to evaluate the reports of explorers. He had been an officer on Cook's last two voyages, had served in North America during the American Revolution, and had spent three years in command of the *Bristol* in the Indian Ocean. He had sailed many oceans and seen many peoples. Comments in the *Monthly* on books of voyage and discovery take on new meaning when one realizes that the author was Captain Burney. But, aside from occasional excursions into the field of public credit and taxation, in which he took a layman's interest and on which he himself wrote a pamphlet or two, his reviewing efforts are confined to the one great subject on which he was the acknowledged authority.

With his father this is not the case. Charles the elder was drawn into the circle of Monthly Reviewers in November of 1785, and for nearly seventeen years used its columns for the discussion of all manner of things. He commenced reviewer, to be sure, as England's leading historian of music, and he continued to be Griffiths' expert in that field. But he was a man of too many interests to be confined within his professional sphere, and in Griffiths he had an editor who subscribed to the old idea that on matters general and literary a man of intelligence and taste might venture to pronounce his ideas with impunity. As a result, the pages of the *Monthly* afford ample material from which to construct a picture of Dr. Burney as critic.

Under the firm guidance of "the worthy Mr. Griffith," the theory and practice of reviewing had changed little for the *Monthly* since the day, years before, when Dr. Johnson had enlightened his politely curious sovereign concerning the characteristic features of the Monthly Reviewers as distinguished from their brethren on the *Critical*. Griffiths still expected his reviewers to possess some expert knowledge—one Burney for music, another for classical scholarship, and a third for voyages and explorations. He still expected them to read a book before they reviewed it. And he still held to the old-fashioned view (soon to be blown into limbo by the smart boys of the *Edinburgh* and *Quarterly*) that the reviewer's function was not to write a clever essay of his own but to characterize the book under review, pass judgment on its excellencies and defects, and provide the reader with extracts sufficiently copious to enable him to make his own conclusions.

In its emphasis on conscientious thoroughness rather than superficial brilliance, this ideal was congenial to Dr. Burney. He tells us that his history of music was thirty years in meditation, twenty in writing and printing, and that in its composition he taxed every amusement and social enjoyment, even drawing deeply upon his sinking fund—sleep. And when, in his seventy-sixth year, he made himself responsible for the articles on music in Chambers' *Cyclopedia,* he wrote, "I had a mind to see what I could really do in twelve months, by driving the quill at every possible moment that I could steal from business or repose, by day and by night, in bed and up; and, with all this stir and toil, I have found it impossible to finish three letters of the alphabet!"

His reviews were prepared in this same painstaking fashion, and it is not difficult to believe Fanny's assertion that they "seized upon every spare moment." If, as Dr. Johnson implied, the Monthly Reviewers were dull because they confined themselves strictly to an account of the book under review, Dr. Burney was probably the dullest of them all. His formula for reviewing was thorough if not exciting. He read the book. He then read everything that the *Monthly* had ever said about previous works by the same author. He then wrote his review, paying far more attention to specific facts and details than to grace of style or literary form. His resultant formula was (a) a review of the *Monthly's* earlier comments on earlier works of the author, (b) a characterization and general criticism of the present work, (c) page-by-page, or poem-by-poem, comments on details, (d) extracts submitted for the reader's judgment, and usually (e) a list of Scotticisms, Gallicisms, and colloquial barbarisms marring the purity of the author's language. This procedure inspires confidence in the reviewer's competence, judgment, and thoroughness; it does not tend, however, to produce a sparkling literary essay.

Constructed thus, his reviews of books on music seem admirably calculated for the instruction of the contemporary reader but are of little interest to the general reader of the twentieth century. They deal thoroughly and authoritatively with the works under discussion. On arguable matters of controversy they present the author's position and consider it with courtesy—often, however, with a reference to Dr. Burney's *History* and a candid statement that the reviewer is in agreement with Burney. Only when the author is maintaining some fantastically untenable theory, such as the antiquity of Welsh or Irish music, does the reviewer become derisive or sarcastic. But when all is said and done, however admirably they fulfilled their original purpose, these reviews deal with a specialized subject and forgotten scholarly controversies.

A second major group of the doctor's reviews—those concerning Italian literature, music, art, and drama—can also be dismissed with only passing mention. He seized every chance to urge upon the English reading public the advisability of a more intimate acquaintance with the Italian culture which he loved. To the extent that articles in the *Monthly* inspired among the English a greater interest in things Italian, the credit must be his. But, again, this

must seem to the modern reader a matter of rather remote historical interest.

A third group of his reviews deals with the biographies, memoirs,
and collected editions of the works of men with whom he had
been intimate. Much of the material in these reviews takes on new
interest when rescued from anonymity and assigned to Dr. Burney.
Here we may best resort to the reviewer's method of offering extracts. The following passages offer Burney's comments on Johnson's conversation, his dissent from Boswell's remarks on the
Doctor's superstitions, his rather startling conclusion concerning
Johnson's attitude toward poetry, his thoughtful analysis of Johnson's religion, and his estimate of Johnson's final position in the
eyes of posterity. Considering their source, we certainly must grant
them all a place in the great library of Johnsonian gleanings.

The sentence passed by this biographer [Anderson] on Johnson's conversation we think not merely severe, but unjust. It was only in large companies, at
times when he was irritated by arrogance, and when all were treasuring up
his decisions, that he talked for victory: but when his opinions were modestly
asked by his friends in private, even by Boswell himself, who put questions to
him which no one else had the courage to do, we may be 'sure that he spoke
the sentiments of his conviction';—and on these occasions he frequently became so eloquent, copious, and accurate, that he seemed reading a well-written
book. If Dr. A. does not allow that his conversations with Boswell were
'much distinguished by flashes of wit and humour,' we know not where to
seek these qualities. We imagine, however, that, if Dr. A., who seems so
desirous of being candid, had ever heard Johnson converse with those whom
he loved, and who respected him, we should not have had [Anderson's re-
marks] on the subject. . . .

His anxiety to ascertain the immateriality of the soul, and the doctrine of
a future state, accounts for his solicitude to give authenticity to stories of ap-
paritions, and his eagerness to credit the existence of second sight, while he
appeared scrupulous, and sceptical as to common facts.

. . . the principal of which [Johnson's defects as a critic] are certainly the
offspring of prejudice, and want of taste for almost all poetry except heroic
and didactic. Perhaps his defective sight prevented him from studying nature,
and from enjoying 'the silent beauties of creation.'

. . .—and perhaps the present liberality, enlargement, and indiscriminate
toleration of all religions and all sects, do not arise so much from *respect* for
the religion of others, as from *indifference* for our own. Johnson was so much

in earnest in his religious belief and practice, that deviations from the rites and ceremonies of our own church were offensive to him; particularly, if those deviations leaned towards what he thought the irreverent plainness of Calvin, or the total incredulity of French philosophers. To the supererogation of Catholics, Methodists, and Moravians, he was extremely charitable: but for the plain coat of JACK, without button or loop, he had no reverence. Yet there were individuals among Dissenters whom he highly respected: such as Dr. Watts, Dr. Robertson, Dr. Beattie, Dr. Blair, the late Dr. Rose, and several worthy ministers of the church of Scotland, with whom he made acquaintance in his tour to the Hebrides. Much of his pretended abuse of the Presbyterians and Whigs was more playful than malignant. If he talked of *Presbyterian dogs,* and *stinking Whigs,* he meant no greater reproach than the Dissenters and Whigs themselves, who ever denounced him as a *furious Jacobite,* or *rank Tory!* Speaking of his own eye, of which he had long lost the sight, he frequently said, "the *dog* was never good for anything"; and for his having neglected the performance of some friendly office for an acquaintance, during his own sickness, he excused himself by saying, "Sir! every man's a *scoundrel* in sickness; he only thinks of himself."

We were never partial to Dr. Johnson's politics, nor to his prejudices, and we have frequently combated his opinions: but we ever must allow him to have been a great moral writer, and a man of genius, learning, probity, and piety. Where his prejudices do not operate, his criticisms are so deep, just, and original, that in all probability they will long guide the public taste; which they are the more likely to do, as he must ever be ranked himself among our prose writers of the first class: nor can he with justice be denied a distinguished place among our poets, of the second class, at least.

There remains another group of reviews, perhaps the most interesting of all, in which Dr. Burney discusses contemporary literature. Fanny, of course, assures us frequently that her father was highly esteemed as a literary critic; for example,

Dr. Burney had too general a love of literature, as well as of the arts, to limit his admiration, any more than his acquirements, to his own particular cast; while the friends just mentioned [Dr. Johnson, Mr. Burke, and Sir Joshua Reynolds] regarded his musical science but as a matter apart; and esteemed and loved him solely for the qualities that he possessed in common with themselves.

And to Griffiths, therefore, there seemed nothing anomalous in entrusting to the historian of music the task of criticizing literature. Literary criticism had not yet become a profession and developed its own professional jargon. Literature was written for the delight and instruction (or instruction and delight) of all intelligent and civilized men; Dr. Johnson himself questioned "if there be in the world such another man, altogether, for mind, intelligence, and manners, as Dr. Burney"; why should an editor not look to him for comment on the collected works of the late Poet Laureate, or on that strange production entitled *Lyrical Ballads?*

In general, Dr. Burney's critical principles conform to the accepted taste of his generation. He commends Dr. Aikin's language in terms reminiscent of Johnson; it "is indeed, both forcible and natural; and though he never labours to attain elegance, he very seldom descends to colloquial familiarity." In discussion of poetic theory and practice he constantly looks back to Dryden and Pope for yardsticks by which to measure contemporary work. Sotheby's *The Battle of the Nile* contains "lines which would not disgrace Dryden," but is disfigured by such lines as "Dids't rush in triumph down, and spoil the slain." "*Dids't* [comments Burney] has scarcely been admitted in good poetry, since it was stigmatized by Pope: 'While expletives their feeble aid *do* join.'" In a passage which reads like a paraphrase of Dryden's remarks on the subject, he makes the distinction between the French taste formed by *rule* and the English by pure *genius,* and proceeds to explain that Shakespeare pleases Englishmen "in spite of his ignorance or contempt of the unities, and all his wildness, puns, and absurdities, to which we are less blind than *habituated.*" He regards the sonnet as an unsuitable medium for English verse:

When Englishmen first read a sonnet, their ears are generally dissatisfied. The disposition of the rhymes is so different from that to which we have been accustomed, that we never enjoy this texture till we have habituated ourselves to bear the disappointment primarily excited.

Obscurity also seems to belong to the sonnet, which is seldom clear at the first reading. . . .

He concurs with Pope's objection to "the repetition of the same rhymes within four or six lines of each other, as tiresome to the ear through their monotony," and his musician's ear insists that this objection "is equally cogent with respect to blank verse, and to prose; where an important word continues vibrating on the ear during the perusal of at least five or six lines."

From all this it is clear that Dr. Burney accepts the critical standards of his time. His distinction as a critic—for I think he has distinction—lies in the clarity with which he perceived, and the continuous vigor with which he opposed, the fallacies that were reducing the poetry of the later eighteenth century to imitative sterility. Here again, to be sure, he is but following Dryden in pointing out that adherence to the mechanic rules can never by itself produce the living beauties of literature. But this was precisely the fallacy by which too many poets of the time were guided. The notion was all too prevalent that any idea became poetry once it was expressed in regular, rhyming, iambic couplets. "Its being in rhyme," says Burney, "is the only mark of poetry with which this play is stamped." Or again, "Common thoughts, expressed in common language, and unembellished with poetical imagery, will probably not obtain much public favour by a mechanical arrangement of syllables, into what is called verse." Many thoughts, as some poets of his generation failed to realize, have not within them the stuff of poetry and are much better left in prose.

Dryden had also said that the rules "will raise perfection higher where it is, but are not sufficient to give it where it is not." Burney perceived that his generation had forgotten this fact, tending to applaud as poetry feeble thoughts if they were couched in regular verse. He stressed even more than Dryden, because he felt that the poets of his time had lost sight of it, the necessity of originality—Dryden called it invention—in the poet. The test of a poet lies in his ability to work within the rules but at the same time to find freedom of expression. On this count Burney condemns the poetry of Thomas Warton, the Poet Laureate; all his poems seem "cast in the mould of some gifted predecessor." Of all the major poets of his lifetime, Warton seems to him the last in point of originality.

The first—and here we are back to Dryden's notion of genius transcending the rules—is Christopher Smart.

His errors are those of a bold and daring spirit, which bravely hazards what a vulgar mind could never suggest. Shakespeare, Milton, and Dryden, are sometimes wild and irregular; and it seems as if originality alone could try experiments. Accuracy is timid, and seeks for authority. Fowls of feeble wing seldom quit the ground, though at full liberty; while the eagle, unrestrained, soars into unknown regions.

There Dryden and Dr. Burney, and all good critics, speak as one
—the rules are made for lesser men; the genius breaks them all and,
unrestrained, soars into unknown regions.

Only once, in his career as a reviewer, was Dr. Burney's critical
equilibrium disturbed. The *Lyrical Ballads* disconcerted him, as
they would certainly have disconcerted the other members of the
Club. Judged by the well-established critical precepts which had
served his century so well, they were certainly not, in either matter
or manner, poetry. The stuff of poetry was not to be found in
"rustic delineations of low-life"; "the elevation of soul, when it is
lifted into the higher regions of imagination, affords us a delight
of a different kind from the sensation which is produced by the
detail of common incidents." At its best, such subject matter can
produce nothing better than *Poésie larmoyante*. As for manner,

Though we have been extremely entertained with the fancy, and facility, and
(in general) the sentiments, of these pieces, we cannot regard them as *poetry*,
of a class to be cultivated at the expence of a higher species of versification,
unknown in our language at the time when our elder writers, whom this
author condescends to imitate, wrote their ballads.—Would it not be degrad-
ing poetry, as well as the English language, to go back to the barbarous and
uncouth numbers of Chaucer? Suppose, instead of modernizing the old bard,
that the sweet and polished measures, on lofty subjects, of Dryden, Pope, and
Gray, were to be transmuted into the dialect and versification of the four-
teenth century? Should we be gainers by the retrogradation? *Rust* is a necessary quality to a counterfeit old medal: but, to give artificial rust to modern
poetry, in order to render it similar to that of three or four hundred years ago,
can have no better title to merit and admiration than may be claimed by any
ingenious forgery. None but savages have submitted to eat acorns after corn
was found.

And yet Burney was disturbed, because he recognized in the
Ballads—concerning each of which he gives his characteristically
methodical comment—the presence of that genius and originality
for which he was always searching. Even the strangest of these
poems had something which was lacking in Thomas Warton:

The author's first piece, the *Rime of the ancyent marinere,* in the imitation of
the *style* as well as of the spirit of the elder poets, is the strangest story of a
cock and bull that we ever saw on paper: yet, though it seems a rhapsody of
unintelligible wildness and incoherence, (of which we do not perceive the

drift, unless the joke lies in depriving the wedding guest of his share of the feast,) there are in it poetical touches of an exquisite kind.

Finally, in closing his long review, the old Doctor writes:

So much genius and originality are discovered in this publication, that we wish to see another from the same hand, written on more elevated subjects and in a more cheerful disposition.

Forty years had passed since that spring day in 1758 when Charles Burney and Samuel Johnson first met, drank tea together, and discussed Shakespearean criticism. Now, standing on the threshold of the new literary era, Burney was still a practising critic, and in the sentence above writing what may well stand as the *ave atque vale* of the Literary Club and Doctor Johnson's circle to the romantic generation of the future.

PART II

THE NOVELISTS

THE NOVELISTS AS COMMENTATORS

Irma Z. Sherwood

NO one reasonably well acquainted with the moral tone of the age could fail to label the quotations which follow "eighteenth century" in tenor; and few persons, I imagine, could spot the source of each quotation or even guess at the kind of writing from which it was taken.

A youthful mind is seldom totally free from ambition; to curb that, is the first step to contentment, since to diminish expectation, is to increase enjoyment.

All *pleasures* are greater in the *expectation,* or in the *reflection,* than in *fruition;* as all *pains,* which press heavy upon both parts of that unequal union by which frail mortality holds its precarious tenure, are ever most acute in the time of suffering.

The recollection of past happiness rather heightens than alleviates the sense of present distress.

It has been a thousand times observed, and I must observe it once more, that the hours we pass with happy prospects in view, are more pleasing than those crowned with fruition. In the first case, we cook the dish to our own appetite; in the latter, nature cooks it for us. It is impossible to repeat the train of agreeable reveries we called up for our entertainment.

Indeed the sensations of pleasure it [i.e., a sanguine temperament] gives are much more constant, as well as much keener, than those which that blind lady [Fortune] bestows; Nature having wisely contrived that some satiety and languor should be annexed to all our real enjoyments, lest we should be so taken up by them as to be stopped from further pursuits.

The subject matter and the similar formality of expression in all these quotations might even lead the reader to attribute them to one author. Certainly their neat, aphoristic finish seems characteristic of the conduct book, the periodical essay, or even the sermon. The fact is that each has been taken from the context of story—from

Evelina,[1] *Clarissa Harlowe,*[2] *The Fool of Quality,*[3] *The Vicar of Wakefield,*[4] and *Tom Jones*[5]—in that order.

The similarity of sentiment and expression in novels as diverse as those cited is no mere coincidence. For the eighteenth-century novelist felt it his privilege—nay, his duty—to punctuate his story with wise and pithy comments on human conduct. Nor did he confine his digressions to brief aphorisms of this type. The life history of a minor character, a sermon, a fable from a book which, conveniently enough, some character happens to be reading, or an enlightening conversation on a set problem (in epistolary novels, often one which is remembered word for word)—all such insertions were considered perfectly permissible, whatever their effect on the main current of the story, if only they served to illustrate some moral truism. Fielding's famous prerogative, "to digress, through this whole history, as often as I see occasion,"[6] was adopted by many a lesser writer, often with disastrous results.

The reasons for the prevalence of this digressive habit, a habit which helped to determine the characteristics of the eighteenth-century novel, are not far to seek. In a century dominated by the spirit of criticism, few writers had enough self-restraint to let their characters' actions stand unannotated; an action illustrated a principle of human conduct, desirable or undesirable, and the writer felt called upon to underline that principle for the edification of his readers. Edification, with the story regarded as "a vehicle to the instruction,"[7] was generally the author's avowed object, and indeed the whole bias of the century in favor of a moral purpose in art demanded at least the profession of this intention.

Had this moral tendency been confined to a central ethical theme, the novelist's design upon his readers would have been far less palpable. Usually, however, the author regarded the moral by-path as quite as attractive and edifying as his main route. Even in

1. Letter IV.
2. Vol. VII, Letter XCIV. (All references to Richardson's novels are to the Shakespeare Head Edition [Oxford, 1929–31], 18 vols.)
3. Chap. vii.
4. Chap. x.
5. Bk. XIII, chap. vi.
6. *Tom Jones,* Bk. I, chap. ii.
7. Preface to *Clarissa Harlowe,* I, xv.

those great novels of the century in which the theme is clearly defined and the unity is firm—achievements the more surprising when one considers the crude attempts at storytelling which preceded them and the disintegration which followed—these fascinating byways are not completely eschewed.

In *Clarissa Harlowe,* for example, much of the abstract moral theorizing, particularly the heroine's own, is directly related to the theme of Clarissa's purification and ennoblement by suffering. The "chain moralizing" in which minor characters indulge is, on the other hand, often grossly irrelevant—irrelevant to the theme, the action, and the development of the character who pens the remark. Self-contained essays such as Belford's comments on the Bible,[8] comments tenuously attached to the novel on the pretense that they were occasioned by a perusal of a "Meditation" of Clarissa's, are clearly nothing but extra sermons thrown in for good measure. Beginning with a comment on the superiority of the Bible to all other books, Belford proceeds to discuss the Bible's admirable style, the unreasonableness of man in seeking knowledge in less perfect books, the perversity of mankind in general, and the ignorance of wits who praise pagan authors and censure the Bible. Thus for three pages the Richardsonian moralizing snowballs on, one idea adhering to another, while the story languishes.

Although in general he exercises a much more conscious control over his material than does Richardson, Fielding too is sometimes led far afield in the pursuit of a didactic idea. In *Tom Jones,* it is true, his remarks are usually connected with the narrative and confined to a paragraph or two. In *Amelia,* however, the philosophical comments are sometimes expanded into complete social essays. Often, indeed, the essay completely overshadows the incident; and there are many incidents (like Dr. Harrison's solicitation of a powerful nobleman in Booth's behalf) [9] whose only *raison d'être* is the essay to which they give rise.

The commonness of this digressive habit, examples of which can be found in virtually every eighteenth-century novel, can be attributed not only to the spirit of criticism and the spirit of morality

8. Vol. VI, Letter **XCVI.**
9. Bk. XI, chap. ii.

which dominated the age but to the fact that the novel was a new literary type. Working in a new genre whose purpose, methods, and limitations were ill-defined, the novelist felt called upon to interrupt his narrative to justify what he was doing. Such justifications, even in the work of a master craftsman like Fielding, are symptoms of a defensive attitude. In *Tom Jones,* in addition to the "prolegomenous" chapters wholly devoted to an explanation of his plan, Fielding frequently inserts in the narrative comments such as the following: "And here, in defiance of all the barking critics in the world, I must and will introduce a digression concerning true wisdom, of which Mr. Allworthy was in reality as great a pattern as he was of goodness." [10] Passages of "defiance" and explanation, common punctuation marks in the novels of the period, are natural enough in a medium in which the artist, without the security of a tradition behind him, sometimes felt ill at ease.

Natural enough too, and for the same reason, is the extent to which the eighteenth-century novel tended to borrow methods from other literary forms. Methods already proved satisfactory in the periodical essay, the conduct book, the sermon, the polite letter, the epic, and the drama all found their way into the novel. That a new genre should have its roots in older, established forms is one of the laws of literature and, by and large, a sign of strength rather than of weakness. Weakness accompanies such dependence only when the older methods, instead of being adapted, are simply lifted and, with all their sins upon them, inserted into the new form. The conduct book and the sermon, in so far as they had suggested ethical themes; the polite letter, in so far as it had familiarized writers with sketching everyday scenes, reporting chitchat, and analyzing personal feelings; the essay, in so far as it had fostered the creation of story—all were rich sources of inspiration for the newly launched novel. In so far as these same forms, however, emphasized explicit didactic summary, their influence on the unity of the new art form was unfortunate.

The influence of the essay illustrates the point clearly. The eighteenth-century periodical essay had perfected the technique

10. Bk. VI, chap. iii.

of introducing a general ethical premise, of illustrating that premise with a pertinent example, and of drawing the whole together by hammering home a concluding lesson or caution. The method lay at hand, fully developed, for the novelist who wished to enforce his general principles with specific illustrations and exempla. A lesson which would be perfectly acceptable in the periodical essay is, however, often felt to be an intrusion in the novel. A novelist creates a new character only to illustrate his point—and then promptly forgets about him; he summarizes neatly, in finished eighteenth-century style, an admirable precept—which has nothing to do with the main theme. Writers were slow to realize that the artistic exigencies of the essay and of the novel differ; that the preoccupation with generalities and the artistic self-sufficiency of a portrait or narrative in miniature were often unsuited to the novel which, moving in larger and more complex rhythms, develops by a principle of relativity.

When essayists like Fielding, Goldsmith, and Johnson and writers of instructive manuals like Richardson turned to novel writing, they were influenced by their earlier training. As they felt their way in the new medium, they regarded themselves not only as tellers of tales but as critics and philosophers, preachers and reformers. This attitude concerning the function of the novelist, an attitude most clearly evidenced in the pat digressions, could not fail to have far-reaching effects—on the movement of the story, on the characters, and on the style of writing.

Pauses (or even dead stops) in the main action are common occurrences in the eighteenth-century novel. Leaving main characters waiting while a minor character, simply for the principle his tale illustrates, tells his life history; sandwiching into the narrative prayers, meditations, fables, sermons, and even numbered codes of conduct; [11] gathering together a group of characters, usually at some social function, for no reason other than the round-table discussion of a moral topic—the introduction of any of these devices inevitably slows down the machinery and impairs the unity of the novel.

11. Pamela's classification of Mr. B.'s concept of the ideal wife into forty-eight formal rules is an outrageous example (*Pamela*, II, 290–294).

Even the picaresque novel, loose as its plan is and exempt as it must be from most considerations of unity, is affected structurally by the insertion of such extraneous material. The detailed history of Mr. Melopoyn, the unfortunate author whom Roderick Random meets in the Marshalsea jail, undoubtedly serves as a convenient outlet for Smollett's own rancor and as an exaggerated illustration of the hard life of a Grub Street hack. Melopoyn's life history is but tenuously connected with the hero's affairs, however, and Smollett himself seems to feel that he has gone too far afield, for at the conclusion of the narrative Melopoyn apologizes for it. "I ought to crave pardon for this tedious narration of trivial circumstances, which, however interesting they may be to me, must certainly be very dry and insipid to the ear of one unconcerned in the affair." [12]

Dry and sometimes insipid these long pauses in the narrative tend to be, more particularly in novels which have some pretensions to unity. In *Amelia,* for example, both the character of the heroine and the singleness of moral theme—Fielding's insistence throughout that social wrongs have their roots in personal selfishness—are unifying elements. The serious purpose of the novel as a whole makes much of the moralizing appropriate. Yet even a reader tolerant of moralizing feels that he has reached an arid stretch indeed in the set conversations between Dr. Harrison, a young clergyman, and the latter's father.[13] The questions discussed, the Christian doctrine of forgiving enemies and the proper conduct for a clergyman, have little to do with the theme; and, a more serious lapse, in no way are these conversations linked to the fortunes of the heroine. The morality is undoubtedly edifying; but the story languishes.

The mention of Dr. Harrison in *Amelia* immediately suggests a second result of digressive moralizing—a result less obvious than the interruption of the narrative but nonetheless pervasive. No character, however fully he may be conceived, can perform the function of mouthpiece for the author's favorite truisms and pet crotchets without suffering some blurring of personality. Although

12. Chap. lxiii.
13. Bk. IX, chaps. viii and x.

obviously it is the mentor characters and exemplary characters who suffer most from being called into service as oracles, minor characters, heroes (including picaresque heroes), and villains themselves do not escape unscathed.

The role of the mentor character would be difficult enough even if he were not constantly called on stage to make wise speeches. His actions, demonstrations of the author's theories put into practice, are above reproach; his function as *deus ex machina,* his readiness to extricate heroes and heroines from their difficulties, is often the pivot on which the whole plot turns. When, in addition to these duties, he is expected to make judicious pronouncements on every development in the story and to be a fountainhead of advice, it is little wonder that his own personality remains stiff and mechanical.

The comments of a mentor character are almost invariably longer and more formal than those of other characters. Mr. Villars, to take a single example at random, constantly writes to Evelina in the following strain:

Let no weak fears, no timid doubts, deter you from the exertion of your duty, according to the fullest sense of it that Nature has implanted in your mind. Though gentleness and modesty are the peculiar attributes of your sex, yet fortitude and firmness, when occasion demands them, are virtues as noble and as becoming in women as in men: the right line of conduct is the same for both sexes, though the manner in which it is pursued, may somewhat vary, and be accommodated to the strength or weakness of the different travellers.[14]

And Allworthy, without hesitation, launches into stately discourses, such as his four-paragraph sermon on matrimony,[15] which, both in style and length, must have tried the patience of his audience. It is true, of course, that formality of expression, strange to the modern ear, characterizes eighteenth-century writing as a whole. Yet even in novels formal in their general tone the letters and speeches of mentor characters stand out by reason of their greater formality.

Exemplary characters suffer from the same disabilities as mentors—and for approximately the same reasons. The Clarissas and

14. Letter XLIX.
15. *Tom Jones,* Bk. I, chap. xii.

Grandisons that people the eighteenth-century novel not only act the parts of but speak with the tongues of angels—prudent, respectable angels, to be sure, and angels performing the author's bidding. With advice, definitive opinions, and pat aphorisms constantly on their lips, the conversation of model characters is sometimes more amusing than edifying. Lord Orville, in a simple question to Evelina concerning two dubious female companions in whose company he saw her, is capable of expressing himself in the following manner: "I should not, however, upon so short an acquaintance, have usurped the privilege of intimacy, in giving my unasked sentiments upon so delicate a subject, had I not known that credulity is the sister of innocence, and therefore feared you might be deceived." [16] "Credulity is the sister of innocence"—how frequently these neat phrases are uttered by model characters!

Besides being formal in style, the wise observations of a model character are often made on subjects having nothing to do with the plot, are listened to by a group of respectful admirers, and not infrequently have the power of reforming the unregenerate. With all these counts against them, the surprising thing is not that model characters in general should be stiffened and stylized but that any model should escape the ordeal with his humanity intact. The reader's belief in Clarissa, despite her penchant for delivering sermons and despite the adulation of her admirers, is a tribute to Richardson's artistic power, to the consistent concept of virtuous womanhood which his imagination created. Similarly, the credibility of Dr. Primrose as a person, despite his saintlike conduct and the unfailing wisdom of his remarks, is a tribute to Goldsmith's naturalness and sense of humor, to his surrounding Primrose with a family no more inspired by the good parson's example than ordinary mortals would be.

Whereas the mentor character and the run-of-the-mill exemplary character may be stiff and unnatural, however, they are at least consistent. When heroes and villains, on the other hand, are required to assume mouthpiece duties, their characters often suffer from the obvious disparity between their actions and their wise pronouncements. Joseph Andrews delivers speeches—his discourse

16. Letter LIII.

on charity is a notable example [17]—too well reasoned and too formally expressed for any footman, however good natured. Tom Jones's observations on human nature at the conclusion of the Man of the Hill's account [18] represent Fielding's mature judgments, not those of the ebullient young hero. In *Amelia* Booth's actions are those of a likable but weak young man, irresolute and easily influenced; his lengthy pronouncements on a variety of weighty subjects are the conclusions of the author, the fruit of a lifetime of thought and experience. When attributed to an unsuitable character, remarks wise and worthy of attention in themselves can change a normal young man into an opinionated prig.

Even Smollett's heroes lose something of their vigor and consistent "picaresqueness" by reason of their mouthpiece function. They are thrust into situations created neither for the sake of the adventure nor for the sake of character development but simply to give the author a chance to "expatiate." The method by which such observations are introduced varies but little: a person whom the hero meets in the course of his wanderings is sketched quickly. Whether he tells his life history or merely steps on stage to act his brief part, he is likely to be only the shadow of a character. The author is using him as a tool. Prefacing his remarks with some such phrase as "I could not help thinking," the hero comments— and at length—on the principle of human conduct illustrated by the actions of the minor character. Roderick Random's vigorous comments on the absurdity of a soldier's sacrificing himself for the glory of a prince [19] and on the effrontery of ill-informed travelers who praise foreign countries at the expense of their own [20] follow this pattern. In both instances the hero's opinions, sane and well reasoned, are given at length. Whereas the motives for a picaresque hero's actions—whether vanity, avarice, anger, desire for revenge, lust, or occasionally true affection—are invariably emotional, his observations frequently give evidence of a mature reasoning power. This dualism, comparable to the dualism of Fielding's heroes, stems from the same source—the author's com-

17. Bk. III, chap. vi.
18. Bk. VIII, chap. xv.
19. Chap. xliii.
20. Chap. xlv.

pulsion to speak, with all his own vigor and maturity, through the mouth of an unsuitable character.

Villains themselves, the characters most incapable of functioning as moralists, are sometimes required to serve as mouthpieces. Thoughtful villains (and there is strong justification for including picaresque heroes in this classification) are common in the eighteenth-century novel. The villain's moralizing, whether he postpones it until after his reformation or whether he unashamedly sandwiches it in between vicious deeds, produces incongruous effects. The reformed villain is perhaps the more incongruous—or at least the more amusing—of the two types. The sudden and unconvincing metamorphosis in the character of Mr. B. when once he has honorably proposed marriage to Pamela is as much due to his newly found ability of expounding moral principles as to Pamela's domesticating influence. Throughout the seduction period Mr. B. the ravisher is, obviously, an unsuitable instrument for enforcing Richardson's moral code. As soon as he enters the bourgeois pale, however, Richardson discovers his usefulness as a theorizer on the ideal conjugal existence. On the fourth day of his marriage he is already capable of expatiating on such minutiae of conduct as the necessity for a wife's carefulness in dress, the advisability of keeping regular hours, and the proper conduct for a wife in receiving her husband's guests.[21] The reader must assume that somewhere in the course of his early rakish existence he has had the leisure to formulate the abstract principles on which these specific instructions are based. In assigning to him this new role of the perambulating conduct book Richardson has, in fact, created a new character. There are two Mr. B.'s—not one.

Although the characters of unreformed villains are not so likely to split in two, they also exhibit inconsistencies. Lovelace, that archetype of the thoughtful villain, moralizes and reflects almost more than he plots and schemes. When his reflective power takes the form of cynical observations on human conduct or of involved sophistries to justify his baseness, the concept of his villainy is enhanced. On the other hand, when he gives voice to opinions that obviously receive the author's support, he is unconvincing. In this

21. *Pamela,* II, 177–183.

latter role he is made to expatiate on such subjects as the veneration due religion,[22] the mean-spiritedness that attends guilt,[23] the force of education in the development of virtue,[24] and the fitness of keeping the Sabbath.[25] It is interesting to note that Richardson was aware of a certain inconsistency in attributing the last opinion to Lovelace. In the *Moral and Instructive Sentiments,* a book of wise observations gleaned from the novels and classified according to subject, he notes: " 'There is something beautifully solemn in Devotion,' *says even* Lovelace." [26]

Yes, even Lovelace may be said to have some right to join that illustrious body of eighteenth-century characters who speak not with their own convictions but with those of their authors. Mentor characters and exemplary characters, heroes and villains, minor characters and sometimes those who appear only once on the stage —all are on call as observers and commentators.

A character's wise observations, as has already been noted, tend to be distinguished from the rest of the narrative by a greater formality of style. A person who normally expresses himself in a credible, conversational idiom suddenly strikes a pose and begins speaking Johnsonian English when the author is using him to give vent to his own opinions. This increased formality of style distinguishes not only mouthpiece speeches but moral and philosophical observations of all kinds, however introduced. Polysyllabic words, balanced phrases, parallel structure, emphatic repetition, and studied comparisons all serve to give warning to the reader that he has reached a section which the author believes deserves special attention. A passage such as the following is as clearly underlined by its style as if it were printed in red or in italics. "TRUE GENEROSITY is not confined to pecuniary instances: It is *more* than politeness: It is *more* than good faith: It is *more* than honour: It is *more* than justice: Since all these are but duties, and what a

22. *Clarissa Harlowe,* Vol. VII, Letter I.
23. Vol. VII, Letter LXXIII.
24. Vol. IV, Letter L.
25. Vol. III, Letter LXIII.
26. P. 195. The full title of this volume is *A Collection of the Moral and Instructive Sentiments, Maxims, Cautions, and Reflections, Contained in the Histories of Pamela, Clarissa, and Sir Charles Grandison* (London, 1755).

worthy mind cannot dispense with. But TRUE GENEROSITY is Greatness of Soul." The speaker is not a doctor of divinity, addressing
a congregation from the pulpit, but Clarissa Harlowe, replying
to Lovelace's promise that he will be generous.[27] While Clarissa is,
admittedly, a more polished rhetorician than some of her fellow
commentators, a comparable stylistic self-consciousness, if in less
exaggerated form, is characteristic of "worthy" observations in
general in the novel of the period. Such observations are further
contrasted with the narrative by the author's frequent use of introductory and concluding phrases, phrases equivalent to marginal
figures pointing out the stopping place. "Let me here observe" or
"one cannot help but reflect" is a sure sign that a philosophic passage is to follow; "but to return to my narration" or "enough has
been said" is an equally clear indication that the sermon is over,
that the story proper is to be resumed.

The direction of the reader's attention, by stylistic devices, to the
wisdom of an observation reinforces the two results of digressive
commentary previously discussed. The stylistic underlining emphasizes the pauses in the narrative and, if the words are spoken,
stiffens the character of the speaker. Thus the total result of these
liberal comments is to focus attention on the mechanism of the
work and on the author's attitude toward his material, rather than
on the material itself. However vigorous and successful the narrative may be, the novelist is deliberately applying the reins to the
reader's imagination in following that narrative. In the last analysis, he is requiring the reader to do much more than stop occasionally and listen to a digression; he is asking him to remember constantly that the story is not completely the real thing—that it is
illustrative, that it is edifying, that it will furnish him with some
useful rules.

In the best novels of the century, to be sure, the commentary does
not smother the story; the author knows where he is going and
does not permit his novel to degenerate into a commonplace book.
Yet even in unified novels like *Clarissa Harlowe* and *Tom Jones,*
brilliant works of the imagination though they are, the author's
shadow keeps intruding itself between the reader and the imagina-

27. Vol. IV, Letter XIX.

tive world of the novel. The world is pictured and its inhabitants are set into motion; but they are at the same time manipulated, dissected, and discussed. To enlarge immeasurably the pleasure and power of literature, to open up a whole new continent in the world of letters, to create the novel—that was the enduring work of the eighteenth century. To achieve a complete fusion between the critic-moralist and the creative artist was beyond its capacity.

FROM *PAMELA* TO *CLARISSA*

William M. Sale, Jr.

D URING periods of history in which men have felt a sense
of disrupted society, a sense of class differences, the novelist has usually been quick to respond to this feeling. If
the disruptive forces are held in check, if they seem only mildly
active, the novelist will usually content himself with recording
the contrasts that are evident in the intermingling of classes. His
mood will be in the main good-tempered as was that of William
Dean Howells. On the other hand, if the disruptive forces are—or
are felt to be—violently active, the novelist may accentuate class
differences and move beyond contrast to the point of conflict—to
such conflict as is clearly evident in the novels of Zola. Samuel
Richardson, whether or not he was the father of the novel, was
certainly the first novelist deliberately to show in his fiction an
awareness of the disturbing forces at work in his society, for he was,
both as man and novelist, acutely sensitive to class differences. During the two hundred years since he wrote *Pamela,* and especially
during the last hundred years, many men, feeling somewhat as
Richardson felt, have turned to the novel as a particularly effective
form for the expression of this feeling. They sometimes elected to
show how the representatives of an older culture received the impact of the "new" man or woman, as in such markedly different
novels as *The Age of Innocence* and *The Sound and the Fury.* At
other times they showed the "new" man or woman either embarrassed, confused, or hurt in mind and spirit, as George Meredith
and Henry James have done. Some novelists have seen the contrast
or conflict in terms only of the immediate conditions that confront
their characters; others have seen these conflicts in the perspective
of time where the fate of their characters may seem analogous to
the fate of man.

Patterns evolving from the interpenetration of classes have under-
gone such various and subtle mutations since *Pamela* was pub-

lished in 1740 that Richardson's simple pattern may now seem un-
believably naïve. Those critics of Richardson who have found his
pattern too simple have been led to call him a snob, but to be called
a snob is the usual fate of any novelist who makes some degree of
common cause with a social class superior to his own. Howells,
James, Scott Fitzgerald are names that come at once to mind. Furthermore, the critic's motives in accusing an artist of snobbery
are not above question. The accusation frequently represents the
exercise of the critic's prerogatives in the service of convictions that
are only remotely related to those he has about the art of fiction.

When not criticized for the simplicity of his pattern, Richardson
is taken to task for having defined the problems of his characters
too explicitly in terms of his age. But the critic who can see his
novels only as time-bound documents may be a man as hopelessly
rooted in his own era as he would argue that Richardson is rooted
in the eighteenth century. Moreover, critics so disposed frequently
seek to validate a novelist's work by referring it to other sources
of knowledge about an age, without realizing that we frequently
understand what the other sources mean only by reason of the light
thrown by an age's fiction. To say that Richardson reflects his age
is a manner of speaking which is sometimes useful, but if it results
in setting him apart from his age, we may fail to see that his age
was, among other things, Richardson and his fiction.

To propose these counterthrusts to Richardson's critics is not,
however, to deny that in one sense Richardson's novels are inex-
tricably bound up with the conditions of his age. It is the critic, not
the novelist, who cannot afford to be provincial. The more conscientiously the novelist devotes himself to the exact rendering of
his material, the greater the chance he has of finding in that material the measure of common humanity and the meaning of human life. It is, then, the purpose of this essay to urge a close examination of Richardson's novels in their own terms, though this examination is to be made from a somewhat different point of view
than that of the critics who have found little in his fiction but
historical significance. If we can see more clearly how his fiction
rendered the conflicts he saw in his own society, we may see more
clearly the meaning that his fiction had for his century and that it

may have for ours. The inadequacy of his pioneering technique should not blind us to his intention, or result in our failure to see what his subject was. Through such an examination some light may be thrown on the tradition of the novel. Though we know that his "influence" can be found only in the second-rate imitations of his novels in the latter half of his century, we can find analogues to Richardson in the modern novel—the novel which began to be written after 1850 when English fiction escaped from the domination of Richardson's more vigorous contemporaries, Smollett and Fielding.

Literature is not a transcript of life but life rendered at the remove of form. To secure this remove the novelist must, among other things, create the images, the symbols, by which he can indirectly communicate his ideas and emotions. With the passing of time a wider and wider gap may open up between the image and the idea it is designed to communicate. To the extent—and only to the extent—that we can close this gap can the literature of the past become available for us. If the symbol can be apprehended only as literal fact, then literature does become merely a transcript of life: the *Divine Comedy* is read as apologetics, Chaucer's Criseyde is thought to be a facile opportunist, and Hamlet a victim of Elizabethan melancholia. It is not always easy to close this gap in the fiction of Richardson, but if the imagination does not fail us we may perhaps be able to recover his novels for our century.

We know that Richardson's characters and incidents were effective symbols for his contemporaries; this fact is attested by the avidity with which they were seized upon. He was providing new insights. He was realizing for his generation the emotions engendered by the conditions of life that defined his generation's hopes and that set limitations upon the fulfillment of those hopes. Before his novels appeared, however, eighteenth-century Englishmen were sufficiently aware of the fact that their vital social problem was the interpenetration of the emergent middle class and the surviving aristocracy. His contemporaries had read authors who sought to educate the middle class in the manners and decorum of the disappearing aristocracy; they had been amused by authors who pointed up the gaucherie of the new man and woman, the new peer. They had their Emily Posts who offered instruction in manners and their Henry Menckens who bumped the boobs. Satire flourished, and when class conflicts were observed with sufficient detachment, the comedy of manners was achieved. The problem was considered in many moods, prevailingly optimistic. But Mandeville treated it cynically, and Swift, beset by some of its aspects, was driven at times to seek the relief of the sardonic. Even the elegiac mood might have found expression, had the aristocrats possessed an able spokesman and had the age been less optimistic. Had not the more violently revolutionary element in society been drawn off into America, the social conflicts might have given rise to a genuinely revolutionary literature. But despite these lacks, there was no dearth of literature to reflect an interest in this social problem. Richardson caught the attention of his readers not by introducing a novel subject but by defining the subject in a new way and by rendering it in a different spirit.

Before the appearance of *Pamela,* fiction of two sorts existed. The eighteenth century kept the romances alive after a fashion, but by their flickering light the aristocrat and his world seemed little more than an artifact. Defoe introduced a fiction which, by contrast with the romances, was vigorously alive, but his characters, like their creator, lived outside the social pale. They "accepted the universe" and fulfilled their destinies in a defiance of society which called forth little soul searching. Though Defoe always took care to tuck them into the orthodox social structure in the final pages of his novels, he produced in so doing a conclusion that stood at odds with his central action. With the romances dead and with Defoe's pirates and prostitutes living outside the pale, it remained with Richardson to bring the heirs of a seventeenth-century Church of England piety into the world of the fatally attractive and profligate aristocrat.

Like James and like Meredith he preferred women for his central characters—the new women, products of a time when a new freedom seemed attainable but was certainly not attained. Richardson brought his heroines into the orbit of the aristocrat, just as Henry James brought the morally sensitive products of a new American civilization into the ancient and enchantedly evil gardens of Europe. He chose, as central symbolic incident, the real or threatened seduction of his heroines, just as Meredith chose the curious psychological violation of his heroine for the central incident of *Diana of the Crossways,* and just as James again and again exposed his heroines to a violation of the spirit, a deflowering of the human soul. Like James's heroines, Richardson's sought union with, not opposition to, those aristocrats who threatened their integrity. In the exploration of this subject lay the novelty of his fiction for his generation. In this respect his fiction shows an affinity with the modern novel.

Because Richardson chose physical seduction as his important symbolic act, he has been accused on the one hand of trying to satisfy vicariously desires which his circumscribed life denied, and on the other hand of a coarseness of moral sensibility. The former charge is irrelevant; the latter is more serious. It is interesting to speculate on why we are so unsympathetic with a heroine who seeks to preserve her virtue. It is true that we have often been confronted in our own fiction with the paradox of the unchaste virgin and of the chaste prostitute. Perhaps such paradoxes have effected a healthy reorientation of our sympathies; they need not, however, lead us to denigrate all virgins who cherish their chastity. Certainly all readers are not completely above "worldly" considerations, or in dire need of the flattery of being allowed to think that they are. But our difficulties with Richardson probably stem from the fact that we are the heirs of romanticism, which made the intensity of an experience the measure of its worth. It is somewhat provincial to impose upon his art the strictures of the romantic aesthetic. He clearly wants to measure the importance of his heroines' experience by the effort that it calls forth to measure up to a standard, however distressed they may be in mind or in spirit during the experience. Furthermore, his heroines meet the threat of seduction while seeking a union with those who represent—or are thought to represent—a way of life more gracious and more distinguished than that to which they were born. Were they made of the finer stuff of earth, they would not feel their lives incomplete, or be seeking to complete them.

The representatives of two modes of life are brought into conflict in Richardson's novels. The men and women are attracted to each other; they seek union, but they seek it on their own terms. The mode of life of these characters in conflict must be realized for us, but in effecting this realization Richardson is not altogether successful. He is reduced to blending romantic material with the realism of Dutch genre painting. This blend disturbed his Victorian biographer, Clara Thomson, who professed to be reminded of "rusty armour hung on the staircase of a semi-detached villa." It is true that the blend is not always happily achieved, but Miss Thomson's metaphor discloses her lack of a sense of history while it records her aesthetic distress. Richardson's heroes are no more knights in armor than his heroines are Victorian suburbanites. Eighteenth-century society, despite the shock that it caused in Miss Thomson, tolerated its Lovelaces; and Richardson's correspondence shows his excited interest whenever the doings of young aristocrats percolated down to him through the letters of girls who were on the fringes of the society in which such men moved. It is obvious that Richardson knew little at first hand of the life of the English aristocracy. But this lack of knowledge is not fatal. His taste for aristocracy, like that of his heroines, is an index of his need to make common cause with a superior social class. This need of the author is no more apparent in Richardson than it is in Shakespeare or in James.

But the need to make some sort of common cause with the English aristocracy did not mean that a complete absorption within its world was possible, however desirable in some respects such an absorption might seem. This was what Richardson learned between the writing of *Pamela* and *Clarissa.* The subject of the two novels is not radically different, but for many reasons he was unable to realize this subject in *Pamela,* whereas in *Clarissa* it had taken full shape. Had he come to the writing of *Clarissa* without the experience provided by the earlier novel, he might well have failed to preserve the sharp outlines of his subject and might indeed have never discovered its real importance. It is in the importance of the subject, fully grasped in *Clarissa,* that Richardson differentiates himself from Fielding. *Tom Jones,* for all its display of talent and for all the ingenuity of its construction, has a subject which is not fully worth the care and attention that Fielding lavished on it. It is Fielding himself and not the subject of his novel that continues to win our admiration, whereas all the irritation that we may feel with the author of *Clarissa* should not prevent our seeing that its subject is of the first importance.

In both *Pamela* and *Clarissa* Richardson chose to see his world in the microcosm of the family. Families were, as he said, but "so many miniatures" of the great community of the world. Tyranny, treachery, loyalty—duty and responsibility, right and prerogative—all these aspects of life he sought to comprehend within the world of the family. His concept of the family was never quite broad enough for the uses to which he wanted it put, but this constricted vision is more apparent in *Pamela* than in *Clarissa*. The master-servant relationship in the household is not so flexible as the father-daughter relationship which he uses in *Clarissa*. In order to maintain the conflict in the earlier novel, Richardson had in some degree to sacrifice the character both of Pamela and of her master. In eighteenth-century England a servant is not bound to her master as Pamela seems at times to feel that she is bound; nor do we find it easy to accept the highhanded fashion in which Mr. B. abrogates the laws of his country in carrying through an abduction. In the earlier sections of *Pamela* the heroine seems to be trumping up excuses in order to keep Richardson's novel going; in later sections, she is a prisoner with her freedom of choice so restricted that the novel becomes in large part an adventure story. The dual role of master and of lover which Mr. B. has to play clouds the main issue of the novel. Were he cast solely as lover, we could see more clearly that his dilemma arises because he falls in love with the girl he should seduce. Were he not Pamela's master as well as the man she wants to marry, Pamela would seem far less the schemer than she too often shows herself to be.

Richardson encountered these difficulties—and others to be mentioned later—because the main outlines of his story were determined before he started to tell it. He chose to follow a story from real life in which a master finally married the serving girl he tried to seduce. When Richardson turned to the reworking of his theme in *Clarissa,* he created his own story and held to it in spite of the advice and entreaty of his friends who sought to reshape it for him. Again he chose the microcosm of the family, but he wisely placed Lovelace outside the domestic orbit of the Harlowes. Furthermore, he idealized the Harlowes just as he idealized Lovelace. The Harlowes, if you will, are essentially London middle-class tradesmen with the tradesman's narrowness of soul and smallness of mind. As Tucker Brooke said of *Lear,* Shakespeare's characters in that play are those whom he could only have understood "from sympathetic observation of the life before his windows and which few have been able to reproduce save by means of the closest transcription." Brooke shrewdly observes that Lear and his daughters are essentially bourgeois types. So are the Harlowes. But Richardson moves them from the city to the country; he wants us to see not the fact but the essence of their materialism, of their penny pinching, their selfishness. If we compare the idealized treatment of the Harlowes with the more direct transcription that Richardson employs for the middle-class Danbys of *Grandison* or for the tradesmen's daughters, Sally Martin and Polly Horton, of *Clarissa,* we can see clearly that the Harlowes are larger than life. The stultifying atmosphere of Harlowe Place is so pervasive that even the kindly instincts of some of the clan prove abortive. Clarissa alone is a free spirit, struggling desperately to preserve her integrity and her independence of mind and soul. She is set apart from the Harlowes more significantly than Pamela is set apart from her parents or from her companions belowstairs.

To make this distinction between Clarissa and her family a sharp one is only part of the task that Richardson had to accomplish in the first two volumes of his novel. Though her father's inhumanity seems intolerable, we must see that Clarissa can never escape from the fact of his fatherhood. She cannot, as Pamela could, quit her master. Though she finds it imperative to incur her father's curse in following the law of her own being, this curse lies upon her like a leaden weight, and Richardson takes pains to make clear that she cannot free herself from its weight until her soul speeds its way to heaven. Pamela's power of choice was removed, but choice is given to Clarissa. To make us see that she cannot escape from the consequence of her choice is a responsibility that the novel accepts and which it continuously makes clear. The burden of this curse is analogous to the burden of the traumatic experiences which pursue Diana Merion relentlessly and which result in her betrayal of both Warwick and Dacier. Both Diana and Clarissa are, by contrast with the other characters of their world, emancipated; but Diana, so often the ally of the Comic Spirit, is also its victim. Clarissa, despite the clarity of her mind, is the victim of the curse incurred when she defies her father and elopes with Lovelace. This aspect of the situation, so dimly grasped in *Pamela,* is clearly realized in *Clarissa.*

It is her fate to defy her father; it is also her fate to be attracted by the free spirit of Lovelace, who stands in such marked contrast to the Harlowes. Lovelace moves in a world of larger freedoms, of wider spaces. His values, however reprehensible, are not the countinghouse values of the Harlowes. Clarissa allows herself to hope that in union with him she will in some way complete her life. She knows and tells us in so many words that in marriage with Solmes, her family's choice, her life will stop. So this passionate pilgrim, like Isabel Archer, is driven to link her destiny with her Osmond. In our century the slackening of family ties has perhaps resulted in making less effective Richardson's symbol of the parental curse. In like manner, the steady democratization of modern society may make it difficult for us to accept an aristocratic rake at Richardson's evaluation, equivocal though that evaluation may be. Aristocracy meant to Richardson a distinction of personal existence. That he should have seen this distinction only in the acts of the attractive libertine is a commentary on his age. In their pursuit of women these energetic sons of the older families perpetuated a mode of life which had flourished during the Restoration. With political action frequently denied them, they flagrantly asserted the *droit de seigneur,* flinging their tattered banners from the falling walls. These gestures both attracted and repelled the creator of Lovelace. He caught fleeting glimpses of them outside his windows, and he idealized them as he did the Harlowes; he heightened the qualities that made them both attractive and repellent. But with them he had to make some kind of common cause if his vision of human potentialities was to extend beyond the narrow confines of his own middle-class world.

The degree to which he could make such cause and the success which could attend the attempt were matters that Richardson had not clearly thought through when he wrote *Pamela*. When he allowed the marriage to take place between Pamela and Mr. B. he did not really resolve his conflict. He merely put an end to it. It is true that he postponed marriage as long as his inventive genius would permit; he even borrowed all the antiquated machinery of romance to keep his story going through the long Lincolnshire episode. But, following his story from real life, he had eventually to bring his characters to the altar. It is difficult to see how Richardson might have avoided the marriage, but to include it is to suggest that a large part of the antecedent action is much ado about nothing. Richardson, of course, recognized the specious optimism implied in the marriage and tried to recover his subject. He devoted his second volume to the conflicts experienced by Pamela because she was the maid who had become the mistress. But the mood of the second volume is that of social comedy, and despite all his efforts the effect is that of anticlimax. To ignore the second volume, as so many critics of Richardson seem to do, is to fail to see, however, the efforts that Richardson made to preserve Pamela's integrity.

Richardson saw clearly what both Pamela and Mr. B. had lost when he turned to Clarissa's story. He would not allow his friends to persuade him to close her story with a wedding. In the course of the action Lovelace tried by several sets of arguments to persuade himself that he should and that he should not marry Clarissa. But he knew that such a marriage would represent a compromise with his own world and its values. If the pressure of opinion or the force of circumstances juggled him into marrying Clarissa, such a marriage would compromise his principles. Accommodations of this sort were possible in the world of the Harlowes but not in his world. In like manner, Clarissa knew that marriage with Lovelace was no resolution of her dilemma, though she found it very difficult to make the Anna Howes of her world understand this. Marriage was not the reward her virtue deserved. This pair cannot be tucked into the social structure as Defoe tucked his characters. There are moments when both Clarissa and Lovelace are tempted by the thought of their union; and marriage, as a symbolic act, is kept constantly in the forefront of the novel. But this story is no "love" story. It is not love for which Clarissa's old pious world is well lost; it is for a chance to live life more completely in conformity with an ideal of conduct. Clarissa is no more a girl in search of a husband than is Isabel Archer. She is—if I may risk a dangerous abstraction—humanity desperately if futilely seeking freedom in a world where duty and responsibility are constant limitations upon that search.

The theologians of Richardson's day were busy accommodating the new science to a world which many of them still believed was ruled by the God of their fathers; the political thinkers were accommodating a new constitution within the framework of the theory of divine right. Even the new industrialism was seeking to accommodate itself within the antiquated structure of the guild system of master and apprentice. Pamela, the embryonic new woman, is fitted somewhat too easily into the older social structure. But Richardson, like Swift and Johnson, finally saw that the optimism of his age was a facile optimism, that the attempts to preserve the old faiths by accommodation were sure indications that these old faiths were moribund. Clarissa can find no hope in this world; she must depend on heaven.

It is her dependence on heaven that is the final cause for the disturbance of many modern readers. The central irony in *Clarissa* is easily recognized, but her faith in heaven is felt to mitigate the sharpness of this irony. And indeed it does. We accept more readily James's secularized versions of a similar theme in which at the end the heroine receives the kiss of death. His heroines have fulfilled their tragic fate as inevitably as has Clarissa, but they have not her hope of heaven. In the closing sections of James's novels his heroines are frequently above or beyond life, even as Clarissa is during the last two volumes of her story. They are beyond earthly considerations; they live in an atmosphere as rarefied as that of heaven itself. The secularized version may be more acceptable to some modern readers, but the intent of the two novelists is not markedly different.

Certainly in the charity of our imagination we should be able to understand Richardson's intent, despite his pious vocabulary and his pious symbols. He wants us to see that Clarissa is a child of heaven, finally removed alike from the world of the Harlowes and of the Lovelaces. The need of heaven was imperative. In this world Richardson could not, as did many of his contemporaries, find room in which to fit everything and a place in which everything might fit.

HENRY FIELDING, CHRISTIAN CENSOR

James A. Work

FOR the better part of a century now the more enlightened critics of Henry Fielding have hailed him as an upright man, a great moralist, and an earnest worker for reform. But no one has yet explained his driving force, the spiritual urge that actuated and gave direction to his life.

An obvious motive underlying much of Fielding's work was the necessity of supporting himself and his family: he must choose between being a hackney writer or a hackney coachman. Even so, money does not appear to have been a major factor in his choice of professions. He did not marry for money; he did not come to terms with Walpole; and there were easier ways—more popular ways—to make money, even with the pen, than those he took after 1737. For a deeper impulsion we have still to seek.

Mr. Cross, the great apologist for Fielding's personal life, restricted himself to an objective recapitulation of the steps by which "the wit and humorist" became "the moralist and reformer." M. Digeon suggested a religious motivation when, on partial evidence, he asserted that Fielding was a deist who late in life became converted to Christianity; and Maria Joesten, working under still greater limitations, propounded the incredible thesis that throughout his life Fielding was actuated by Stoicism pure and unchanging —though he did not disdain "die gelegentliche Bundesgenossenschaft mit christlichen Versittlichungsbestrebungen, um die eigenen Zwecke zu fördern." Neither of these suggestions, however, will square with the facts. Nor have more recent studies of the novelist been more perspicacious. Mr. Willcocks retails the story of a "Harry" who "was so intent on the face of the Sphinx that he forgot the depths of the sky behind it"; Mr. Pritchett complacently accepts his subject as "the shallowest of philosophers," who held "that self-love and self-interest are the beginning and end of human motive, and that the only real and virile view of human nature is the low one"; and Mr. Maugham, who is frankly bored by "what [Fielding] has to say about this, that, and the other," and who—presumably to titillate the prospective reader of his abridgement of *Tom Jones*—vilifies his author's morals even beyond the capacity of an Arthur Murphy, fails utterly to catch the nobility of Fielding's mind.

In a re-examination of Fielding's works, I have been impressed by the number of religious passages they contain, passages not merely moralistic but dealing specifically with the first and second members of the Trinity and with the beliefs, virtues, rewards, and punishments of Christianity. As a result I have become convinced that the motivation of Fielding's activity as moralist and reformer lay at least in part, and perhaps in large part, in his Christian beliefs and feelings: in his conscious and conscientious, though unpublicized, intent to follow in his own life "that total of all Christian morality . . . 'do unto all men as ye would they should do unto you,' " and to practice "the greatest virtue in the world (according to the tenets of [Christianity]) . . . charity."

In Fielding is God's plenty. It is quite possible to pluck from his works passages dealing with the large common ground held by both deists and orthodox low-church Anglicans, and from such passages alone to argue him a deist. Or to concentrate attention on his admiration for "the best of the heathens" and his references to "human philosophy" (the adjective is implicative) and on such partial evidence to conclude him a Stoic. What Digeon and Joesten both unhappily overlook are Fielding's direct and explicit repudiations of both the deistic and the Stoic positions, as well as his repeated declarations of Christian faith.

Treating the deists, at times by themselves and at times lumping them in with atheists and Mandevillians as freethinkers or, as he contemptuously calls them, *"political* philosophers," he vigorously opposes their views, both by reasonable argument and by irony and scorn worthy of Swift. Their denial of God's providence, he declares, "if it is not downright atheism, hath a direct tendency towards it; and, as Dr. Clarke observes, may soon be driven into it." Stoicism he valued for its utility in steeling the mind against misfortune, but his social consciousness as well as his Christianity rejected it as a way of life. "Philosophy makes us wiser, but Christianity makes us better men." The Stoics, Fielding concluded, were unchristian both in their doctrines and in their steadfast self-contemplation, which rendered them insensible to "the virtues or vices, the happiness or misery of the rest of mankind." Though he honors the philosophers of "the heathen systems" he parts company with even the most upright men of "those unenlightened nations, who walked only by the law of nature, without the assistance of revelation"; for their highest ideals of conduct fall short of the Christian doctrine of forgiving those who have trespassed against us, and they have neither the consolations of divine love nor the prospect of heavenly bliss to sweeten their lives.

From a careful reading of his works it is clear that by the time of *The Champion,* when he first spoke out in his own voice, Fielding was in all significant points an orthodox believer in the rational supernaturalism of such low-church divines as Tillotson, Clarke, and Barrow, and that he experienced no important changes in belief throughout the remainder of his life.

God, as Fielding understood and preached him from at least 1739 on, is holy and true, omnipotent and omniscient. He is filled with benevolence or charity—the virtue in which man can most nearly approach Him, and which enables Fielding to refer, quite literally, to "the impious severity of our laws"; but He is also just, and watches constantly over human affairs, concerned to reward and punish each man according to his desert. Contemptuously, Fielding rejects the deistical concept of "a lazy, unactive being," who "slumbers on His throne." Over and over he asserts God's interest in man's every act, and asks whether the heart of man could "be warmed with a more ecstatic imagination than that the most excellent attribute of the great Creator of the universe is concerned in rewarding him." So personal a God as this must have means of communication with His creatures. Accordingly, men can approach Him in prayer—which Fielding in one place refers to as conversation with God; and He can make His will known to men by "supernatural and miraculous" interposition in human affairs, by His "positive revealed laws," and by "those secret institutions, which [He] hath written in the heart and conscience of every man."

All of this, of course, was perfectly orthodox low-church doctrine. Equally orthodox were his beliefs concerning the Trinity and Christ. The former, like the other mysteries recognized by the supernatural rationalists of the Established Church—mysteries which are above human reason but not repugnant to it—he accepts on faith. To the latter, "the divine Founder of our religion," "the divine Lawgiver of the New Testament," he attributes those qualities of benevolence and mercy which he attributes to God and, in addition, good nature: Christ is the opposite of "a sour, morose, ill-natured, censorious sanctity." Humility, however, is the special virtue of "our blessed Saviour," who "died for the sins of mankind."

These concepts of the Deity were fully revealed in Fielding's writings between 1739 and 1743. Falling into the language of his time, and occasionally for the sake of impressing on his readers the extent of God's power, he sometimes refers to Him as the great God of nature; but He is not the God of the deists or of the pantheists. When in revising *Jonathan Wild* in 1754 he made the change that caught Digeon's eye—altering "proofs of a Supreme Being" to "proofs of Christianity"—he made it not because his view of God had changed but because his increasing conviction, late in life, that man's *only* hope lay in Christianity predisposed him to stress the word. For at least fifteen years his belief had been fixed in a revealed religion, in a miracle-working and personal God, and in salvation through Christ.

Orthodox, too, were Fielding's beliefs concerning the rewards and punishments, both temporal and eternal, which his all-observing God justly metes out to men. Of the various temporal rewards, those most precious to a Christian are the satisfaction of a good conscience, the "transports" of believing that he is acceptable to God, the "ecstasy" of imagining that God is "concerned in his happiness," and the assurance of bliss beyond the grave—all of which contribute to "those exquisite raptures which the coolest enthusiast in religion enjoys." Complementary to these rewards are the temporal punishments of wickedness, which include the sense of guilt which comes from a bad conscience and the dreadful prospect of "endless misery" beyond the grave. But the temporal rewards and punishments of virtue and sin were as nothing in Fielding's eyes, as in those of the orthodoxy of his time, compared with the eternal bliss and torments of heaven and hell. The evidence of *The Champion,* in which he refers his readers to Tillotson and Clarke, and writes paragraph after paragraph in their vein, is full and conclusive that by 1740—two years before the death of Charlotte and the composition of the essay *Of the Remedy of Affliction for the Loss of Our Friends*—Fielding believed, literally and simply, in the individual immortality of the soul, and in its certainty of enjoying an earned "eternal happiness" in heaven or suffering a deserved "eternal misery" in hell.

The evidence is clear that from 1739-40 on Fielding's religious beliefs were in all essentials conservative, consistent, and orthodox. And as far as one can tell, they had always been so. Whether during his salad days he ever sought to rationalize his gratifications of the flesh by espousing the "natural religion" he later satirized, we do not know. But as far as one can judge from his ancestry, from the character of his grandmother, from the recently discovered testimony concerning his childhood, and from his life at Eton, his early religious training was orthodox and thorough. And the evidence of his plays, in so far as it can be used, supports the presumption that his views on Christianity had been fixed long before 1739.

This presumption is heightened by a consideration of his library, the sales catalogue of which lists fifty-odd works of a religious nature—theological treatises, sermons, discourses, theologicophilosophical works, and commentaries—and over forty works on religious history and biography. It is likely that other theological works were carried to Portugal, to use in finishing his reply to Bolingbroke, and were disposed of there. The probability is that so extensive a collection (which runs to many volumes) on a subject not professionally necessary to him was the gradual accumulation of a lifetime; most of his editions were available before the 'forties, and lack of funds would have made unlikely a very large acquisition of such works during his later years. Furthermore, the references to religious writers and the frequent use of Biblical matter in his works from *The Champion* on suggest an early familiarity with religious writings.

Fielding's reading included divines such as Trapp, Sherlock, Clarke, Cumberland, and Cudworth; philosophers of religion such as Grotius and Locke; and deists such as Tindal, Toland, and Bolingbroke; but his great favorites were, during his early years, "the witty Dr. South," during his later, "the divine Dr. Barrow," and throughout his mature life, Hoadly and Tillotson. Except for acknowledged quotations, however, I have found no evidence of his writing with religious works open before him. The many religious and moral passages in his works are not paraphrases, consciously added to his own material, but are natural outpourings, by an alert religious and moral sense, from a well-stored mind.

But Fielding's religion, it is almost superfluous to observe, was not merely a matter of belief. To him "faith without good works" was mere hypocrisy. Accordingly his mature life was one of strenuous activity both in the personal practice of Christianity and in the conversion of others to Christian faith and life.

It is unnecessary to pause here on his practice of "that virtue without which no man can be a Christian," which he recommended to others and which he defined as "the relieving the wants and sufferings of one another to the utmost of . . . our power." Well known are his gifts to the needy, his establishment of subscriptions for unfortunate men, his support of the Foundling and the Lying-in hospitals, and his distributing free copies of his *Interposition of Providence* to further his campaign against murder. He gave, to the extent of his power, of his money, of his time, and of his pen. But his most valuable contribution to the cause of Christianity was made with his pen.[1]

" 'Tis the worst abuse of the press," he wrote in 1739, "to propagate doctrines that visibly tend to the entire extirpation of all society, all morality, and all religion"; and it is not too much to say that a major motive underlying his chief writings from that time

---

1. "Whatever our talents are, let us convert them to the good of mankind. Charity is not confined to giving alms. If so, perhaps it would be but little within your reach *or mine*. But the divine founder of our religion never intended to restrain a virtue so essentially necessary to a Christian, to the rich alone. As one man's talent lies in his purse, another's may lie in his pen; a third may employ his tongue, and a fourth his hands for the service of others, nay the most impotent may perhaps fully exercise this virtue even with their wishes, most certainly they may with their prayers."

on was to reform the individual and society, to exalt morality, and to defend orthodoxy.

He was not a theologian, and was much less interested in Christianity as doctrine than in Christianity as a way of life.[2] Like his beloved Dr. Barrow, he for the most part "avoided controversy and preached morals." With his fictional characters he went below their actions and distinguished, as Coleridge has remarked, between what a man does and what he is. But of actual men and women, whose hearts cannot be probed, their actions, he declared, are the justest interpreters of their thoughts and the truest standards by which we can judge them. "By their fruits you shall know them," he observed, "is a saying of great wisdom, as well as authority." As a consequence the religious passages in his writings were most frequently designed with the Christian view of amending men's conduct. And since charity was to him the essential Christian virtue, he unceasingly urged that virtue in particular upon his readers.

Taking, generally, the orthodox view that man is formed capable of both good and evil, Fielding was certain that individuals acquire their "iniquity rather from the general corruption . . . than from any extraordinary disparity in their own nature." Consequently his attacks were usually directed against the common social evils —the "education, habits, and customs"—of his day. But his deepest motive underlying these attacks was not, I think, a desire to serve society in the abstract but an active passion to salvage the virtue of the individuals who made up society, and to save from perdition precious Christian souls. In spite of environmental pressures the individual himself, Fielding was sure, could by the exercise of his free will "greatly" control his passions and perfect his nature. Not mere rhetoric was his ejaculation, "consider, O wicked man, thy immortal soul." And when he observed, in comment on a freethinker, that "every gentleman hath a right to be damned in his own way," he meant just that: simple and literal damnation of the individual.

The practical effect of Fielding's Christian motivation is apparent

2. Accepting on faith the superrational portions of Anglican belief, he opposed, as Swift had done before him, what seemed to him to be futile—if not actually impious—speculations on abstruse religious and philosophical points.

in his major and many of his minor works. It is unnecessary to review here his serious addresses to his "young readers," and his frequent brief sermons on Christianity, as well as on morality, in both his fiction and his essays. Suffice it to remark that in addition to his attacks on such vices of the times as gaming, dueling, gin drinking, and masquerades, he dwelt, usually fully and with iteration, on each of the Ten Commandments—"that first and most perfect table of law"—and on most of the points of conduct treated in "the excellent and divine Sermon on the Mount"—which, he intimates, "contains all that can be said or thought" on matters of morality. And we may note his attention to more formal aspects of Christian conduct: his opposition to oaths, blasphemy, and the irreverent mention of religion; his vigilance to punish "all offences committed immediately against the Divine Being"; and his strong advocacy of attendance at Church.[3]

Characteristic of his Christian purpose was his establishment of *The Champion* to expose and punish "whatever is wicked, hateful, absurd, or ridiculous," and to exalt "purity and good manners." It is significant that of the sixty-two leading articles he is known certainly to have written for this periodical, the first of his works in which he could speak directly and personally to his reader, a full dozen deal specifically and extensively with religion or religion and morality, and something over a dozen more touch briefly but specifically on similar topics. *The Journey from This World to the Next* was written to teach "that the greatest and truest happiness which this world affords, is to be found only in the possession of goodness and virtue." The *Essay on Conversation,* the *Essay on the Knowledge of the Characters of Men,* and the *Remedy of Affliction for the Loss of Our Friends* are among the most truly Christian writings of the period. *The True Patriot* Fielding undertook from religious as well as patriotic motives, and concluded "with the secret satisfaction which attends right actions." In *The Covent-*

3. The traditional picture of Fielding is hardly that of a churchgoer; yet when one considers the number of church services in his novels, his many references to sermons, his supporting in his periodicals of proclaimed days of fasts and prayers, his careful provision and eloquent argument for holding regular and frequent church services in his proposed County House, and his satisfaction with the character of the religious services held aboard the *Queen of Portugal,* one cannot avoid the conclusion that he was well acquainted with, as well as disposed toward, divine worship.

Garden Journal he aimed at the "glorious" purpose of "serving the noble interests of religion, virtue, and good sense," presenting extensive discussions of religious or religious and moral matters in fifteen of the sixty-odd leaders which came from his pen, and touching briefly but specifically on such subjects in nine others. Equally disinterested and Christian were his labors in preparing his *Examples of the Interposition of Providence,* his *Enquiry into the Causes of the Late Increase of Robbers,* his *Charge Delivered to the Grand Jury,* and his carefully elaborated *Proposal for Making an Effectual Provision for the Poor.*

All of his novels Fielding designed "to recommend goodness and innocence" and "promote the cause of virtue." His admirable characters are invariably practicing—and frequently preaching—Christians; his despicable are more often than not religious hypocrites. It is worthy of note, however, that his last novel, in addition to being the most grave, is the most overtly and immediately concerned with Christian conduct, and that his last hero finds salvation only in religion. Tom Jones, for all his impertinent sermonizing, is for the most part a "good man" on the purely human level. But by the time he wrote *Amelia* Fielding felt that his readers needed stronger medicine than mere benevolence, so he gave them a conversion and Dr. Harrison on the hope and fear of heaven and hell.[4]

Increasingly, Fielding came to believe that the chief cause of England's political and moral evils was the "general neglect (I wish I could not say contempt) of religion"; and with increasing seriousness and deliberateness and directness, therefore, he preached Christianity and Christian charity in his works.

It is appropriate that Fielding's last labor—"the most difficult piece of writing that he had ever undertaken"—which was undertaken, when he was in his last illness, solely for the public good, was in defense of orthodox Christianity against the attack of one who had sported with "the eternal and final happiness of all mankind." "It must always be remembered to the honour of Mr. Field-

---

4. Fielding believed with Dr. Harrison (and with Locke, and Tillotson, Barrow, Clarke, and many another orthodox divine) that most men act from their passions rather than their reason and are therefore to be reached only by that religion "which applies immediately to the strongest of these passions, hope and fear."

ing," wrote one of his contemporaries in *The Evening Advertiser* for April 16–18, 1754,

that, while he is sinking under a complicated load of dangerous disorders, and is so near the verge of eternity, that at night there is but little probability of his surviving to the next day; he devotes the whole strength of his faculties to the honour of God, and the virtue and happiness of the human soul, in detecting the pernicious errors of the late Lord Bolingbroke . . . the disgrace of his country, and the enemy of mankind.

Fielding does not present himself to us as an enthusiast. Although he refers, as we have seen, to "those exquisite raptures which the coolest enthusiast in religion enjoys," his own faith was apparently based, like that of Square and Booth, on a rational acceptance of the doctrines of Christianity. He reveals no ecstasy in those writings which were intended for publication. And of his writings those are all that we possess. We would have a very different idea of Johnson's religion did we know nothing of his prayers and meditations and of the testimony of his close friends. In their works intended for the public eye both men were controlled by a sense of decorum and fitness. On Fielding's inmost thoughts and feelings it would perhaps be futile to speculate. But many times from 1739 on he publicly proclaimed his belief in the doctrines and virtues of Christianity, and his mature life, as far as we know it, was one of the practice of those virtues. I find no reason to doubt the sincerity of his professions of faith. And the conclusion seems inescapable that this faith, which tempered almost all of his writings, was a significant motivating force in his entire active life.

Fielding never wrote as other than a layman. He accepted in general the rational supernatural beliefs of the more conservative of the latitudinarian churchmen whom he delighted most to read, and did not enter the theologian's domain of speculation. But within these limitations—which, to a man of his sturdy common sense were no limitations—he applied his analytical and creative powers to the propagation of Christian doctrine and conduct, which he treated with a fullness and wisdom and force—with an idealism and a hardheaded practicality—which made him the nearest successor to Swift and the most important Christian moralist of his generation.

SMOLLETT'S SELF-PORTRAIT IN *THE EXPEDITION OF HUMPHRY CLINKER*

Lewis M. Knapp

THE impressive merit of *Humphry Clinker* is largely due to the fact that it embodies the breath and finer spirit of its remarkable author. Properly to understand Smollett is to realize that interlocked within him were two distinct trends. One comprised his capacity for reason, his ability to create literary satire not always dripping with anger, and his concern over being a sensible and decorous gentleman rather than a "singular" author tinged with grubstreet eccentricities. The other trend included his ebullient emotionalism, expressed in some of his personal correspondence, in his fiercest satire, in his best verse, and in his miniature self-portraits, found, for example, in the preface to *Count Fathom,* and in *Humphry Clinker*. Smollett's notorious temper resulted in the ruthless personal satire in his early verse and fiction. Of this unfortunate lack of rational control Smollett was keenly aware. In his youth, in particular, he was not always a canny or a closemouthed Scot: he confessed the "Weakness and Leakiness [loquaciousness]" of his disposition to his friend Carlyle in 1749. Moreover, Smollett was subjected to bitter conflicts and frustrations. Add to all this the fact that no writer of his time disciplined himself by such an exhausting schedule of professional composition, and it is obvious that there developed within him powerful psychological tensions, for which some type of release was sorely needed.

How Smollett vented his rages no biographer can wholly say. It is clear that he did not forfeit the affection of his wife, or the devotion of Tolloush, his servant. And it is safe to say that he released many of his tensions in the more splenetic outbursts of his correspondence, reviews, and occasional literary libels.

There is, however, in the extensive body of Smollett's creative work vastly more than the element of angry satire. There are many pages of comical farce, and there is a large amount of dispassionately objective realism. Most of this realism is rooted, I believe, in his personal observations and experiences. Thackeray's suggestion, offered nearly a century ago, that Smollett "did not invent much . . . but had the keenest perceptive faculty, and described what he saw with wonderful relish," has been confirmed repeatedly, and appears to be especially applicable to the brilliant panorama of persons and places etched in the pages of his last novel written in his final years.

Unfortunately, there is no way of ascertaining precisely when Smollett wrote *Humphry Clinker*. During the spring and summer of 1766, while on his travels in Scotland, he may have kept a journal, from which he later drew details for its Scottish scenes and characters. While he was at Bath and at London from 1766 to 1768 it is probable that he recorded some of the material contained in the epistles written by Bramble and his entourage in those same centers. There is undeniable proof, to which I shall allude later, that he could not have prepared his satire on Paunceford (found in the latter half of the first volume) until the spring of 1768. It is possible that he worked upon some parts of *Humphry Clinker* before leaving for Italy in the autumn of 1768. Yet there is no certainty that he had progressed very far with it because of the fact that before he left England he supposedly completed *The Atom,* which, according to newspaper publicity, was in the press by December, 1768. If this very violent and unpleasant political allegory, traditionally attributed to Smollett (there is no sign that he ever acknowledged it), was motivated by his failure, about July, 1767, to obtain a consulship at Nice, then it must be assumed that he concentrated upon *The Atom* during his final year in England, having laid aside, perhaps, whatever fragments of *Humphry Clinker* he had previously prepared. Consequently, good grounds exist for accepting the Italian tradition that he completed *Humphry Clinker* at his mountain villa near Leghorn. In other words, it is fairly certain that from 1768 to 1770 Smollett labored intermittently on his best novel.

Humphry Clinker contains a kaleidoscopic variety of localities, characters, and social criticism. Because its plot is as stereotyped and fragile as a sprig of dry heather, its outline is easy to follow.

The style, even when distorted by comic malapropisms, is somewhat varied to suit the several letter writers, and is usually admirable whether in achieving humor, farce, pathos, irony, or slashing satire. Permeating and vitalizing the entire opus is the *élan vital* of Smollett, who found in his final work a pliant medium through which to project his personal experience, temperamental traits, and characteristic ideas, during the days of his physical decline. Significant it is that about 40 per cent of this novel consists of letters written by Bramble, who, in the essential traits of his character, is Smollettian; it is also significant that some 50 per cent of the book is made up of letters composed by Jerry, Bramble's nephew, and one given to amusing but sympathetic comment on his uncle. Consequently Smollett provided for himself two media (and the lips of Lismahago as well) for his varied self-revelation.

After introducing Bramble and his traveling group, Smollett held them at Bath during the April and May of their expedition. Smollett, of course, had resided at fashionable Bath in Gay Street from 1766 to 1768. The critical Bramble described this street as "so steep, and slippery, that, in wet weather, it must be exceedingly dangerous, both for those that ride in carriages, and those that walk afoot; and," he added, "when the street is covered with snow, as it was for fifteen days successively this very winter, I don't see how any individual could go either up or down, without the most imminent hazard of broken bones." This comment is a neat example of Smollett's recollection of actual conditions because the allusion to snow "this very winter" referred to the extraordinary snowdrifts in Bath in January, 1767. (See *The Whitehall Evening Post: Or London Intelligencer* for January 15, 1767.) Furthermore, through the amusing associations of Bramble and Tabitha with the diminutive Derrick, Master of Ceremonies at Bath, Smollett recalled, surely, his own observation of Samuel Derrick from 1765 to 1768. There is good reason to assume that Smollett knew Derrick fairly well: he subscribed for his *Original Poems* in 1755, and seems to have hired him as a minor contributor to *The Critical Review*. In the delectable scenes, depicted by Jerry, of the most cordial reunion between Bramble and the great actor, Quin, there is every indication that Smollett was again utilizing personal experience:

this time he recalled, as Professor Buck showed, his joyful reconcili-
ation with Quin in Bath shortly before the latter's death in January,
1766. Young Jerry averred with emotion that he "would give an
hundred guineas to see Mr. Quin act the part of Falstaff," where-
upon Quin responded, "And I would give a thousand . . . that I
could gratify your longing." And many would give guineas today
to peruse an authentic account of anecdotes exchanged by Quin
and Smollett at The Three Tuns over the claret and a John Dory.
Equally enjoyable would it be to learn more about Bramble's
ecstatic meeting with those crippled army and navy eccentrics,
Rear Admiral Balderick and Colonel Cockril, whose real identities
and histories remain obscure.

To such pleasant associations at Bath there was one notable exception recorded by Smollett, namely, his observation of a considerable ingrate disguised in *Humphry Clinker* under the connota-
tive title of Paunceford. By a roundabout device in Jerry's letter of
May 10, Smollett, under the pseudonym of Mr. Serle, wrote a
bitterly satirical account of Paunceford's callous ingratitude.
Smollett declared that he had been most generous to Paunceford
in the old days but that the latter, though he had recently returned
with his pockets full of gold from India, made not the slightest
gesture to repay him. At long last the identification of Paunceford
is complete: he was one Alexander Campbell, who returned from
India to Bath with a fortune in the spring of 1768. Further details
about him are available in my recent biography of Smollett.

Having completed the episodes set in Bath, Smollett transferred
Bramble and his party to London for a stay of some two months.
For this rich section of the novel he again dipped into his own
memories of London and of Chelsea. He pictured such celebrities
as Chatham, "the grand pensionary," and the Duke of Newcastle
as in association with the Duke of Cumberland, who died in 1765,
thus implying that in his satire of them he relied on what he had
seen or heard of them before going to France in 1763. From a still
earlier period he reconstructed certain events in his own life in
Jerry's memorable description of Mr. S——'s Sunday dinners at
Chelsea, where Mr. S—— (Smollett himself, of course) regaled
his hack writers for *The Critical Review* and for other projects

with "beef, pudding, and potatoes, port, punch, and Calvert's entire butt-beer," and was amused by their many eccentricities. This scene, the humorous episodes embedded in it, and Smollett's concluding self-vindication (see the end of Jerry's epistle from London, June 10) are all essentially autobiographical: they certainly display the author himself about 1760 as painted by his own hand some eight or ten years later, when as a chronic invalid he dreamed of his days of boundless vitality.

Similarly, Smollett must have enjoyed the recollection of personal experience embodied in the mellow chapters describing Bramble's expedition to Edinburgh and Glasgow and his tour of the Highlands. The varied social joys of Bramble during this trip were essentially those of Smollett, the seasoned continental traveler, now returning for a last breath of Scottish air and for a happy view of his circle of friends and relatives, some of whom he had visited in 1753 and in 1760. I do not imply that Smollett had the strength to participate in every activity experienced by Bramble. Nor do I infer that Smollett later composed all the letters from Scotland with aids to his memory, such as manuscript journals or printed accounts of that Arcadian land north of the Tweed. Nevertheless, indelible memories of that summer he surely cherished: the hours with his mother and his sister, not alluded to in the novel; his visit with his cousin, the Commissary, at Cameron House on Loch Lomond, so glowingly painted; his farewell sessions with old friends like Dr. Moore, "Jupiter" Carlyle, and others; and at least a glimpse of the Highlands, where, to quote Bramble, all was "sublimity, silence, and solitude."

Such, in general, are the peaks of Smollett's experience and recollection in *Humphry Clinker*. I have still to suggest how this work expresses his character and his social criticism.

One of several reasons why Smollett was fortunate in taking a few hints from Anstey's *New Bath Guide* was that he hit upon the plan of featuring as his central character a valetudinarian in search of health. Thus, through Bramble, Smollett could easily project consciously and subconsciously and with piquant humor certain prevailing moods which he "felt in the blood and felt along the heart." He conveyed through Bramble his own physical distress, his peevish, fretful, and crusty humor, or, to quote Bramble, his "soreness of mind," his excessive sensibility. Smollett never lost his *vis comica,* his capacity to laugh at himself as well as at the follies of mankind. Consider Jerry's diagnosis of Bramble:

He is as tender as a man without a skin, who cannot bear the slightest touch without flinching. What tickles another would give him torment; and yet he has what we may call lucid intervals, when he is remarkably facetious. Indeed, I never knew a hypochondriac so apt to be infected with good humour. He is the most risible misanthrope I ever met with. A lucky joke, or any ludicrous incident, will set him a-laughing immoderately even in one of his most gloomy paroxysms; and when the laugh is over, he will curse his own imbecility.

Read superficially, this appears as a cleverly concocted and exaggerated compound of laughable incongruities, but Jerry's description is, I suspect, very true to the psychology of the novelist in his declining years. Smollett has been called misanthropic; *quasi misantropo* wrote his Italian doctor, Gentili, who observed him in his last illness; and certain critics have labeled him a complete misanthropist. The latter judgment is very dubious; nearer the truth is Jerry's view of Bramble: "He affects misanthropy, in order to conceal the sensibility of a heart which is tender even to a degree of weakness." Indoctrinated in the Augustan age of rationalism, Smollett felt that it was more decorous to appear misanthropic than to succumb to a Shandean emotionalism.

In still other ways Bramble is Smollett's exact portrait. Like his creator, he was compassionate to his relatives and notably generous to the poor. Like Smollett he could enjoy the tender, melting, and humanitarian mood. Like Smollett he was outraged by the noisome filth in the bathing pools of Bath or by the nocturnal stench drifting along the streets of Edinburgh. Identical with Smollett's was Bramble's disillusionment and stoicism as well as his pronounced enthusiasm for the pleasures of a clean country life. Of all these similarities there is abundant proof written large in the pages of *Humphry Clinker.*

In complete harmony with Smollett's oft-expressed views is Bramble's criticism of British and Scottish personalities and manners. Some of the author's criticism was also projected through the

comments of Jerry, but the reactions of Lydia, Tabitha, and Wini-
fred are largely irrelevant, although they are an effective foil to
the central criticism, which, in turn, is both satirical and complimentary. Among the individuals whom Bramble praised was John
Taylor, a young painter at Bath. He also complimented his land-
lady, one Mrs. Norton, in whose house by Golden Square the
Smolletts resided for an indefinite period from 1765 to 1768. Bramble also acclaimed the new Blackfriars Bridge, and the British
Museum, for the improvement of which he proffered suggestions.
In Scotland there was much to admire: the universities of Edinburgh and of Glasgow; at the former center a group of distinguished authors (John Home, David Hume, William Robertson,
Adam Smith, and others); the flourishing city of Glasgow; charming Cameron House, the country seat of Smollett's cousin; and the
romantic beauties of the Highlands. Such favorable impressions,
plus the rich and extravagant comedy of *Humphry Clinker* arising
from incongruities within the characters, as well as from external
caricature, fantastic malapropisms, and highly seasoned anecdotes,
give the book a predominant spirit of mellowness and good nature.
And yet this novel contains samples of Smollett's well-known violence; a louring rack remains in the sunset sky of his art; the
thunder of wrath is often audible; the lightning bolts of satire and
invective still flash and strike home, although not always with
their former power.

It is unnecessary to enumerate all the smaller targets. A pompous
one, Dr. Diederick Wessel Linden, sometime authority on Hyde-
Spaw-Water in Gloucestershire and on the etymology of stench
and of various racial attitudes toward this topic, suffered humiliating treatment from Jerry and from Bramble. Paunceford, Pitt,
Newcastle, and Townshend were larger objects of satire. Harder
hit, however, were two weedlike and boorish Yorkshire squires
named Burdock and Pimpernel.

Smollett, in *Humphry Clinker,* launched his heaviest bolts not
against individuals but against groups of people and against sundry
social institutions. He attacked the tumult and rush of life at Bath
and at London. Like Goldsmith, he warned against the dangers of
unregulated commerce and the great evils of luxury and wide-

spread corruption. He inveighed against the exorbitant cost of living at Bath, and against the adulterated food and drink of London. He struck out at the evils of an unrestricted press and of politically biased juries. Against the vulgarity of Ranelagh and Vauxhall he fulminated repeatedly. He declared that the British public, with no social distinction or subordination left, was rapidly losing its wits. Conservative in politics and fastidious in his tastes, Smollett, like Swift, detested any kind of a mob. Bramble raged against it at Bath:

[The] mob is a monster I never could abide, either in its head, tail, midriff, or members: I detest the whole of it, as a mass of ignorance, presumption, malice, and brutality; and in this term of reprobation, I include, without respect of rank, station, or quality, all those of both sexes who affect its manners, and court its society.

Any mob was repulsive to Bramble, but the worst of all mobs was that composed in large part of the *nouveaux riches,* as it contaminated the streets of Bath:

Every upstart of fortune, harnessed in the trappings of the mode, presents himself at Bath, as in the very focus of observation. Clerks and factors from the East Indies, loaded with the spoil of plundered provinces; planters, negro-drivers, and hucksters, from our American plantations, enriched they know not how; agents, commissaries, and contractors, who have fattened, in two successive wars, on the blood of the nation; usurers, brokers, and jobbers of every kind; men of low birth, and no breeding, have found themselves suddenly translated into a state of affluence, unknown to former ages; and no wonder that their brains should be intoxicated with pride, vanity, and presumption. Knowing no other criterion of greatness, but the ostentation of wealth, they discharge their affluence without taste or conduct, through every channel of the most absurd extravagance; . . . Even the wives and daughters of low tradesmen, who, like shovel-nosed sharks, prey upon the blubber of those uncouth whales of fortune, are infected with the same rage of displaying their importance. . . . Such is the composition of what is called the fashionable company at Bath; where a very inconsiderable proportion of genteel people are lost in a mob of impudent plebeians, who have neither understanding nor judgment, nor the least idea of propriety and decorum; and seem to enjoy nothing so much as an opportunity of insulting their betters.

To this brilliant exposé of the evils of the urban Vanity Fair in eighteenth-century England must be added a cluster of other satirical scenes in other novels by Smollett. Modern social historians now admit that he was not guilty of exaggeration.

In contrast to the folly and depravity of urban life is Smollett's idealized picture of country life in several letters in *Humphry Clinker* dealing with the unfortunate Mr. Baynard and the very fortunate Mr. Dennison. Of course it was "in character" for Bramble, the Welsh country squire, to idealize the country, but there is no doubt but that Smollett enjoyed the rural air of his Chelsea garden and hoped at one time to end his days by the shores of Loch Lomond.

To appreciate his concluding outlook on life it should be recalled that the death of his daughter (his only child), in 1763, had been a heavy affliction. Added to this was his cruel illness, a combination of asthma, rheumatism, and tuberculosis, which first affected him about 1759. How ill he was has not always been recognized. Upon his return in 1765 from his sojourn at Nice he wrote to Dr. Moore that he had "brought back no more than the skeleton" of what he had been. Gone forever were long stretches of Herculean labor in his study at Monmouth House. In the irrecoverable past lay the hours in which he had entertained the tavern table with repartee and salty anecdotes preserved by no Boswell. At Bath in 1766 he was dangerously ill, and in Scotland that same year he was benumbed by a kind of stupor or *coma vigil,* as, with probable exaggeration, he described it. During the spring of 1767 he improved temporarily. In the brilliant Italian sunshine (at Pisa, Florence, Lucca Baths, and Leghorn), thanks to his indomitable will, he clung to life, his vitality apparently improving until he was struck down by an intestinal infection in September, 1771.

Despite his physical weakness and suffering, and despite the fact that as a doctor he must have realized keenly enough after 1766 that his years were limited, Smollett appears not always to have been psychologically depressed, at least not unduly so when he set pen to paper to create what Thackeray called "the most laughable story . . . written since the goodly art of novel-writing began." Inevitably, however, the sheer physical labor of composing *Humphry Clinker* was an ordeal. It "Galls me to the Soul," declared his widow in 1773, "when I think how much that poor Dear Man

Suffered while he wrote that novel." Yet it seems certain that Smollett enjoyed his final writing. It enabled him to recapture in imagination many exciting scenes and moods now recollected in relative tranquillity; it heightened for him what Bramble called "the humor in the farce of life," which he was determined to enjoy as long as he could; and it allowed him to express a considered appraisal of British and Scottish society so well known to him not only through books but also from his extremely keen observation as a traveler. In part, at least, *Humphry Clinker* was a happy escape from a painful and frustrating existence. Remembering Quin, at Bath, Smollett had Jerry write, "My uncle [Bramble] and he [Quin] are perfectly agreed in their estimate of life, which Quin says, would stink in his nostrils, if he did not steep it in claret." In similar fashion, Smollett sweetened the stench of political and social corruption and mitigated his own physical distress by the rich vintage of his creative imagination.

LAURENCE STERNE, APOSTLE OF LAUGHTER

Rufus D. S. Putney

I LAUGH till I cry," Laurence Sterne wrote David Garrick, "and in the same tender moment cry till I laugh." The statement epitomizes his literary career. "Everything in this world, said my father, is big with jest—and has wit in it, and instruction too—if we can but find it out." To find it out *Tristram Shandy* was written, but though we laugh often in making the discovery, that novel impresses us with the pathos of life rather than with its comedy. As Sterne approached the end of *A Sentimental Journey,* he wrote to Mrs. James: "I told you my design in it was to teach us to love the world and our fellow creatures better than we do— so it runs most upon those gentler passions and affections which aid so much to it." But if the comedy of life ends in pathos, Sterne's delineation of its pathos is comic. To a gay young woman named Hannah, Sterne sent this challenge: "I have something else for you, which I am fabricating at a great rate, & that is my Journey, which shall make you cry as much as ever it made me laugh—or I'll give up the Business of sentimental writing—& write to the Body." His hopes were fulfilled beyond his expectations. The echoes of the deluge with which countless Hannahs of both sexes once saturated the pages of *A Sentimental Journey* still drown out the sound of Sterne's laughter.

We are likely to be misled by reading "sentimentalist" on the label affixed to Laurence Sterne. The term, unless the word be used in its unsentimental eighteenth-century sense, is never appropriate to the writer and only occasionally so to the man. To call Sterne a sentimentalist is to ignore the hard core of comic irony that made him critical of the emotional vagaries of his own life and of his imagined characters. The reputation for lachrymose sensibility has been fastened unjustly to Sterne by a misunderstanding of *A Sentimental Journey,* fostered by uncritical dependence on the four letters supposed to have been written to Elizabeth Lumley before she became Mrs. Sterne and on the *Journal to Eliza*. Of the two, the letters to his wife are the more damaging because they appear to push back his cardiac instability to 1740 or earlier. Professor Lewis P. Curtis has demonstrated, however, that they could not have been written as we now have them at the date conventionally assigned. Neither the letters nor the *Journal* prove Sterne's excessive sensibility. More manly men than he had tears to shed indiscriminately on real or fictitious woes, and his prompt though somewhat inactive compassion was the result of the hardships and frustrations of his own life. Like Pope and Swift, he was anti-intellectual because he knew that reason often deludes the reasoner and solves only minor problems. He did not subscribe to the philosophical cult of feeling. On the contrary, as Herbert Read has shown, Sterne's sermon, "The Abuses of Conscience," insists upon Christian authority as the proper measure of virtue. Man's propensity to self-delusion makes his feelings deceptive guides to right conduct. In his final judgment upon himself Sterne reiterated the fallibility of the emotions. To Mrs. James he wrote in March, 1768, shortly before his death: "If I die cherish the remembrance of me and forget the follies which you have so often condemn'd—which my heart, not my head betray'd me into."

Sterne doubtless knew that Mrs. James would more readily forgive the mistakes of the heart than the perversions of the mind, but the self-criticism this passage displays was constant, not unique. Once his effusions of feeling were past, Sterne could and did view his behavior with impartial irony. In 1764 he sent John Hall-Stevenson an account of a love affair identical in all respects to his courtship of Eliza—even to the hemorrhages of the lungs with which he lamented the departures of both ladies:

I have been for eight weeks smitten with the tenderest passion that ever tender wight underwent. I wish, dear cosin, thou couldest conceive (perhaps thou can'st without my wishing it) how deliciously I canter'd away with it the first month, two up, two down, always upon my hânches along the streets from my hôtel to hers, at first, once—then twice, then three times a day, till at length I was within an ace of setting up my hobby horse in her stable for good and all. I might as well considering how the enemies of the Lord have blasphemed thereupon; the last three weeks we were every hour upon the doleful ditty of parting—and thou mayest concieve, dear cosin, how it alter'd my gaite and air—for I went and came like any louden'd carl, and did nothing but mix tears, and *Jouer des sentiments* with her from sun-rising even to the setting of the same; and now she is gone to the South of France, and to finish the comedie, I fell ill, and broke a vessel in my lungs and half bled to death. Voila mon Histoire!

Love, as Trim told Uncle Toby, is "the most serious thing, an please your honour (sometimes) that is in the world." But not after love has ended. Just as Sterne in this letter laughed at his folly, he mocked in the *Sentimental Journey* the foolish figure he had cut with Eliza Draper.

Though Sterne during the final years of his celebrity often wept to demonstrate the soundness of his heart, he had no faith as a writer in the moral efficacy of tears. In the cathartic effects of laughter he felt complete assurance. "If 'tis wrote against any thing, —'tis wrote, an' please your worships, against the spleen," he re-marked in volume four of *Tristram Shandy,* "in order, by a more frequent and a more convulsive elevation and depression of the diaphragm, and the succussations of the intercostal muscles in laughter, to drive the *gall* and other *bitter juices* from the gall bladder, liver and sweet-bread of his majesty's subjects, with all their inimicitious passions which belong to them, down into their duodenums." His insatiable love of laughter and belief in its worth distinguishes him from Meredith. Otherwise he had the same confidence in the value and healthiness of comedy.

Begun to please himself in the conviction that what he liked the public must also relish, *Tristram Shandy* is one of the funniest of English novels. Sterne's zest for laughter infects every part of the book, characters, style, incidents, satire, and structure. There is an abundance of sentiment as well, but his diffidence in the presence of pathos transmutes sorrow into mirth. Walter and Toby Shandy and Trim are the figures best remembered and loved. The most gracious events are those that take place on Uncle Toby's bowling green where he and Trim re-enact for the good of the nation the victories of English arms abroad, until the Treaty of Utrecht puts an end to glorious war and allows that daughter of Eve, the Widow

Wadman, to shatter their masculine Paradise. No less memorable
are the scenes at the fireside in Shandy Hall, where the two affectionate but incompatible brothers meet to smoke, to snooze, to talk,
and inevitably to vex one another. While Walter "crucifies Truth"
in his impetuous quest for evidence to support his extraordinary
hypotheses, benign, sensible, brave, modest, orthodox Uncle Toby
finds ample vent for the outrage done his modesty, religion, and
common sense in puffing on his pipe or whistling the "Lillibulero."
But Walter's patience snaps faster than his pipestems when an inadvertent word sends Toby rushing into discourses on fortifications
and ballistics, or when Uncle Toby's naïve questions interrupt Walter's eloquence:

'Tis pity, said my father, that truth can only be on one side, brother *Toby,*—
considering what ingenuity these learned men have all shewn in their solutions of noses.—Can noses be dissolved? replied my uncle *Toby.*—
    —My father thrust back his chair,—rose up—put on his hat,—took four
long strides to the door,—jerked it open,—thrust his head half way out,—shut
the door again,—took no notice of the bad hinge,—returned to the table,—
pluck'd my mother's thread-paper out of *Slawkenbergius's* book,—went
hastily to his bureau,—walk'd slowly back,—twisting my mother's thread-
paper about his thumb,—unbutton'd his waistcoat,—threw my mother's
thread-paper into the fire,—bit her sattin pin-cushion in two, fill'd his mouth
with bran,—confounded it;—but mark!—the oath of confusion was levell'd at
my uncle *Toby's* brain,—which was e'en confused enough already,—the curse
came charged only with the bran—the bran, may it please your honours,—
was no more than powder to the ball.

If Toby, Walter, Trim, and Yorick are Sterne's most praised
characters, the most neglected is Tristram himself. The chief cause
for this neglect has been the identification of Tristram with Sterne,
who complained toward the end of his life that "The world has
imagined, because I wrote Tristram Shandy, that I was myself
more Shandean than I really ever was." Tristram, as Edwin Muir
some years ago demonstrated, is the projection of a mere fraction
of Sterne's personality, not a portrait of the real man. To write *The
Life and Opinions of Tristram Shandy, Gent.,* Sterne assumed the
character of Tristram as he was later to wear the more subtle
disguise of a revamped Yorick to write *A Sentimental Journey.*
His imaginative fidelity to these created roles beggars praise, giv-

ing unity to the novels and making plausible their eccentricities.
The assumption of Tristram's mind provides also the chief structural device of the book. In the fragment we possess, very little of
Tristram's life is narrated, but he was once destined to play a larger
part than Sterne's fate allowed him to fulfill. Up to chapter xx of
Volume VI, the misadventures of Tristram's life provide the skeleton on which the digressions are hung, and his is the mind so lost
in the flux of thought, as explained by Locke's theory of the association of ideas, that each mischance he suffers leads into tangential
mazes. What Sterne once designed, after he had given up the notion reported by Stephen Croft of traveling Tristram all over Europe and returning him home at last a complete English gentleman,
can be learned from the first volume:

But I was begot and born to misfortunes;— . . . so that I was doom'd, by
marriage articles, to have my nose squeez'd as flat to my face, as if the destinies
had actually spun me without one.

How this event came about,—and what a train of vexatious disappoint-
ments, in one stage or other of my life, have pursued me from the mere loss,
or rather compression, of this one single member,—shall be laid before the
reader all in due time.

This and other passages in the novel make it clear that as he commenced the book Sterne intended to follow Tristram's career into
manhood with a series of humiliations and petty disasters.

The abandonment of this scheme in the middle of Volume VI
for the interpolation of Uncle Toby's wars, his amour with the
Widow Wadman, and Tristram's travels has obscured the structural unity (on the principle of the association of ideas) that prevailed for the first five and a half volumes. All but a few brief
and unimportant digressions are connected with the accidents that
befall Tristram. Mrs. Shandy's ill-timed question leads to the
discussion of the rights of the homunculus, to the date of his conception, and to Walter Shandy's theory of geniture. The date of his
birth involves its method, and that brings in the local midwife,
whose existence in the neighborhood requires a description of
Parson Yorick and his reasons for establishing the old woman in
her vocation. Her role in Tristram's misfortunes would be inexplicable, in view of Dr. Slop's proximity, without a knowledge of

his mother's marriage settlement. Tristram's name results in an exposition of Walter's theory of names with the history of Aunt Dinah, and Tristram's quasi-logical comment that one cannot be christened before one is born reminds him of the decision of the doctors of the Sorbonne on that subject. While Walter and Toby are awaiting Tristram's birth, they begin a discussion of Mrs. Shandy's reason for rejecting Dr. Slop which cannot be understood until Toby's character has been elucidated. The accident to Tristram's nose in volume three is responsible for the discussion of Walter's theory of the importance of noses with the reasons therefore and an account of his collection of books on the subject. From his favorite work the tale of Slawkenbergius is gleaned. The remainder of the fourth volume follows from the mistake at the christening which reaches its culmination in the ludicrous happenings and talk at the Visitation Dinner. The news of Bobby's death soon after focuses all Walter's hopes upon Tristram. Hence his father begins writing the Tristra-*pœdia,* upon which he has made considerable progress before Tristram at the age of five suffers his misadventure with the window sash. The arrival of Yorick, Toby, and Trim to explain the defective window not only gives Walter a chance to express his views on circumcision but also provides an audience for the reading of the Tristra-*pœdia.* That introduces the need for a tutor, and Uncle Toby recommends Le Fever's son. Who he is necessitates telling his father's story. The mad rumors about Tristram caused by his last accident make Walter resolve that his son shall be put into breeches, a determination which leads to an account of Walter's researches upon clothes and a description of his beds of justice at which affairs important to the family are decided. Up to this point *Tristram Shandy* is as thoughtfully constructed and as unified as *Tom Jones.*

The probable cause for the alteration in Sterne's design was the clamor against the double entendre and downright indecencies of the second installment. Possibly he also realized that Walter's hypotheses were growing slightly stale. Still the compromise he made was minor. He shifted his subject to the more poignant humor of Uncle Toby's activities, but the consistency of Tristram's character as narrator and consequently the tone and comedy were scrupulously maintained. For Tristram is himself a comic character in whom are blended the diverse strains of the Shandys. From Uncle Toby he inherited pity, from his great Aunt Dinah lasciviousness. His obligations to his father are so great that they require a separate paragraph.

That Tristram would "neither think nor act like any other man's child" was the conviction to which Walter Shandy was led "upon his observing a most unaccountable obliquity, (as he call'd it) in my manner of setting up my top, and justifying the principles upon which I had done it, . . . with a thousand other observations he had made upon me." Never stopping to reflect that his son could be only extraordinary, Walter accounts for Tristram's eccentricities in terms of his favorite theories of geniture, obstetrics, names, noses, and education. In the depiction of father and son Sterne employed his subtlest skill in characterization. Tristram's taste for the oddities of knowledge, his unpredictable attitudes toward persons and things, rival his father's. He has his father's relish also for witty indecencies, and the same irreverence. His representation of Walter's strange opinions is half serious, half playful, for he half believes himself that they explain the idiosyncrasies he enjoys. Besides, he has hypotheses of his own, though like everything else about Tristram when compared to his father, they are diminutive and trifling. Knots, swearing, plackets, buttonholes, chambermaids, chamber pots, and chapters are the sorts of things he theorizes about. Finally, Walter had the zeal or anger (two names for the same quality) to make him a satirist. Uncle Toby's benevolence had eradicated the harshness from Tristram, who thus sums up the difference between himself and his father:

For my hobby-horse, if you recollect a little, is no way a vicious beast; he has scarce one hair or lineament of the ass [the lower passions in Walter's terminology] about him— 'Tis a sporting little filly-folly which carries you out for the present hour—a maggot, a butter-fly, a picture, a fiddle-stick—an uncle *Toby's* siege—or an *any thing,* which a man makes shift to get astride on, to canter it away from the cares and solicitudes of life— 'Tis as useful a beast as is in the whole creation—nor do I really see how the world could do without it—

—But for my father's ass—oh! mount him—mount him—mount him— (that's three times, is it not?)—mount him not:—'tis a beast concupiscent— and foul befall the man who does not hinder him from kicking.

Some have complained because Sterne's "filly-folly" did not kick like Walter Shandy's ass. The censure that *Tristram Shandy* lacks high purpose because Sterne undertook no reformations is idle criticism. There is a quantity of sportive satire, although Dr. Burton and the Pope might have detected occasional bitterness, but satire is not what we seek in *Tristram Shandy*. The greatness of the novel and its abiding charm reside in Sterne's humor, that mixture of pathos and wit that sheds its warm glow over the representation of the frailties and foibles as well as the strength of man's nature, matters upon which Sterne was far better informed than most of his critics. More truly than *A Sentimental Journey, Tristram* "teaches us to love the world and our fellow creatures better than we do."

On the success of *Tristram Shandy* Sterne gambled everything he had—money, his reputation as a clergyman, and his hope of rising in the Church. Friends warned him of his peril in publishing such a book. "Get your Preferment first Lory," one said, "& then Write & Welcome." A note of quiet desperation, induced by forty-six years of obscurity and frustration, pervades his answer, "But suppose preferment is long acoming (& for aught I know I may not be preferr'd till the Resurrection of the Just) and am all that time in labour—how must I bear my Pains?"

The intoxicating popularity of the novel permitted Sterne to discover what Pope had found before him. "The greatest advantage I know of being thought a wit by the world," Pope had said, "is, that it gives one the greater freedom of playing the fool." Sterne possessed an impulse to folly that had driven him, while his reputation was merely local, to play the fool agriculturally, politically, clerically, and domestically. Some of the motives for this conduct one should not try to explain. During the years of his fame, however, he deliberately adopted and emphasized his favorite role. "I wrote," he told one of his friends, "not to be fed but to be famous." To the obscure Yorkshire parson the idea of fame included posthumous reputation if it could be had, but most of all it meant contemporary celebrity, the outward and visible sign of which not infrequently is food of superior quality eaten at the tables of the great. If his book had brought him renown,

Sterne resolved that he would whet the appetites of his readers by his life. He therefore undertook to advertise his novel by impersonating the character of Tristram Shandy.

The experiment was only partially successful. He won and kept the friendship of David Garrick, Lord Bathurst, and many more, but the spectacle of a reverend clergyman acting the part of a licentious jester shortly aroused the ire of others. Recovering from the panic that made him present Sterne a purse of guineas as insurance against a lampoon, Bishop Warburton solemnly pronounced him "an irrecoverable scoundrel." In and out of print Oliver Goldsmith raged against the man and his work. Whitfield thundered, "O *Sterne!* thou art scabby, and such is the leprosy of thy mind that it is not to be cured like the leprosy of the body, by dipping nine times in the river Jordan." The more dignified Dr. Delany was reported to be much offended with "the man Sterne," and Dr. Dodd, who was soon to hang for forgery, protested in execrable verse,

> Is it for this you wear the sacred gown,
> To live and write the Shandy of the town?

Sterne could afford to be amused as long as people bought his book, but after 1762 *Tristram Shandy* ceased to pay profits of the size Sterne needed, and the critics began dunning him for his arrears of pathos. A new book was necessary to recoup his literary fortunes without sacrificing, since tears were alien to *Tristram Shandy,* his integrity as an artist. As nearly as can be determined, Sterne conceived *A Sentimental Journey* during the summer of 1766 while he was busy with the last volume of *Shandy*. It was written throughout the summer and fall of 1767.

During that year Sterne suffered a dangerous illness and his love affair with Eliza Draper. Too much effect has been attributed to both in explaining why Sterne, always sentimentally chaste in *Tristram Shandy,* seems emotionally wanton in *A Sentimental Journey*. He had recovered entirely from the lady and temporarily from the disease by the time he produced most of his book. The exuberant gaiety of his work belies its origin in depression and despair. As for Eliza, she was merely another in the long list of

Sterne's sentimental mistresses. They met in January. By February Sterne, following his usual procedure in such cases, had persuaded first himself and then the lady that he was in love. An idealized but essentially accurate description of the beginning of his infatuation can be read in Yorick's description of his enamorment:

It had ever, as I told the reader, been one of the singular blessings of my life, to be almost every hour of it miserably in love with some one; and my last flame happening to be blown out by a whiff of jealousy on the sudden turn of a corner, I had lighted it up afresh at the pure taper of Eliza but about three months before, swearing as I did it, that it should last me through the whole journey. Why should I dissemble the matter? I had sworn to her eternal fidelity; she had a right to my whole heart; to divide my affections was to lessen them; to expose them, was to risk them: where there is risk, there may be loss.

Six or seven months in affairs of this kind meant eternity to Sterne. Eliza sailed for India in April. By the end of July long gaps appeared in the *Journal,* in which he had vowed he would keep a daily record of his love. On August 4, when he shut up the *Journal* with a lie to Eliza about the date of his wife's homecoming, he had found out what he had just written or soon would write in the drummer's letter to the corporal's wife:

> L'amour n'est *rien* sans sentiment.
> Et le sentiment est encore *moins* sans amour.

Once he had made this discovery Sterne ceased playing at sentiments in the *Journal.*

To write and to laugh were still synonymous for him. He now solved his literary dilemma with a hoax by which he persuaded his contemporaries that the comedy he must write was the pathos they wished to read. He accomplished this by making Yorick weep in order that "in the same tender moment" he himself might laugh. For Yorick is a dramatically presented comic hero with a heart as erratic as Tristram's head. He is not to be regarded, Edwin Muir and W. B. C. Watkins have shown, as a sympathetic portrait of his creator. Occasionally Sterne's identification of himself with Yorick becomes almost complete. But for the most part the writer records with amused irony the false, ludicrous, or humiliating postures into which Yorick is thrust by his intrepid sensibility. Far from being a manual of sentimental and civilized behavior, as Peter Quennell has lately described the book, *A Sentimental Journey* displays the errors, equivocations, and dilemmas into which Yorick is betrayed by the instability of his heart. For Yorick, unlike the benevolent monsters spawned in imitation of him, runs the full scale of human emotions. He is vain, libidinous, servile, proud, greedy, and fickle as well as humane, faithful, honest, humble, and loving. The gift of his snuffbox mitigates but does not excuse his injustice to the Monk. His somewhat tardy continence scarcely offsets the infidelities to Eliza he commits in spirit. He gives alms to the wrong people and hires a valet for preposterous reasons. Compassion for the master of the dead ass leads him to curse his postilion. He buys the caged starling but does not free it, and purchases popularity with obsequious flattery. He goes, like "the Knight of the Woeful Countenance," in quest of a melancholy meeting with Maria, and his pity for her misery ends in con-cupiscence. At such incongruities Sterne could not help but laugh.

It has been duly noted that Sterne immortalized Eliza by mentioning her name on five occasions in his novel, but I think no one has pointed out the ambiguous role he assigned her in his love comedy as the mistress to whom Yorick could scarcely be true. In two instances her name merely lends the book the piquant impropriety that Jenny had given *Tristram Shandy*. Her other appearances are more amusing. Tormented by his inability to read the Old French fragment, Yorick seeks a remedy for his vexation in correspondence. He writes Eliza, but only as an afterthought. He writes Eugenius first. Elsewhere she is a clog hindering his pursuit of the women that attract him. Commenting on Maria's departing figure, Yorick says,

Affliction had touch'd her looks with something that was scarcely earthly—still she was feminine, and so much there was about her of all that the heart wishes or the eye looks for in woman, that could the traces be ever worn out of her brain, and those of Eliza out of mine, she should *not only eat of my bread and drink of my own cup,* but Maria should lie in my bosom and be unto me as a daughter.

Earlier, tempted by visions of the joys a visit to Madame de L—— offers, Yorick suddenly remembers Eliza and his vows of constancy. Falling on his knees he swears he "would not travel to Brussels, unless Eliza went along with me, did the road lead towards heaven," then wryly adds, "In transports of this kind the heart, in spite of the understanding, will always say too much." His fidelity reasserted, Yorick writes gallantly to the lady and hastens on to Paris to expose, risk, and lessen his affections with the beautiful *grisset,* the *fille de chambre,* the Marquisina di Fagnani by interpolation, Maria at Moulines, and the lady who shared his room in the Bourbonnois. In the "Business of sentimental writing" Sterne used Eliza as the symbol of delicate, disinterested, romantic love. In the semiprivate comedy that made him laugh Eliza provides a standard to measure the vagaries of Yorick's heart.

Priesthood was a fortunate accident in the career of Laurence Sterne. Most of the materials for his fiction came from his own far from exemplary life. Yet if he did not practice, he believed sincerely what he preached. Thus his clerical vocation gave him the absolute ethical code that made possible the dispassionate judgment comedy requires. His own behavior after his residence in France in 1762 often resembled Yorick's; his literary account of it is the self-mockery of *A Sentimental Journey.* The disparity between his practice and his professions enriched *Tristram Shandy* in another, less tangible way. Only from the knowledge of his own trials and failures could have come his humorous pity for the frailties of other men. Sterne cannot have added a cubit to the spiritual stature of the Church of England. By making him take thought it added many to his greatness as a writer.

FANNY BURNEY'S *EVELINA*

Edwine Montague and Louis L. Martz

A. It's a disturbing experience to reread *Evelina* like this, just after finishing *All the King's Men*. Two popular novels, each fairly representative of the better writing of its time, but see what they represent. Here's Warren's book, concerned, at one level, with the problems of political action, and at a deeper level obsessed with the rediscovery of evil—original sin—the necessity for spiritual rebirth; violent passion, violent death, violent language, all probing into the anxieties of modern secularized man. Then there's *Evelina,* filled with these agonies: to be forced to admit to a lord that one lives—"in Holborn"; to have a baronet hear a silversmith's daughter call one "cousin"; to have to go up "two pair of stairs" to dine; to violate the rules of a ball; to be forced to sit in the upper gallery in "pit" dress . . . I wonder. Does *Evelina* really deserve its fame? Did it ever really live in its own right?

B. How can you doubt it? That edition you're reading ought to prove that the book's a "classic." The Clarendon Press wouldn't have asked MacKinnon to provide those elaborate notes if the novel hadn't proved its worth through 150 years.

A. This edition has a perversely opposite effect on me. I have a feeling that MacKinnon mistrusts the book, and is providing crutches to help it along. He practically admits that he's using it as a series of pegs to hang a commentary on, and he says flatly here in the preface: "the interest of the book lies not in the story, and the drawing of character, but in the picture it affords of contemporary life and manners." That doesn't sound to me like a declaration of literary merit—though it may be true that the book is useful to a social historian.

B. It has literary importance, though, as a link between *Humphry Clinker* and *Sense and Sensibility;* certainly it's the best English novel to appear between those two. Don't you think she's using *Humphry Clinker* as a base for operations in the direction of Jane Austen?

A. You might say something of the sort, though her epistolary method is really a blend of Richardson and Smollett. Still, she does seem to follow *Humphry Clinker* in giving satirical views of social life at London and the "Hotwells," and also in trying to distinguish her correspondents by giving the letters different tones. But that's one trouble; she can't carry it off. The only letters that have a stamp of character are Evelina's; Mr. Villars' rhapsodies are only embarrassing. It might as well be written entirely in *Pamela's* way: everything that counts is given through Evelina.

B. True—you don't get the complexity and variety of *Humphry Clinker,* but you do get a single, focused view—a sensitive, feminine view—of the problems raised in a small social circle, and that seems to me to lead the way toward Jane Austen.

A. Oh, I'll grant the book its place in literary history. But isn't that rather like granting the usefulness of knowing about Kyd or Davenant or Cowley?

B. But *Evelina's* never stopped having its readers. My Everyman edition shows eight printings between 1909 and 1931, and there were at least two dozen nineteenth-century editions. I don't think it's just a book for graduate students of the novel or the Age of Johnson. There's something essentially good about the book that has drawn out all those editions.

A. Don't you think a lot of people read the book—or start to read it—simply because Fanny Burney wrote it? Evelina has a good deal in common with the young Fanny Burney; people who enjoy the *Diary* enjoy finding Fanny Burney in the novel too; and so the book becomes a kind of appendix to the *Diary*.

B. Right there you're finding more power in the book than you've admitted so far. You're admitting that the book creates, or conveys, a certain personality. Whether you call her Fanny Burney, or Evelina—the personality is there—the Young Lady entering the World. And don't deny me the pleasure of reading one work in the light of another by the same author. I enjoy feeling the typical Burney phrasing and point of view in Evelina's letters; the parallels place the novel in a concrete setting in my mind—the world I know from Fanny Burney's *Diary*.

A. But—

B. Oh, I know, you're going to say the novel ought to create its own world. It does. What we know about Fanny Burney simply extends the significance of the things we find in the book itself. MacKinnon's notes work the same way, if you'd take the trouble to read them.

A. Sometime I will: I'd like to know about Cox's Museum. But the rather surprising fact is that that's the only place where I've really felt the need of a note (up to p. 283, at least, where Mr. Macartney's "affecting letter" has stopped me dead). Not that I know so much about Ranelagh or Vauxhall or the Pantheon—but where you absolutely have to know a detail to interpret the action properly, Fanny Burney gives it to you, almost as if she were thinking of posterity—or a French translation. Take that incident where the girls are having their troubles in the dark alleys of Vauxhall. Burney sets down the one essential aspect of the scene in Evelina's first comment on Vauxhall: "The Garden is very pretty, but too formal; I should have been better pleased, had it consisted less of strait walks, where 'Grove nods at grove, each alley has its brother.'" Pope's line neatly gives us all we need to know to follow the incident.

B. True—but later, when they're looking at the Hayman paintings in the room off the Rotunda, you can't get the full humor of Mr. Smith's display of ignorance unless you realize that the paintings deal with British military and naval victories.

A. So that's why there's so much talk about generals? Still, the text itself makes the main point clear: Mr. Smith can't tell Neptune from a general. And the same thing's true of social customs. You always know when a custom has been breached, and usually you're told exactly what that custom was.

B. That's certainly true of Evelina's first faux pas: refusing the dance with Lovel, and then accepting a dance with Lord Orville later on. Evelina explains the whole thing to herself near the end of that letter: "A confused idea now for the first time entered my head, of something I had heard of the rules of an assembly; but I was never at one before,—I have only danced at school,—and so giddy and heedless I was, that I had not once considered the impropriety of refusing one partner, and afterwards accepting another. I was thunderstruck at the recollection." So her character and situation are clearly defined at the outset; and she never stops such rash actions and informative repentances.

A. I suppose Fanny Burney liked to explain such matters very clearly in order to provide a kind of guide for the proper behavior of young ladies entering the world?

B. That's one benefit, then, of the didactic novel: you always know where a character stands. Yet her didacticism never gets out of hand in Evelina's letters (I admit that Villars is unbearable). The "lessons" arise quite naturally out of Evelina's repentant ruminations over the incidents.

A. Next you'll be arguing that the incidents "arise quite naturally" out of the plot!

B. I won't say a thing for the plot—except that it's no worse than most of Dickens' plots, and might be charitably overlooked for somewhat the same reasons that let us forgive his plots. Because the novel has unity and design, of a kind not dependent on the plot.

A. "Spatial form," I suppose.

B. Much simpler than that: if you put aside the introductory and concluding portions dealing with the matter of Evelina's parentage, you can see that the book falls into three well-defined sections, of almost exactly the same length, separated by two equally well-defined interludes. The early editions, in three volumes, make the arrangement obvious. Section I you might call "Introduction to London"—her visit there with the Mirvans, her first glimpses—rather distant—of high society, and her first meetings with her "low" relatives. Then follows an interlude in the country, at Howard Grove, where the Captain's horseplay (dull reading, I admit) serves to set off the high life preceding it. Then follows Section II: the contrasting "low" visit in London with Madame Duval and the Branghtons. Next comes another interlude in the country, this time at Berry Hill, lasting just long enough to rest us and prepare us for Section III, at the "Hotwells," the last, the most complicated, the best-written part of the book—and the highest point of the social scale: Evelina rockets from the Branghtons to the pinnacle of society—the inner sanctum of earls. I think, too, I could show that each of the three sections rises to a climax within its own area: Section I with the horrifying scene of the opera; Section II with the vile use of Lord Orville's coach in Evelina's name, and the dreadful consequences, including the letter that Evelina rashly, and *improperly,* writes to Orville; and Section III, of course, with the complications immediately preceding the mutual admission of love between Orville and Evelina. I think I could show you that each of these big incidents is very tightly built upon the preceding smaller events of each section. The whole arrangement is very deft. Each section begins with fairly simple embarrassments, to establish the new situation, and then the incidents grow in complexity until the climax is reached. The second climax is much more intricate and painful than the first; and the third is by far the most complex of the three, because of the way in which Orville is led to fear that her "sudden reserve" toward him is due to the arrival of Sir Clement.

A. You don't agree, then, with the critics who praise the book for giving something like "a direct transcript of life"? You know it's been praised for simply "transferring reality" into a book with a minimum of artistic modification. Like Thackeray's idea that Smollett "did not invent much, but described what he saw."

B. Yes, and just as unsatisfactory. Her handling of the characters alone ought to show the opposite: there isn't a character in the book who isn't a carefully designed caricature. Lord Orville is Gentility Incarnate; Lovel is the Rude Fop; Sir Clement, the Unscrupulous Beau; Captain Mirvan, the stock seagoing ruffian (duller than most); Du Bois, the stock Frenchman; the Branghtons, types of vulgarity, and so on. They're all types, remarkably single-minded types—like something out of Ben Jonson or Congreve.

A. You have a point there. I was just reading that scene in the theater where they are seeing *Love for Love.* The Captain suggests that Lovel ought to have "taken some notice of one Mr. *Tattle*" in the play. Lovel retorts by asking what the Captain thinks of *"one Mr. Ben,"* and next insults Evelina by asking her what she thinks of "the *country* young lady, Miss Prue." Then Orville tactfully shifts the discussion to the character of Angelica. Certainly you have there a key to where Fanny Burney learned her methods of presenting character.

B. Except for Evelina: it's strange how hard it is to consider her a "character." She's really a sort of "setting," or a stage, for the "characters" proper to play upon. Or perhaps it's better to call her a central point of view.

A. —which is brought out by being played against various aspects of life, represented singly in all the other characters?

B. Yes, so that a given character is of no importance except in so far as he sets up a vibration in that sensitive central personality called Evelina. It's the vibration that counts, not the Lovels or the Orvilles in themselves. That's why the "characters" never get out of control, except for Captain Mirvan, now and then; they all have carefully defined functions. Take Du Bois, for instance: he's not there just to give an opportunity for irrelevant ridicule of the French: he has at least three important functions. His fine manners are a constant foil to the vulgar behavior that surrounds him; his attendance on Madame Duval emphasizes her dubious character and reputation; and finally, his infatuation with Evelina is very neatly contrived to break up Madame Duval's interest in holding fast to such an attractive granddaughter.

A. But what about Macartney? Isn't he a rather sad adventure in the sentimental fashion?

B. Very sad indeed. But you can see plainly why the plot needs him: something humane has to be done for that poor girl, the nurse's daughter, who's been reared as *Miss Belmont*. Macartney is there to provide the "little impostor" with a decent place in life, after Evelina takes the post of heiress. Macartney in himself is badly conceived, and yet I think Burney makes very artful use of him in the last section, where he has those furtive and mysterious meetings with Evelina. You remember how those meetings worry the admirable Orville and distress Evelina because she can't explain them to him.

A. True enough. I've never denied that the book is artfully done. I've been noticing the economy of her phrasing: how she manages to make every word count, even while she maintains the illusion of seventeen-year-old garrulity—and "vibration." It's not a lack of art that bothers me—it's a question of substance. What do all the little shocks and tremors add up to after all? What's the standard of values in the book? Evelina objects to her cousins simply because they are "low" and ill-bred, and she's overwhelmed with shame when Sir Clement discovers her relation to them—yet Sir Clement is plainly "unprincipled" and the cousins are perfectly decent people. How can a book survive such triviality?

B. But Fanny Burney takes full account of that conflict between snobbery and virtue. Remember the scene where Sir Clement boldly visits Evelina and Madame Duval, when the Branghtons are present; he's finally put out of countenance—and out of doors—by the blatant rudeness of the group. Evelina's feelings are quite mixed there: she's ashamed of her relatives—yes—yet gratified that Sir Clement has been cut down; she despises his character, yet she can't overcome her awe at his position and breeding. A nice dilemma, and one that runs throughout the book.

A. I see, you're going to say that the book is "delightful for its naïve picture of unconscious snobbery."

B. I shouldn't make a statement as brash as that, but there's something in it. Don't forget that Fanny Burney said she was not pretending to show the world "what it actually *is,* but what it *appears* to a girl of seventeen." Well, to a girl of seventeen the problems of the world are mainly matters of form, manners, appearances. Evelina comes out of her childhood to discover that the world is a place where one has to know the established modes of behavior, or it becomes a mighty unpleasant spot. That's a universal discovery—accentuated by the situation of Evelina. She's neither upper class nor lower class—a girl of no position. She knows too much of good breeding to be happy with Madame Duval and the Branghtons, and too little to be happy with the "quality" of London and Bristol Hotwells. She goes through the universal sufferings of the person who hasn't yet learned—and often he never does learn—where he "belongs," and how to "belong." I shouldn't call that a trivial subject.

A. I suppose it all depends on how the subject is handled. It's probably large enough for successful comedy, if the author can develop it to show how deeply forms and manners can affect one's existence.

B. And Fanny Burney does. The causes of Evelina's miseries may be trivial—but the results are not. You might even argue that the results are all the more painful just because of the trivial nature of the causes. But let me try to show you what I mean. Look at that opera scene closely. The causes of it are introduced as soon as Letter XXI begins: "In the afternoon,—at Berry Hill, I should have said the *evening,* for it was almost six o'clock . . ." (Notice how Burney keeps the difference between town and country before us.)

. . . while Miss Mirvan and I were dressing for the opera, and in high spirits, from the expectation of great entertainment and pleasure, we heard a carriage stop at the door, and concluded that Sir Clement Willoughby, with his usual assiduity, was come to attend us to the Haymarket; but, in a few moments, what was our surprise, to see our chamber-door flung open, and the two Miss Branghtons enter the room! They advanced to me with great familiarity, saying, "How do you do, cousin?—so we've caught you at the glass!—well, I'm determined I'll tell my brother of that!"

Two discordant elements are introduced at once: discordant with the expected pleasure of the opera, and with each other: Sir Clement's "assiduity" (the word runs throughout the novel); and the Branghtons' vulgarity, which later makes Evelina take refuge in the hitherto unwelcome attentions of Sir Clement. The Branghtons call her "cousin" at once—the fear that Sir Clement—and Lord Orville—will discover her relationship to these creatures lies at the bottom of her actions during the incident. Every word and action of her cousins betrays their ignorance of the "laws and customs *à-la-mode"*—to such an extent that Evelina soon displays some rather complicated feelings:

I was extremely disconcerted at this forward and ignorant behaviour, and yet their rudeness very much lessened my concern at refusing them. Indeed, their dress was such as would have rendered their scheme of accompanying our party impracticable, even if I had desired it; and this, as they did not themselves find out, I was obliged, in terms the least mortifying I could think of, to tell them.

A. A kind of comic hubris?

B. Yes, and also later on, when they arrive at the opera house and she is the only one who knows anything about the place. She's much too proudly conscious of the fact that her dress is "very improper for my company," and she says that if she had not been "too much chagrined to laugh," she would have been "extremely diverted at their ignorance of whatever belongs to an opera."

A. That's rather too much like Lovel's attitude toward her.

B. Then, in the midst of these miseries, after the haggling over tickets, the arrival in the upper gallery, the crude comments of the Vulgar on the opera, we are allowed a single, controlled glimpse of paradise in the pit:

I was then able to distinguish the happy party I had left; and I saw that Lord Orville had seated himself next to Mrs. Mirvan. Sir Clement had his eyes perpetually cast towards the five-shilling gallery, where I suppose he concluded that we were seated; however, before the Opera was over, I have reason to believe that he had discovered me, high and distant as I was from him. Probably he distinguished me by my head-dress.

A. That last sentence is a nice touch.

B. Yes—it explains in a word why she is appalled to see Sir Clement approaching her in the gallery, why she rashly joins him to "avoid immediate humiliation," why, hearing Madame Duval's voice as the old lady descends from the gallery, she flees into Sir Clement's carriage, even though Lord Orville is standing there to see her. The possible results (which come close to occurring) are: loss of reputation, if not loss of virginity, together with the loss of Orville's interest in her. So, it seems, the combination of innocence and snobbery can produce disastrous results for a person who doesn't quite "belong."

A. You're pushing it rather hard to make me feel a moral issue there; but I suppose there is one, of a sort. The helplessness of Evelina makes you feel some mild sense of the world's injustice, the tyranny of forms.

B. Wait until you reread the last part, at Bristol Hotwells; I don't think you'll call it mild at the end. There's a viciousness and savagery in the satire there that's almost Swiftian in places. Do you remember the scene where the men of quality, after pages of haggling over an "important bet"—the prime interest of their lives—finally settle it by having two wretched old women run a race for them? The "poor creatures, feeble and frightened," run against each other and fall, but despite their bruises, the gentlemen (who have been drinking freely) insist that the women hobble along, stumble, and totter, "to the inexpressible diversion of the company."

A. I remember—it seems almost symbolic of the attitude of Sir Clement, Lord Merton, and Lovel toward Evelina: they try to use her—and do use her as far as they can—for their own "diversion." Fanny Burney certainly doesn't play favorites in class: the "quality," except for Orville and the Mirvan ladies, don't come off any better than the tradesmen—perhaps not quite as well. Still, I have a feeling that Evelina would rather be in Mrs. Beaumont's house for all the snubs and worries there, than go back to that *"Hosier's* in *High Holborn."*

B. Surely: that's essential to the nature of snobbery. Evelina snubs the Branghtons, yet resents being snubbed by Lady Louisa and wants to assert her equality. Just so, the Branghtons resent Evelina's attitude toward them, but they court her company because of her superior friends and try to show that they are her equals. It's all painfully true to human experience. But there's more than that involved. The book doesn't condemn Evelina for being anxious to measure up to the manners of the class to which she rightly belongs. Quite the contrary: the whole novel seems to insist that the standards and demands of manners must be and should be met. The book seems to be built on the assumption that a society—I mean a whole social order—stands or falls by its ability to express and maintain a code of manners. The Branghton group is ridiculed because it is trying to go beyond the manners proper to its class, while the satire of upper-class arrogance and brutality is merciless because these people are supposed to be the warders of the code. That code becomes tyrannical only when it's abused—willfully or ignorantly. Innocence itself can't escape the results of its offenses against the establishment: it's a pity, but the rules are inexorable.

A. I know Samuel Johnson would agree with that point of view. But in an age such as ours, can we help feeling that such "codes" are something less than all-important?

B. That's a rather large question for a small evening, but it looms over everything we've been saying. Before we try to settle it, though, I think you ought to read a remarkable article by Lionel

Trilling in the *Kenyon Review* called "Manners, Morals, and the Novel." You may find it rather elusive and not quite cogent, but the main points, I think, strike right at your whole question about the representative differences between *All the King's Men* and *Evelina*. Trilling suggests that our peculiar modern definition of "reality" makes it hard for us to feel the importance of manners; and yet he insists that for the novels of the past the study of manners has been the main tool in their exploration of the nature of reality. I can't possibly summarize his points; but read the article and you'll see that he's talking about *Evelina,* though he doesn't mention it.

A. I will, I will: but first—I think I'd better stay up late and try to finish reading *Evelina.*

ANN RADCLIFFE, OR, THE HAND OF TASTE

William Ruff

I

MRS. ANN RADCLIFFE was a lucky novelist. When she published her books in the last decade of the eighteenth century, she liked tales of terror and the public happened to like them too; she is forever being mentioned as an ancestress of the romantic movement because she loathed cities, loved mountains, and thought gothic architecture was gloomy but sublime; Walter Scott kept her name alive, for a hundred years or so, by writing a biography for an edition of her novels published in 1821; and shreds of her *Mysteries of Udolpho* and *The Romance of the Forest* are preserved in the vinegar of *Northanger Abbey*.

How should one treat this lucky woman? Should one be respectful because she was thought good in her own time, and because three of her novels are still in print? Or should one think of her as a writer of trash? She certainly wrote trash, and yet good critics have praised her—Walter Scott for one. There is nothing a modern novelist can learn from her works, yet she has a vitality that keeps her books alive when better writers have disappeared. I am not going to justify a study of Ann Radcliffe by saying that she invented the modern mystery story, because it is not true. And I shall not say she is worth studying because she inspired Jane Austen's parodies: it would be true to say so, but unimportant. (Her likeness to Jane Austen *is* strong; of that likeness I shall have something to say later.)

Reputation Ann Radcliffe certainly has to this day, and one adds that if she had talent as well she would indeed be the fortunate novelist. And yet I am not sure that she is entirely lacking in talent. To one type of fiction she did "bring the last polish"[1]—as she would have said—if she did not create the type itself. However, I am not speaking of gothic romances, nor of novels so bad that one reads them only to laugh at them. It *is* easy to laugh at Ann Radcliffe; Jane Austen found plenty of material for parodies in heroes who "bound" along mountain sides and heroines accustomed to sink senseless in the arms of the nearest man. Ann Radcliffe, nevertheless, has virtues.

The Romance of the Forest, The Mysteries of Udolpho, and *The Italian* are readable today. If I read the first of *Udolpho* I want to finish it. Will Emily St. Aubert escape from Count Morano who insists on marrying her, I ask; will Emily's aunt, Mme. Montoni, be murdered, or will she surrender her property to her new husband? And, once the aunt *has* been murdered, will Emily save her new legacy? Will she escape from the Castle? Who is the mysterious singer under her window? What made her faint when she lifted that black veil from a frame? I was annoyed, during one reading, when my light flickered out before I could discover why the Marchioness de Villeroi died with a blackened face. But there is a rule about these novels of suspense which applies as well to Ann Radcliffe as it does to that once popular writer of thrillers, Sheridan LeFanu—today's cheap stories of horror are easier to read than yesterday's. Let Sir Walter Scott unwittingly give the reason for this decay of interest in elderly thrillers, when he writes of *The Italian:* ". . . but the fine scene, where the monk, in the act of raising his arm to murder his sleeping victim, discovers her to be his own child, is of a new, grand, and powerful character."[2] Such a scene, of course, is no longer new to us, and since it is not new, it is neither grand nor powerful.

Scott says nothing of what annoys us most in Ann Radcliffe today, her language. He knows her poetry is worthless, and delicately writes: "The language does not become pliant in Mrs. Radcliffe's hands."[3] Perhaps he meant this to apply to her prose as well, prose where winds always sweep along "hollow gusts,"

1. Ann Radcliffe's critical terms are so much better than those I can discover today, or make up, that I shall use her own words, taken from her novels, as often as possible.
2. Sir Walter Scott, *Miscellaneous Prose Works* (Edinburgh, 1834), III, 352.
3. *Ibid.,* III, 385.

glades are "romantic," scenes "ever wild and solitary." Ann Radcliffe liked to march her adjectives in pairs: in her works expressions are "artless and simple," her heroine remembers "in melancholy and dejection," and appearances are "forlorn and desolate." Women are either "tranquil and composed" or "disturbed and uneasy," and when they are uneasy they show it by "quitting the room instantly, their hands clasped in an agony of despair." I think Ann Radcliffe would have called her style one of "modest elegance," and she referred too often to "elegance and propriety of thought" to try anything novel in language. Her figures of speech were already dead when she used them, for her novels are the charnel house of the poetry popular in the eighteenth century, and if she occasionally uses a fresh image, time has killed its beauty, as time has ruined those situations which once "thrilled bosoms with a kind of pleasing dread."

What Scott reluctantly criticizes in Ann Radcliffe is her use of denouement. He says she cheats. She cheats, also, when she will not tell us what happened to LaMotte on his solitary walks in *The Romance of the Forest,* though she has faithfully described his other actions. She cheats when she writes of Emily St. Aubert:

As she mused, she saw the door slowly open; and a rustling sound in a remote part of the room startled her. Through the dusk she thought she perceived something move . . .

The silence which again reigned, made her ashamed of her late fears, and she believed that her imagination had deluded her, or that she had heard one of those unaccountable noises which sometimes occur in old houses. The same sound, however, returned; and, distinguishing something moving towards her, and in the next instant press beside her into the chair, she shrieked; but her fleeting senses were instantly recalled, on perceiving that it was Manchon who sat by her, and who now licked her hand affectionately.

When Ann Radcliffe ought to explain why her heroine faints before a horrid picture, says Scott, she will forget the explanation or be matter-of-fact. Scott thinks she should either give an adequate and rational explanation or trust in the supernatural. Actually he might have said that Ann Radcliffe was never sufficiently thrilling. She did not have enough gothic monasteries, not enough murders; her villains died too soon or reformed too easily; her castles have too few secret chambers, and even the Italian inquisition does not use enough torture; girls are pursued through wild forests but no one ever catches them; they are kidnaped but are returned intact; her heroes are sentenced to die but are reprieved before they reach the scaffold. In short, her novels do not have enough blood.

True, she might have tried to make what horrors she has more intense, but it would take an artist like Scott to do such a thing; Ann Radcliffe does not have the power.

II

I am sure that Ann Radcliffe would not have minded Scott's criticism, so gentle was it. And how pleased she would have been at his praise of her set pieces, the elaborate descriptions of sunset in the Alps or of mist hovering around a gothic abbey. ("How infinitely inferior all the splendour of art is to the sublimity of nature," she said.) For it was these set pieces that she wrote with love. And I am convinced that she thought of herself, not as a writer of "those improbable fictions that sometimes are exhibited in a romance," but as quite another sort, one who "writes books which elevate the mind, and interest the heart." She thought of her own mind as one "enriched with taste, enlightened by science, and enlarged by observation, a benevolent, mild, and contemplative mind adorned by elegant literature." (At least, whenever she praises the taste in literature of her heroines, it is in these words.)

She was, in brief, a lady writing for ladies and gentlemen. And the work she did best might well be called the novel of taste. What does she mean by "taste"? "Virtue and taste are nearly the same," she writes, "for virtue is little more than active taste." Whenever a musician in her novels "touches a lute with sweet pathos," it is done "by the hand of taste." (She has no higher praise.) Every one of her books was written by this hand of taste. Not once in all her novels is there a breach of correct manners unpunished. There *are* horrid incidents in *The Romance of the Forest*. Adeline St. Pierre is abducted, and she makes an appointment to meet a man to whom she is not betrothed. (Later she regrets both episodes.)

Emily St. Aubert is sorry that her aunt has been murdered and is apprehensive of the future at the hands of her stepuncle, but she is furious that he should leave her in his castle unchaperoned. ("I can no longer remain here with propriety, sir, said she.") And when she finally agrees to sign away her aunt's inheritance if she is allowed to leave the castle, she is vexed at Montoni's theft (once she has signed away her property he laughingly refuses to let her go), but "The deliberate villainy with which he violated the solemn engagement he had just entered into, shocked Emily as much as the certainty that she had made a fruitless sacrifice, and must still remain his prisoner." Indeed, the story of her misfortunes begins not with a kidnaping but with a tasteful sermon from her father on the evils of sensibility; she has been too fond of giving way to her imagination, and she feels things too deeply. "Above all, my dear Emily, said [her father], do not indulge in the pride of fine feeling, the romantic error of amiable minds. Those who really possess sensibility ought early to be taught that it is a dangerous quality, which is continually extracting the excess of misery or delight from every surrounding circumstance." She promises to reform and does reform; no later reference is made to the fact that her extreme sensibility might have caused any of her trouble. On the contrary, it is the lack of sensibility in her tormentors that makes her life unhappy.

As correct as Emily St. Aubert's ethics and manners is the conduct of the hero, the Chevalier Valancourt. At the beginning he is ingenuous; he had no experience of Paris, but his "manly frankness, simplicity and keen susceptibility to the grandeur of nature" and "the strong indignation which he felt and expressed at a criminal or mean action" are all tokens of a good character. After her father's death Emily is tempted to marry him without the consent of her relatives, but she refuses. Though Juliet could run away with Romeo, Emily must preserve all the forms of etiquette so that she can keep what Juliet lost, "the luxury of conscious worth." And in the end the hero wants the same luxury. Very close to the last page of the story we are alarmed lest the hero and heroine never marry at all. He has returned from Paris with a countenance that had "all its wonted intelligence and fire; but it had lost much of the simplicity, and somewhat of the open benevolence, that used to characterise it," and there are many scandals about his name; he is said to have borrowed heavily, to have gone to jail in consequence, and (but with no foundation in fact) to have carried on an intrigue with a married woman. As Mrs. Radcliffe says, these scandals "being such as Emily could not name to the Chevalier he had no opportunity of refuting them," and it takes a series of heavily condensed revelations to clear his name. Emily felt that she could not marry a man unworthy of her; indeed, she *knew* that true love and unworthiness of character never go together, and so she must wait for these elaborate explanations before her love can return.

Why anyone should think of *The Mysteries of Udolpho* as merely a gothic romance, when it has such sermons on the dangers of sensibility, and the pictures of good taste in scenery and manners I have described, I do not know. The first chapters (i–xviii) are mainly concerned with the tender scruples that compel Emily to leave Valancourt without marrying him; by chapter xxxiv her troubles in the Castle of Udolpho are over, and her troubles with true love are to continue to the end of the book (chapter lvii). Two thirds of the book, therefore, is about the course of true love and not about gothic horrors at all.

III

What have the rules of good taste to do with Mrs. Radcliffe's clichés? Clichés they may be, but they are also the well-worn, much-loved phrases of poetry she knew by heart, every phrase in the best of taste, and chosen from select authors. Indeed, she has written an anthology of good poetical phrases, and by reading the chapter headings of her novels and nothing else one can recognize the source of her quotations and most of her inspiration. Her inspiration is from Milton, Collins, Walpole, Warton, Beattie, Seward, Mason, Gray, Thomson, Goldsmith, Homer (in Pope's translation), and her favorite—Shakespeare. So chaperoned by the masters of English literature, and in their easily remembered words, she tells her stories. For her plots she goes to Samuel Richardson, whose themes she has taken over and, as she might say, softened, refined, and rewritten with taste and elegance.

One must, however, be fair to Mrs. Radcliffe in this matter of words. It is true she writes a dead language, but it is a clear one. There is no mystery in any of her books, no voice at midnight, no burning spear, no frightening picture, which she is not capable of explaining neatly and clearly. Never again will there be Ann Radcliffe's combination in fiction of cool temper and exciting incidents, or a discussion of the romantic and mysterious carried on with such cheerful lucidity. In her frigid tales of terror, clarity and good sense go with correctness and elegance, qualities which, of course, can allow no room for the supernatural.

And if it is true that she does not always build her stories to an appropriate climax and punish the wicked as a modern thriller would do, again she has the justification of taste. For good taste means that the wicked are wicked only so long as the story demands it; when virtue is ready to triumph the villains are lightly dismissed. It would be vulgar to triumph over Montoni; let him drift out of the story and completely disappear in these few words:

Orsino was found guilty, condemned and executed upon the wheel; but nothing being discovered to criminate Montoni and his colleagues on this charge, they were all released except Montoni, who, being considered by the senate as a very dangerous person, was, for other reasons, ordered again into confinement, where it was said he had died in a doubtful and mysterious manner, and not without suspicion of being poisoned.

It would be in bad taste to give a long, painful end to the Marquis who tried to seduce Adeline St. Pierre so he kills himself in a sentence. Nothing to excess in an ending is Ann Radcliffe's rule, and it is a very ladylike one. Her successors, such as M. G. Lewis, were to carry her settings, and her themes, to the logical end of overpowering horror. But Mrs. Radcliffe would have been incapable of writing as Lewis did when he killed the villain of *The Monk*:

As [the fiend] said this, darting his talons into the monk's shaven crown, he sprang with him from the rock. The caves and mountains rang with Ambrosio's shrieks. The demon continued to soar aloft, till reaching a dreadful height, he released the sufferer. Headlong fell the monk through the airy waste: the sharp point of rock received him, and he rolled from precipice to precipice, till, bruised and mangled, he rested on the river's banks. Instantly a violent storm arose: . . . the waves overflowed their banks; they reached the spot where Ambrosio lay, and, when they abated, carried with them into the river the corpse of the despairing monk.

Such an end fits a villain, but Mrs. Radcliffe's phrase for it would be "coarse."

Like every writer of romance with an interest in correct manners, she warns us against that insidious form of fiction where readers are "resigned to the illusions of the page," and especially she dislikes "a sentimental novel on some fashionable system of philosophy." She furnishes her readers romance and sentimentality—with the warning that they are upsetting. "Don't eat sweets," she says as she hands over a five-pound box of chocolates. I think she was sincere in this distrust of novels for their effect on susceptible readers. She often talked of "the pure delights of literature," and she was not seduced into making them less pure. She disliked people or books with "qualities which throw a veil over folly, and soften the features of vice into smiles." And if no one in her time would write books denouncing such follies, she would supply the need herself.

IV

Ann Radcliffe's fiction can be read today as the embodiment of good taste. Other novelists have talked about taste and elegance, but only Ann Radcliffe makes the two words so consistently the backbone of all her fiction. Even if she wrote gothic romances, the gothic trimmings interested her less than the moral principles she taught; she wanted to write in the grand tradition of eighteenth-century letters—and be a moralist.

The novel of taste, then, is Ann Radcliffe's contribution to English literature, for in three novels she has combined adventure with the most high-principled characters in fiction. She has made the best of all possible worlds; her subject is shocking and her morality flawless. No matter how often her story threatens to be about horrid deeds, her heroine stands in the foreground of her books, pure, tender-minded, elegant, and conscious of the etiquette each situation demands. In later fiction Ann Radcliffe has many sister and some brother novelists. Where one meets a little talk of adventure in novels but a great deal of talk about virtue, and where virtue seems identical with elegance and good taste, there you will find a parallel to Ann Radcliffe.

In the nineteenth century the best novelists have little to do with elegance and good taste. I doubt if Dickens knew the meaning of the word "taste." And in Emily Brontë's world there is not room for passion *and* for good taste. Accordingly her people behave as they please. And they please to behave brutally. Walter Scott knew much about taste, but it has nothing to do with "elegance" and considerations of it do not shape his stories. If he learned anything from Ann Radcliffe it was how to fill her empty armor with living men. Of all these great figures Jane Austen is closest to Ann Radcliffe.

Some critics justify Ann Radcliffe by saying that she inspired *Northanger Abbey.* And it is true that whenever I read the novels of Ann Radcliffe I see the shadow of Jane Austen; yet it is not because Jane Austen made such delicious fun of her predecessor but because there is more of Ann Radcliffe throughout Jane Austen than people realize. Jane Austen was a lady of taste, too, and those favorite words of Mrs. Radcliffe's, such as "principles, sensibility, and elegance," occur as often in her works as they do in *The Mysteries of Udolpho.* Lady Russell of *Persuasion,* for example, is a woman who would have delighted Mrs. Radcliffe, for Lady Russell "was of strict integrity herself, with a delicate sense of honour; . . . she was a benevolent, charitable, good woman, and capable of strong attachments, most correct in her conduct, strict in her notions of decorum, and with manners that were held a standard of good-breeding. She had a cultivated mind, and was, generally speaking, rational and consistent; but she had prejudices on the side of ancestry." Though Ann Radcliffe would not have added the disparagement, the first section might have been written by Ann Radcliffe.

One of Jane Austen's finest—and least appreciated—comic creations is Mary Bennet, the moral Mary Bennet who says, when her sister Lydia has eloped with Wickham: "Unhappy as the event must be for Lydia, we may draw from it this useful lesson; that loss of virtue in a female is irretrievable—that one false step involves her in endless ruin—that her reputation is no less brittle than it is beautiful, and that she cannot be too much guarded in her behaviour towards the undeserving of the other sex." And it is surely a proof of Jane Austen's genius that she made the enchanting Elizabeth a true sister of Mary even to the habit of moralizing elegantly. "You shall not, for the sake of one individual, change the meaning of principle and integrity," says Elizabeth after the hasty engagement of Charlotte Lucas, "nor endeavour to persuade yourself or me, that selfishness is prudence, and insensibility of danger, security for happiness." Mary and Elizabeth Bennet are indeed sisters, and both are related to Emily and Adeline.

I cannot prove that Jane Austen wrote in the tradition of good taste because Ann Radcliffe considered it so important. Indeed, I have no intention of proving such an inheritance. My point is that Jane Austen, instead of being the enemy of the vulgar Ann Radcliffe, is closely akin to her. The reasons for such a resemblance are simple: both were raised in the eighteenth century; they read the same type of books; both originally wrote for the same audience; and their point of view toward decorum is feminine. (In *Persuasion* Jane Austen wishes, with Anne, that Charles Musgrove, who enjoyed life immensely, could have had "more usefullness, rationality, and elegance to his habits and pursuits.") When Emily St. Aubert blushes for the low conduct of her aunt, Mme. Cheron, I think of Elizabeth Bennet blushing for her mother. The lines from *Persuasion* about the integrity, sense of honor, decorum, and manners of Lady Russell are in the best of taste and have nothing much to do with the story. It was Lady Russell's respect for fortune and background which led her to break the early engagement between Anne and Frederick Wentworth; this characterization of Lady Russell is only for our entertainment—and moral profit.

Ann Radcliffe's preaching is insistent and wearisome, while Jane Austen's is one of the decorative touches her readers forgive and forget. Could Ann Radcliffe have written so genuine a passage of morality as this one about a dead war hero? "The Musgroves had had the ill fortune of a very troublesome, hopeless son; and the good fortune to lose him before he reached his twentieth year."

V

When Ann Radcliffe wrote an introduction to *The Romance of the Forest* she rejoiced about "the attention given in the following pages to the cause of morality." But perhaps modern readers do not want to learn how to hate "corrupted sentiments," "monkish superstition," and "the vicious pleasures of society," or to love "a sweet union of conscience and reflection," or "modest elegance," or "mild virtue." Perhaps a modern reader would prefer the small sections of her novels which actually deal with gothic horrors. There they will find picturesque settings and harmless villains; and there—to use Ann Radcliffe's own words for the last time—they will find exciting fiction written with a "tincture of soft and interesting melancholy" in a "manner so warm, yet so artless."

PART III

THE POETS

EDWARD YOUNG

Margery Bailey

It is midnight, in a walled space which exhales the dank effluvia of the tomb. The obsequious ivy . . . the flitting bat . . . the raven (or, the owl, that fatal bellman) . . . A faint gleam of lantern light pierces the Stygian shade: it illumines one who bears a rigid burden swathed in white. He disposes it beside a leaning stone, and is lost to sight beneath the twisted branches of a melancholy yew. The dismal impact of a spade is heard in the deep obscure, and when the laborer turns again, the lantern sheds its feeble light upon a yawning cavity—Oh Heaven, he bore a corpse, and digs a grave!

This is no translation of some macabre Gallic or Teutonic dream. It is no nightmare of Radcliffe or Poe, not a page from the darker chapters of Dickens, nothing of boyish terrors remembered by Mark Twain—though this picture haunted all these writers and their coevals. It was the depressing legend with which the eighteenth- and nineteenth-century taste for horrors clouded the figure of Edward Young, author of *The Complaint, or Night Thoughts on Life, Death, and Immortality.*

He was the Reverend Edward Young, son of a Hampshire clergyman, product of Winchester and Oxford, friend to Addison, Pope, and Swift, royal chaplain twice over, and clerk of the closet to the mother of George III. In his most famous poem he alluded grimly to the death of his stepdaughter in France and his unseemly skirmish with Roman Catholic authorities in the effort to procure decent burial for her Protestant remains; a newly imaginative audience, trained in the dim pensiveness of Lady Winchilsea and Parnell, received the passage with rapture. Protestant piety enlarged upon it, allusion and engraved illustration embroidered it beyond all bounds. There is no old churchyard along the eastern seaboard of the United States which has not at least one virginal headstone (and many have three or more) bearing Young's next to worst lines, on the lost "Narcissa":

> Early, bright, transient, chaste, as morning dew
> She sparkled, was exhaled, and went to Heaven.

If Young is mentioned at all in modern times, he is bracketed with Gray and Blair and cheerfully forgotten as one of the Graveyard School.

All this is but Horatio on the battlements, a piece of him. In the poet's own days—and they were long days, from 1683 to 1765, spanning the day of Congreve, the day of Thomson, Fielding, and Collins, the day of Goldsmith and Johnson—he was accorded a larger field and higher place. As a moralist he was paired with Johnson, and to many minds the poetry of *Night Thoughts* surpassed the prose of *Rasselas*. His satires held a niche at the elbows of Pope and Swift. His three tragedies, esteemed with reason as mountain peaks above the desert century after Otway and Rowe, kept their place both in drama collections and on the stage, performed by such actors as Booth, Nance Oldfield, Wilks, and George-Anne Bellamy. Six years before he died Young addressed to Samuel Richardson his modest *Conjectures on Original Composition,* which the public welcomed as the voice of a new aesthetics. In its break with authority and rules in favor of the native genius which must discover and reverence itself, and its open trust of imagination and passion, the energetic treatise laid down the sane essentials of the revolt in poetry almost forty years before the publication of the *Lyrical Ballads.*

These conclusions were written down in 1759 but they were not a late conversion to new truth. In part because of his devotion to Shakespeare and Milton but more largely because of his own nature, Young had worked on these grounds from the first; they are traceable in everything he wrote. The forms he used are conventional and in some instances, notably his stiff lyrics, induce a *rigor artis* which befools even a friendly eye into seeing him as a strict Augustan; but his characteristic work shows a vigorous individual straining at the bonds of correctness and regularity, and often breaking through them to assert himself. The struggle which is implicit in such a meeting of opposites in one mind is never missing. There was in Edward Young a good deal of Prometheus bound.

Like Swift, Young was too large a man for the limitations of his era and instinctively in a state of rebellion against it. Upholding the fixed order which Englishmen of 1700 thought necessary to keep their world from chaos, he still chafed at the restricting channels through which alone a man of ability could find an outlet for his quality and training. He did his best to seek preferment, he found a public in literature, he was faithful to his duties in the Church which he entered as an avenue to high experience; but these things were barren of what his spirit demanded—the enlarged life of great responsibility and action. His entire career, under its surface of relative successes, was the restless search of a proud and independent man, conscious of strength, talents, and breeding, to find the fullest use for his capacities; and his writing records it, directly or otherwise. He attempts to chasten the sense of power fusting unused, only to have it break out afresh, until the conflict is resolved in an exaltation of spirit which made Edward Young the most beloved among the poets of his time.

He did not publish until he was thirty, when experience with patronage had shown him the relative values of place and merit and taught him that one must bow to the other. His lessons did not make him an adept. All three of the long poems of 1713 were candidly written to obtain advancement, but their purpose was blunted by the somewhat tactless vigor with which the poet's independence asserted itself. Correctly topical and complimentary, *An Epistle to Lord Lansdowne* hailed the peace with France and showed a readiness for foreign service; *The Force of Religion* was a bid for preferment from the Whigs at home, in the guise of a narrative poem on Lady Jane Grey. More remotely, *The Last Day* was evidence that Young would consider taking orders in the Church if necessary. But in the first of these, while saluting a handful of soldiers and diplomats and suggesting an interest in foreign problems by passages on British merchant captains or French life and art, Young puts his greatest warmth into his lines on Shakespeare as the national voice—in terms moreover of *Othello, Macbeth,* and the romances, rather than *Henry V,* fit matter for conquerors. Worse, he celebrates peace by a touching picture of crippled and forsaken veterans and an obstinate view of a Christian unity of nations rather than by a suitable sketch of triumphant Britons riding whirlwinds and directing storms. Mr. Secretary Addison did these things much better.

The Force of Religion ignores the opportunities which the poet might have found with his friend St. John, intriguing hopefully with the Catholic Stuarts, and plumps for the Protestant succession in the eager speeches of Lady Jane—so far, a shrewd course; but his heroine is more to Young as a character than as a queen, and in phrasing more freely poetic than any other to be found at the time (for years before and after it there is nothing to match his line, "the hollow wind and melancholy rain") he causes her to bid a throne good night without regret as a thing of little moment beside stability of soul. Who without impertinence could offer place to a man who wrote so?

The Last Day is oddly divided between an unpleasant and material vision of doomsday (in which skeletons nervously articulate themselves while their disembodied spirits idle about the pole awaiting them) and an ethical appeal which is scarcely in terms of fundamental Christian doctrine. No conservative churchman, on either score, would offer encouragement to the author; and no churchman did. The poem has many strokes of dignity and force, one suggesting that Young had been moved to his theme by the humble majesty of Shirley's meditation on the glories of our blood and state:

> From our decays a pleasure to receive,
> And kindle into transport at a grave!
> What equals this? and shall the victor now
> Boast the proud laurels on his loaded brow?

But the last lines of the poem, in fervor and directness, are Young's, and Young's only, on the theme of true greatness which has marked all this early work and is to remain his dominant note:

> Have ye not seen th' eternal mountains nod,
> An earth dissolving, a descending GOD? . . .
> For whom these revolutions, but for man?
> For him Omnipotence new measures takes,
> For him through all eternity awakes. . . .
> 　　Think deeply, then, O man, how *great* thou art,

Pay thyself homage with a trembling heart;
What angels guard, no longer dare neglect;
Slighting thyself, affront not GOD's respect:
Enter the sacred temple of thy breast,
And gaze, and wander there, a ravish'd guest:
Gaze on the those hidden glories thou shalt find,
Wander through all the glories of thy mind . . .

This is more than a justification of the ways of God to man. In its stimulus to human dignity it shows how much Young shared both the discipline of the classic spirit and the urge to wonder which was later to be called romantic. With Swift, Pope, Chesterfield, and the rest of his generation, he considered man a creature stumbling in the darkness of a middle state yet greatly gifted with a soul and with reason to guide it; but where Pope soothes his fellow men with the assurance that their defects are part of a perfect plan, and Swift, amazed and furious that they are incapable of control, essays to shame them into decency, Young boldly attempts to exalt humanity into self-command. It is this vigorous masculine challenge, typical of the man himself, and not graveyard melancholy which gives him a stature beyond that of a mere moralist.

In 1714 a poem addressed to Addison on the death of the Queen brought some attention to the poet, but still he did not find the responsible place and service which should absorb his energies and give the opportunity for action which a man of his breeding craved. He was nearing forty when he turned to drama and satire for recognition from a general audience.

Young's plays have their limitations, largely the limitations of current taste, but they do not fall into the tepidity or stiffness which marked other playwrights under the first Georges. His masters were Shakespeare, Corneille, and Otway, and his dialogue has a tensity of emotion which does them credit; yet the general effect of *Busiris King of Egypt* (1719) and *The Revenge* (1721) is that of the Caroline heroic play minus the rhymed couplets. It is not the heroes and heroines who produce the impression, though the men have fine contemplative lines and the women are austere developments of Young's staunch Lady Jane; they move within human bounds and with understandable emotions. It is the villains who escape all measured courses. Yet these are not villain-heroes in the Elizabethan sense, for though they crush others and, rather arbitrarily, are crushed in turn, they have about them less of the interesting criminal or conqueror than of a terrifying natural force which has a majesty beyond morals, and suffers more than mortals may through a grinding restlessness.

Busiris is a tyrant on a wrongfully gained throne, Zanga a combination of Othello-Iago who seeks vengeance for a blow from his Spanish master which he cannot return. The first plans nothing, develops no whit up to his cutting-off, and the other pursues a well-organized dramatic action from motive to crime to remorse; but both are remarkable for the quality they have in common, a lonely consciousness of power beyond the reach of the normal people surrounding them, a sense of energy more immense than force or violence, seething in unused fury. They have the anguish of eminence which *Cato* attempts in vain to convey; it is the futility of possessing a vital force which is doomed to face no foeman worthy of itself, to trickle sedately through a daily round, to eat itself away for lack of immediate and commensurate action. The one outlet afforded them is high and splendid discourse: Zanga speaks with a remote and controlled iciness which is august in its withdrawal from human emotions; and from Busiris comes not only a sardonic assurance of his wretchedness in singularity but a description of his empire which for echoing splendor can be matched only by the brief hint of Xanadu a century later. Beside these self-lacerated giants the titans of Marlowe seem boyish and the heroes of Dryden and Crowne merely noisy. They are originals, and they are so because they have about them something of the crippled thunder which rolled at the poet's own heart. Too easily called pride, soured ambition, resentment, it is the weariness of spirit which falls upon the large nature, knowing itself forceful and commanding and unable to prove itself completely. This (not hypochondria, which merely results from it) is the English Malady. This is the spiritual disorder which beset Edward Young and Jonathan Swift, who loved the action of the world as athletes love a trial of strength, and found themselves but hollow onlookers at the games.

Though the tragedies brought no greater introduction to public affairs than the occasional pieces composed during the same years, they won for the poet an attentive audience, and the satires of 1725 to 1728, collected under the title *The Universal Passion, or The Love of Fame,* fixed his reputation as one of the leading wits. In general form they are conventional hits in the manner of the still fashionable "characters," but otherwise they are much beyond their own day—more heart-engaging than the acid of Dryden and Pope, more pictorially individualized than anything by Prior, more warmly human and intimate than the work of anyone save Goldsmith. His bouncing squire, his book collector who never reads, his churchgoer correctly civil to God, are all set forth in impeccable couplets but with a tolerant good nature which seems a forecast of romantic genre portraits. An even stronger suggestion of the new age is the unexpected subjective quality of the conclusion to Satire II, a half-sad criticism of the poet's own love of fame and its defeats; the closing lines offer to his audience and himself a resolution of unrest in a theme which is to dominate his greatest work later on—the evanescence of human life with all things material, the powerlessness of power, and the fleeting worth of place. The passage utters the same passionate groping toward acceptance that Eugene O'Neill's scientist attempts centuries later— "O God, make me willing to be resigned, make me willing to be an atom"—and the same wistful absence of hope to find the balance between the fullness of life and a complete rejection of it.

The Love of Fame is the last of Vanity Fair. The two *Epistles to Mr. Pope* of 1730 were, in spite of their undeniable wit, grave criticism of the superfetation of the press, an ethical *ars poetica* of sorts, emphasizing rather the author's duties to himself and his public than the niceties of form and style. These satires may be taken as the first conscious statement of men dedicated to what is to be the new métier—the lesser gentry and the men of leisure who were learning how much power and responsibility lay in serious writing and who glorified the Augustan age by raising themselves from pamphleteering hacks and dilettanti to the status of professional men of letters.

But though the sense of accomplishment was there the means of secure life was not, and by the time the *Epistles* appeared Young had bent his neck to necessity and taken orders in the Church. Almost at once he was established in the parish of Wellwyn and had his first appointments to the royal family; he was on the eve of a fortunate and happy marriage which brought to him a cherished stepdaughter as well as a wife. And he was forty-seven years of age. Resolutely he arranged his existence to meet the requirements of his cloth: the last of the plays was discreetly impounded; the sermons multiplied. The poems of the next years were commemorations of national events, without much heart or splendor in them—a psychologist would observe with interest that most of them concern the sea. As men's lives go, Young was a happy man. In less than a decade the happiness had collapsed with the death of wife and daughter. Aging and desolate, the poet reached toward serenity by composing the first of the *Night Thoughts* and stumbled into a fame he had never dreamed of. For the twenty years which remained to him after the publication of "Night the Ninth" and last, he was to know his home a place of pilgrimage and himself possessor of what then seemed an undying name.

The Complaint, or Night Thoughts, is not epic, elegy, or theological essay; it is, in terms which would have been impossible to an earlier generation, a startlingly personal record of grief and the hope of discipline to be derived from it, loosely arranged in reflections, exhortation, imaginary arguments with one "Lorenzo," and brief descriptive or narrative passages. The general audience found it a heartening consolation in the sorrow which touched every household almost yearly in those days of large families, constant epidemics, and haphazard medicine; the intellectual world, in which the new science and the "religion of nature" had produced a nervous skepticism that made fear of death acute, leaned on it as a bulwark against uncertainty. To men of that time the melancholy of the poem, which strikes the modern ear as elaborated and overstrained, seemed merely touching evidence of Young's personal nearness within their common experience; its great value lay in its view of death as a challenge to intensified life and its frank testimony of a man's wrestling to find himself and his God.

The actual inner travail was more than Young, with all his un-

Augustan candor, was willing to reveal in its nakedness, and he used the debates with Lorenzo to veil it. Critics have expended fruitless effort to establish the identity of this worldling for whom the parade of rank and the new mechanistic philosophy have a persistent fascination; he is none other than the untamable half of Edward Young himself, and the arguments with him sum up the long campaign for satisfaction or mastery of that pride of strength which the poet knew to be his daemon. The aim of the argument is not to throttle Lorenzo into passive resignation but to make him accept service in the only fields where fulfillment lies.

With a moral energy more humanly compelling than Pope's uncertain logic or the imperial grandeurs of Milton, Young reiterates his early thesis of self-reverence: man is the object of infinite care, and hence august, though his highest earthly greatness is the completion of simple manhood; this he attains, whether king or laborer, only through unending and vital combat against false hungers and impulses, and even against his own half-virtues. *The Complaint* does not reject life, as Longfellow and his peers object. The nature of man and the nature of the physical world are held up as miracles which far outshine what is usually termed miraculous ("a satire on mankind," says Young with a shade of deistic scorn) and which, well considered, lead men to the Creator and Preserver of all things and His endless verities. This is in the main the familiar orthodox tradition but put forth with such virile energy and fervor as to give it a new sublimity. In disciplining his resentment at what life had brought to him Young finds at last what life had long denied—scope for the wings of his insistent spirit.

The Complaint has many of the faults of rhetorical verse, largely because of Young's obedience to Longinus, and it suffers to some degree from the limitations which Johnson held to be inseparable from religious poetry; but its austere ecstasy is gripping, particularly when it is heightened, as in the noble supplications to the Creator, by devices of dramatic contrast and incisively graphic wording:

> . . . THOU, who didst put to flight
> Primeval darkness, when the morning stars

Exulting, shouted o'er the rising ball:
O THOU! whose word from solid darkness struck
That spark, the sun; strike wisdom from my soul.

These stern flights are rarely extended; Young wishes his thoughts to be memorable, not merely beautiful, and he is willing to sacrifice melody to a concise exactness of simple phrasing which should strike the mind and lodge there, seed for future meditation. What the romantics expand into pages Young packs into a line—"Man is to man the surest, sorest ill"—or into a couplet:

Earth's highest station ends in "Here he lies";
And "dust to dust" concludes her noblest song.

He does not hesitate to repeat a good thing and in another context paraphrases these lines in what seems an ironic autobiography:

Milk and a swathe at first his whole demand,
His whole domain at last a turf or stone—
To whom, between, a world may seem too small.

A certain weighty emphasis gives many of such compact generalizations an element of final pronouncement, and a number of them have entered the language as proverbs whose source has been forgotten: "Man wants but little, nor that little long . . . " "Procrastination is the thief of time . . ."

At present both the rhetorical and the sententious are out of fashion, and Young's work is set aside, distastefully labeled "bombast" or "copy-book verse." But that is to overlook its stately, sonorous directness, the great art of its simplicity and precision. It is the sort of thing which can be written only by a man who is sure of his own ideas and who can distinguish an idea from a sentiment; one, moreover, who is keenly aware of the essentials which are the root of all definite form. Fashions change. Young's poetry comforted Boswell; it influenced Wordsworth and the great hymn writers and inspired some of the most glorious designs of William Blake; it was household counsellor to both old and new worlds and rolled across the Western plains in a company which the pioneers' limited possessions made augustly select: the Bible, *Pilgrim's Progress, The Spectator, The Rambler*. What modern writer can hope to have so honorable a life in the century following him?

There is no knowing whether the poet found peace at last in his unprecedented fame. Time could not allow perspective for Young to see how his poetry gave new heart and dignity to a Church which was still too closely allied to national policy, or how in literature he united two great traditions; it is probable that he never grasped how much he had become part of English daily thought and speech. But in those inner courts of the mind where a man must move alone Edward Young must have known the sense of completion which comes to one who has fought the fight and kept faith: he had met his Angel at Peniel face to face and had prevailed.

THOMSON AND DYER: POET AND PAINTER

Ralph M. Williams

I

THE contemporary reader of poetry who had enjoyed the description of natural scenery in Thomson's *Winter* (1726) found a change in the style of description in *Summer,* published a year later, that is of interest to students of Thomson even today. In *Winter* the passages of description are for the most part of single details:

> Sometimes, a fleece
> Of clouds, wide-scattering, with a lucid veil,
> Soft, shadow o'er th' unruffled face of Heaven;
> And, thro' their dewy sluices, shed the sun
> With temper'd influence down.[1]

Or they are of single natural phenomena—the falling of the leaves, or the rising of fog.[2] Even in the few passages in which he does approach the "picturesque," Thomson seems to be describing an action rather than a scene, an activity rather than nature, as in his descriptions of the moon's riding through the sky or the falling of the stream.[3]

This sort of description is often very effective in *Winter,* and no doubt accounts for the four editions of the poem in 1726. But in *Summer* there is relatively little of this; instead, there are ten longish passages which are clearly intended to be well-rounded, complete word-landscapes, each made up of a number of details. Thomson had begun to look at nature as a painter would, with an eye to composition, and had not, as his predecessors had, merely given a

---

1. *The Complete Poetical Works of James Thomson,* ed. J. Logie Robertson (Oxford Edition, 1908), hereinafter known as *Poetical Works;* p. 228, ll. 29–33. The first version of *Winter* is given on pp. 227–238, following the much enlarged final version.
2. *Ibid.,* pp. 229, 230, ll. 45–49, 80–87.
3. *Ibid.,* pp. 230, 231, ll. 88–96, 133–142.

series of single phenomena. I am interested in how Thomson learned of the painter's point of view, and why he decided to use it in his *Summer*.

II

Thomson had come to London late in February, 1725, expecting to support himself at first in the church.[4] When he failed to secure a clerical appointment he accepted a position as tutor to the eldest son of Lord Binning, and by July, 1725, was settled in East Barnet just outside London.[5] Here, in the rather casual manner which he describes to Dr. Cranston,[6] he began and probably completed *Winter*. Early in 1726 he came to London to see his poem through the press. By the middle of June he was preparing a second edition of *Winter* and beginning to work on *Summer*.[7] By August he was three-fourths of the way through his new poem, and in the autumn probably finished his first draft.[8]

Meanwhile his friend David Mallet had been introducing him to various interesting people, the most congenial of whom must have been a young Welshman named John Dyer. Dyer too was a lover of nature and came from a country which had the variety that Thomson had missed at East Barnet.[9] Dyer had been (and perhaps still was) a student of Jonathan Richardson, and, even though he had published a few poems, was obviously looked upon by his friends (and probably by himself too) as a painter rather than as a poet.[10] But most important of all for our present consideration, within the twelvemonth he had returned from a tour of Italy with the usual collection of prints and his own sketches, drawings, and paintings.

Dyer probably met Thomson about the time *Winter* was pub-

4. Thomson to Cranston, April 3, 1725, *The Poetical Works of James Thomson*, ed. Peter Cunningham (Aldine Edition, 1860), hereinafter referred to as *Works;* I, xx.
5. Thomson to Cranston, July 20, 1725, *ibid.*, I, xxiii.
6. Thomson to Cranston, autumn, 1725, *ibid.*, pp. xxvii–xxviii.
7. Thomson to Mallet, June 13, 1726, *ibid.*, pp. cxliii–cxlv.
8. Thomson to Mallet, August 11, and autumn, 1726, *ibid.*, pp. cxlvii, cli.
9. Thomson to Cranston, autumn, 1725, *ibid.*, p. xxvii.
10. See the poetic tributes addressed to him in Richard Savage's *Miscellaneous Poems and Translations by Several Hands* (1726), pp. 26, 58, 209.

lished (March, 1726).[11] By June they were good friends, and Dyer was invited to contribute verses to the second edition, a duty from which, as Thomson says, he "very handsomely excused himself." [12] The closeness of their friendship is indicated, I think, by the fact that it was Thomson (not Savage or Hill or Victor) to whom Mallet wrote to learn Dyer's address when he was in the country during the summer.[13]

In the verses which he addressed to Thomson in 1727 Dyer stresses the "amicable parle" and "tuneful converse" that had made their friendship so happy.[14] His mention later in the poem of Newton and various literary figures suggests that two of their topics of conversation were science and literature, subjects then prominent in Thomson's mind, and painting must have been a third. And in particular they must have considered a topic that was a favorite with Dyer's mentor, Richardson, who insisted that a painter must "have the talents requisite to a good poet, the rules for the conduct of a picture being much the same with those to be observed in writing a poem." [15] One can today easily visualize Thomson and Dyer "at field," talking about the relationship of the two arts: why writing poetry should help a painter, and what the art of painting could do to aid the poet.

I think there can be no doubt that Thomson learned most of what he knew at this time about painting and its possible uses in poetry from Dyer, who was ideally prepared to help through his own writing of poetry, his reminiscences of all he had seen in Italy, and his collection of paintings, sketches, and drawings.[16]

11. Unless one wishes to believe that the Lycidas of the first edition of *Winter*, ll. 298–300 (*Poetical Works*, p. 235), is Dyer because Dyer, in his verses to Thomson two years later, addresses Thomson as Lycidas (l. 22; see n. 14 below); in that case they must have met soon after Thomson's return to London. The description of Lycidas in *Winter* would fit Dyer well.

12. Thomson to Mallet, June 13, 1726, *Works*, I, cxliv.

13. Thomson to Mallet, August 2, 1726, *ibid.*, cl.

14. Helen Sard Hughes, "John Dyer and the Countess of Hertford," *Modern Philology*, XXVII (1929–30), 318–319.

15. [Jonathan] Richardson, *An Essay on the Theory of Painting* (1715), p. 21.

16. It might be argued that Thomson could have learned of painting from his Scots friend, the painter William Aikman, but there is no evidence that they were intimate at this time. If the Mr. Aikman who called on Thomson on August 10, 1726, was the painter, he seems to have been unsympathetic with what the poet was doing and not the man to

That Thomson saw that the techniques of painting could help in verbal description is shown by the change in style from *Winter* to *Summer*. But what advantage did Thomson see in this new type of description? What could make him leave a style which had proved so highly successful for one he had not yet tried?

III

It is in its long, detailed descriptions that *Summer* differs most from *Winter* in their first editions. Occasionally in *Summer* Thomson presents us with what the later eighteenth century called a "landskip" or "landscape," that is, a view near at hand.[17] These usually provide the background or in some way prepare for a bit of narrative, as when the picture of the cattle in the stream, a lovely pastoral scene, leads into the account of the hornets attacking the cows, and the running away of the horse. Much more frequently, however, Thomson gives us a "prospect"—that is, a scene involving in part, at least, some distance, usually in the manner of Claude Lorraine, Salvator Rosa, and the Italian landscape painters. And it is Thomson's use of this that is most interesting.

The "Key" to Thomson's use of these prospects is given at the end of *Summer*—though not in a separate section as was customary in the romances of the time. In a climactic passage Thomson says that Fancy receives

> The whole magnificence of Heaven and earth,
> And every beauty, delicate or bold,
> Obvious or more remote, with livelier sense,
> A world swift-painted, on th' attentive mind! [18]

This is, of course, Locke's theory of sensations, which Thomson and most of the eighteenth century accepted in one form or an-

---

alter his style of writing. Thomson to Mallet, August 11, 1726, *Works*, I, cxlviii. If the Mr. Aikman of Livorno (Leghorn), Italy, in care of whom Thomas Edwards addressed letters to George Knapton the painter and Daniel Wray in October, 1725, and on May 21, 1726, was the painter, he was not in London to influence Thomson. Thomas Edwards' letterbooks in the Bodleian Library, Oxford, Ms. Bodl. 1007, pp. 59, 70.

17. For example, *Summer* (1727), pp. 35–36, 76–77; cf. "Summer" (i.e., the final version of this section of the *Seasons* in *Works* or *Poetical Works* or any standard edition of Thomson), ll. 480–497, 1647–1663.

18. *Summer* (1727), p. 85; cf. "Summer," ll. 1749–1752.

other. As time went on, however, it did receive several modifications, one of them being the notion that the greater the object contemplated the greater would be the idea stimulated. As Edward Young wrote, "Extended views a narrow mind extend." [19] And, as a curious variation of this idea, Professor MacLean notes that "Isaac Watts was most emphatic in recommending to the young the study of astronomy which would accustom them to *'take in vast and sublime Ideas without Pain or Difficulty.'* " [20]

Judged by his use of prospects or "extended views," Thomson, with the aid of his friend Dyer, made a similar modification of Locke's philosophy. Unlike his landscapes, Thomson's prospects in *Summer* are without exception connected with a moral or some other idea which he wished to impress upon his reader's mind. And with one exception the prospect always precedes the idea. It was, I think, Thomson's intention that the prospect should extend the reader's mind so that he could take in the following idea "without Pain or Difficulty."

Let me illustrate. Thomson has organized *Summer* into the sequence of an ideal day.[21] Early in the poem occurs this typically Claudian sunrise scene:

> Young Day pours in apace,
> And opens all the lawny prospect wide.
> The dripping rock, the mountain's misty top
> Swell on the eye, and brighten with the dawn.
> Blue, thro' the dusk, the smoking currents shine;
> And, from the bladed field, th' unhunted hare
> Limps awkward, while, along the forest glade,
> The wild deer trip, and, often turning, gaze
> At early passenger. Music awakes,
> The native voice of undissembling joy;
> And thick around the wood-land hymns arise.
> Rous'd by the cock, the soon-clad shepherd leaves
> His mossy cottage, where with peace he dwells;

19. *Night Thoughts*, IX, 1383.

20. Kenneth MacLean, *John Locke and English Literature of the Eighteenth Century* (New Haven, 1936), p. 57, quoting from Isaac Watts, *Improvement of the Mind*, Pt. I, chap. xvi, "Of Enlarging the Capacity of the Mind."

21. Thomson's use of this Miltonic device may have been influenced by Dyer's use of it in his "Country Walk." Mallet did not entirely approve of it, as is clear from Thomson's letter to him of August 11, 1726. *Works*, I, cxlvii.

And from the crowded fold, in order, drives
His flock, to taste the verdure of the morn.

Having properly opened and prepared our minds for new ideas
with this extended view, Thomson immediately proceeds with this
appropriate moral observation:

Falsely luxurious, will not man awake,
And starting from the bed of sloth, enjoy
The cool, the fragrant, and the silent hour
To meditation due, and sacred song!
And is there ought in sleep can charm the wise?
To lie in dead oblivion, lost to all
Our natures boast of noble and divine:
Total extinction of th' enlighten'd soul!
Or else to feverish vanity alive,
Wilder'd, and tossing thro' distemper'd dreams.
Who would in such a gloomy state remain
Longer than nature craves? When every Muse,
And every blooming Pleasure wait without,
To bless the wildly-devious morning walk.[22]

Later the prospect of devastation wrought by lightning leads into
a passage on the power of God;[23] a Claudian sunset prepares for
a moral comparison between the afterglow, "the day illusive," and
the illusions about life which are held by the cruel and heartless.[24]
But Thomson is not solely a moralist; he has other ideas he wishes
to communicate. A second sunrise scene introduces his apostrophe
to the sun, which contains miscellaneous astronomic and agricultural information;[25] another vista at sunset opens our minds so
that we may be disillusioned of all superstitious beliefs about
the aurora borealis.[26] And in the middle of the poem two prospects
in a row[27] are used to prepare us for his apostrophe to Britain,
a passage Thomson considered important.[28]

22. *Summer*, pp. 12–14; cf. "Summer," ll. 52–80.
23. *Ibid.*, pp. 64–66; cf. "Summer," ll. 1150–1169 (in the collected edition of 1730 and
thereafter, however, the "moral" was reduced from 24 lines to one).
24. *Ibid.*, pp. 74–76; cf. "Summer," ll. 1620–1646.
25. *Ibid.*, pp. 14–20; cf. "Summer," ll. 81–174.
26. *Ibid.*, pp. 80–83; cf. "Summer," ll. 1690–1729.
27. *Ibid.*, pp. 41–51; cf. "Summer," ll. 590–628, 1438–1619 (the original passage was
divided in later editions).
28. Thomson to Mallet, autumn, 1726, *Works,* I, cli.

That Thomson turned to painting rather than to astronomy or some other source for such a rhetorical device is, to me, interesting, for *vertu* seems to have played small part in the background of the *Seasons* at this time.[29] Yet it is a very natural outgrowth of such a friendship as his with John Dyer. For Thomson it was as easy a development of his Lockean philosophy as Young's and Watts's ideas had been of theirs; for Dyer it was the next step from the moralizing on a scene which he had done so gracefully in *Grongar Hill.*

That Thomson looked upon his use of the prospect as a rhetorical or at least stylistic device, not merely an esthetic effect, is indicated, I think, by his later use of it in the *Seasons. Summer,* written when his friendship with Dyer was at its peak, remains the high point in Thomson's use of the prospect. *Spring* (1728) and *Autumn* (1730) combined have about as many prospects as *Summer* alone, with many excellent opportunities left undeveloped,[30] more landscapes or near views, and much more of the shorter style of description characteristic of the first edition of *Winter.* But such prospects as do appear are all used in the same manner. And even as late as 1744, when the description of the prospect at Hagley was first printed, it was inserted in "Spring" so as to precede Thomson's "dissuasive from the wild and irregular passion of love, opposed to that of a pure and happy kind." [31] Thomson's use of the prospect waned, but it continued as it had begun, a rhetorical as well as an esthetic element.

This point has implications that extend beyond Thomson to the entire eighteenth century. Thomson was a serious young man who was keenly interested in the new ideas of his day and in presenting them to the reading public. The *Seasons* were didactic poems and were recognized as such by his contemporaries.[32] I feel certain, therefore, that Thomson would never have used as lengthy passages as some of his prospects are without some such

29. Cf. Alan Dugald McKillop, *The Background of Thomson's Seasons* (Minneapolis, 1942).

30. For example, *Spring,* 1728, pp. 42–43 (cf. "Spring," ll. 832–848), where a shepherd and his sportive lambs are on a mountain brow, the sun is descending, but no prospect develops to introduce the philosophic passage which follows.

31. "The Argument" to "Spring." The prospect is in ll. 950–962.

32. McKillop, *op. cit.*, pp. 5–6.

didactic purpose as I have described. But later poets, being less conscious of having their minds extended, imitated the prospect and more and more frequently left out the moral. This change in attitude is well illustrated by the critic John Aiken, who in 1778 wrote, "Essentially different from a didactic piece, its [the *Seasons'*] *business* is to describe, and the occupation of its *leisure* to teach." [33] Thomson would, I think, have reversed these pairings, for he and Dyer, often referred to as "preromantic" poets, are really much more in harmony with the Age of Pope than the nineteenth century thought. But that Aiken, and many others with him, should place the wrong emphasis on Thomson's work is a beautiful example of how clearly the large shifts of feeling which differentiate periods in literature have their beginnings in many changes as small as the use of a prospect for stylistic reasons—in changes so microscopic that, like the changes which begin linguistic shifts, they often cannot be discovered later.[34]

Literary friendships sometimes last too short a time for sentimental scholars of later centuries; in 1727 Dyer had to write:

> O Thomson, we have long in absence lain
> And long in silence . . .

But this friendship had lasted long enough to provide Thomson with some of the inspiration that made him, as Miss Manwaring says, *"par excellence,* the poet of pictorial landscape." [35] And Professor Tinker, in numerous references in *Painter and Poet*,[36] has shown how well Thomson repaid to later painters the debt he owed to his painter-friend of 1726.

33. J. Aikin, "An Essay on the Plan and Character of the Poem," prefixed to the *Seasons* (new ed. 1779), p. viii.

34. Cf. Frederick A. Pottle, *The Idiom of Poetry* (revised ed. Ithaca, N. Y., 1946), pp. 18–22.

35. Elizabeth W. Manwaring, *Italian Landscape in Eighteenth-century England* (New York, 1925), p. 101.

36. See C. B. Tinker, *Painter and Poet* (Cambridge, Mass., 1938), pp. 76, 129–130, 135, 151–152, 170, 174, 176, for the influence of the various versions of *Summer,* which seems to have been the most popular of the *Seasons* with later painters.

THOMAS GRAY
Donald M. Foerster

OF all the English poets, Thomas Gray was undoubtedly one of the least productive. His life was not cut short before his best verse was written; he was not distracted by the problems and pressures of a business career or a profession, nor was he discouraged from writing poetry by severe and unjust criticism. Yet Gray composed no lengthy epics, no complete plays, nothing more than a few short hymns, elegies, and odes that could all be bound in a thin pamphlet of seventy pages or so.

How does it happen that a man should express himself as well as Gray and yet so rarely? Why was it that even loud popular acclaim and an offer of the poet laureateship did not inspire him to write some ambitious and outstanding masterpiece? A direct reply, a reply that leaves nothing more to be said, could probably not be given. But the letters of Gray, fortunately more abundant than his poems, do at least suggest several possible answers.

First of all, it appears from these letters that Gray was singularly free of the attitudes and motives that usually move men of talent to write and to publish. Though occasionally obliged to borrow, he seems to have been a foe to money, to have been totally indifferent to the market value of his poems. He did not welcome praise; his taste for it, he said, was "not like that of Children for fruit." [1] Nor did he apparently care what posterity might think of him: "what has it ever done to oblige me?" [2] Gray asked.

But a more fundamental reason for his not writing and especially not publishing was that he could not tolerate being called a poet, a professional poet. So little did he like the title that only the endless and earnest pleadings of friends ever persuaded him to print anything. Once or twice, in fact, a poem made its appearance only

---

1. *Correspondence of Thomas Gray,* ed. Paget Toynbee and Leonard Whibley (Oxford, 1935), p. 416.
2. *Ibid.,* p. 566.

because some well-meaning acquaintance had surreptitiously transcribed and then rushed it to a publisher. "I desire you would by no means suffer this to be copied," Gray was perpetually saying; "if you are so loth to publish *your productions,* you can not wonder at the repugnance I feel to spreading abroad mine." [3] He complained bitterly when certain stanzas of the churchyard elegy had the "Misfortune . . . to be made still more publick, for which they certainly were never meant." [4]

This attitude may have been owing, as some have suggested, to a fastidiousness of Gray's, to a desire to appear as a gentleman of leisure who was in no way dependent upon his verse for bread and butter. But the fact is that Gray was, of all our English poets, one of the shyest and most modest. When a volume of his poems was about to come out he asked Horace Walpole whether he did not think it would be less pretentious to print "By Thomas Gray" rather than "By Mr. Thomas Gray"; and as for including his picture in this volume, that "would be worse than the Pillory." "If you suffer my Head to be printed, you infallibly will put me out of mine." [5] Nor could Gray apparently say a good word for any of the verse that he had written. "I . . . find myself (as the Women are of their children)," he said, "less enamour'd of my Productions the older they grow." [6] "The Progress of Poesy" is branded "a high Pindarick upon stilts"; [7] and some years after its composition, the "Ode to Spring" is sent to Walpole with: "all it pretends to with you is, that it is mine, & that you never saw it before, & that it is not so long as t'other." [8] Even the famous churchyard elegy, which earned him the hated title of "Mr. Gray, the poet," is spoken of merely as "a thing with an end to it." [9] Practically everything he wrote, in fact, Gray habitually called "a thing" or "a trifle."

Why, then, did Gray write poetry at all? Who else would have written verses with no apparent motive? Apparent or not, there

3. *Ibid.,* p. 420.
4. *Ibid.,* p. 335.
5. *Ibid.,* p. 372.
6. *Ibid.,* p. 196.
7. *Ibid.,* p. 364.
8. *Ibid.,* p. 250.
9. *Ibid.,* p. 327.

was one motive at least. Temperamentally unable to select and follow a specific profession, disdaining a life that would make him subservient to others, Gray seems to have taken the view—perhaps it could be called the philosophy—that "to be employed is to be happy." [10] "I am persuaded the whole matter is to have always something going forward," he said; [11] "to find oneself business is the great art of life." Apparently it did not matter to Gray how one occupied himself; the important thing was to avoid by whatever means the gloom and introspection that come from having nothing to do. Actually, Gray did not often attain the contentment he was after. His letters are full of complaints about "black and white melancholies," ennui, insipidity, and a sense of never accomplishing anything.[12] "When you have seen one of my days," he tells Richard West, "you have seen a whole year of my life; they go round and round like the blind horse in the mill, only he has the satisfaction of fancying he makes a progress, and gets some ground." [13] "Alas! for one who has nothing to do but amuse himself." [14] Nevertheless, there were few periods in Gray's life when he was not hard at work upon some project, reading and taking notes about Gothic architecture, heraldry, entomology, literature past and present, the histories of Greece, Rome, and England—or occasionally composing verse.

A philosophy of this sort obviously left Gray free to wander where he would, to concentrate upon nothing. Now and again, in a moment of inspiration, he might labor over a few verses, but for him writing poetry was no more enjoyable or important than compiling Greek chronologies or drawing up monthly weather reports for Thomas Wharton. Furthermore Gray had the unhappy tendency of beginning but rarely finishing. Over a period of twenty years or so he turned from the study of classical antiquities to English history, to English poetry, and finally to science, becoming an expert in each field but somehow never quite reaching the point of writing down the results of his research. Similarly he

10. *Ibid.*, p. 520.
11. *Ibid.*, p. 677.
12. *Ibid.*, p. 209.
13. *Ibid.*, p. 34.
14. *Ibid.*, p. 194.

began poems and abandoned them long before they were finished. Many were never completed; indeed, had his friends not urged and pleaded so persistently, "The Bard" would still lack a concluding epode. "Rapidity in writing, & perseverance in finishing" are, he said, "two talents that I want." [15]

What a great difference there is between the attitudes of Gray and a poet like Dryden! Dryden—a professional, eager for money, eager to please a wide public and able to please it; a man who could produce almost at will a new heroic play, a political poem, a translation from the classics—whatever he thought might prove most popular at the time. Gray on the other hand—strictly an amateur, indifferent to reward or praise, more scholar than poet, writing only when he felt a momentary inspiration, writing, one might almost say, only to avoid boredom.

Granted, then, that Gray's temperament, his rather strange attitudes, and perhaps his multiplicity of interests rarely made for self-expression in verse, what reply can be given to our original question? How is greatness achieved by a man who seems almost to have gone out of his way to avoid greatness? Rather than attempt to discuss the merits of each of his poems, an ambitious undertaking indeed, it would perhaps be better to concentrate upon one of his best and most unique compositions, "The Bard."

In 1757, when "The Bard" and "The Progress of Poesy" were first published, there was none of the vigorous applause that had greeted Gray's earlier poems; there was almost dead silence. It was not that people disliked the new odes but rather that they felt puzzled, uncertain what to think. "No body knows what we would be at," Gray remarked; and in a letter to Thomas Wharton he reported that a friend had "overheard three People, whom by their dress & manner he takes for Lords, say, that I was impenetrable & inexplicable, and they wish'd, I had told them in prose, what I meant in verse, & then they bought me (which was what most displeased him) & put me in their pocket." [16] But while the public as a whole had no judgment to offer, critics, poets, and scholars joined in giving the heartiest praise to the odes. The *Monthly*

15. *Ibid.*, p. 533.
16. *Ibid.*, p. 532.

Review was especially enthusiastic; so too, according to Gray's letters, were Warburton, Wharton, Mason, Hurd, Walpole, and Beattie. John Brown, author of *The Estimate,* proclaimed them "the best odes in our language."

Gray thought he knew why "The Bard" appealed to so few. "There is a certain measure of learning necessary, & a long acquaintance with the good Writers ancient & modern . . . without this they can only catch here & there a florid expression, or a musical rhyme, while the Whole appears to them a wild obscure unedifying jumble." [17] One cannot fail to agree with Gray: people without good literary and historical backgrounds have never fully understood the poem. But "The Bard" must have seemed still more perplexing in a time when such strange themes and such strange ways of handling those themes were the exception rather than the rule. For in the year of "The Bard" the primitivist movement was just beginning; only among a handful of Scotch historians and poets were there as yet any lively discussions about ancient poetry and its highly emotional character, about the rhapsodists and bards and the oral transmission of their verses. Nor had many poets attempted to reproduce the enthusiasm and wildness of primitive song. In fact the reading public and even the critics and scholars were still in the habit of regarding an early poet like Homer as one of their contemporaries. It was not until 1760 and after, with the appearance of the Ossianic poems and the many books on original genius, the history of man, and the rise and development of poetry, that the average person was able at all to see what Gray "would be at."

"The Bard" was therefore one of the first of the modern "primitive poems." That Gray succeeded so well in taking a theme from the remote past and in re-creating the enthusiasm and suggestiveness of the Welsh bard is owing in large part to his having been an ardent scholar rather than poet, to his long years of historical study. For in tracing the rise of many nations—Greece, Rome, England, and Wales—he developed several theories about the use of primitive themes in poetry. He came to believe, above all else, that a poem like his own "Bard" should seem old and

17. *Ibid.,* p. 478.

should seem Welsh. Hence he thought it desirable to adhere to historical fact, to introduce real Welsh customs and religious beliefs, real and yet highly suggestive Welsh names. But Gray saw that there were dangers in doing this, that it was easy inadvertently to misuse historical data and thus mar or spoil a poem. In one of his letters, for example, he did everything possible to discourage his friend William Mason from bringing "Woden & his Valkhyrian Virgins" into a poem that pretended to be Celtic, and from having druids fight with toads: "these are things for Fairies to make War upon." [18] Rid your poem of such inconsistencies, he warned, or the advantages of using historical materials will be entirely lost.

Gray felt that there was a second danger in introducing historical fact. For "when we treat a subject, where the manners are almost lost in antiquity, our stock of Ideas must needs be small, & nothing betrays our poverty more, than the returning to, & harping frequently on one Image." [19] Under such circumstances, and under these alone, the poet should fall back upon "pure imagination, & fiction (our favourite provinces) where no Critick can molest, or Antiquary gainsay us." Nevertheless, one should not invent at random. The fictions "must have some affinity, some seeming connection with that little we really know of the character & customs of the People." [20] We know, for instance, that the early Celts had a strange mythology and many quite fantastic beliefs. In a "Celtic poem" therefore, readers would not be at all shocked to find Midnight and the Moon represented as sisters who carried gold and ebony rods and whispered together on the top of a mountain. In fact any fiction of this sort can be used, provided it "be made picturesque, & look almost as if it were true." [21]

To win one's belief that the truth is being told, whether it is actually being told or not—that is, Gray thinks, a primary aim of the poet in dealing with primitive themes. Nor can there be any question that this aim is accomplished in "The Bard." Reference is made not only to actual places but also to a number of figures in

18. *Ibid.*, p. 607.
19. *Ibid.*, pp. 528–529.
20. *Ibid.*, p. 529.
21. *Ibid.*, p. 607.

history—to Margaret of Anjou, Edward I, Henry V and Henry VI, to Urien, Taliessin, and "high-born Hoel." At the same time Gray does not hesitate to use "imagination and fiction." For example, it is said that Cadwallo was able to hush the stormy sea, that Modred's song made Plinlimmon bow its head, and that ravens would not touch the corpses of the bards, so shocked were they at the enormity of the crime. These are strange fictions indeed, but aside from seeming quite appropriate in a "Welsh poem," there can be no doubt that they give "The Bard" the wildness and the picturesqueness which, as Gray said, characterize all early poetry.[22]

But if Gray's study of history was of immense value in the writing of "The Bard," his background in literature was perhaps even more helpful. It was indeed one of the richest backgrounds imaginable, for there was hardly a book of even the slightest importance that Gray had not read at one time or another. Homer, Virgil, Dante, and Tasso in the original, Chaucer, Milton, and Shakespeare, more recent poets like John Phillips, Dyer, Pope, Shenstone, and Akenside, the latest novelists, the French romancers, the Anglo-Saxon, Gothic, and Norse poets of old—his field was a wide one. As Gray once told his friend West, "My life is like Harry the fourth's supper of Hens. 'Poulets a la broche, Poulets en Ragôut, Poulets en Hâchis, Poulets en Fricasées.' Reading here, Reading there; nothing but books with different sauces." [23] Gray did not merely know these books, however; he absorbed them so thoroughly that everything he wrote, perhaps everything he thought too, was influenced by some play or some poem. Even in his letters there are endless quotations in Greek and Latin, endless references to one character or another in Restoration or Elizabethan drama. In fact he cannot speak about the most trifling incident in the most offhand manner without making a literary allusion. For instance, in chiding Walpole because he had so often postponed a promised

22. This passage, which will be referred to again in another connection, reads as follows:

"Cold is Cadwallo's tongue,	Made huge Plinlimmon bow his cloud-topt
That hush'd the stormy main:	head.
Brave Urien sleeps upon his craggy bed:	On dreary Arvon's shore they lie,
Mountains, ye mourn in vain	Smear'd with gore, and ghastly pale:
Modred, whose magic song	Far, far aloof th' affrighted ravens sail;
	The famish'd eagle screams, and passes by."

23. *Ibid.*, p. 210.

visit Gray writes, "I have born, & born, and been fub'd off, & fub'd
off from this day to that day by you, thou Honey-suckle Villain (as
Mrs Quickly says) oh! thou art an infinitive thing upon my score
of impatience." [24] And when the same man wrote him a disap-
pointingly short letter of less than a dozen lines, Gray jokingly
showed his irritation with Congreve's "gadsbud! I am provoked
into a fermentation!"

Gray reveals the same tendency in "The Bard." Image after
image, phrase after phrase, have been taken, sometimes consciously,
sometimes not, from almost every conceivable literary source. In
one letter he quite willingly confesses that the bard's hair which
"stream'd like a meteor" was "almost stol'n" from Milton's description of Azazel's standard, which "shone, like a meteor, streaming
to the wind." "That about the Banners of K: Edward ["They mock
the air with idle state"] has," Gray says, "a near affinity to a line
in Shakespeare's King John, Mocking the air with colours idly
spread." And two lines he admits "pilfering" from *Julius Caesar*.
"Do not wonder therefore, if some Magazine or Review call me
Plagiary: I could shew them a hundred more instances, which they
never will discover themselves." [25] A hundred more have indeed
been discovered. To mention a few, "Amazement in his van with
Flight combined" harkens back to the $\Delta\epsilon\hat{\iota}\mu\rho\varsigma\ \grave{\eta}\delta\epsilon\ \phi\acute{o}\beta\rho\varsigma$ of Homer;
the "sweeping Whirlwind's sway" is probably an echo of Dryden's
"rolling onwards with a sweepy sway"; and "Heard ye the din of
battle bray" reminds one of Milton's "arms on armour clashing
brayed." One cannot, however, justly call Gray a "plagiary." To
paraphrase long passages from the poets is one thing; to appropriate mere phrases and single words is another. In fact one reason for the success of "The Bard" is that Gray was not obliged to
seek safety in the conventional images and expressions of the time;
that, on the contrary, his rich literary background, his wide reading, and particularly his habit of remembering and using the most
striking phrases he came across enabled him to impart to his poem
one thing which he knew most essential: the vigor or force of
primitive song.

24. *Ibid.*, p. 25.
25. *Ibid.*, pp. 476–477.

There is, of course, no mistaking the fact that "The Bard" was written in the eighteenth century: Urien sleeps upon his "craggy bed," the vessel rides proudly o'er the "azure realm," and Snowden has its "shaggy side." But Gray's diction is generally quite different from that of Pope and his imitators. Words are chosen, just as phrases are borrowed, because of their effectiveness, not because they happen to be in current use among poets. Regarding those words that had become archaic, Gray pointed out that "our language not being a settled thing (like the French) has an undoubted right to words of an hundred years old, provided antiquity have not rendered them unintelligible." Other words that he used were given their older meanings, were more properly classical than English. For example, in the line "tomorrow he repairs the golden flood," he used the verb in the Latin sense of "to recover." But here again Gray felt justified: "Our poetry . . . has a language peculiar to itself; to which almost every one, that has written, has added something by enriching it with foreign idioms and derivatives: Nay sometimes words of their own composition or invention." [26] Other remarks about diction, about the sounds and the connotations of words, occur repeatedly in his letters criticizing Mason's poetry. For instance, Gray says that "a *Rill* has no *tide* of waters to *tumble* down *amain,*" that *Zenith-height* is harsh to the ear & too scientific," that "we say the juice of the grape *mantles,* but not the grape." [27] Comments of this kind seem trifling, to be sure; but they do at least indicate how carefully he must have chosen the individual words for his own "Bard," a poem that demanded not only vigorous expression but highly suggestive expression as well. Indeed if one turns to the passage concerning the fate of the bards, what words could better give the effect of wildness than "Made huge Plinlimmon bow his cloud-topt head," or better suggest a scene of desolation and death than *"dreary* Arvon's shore," *"craggy* bed," *"smear'd* with gore," *"ghastly* pale," "famish'd eagle *screams,"* *"cold* is Cadwallo's tongue"?

A most unusual poet was Thomas Gray. Obviously he had the "celestial fire" of the poet, he had examined carefully the "ample

26. *Ibid.,* p. 192.
27. *Ibid.,* pp. 714–715.

page" of knowledge, he had the time and the encouragement to write. And he did indeed produce several of the finest short poems in the English language. Some, like "The Bard," are favorites of literary people; others, like the churchyard elegy, are admired even by those who can barely read. But Gray's accomplishments were clearly limited. An indifference toward his own poems, an inactive and uninspiring life that could only mean discontent and low spirits, a lack of interest in the human causes that stir men to express themselves nobly—these meant that the poetic genius of Gray was to reveal itself only on rare occasions. In fact the more we read his letters, read about things he thought and did in passing "along the cool sequestered vale" of his own life, the greater becomes our wonder that he ever achieved any fame at all. Perhaps we should be content and consider it sheer good fortune that his poetic talent did not entirely "waste its sweetness on the desert air."

SHENSTONE'S READING OF SPENSER

Virginia F. Prettyman

OF the ninety-odd poems which comprise the first collected edition of Shenstone's verse a dozen or more received from the poet's contemporaries the compliments of high praise and imitation, but not more than three are now familiar even to students of eighteenth-century poetry. Of these, the "Lines Written at an Inn" owe their modest fame to Dr. Johnson's fondness for them. The "Pastoral Ballad," a pretty though somewhat faded period piece, gained some currency through being set to music by Dr. Arne. Only "The Schoolmistress" has survived by its own merits.

This poem, which of all Shenstone's works alone bears the stamp of a fresh talent, was begun as an imitation of an imitation of Spenser. In its first version it is a rather crude burlesque, patterned upon Pope's Spenserian imitation, "The Alley." The second version is expanded and somewhat modified in tone. The third, which has been accepted as the standard text, shows an increasing appreciation of Spenser's art and a real understanding of his humorous vein. Shenstone's letters indicate that he made further additions to the poem, additions which modified the burlesque tone still more. The successive alterations were adversely criticized, however, by Richard Graves, who prized the burlesque element and thought the poem interesting only as a parody. Graves unfortunately persuaded Shenstone to discard some fifteen or twenty stanzas of the unpublished third version of "The Schoolmistress"; and as Shenstone's literary executor he may well have been responsible for reproducing this cut version in the posthumous collection of Shenstone's poems, for it seems almost certain that the poet himself would have preserved the additional stanzas. It is possible, nevertheless, to trace in the three surviving versions the growth of Shenstone's knowledge of Spenser, from the superficial acquaintanceship indicated by a mimicking of archaisms to the sympathetic appreciation which enabled him to recapture something of the earlier poet's mood and music.

"The Schoolmistress" first appeared in *Poems Upon Various Occasions,* a little miscellany which Shenstone succeeded in having printed in 1737, soon after he left Oxford. The contents are all imitative. The songs are obviously inspired by Dryden's; the ballads are reminiscent of Prior's; and "Colemira, a Culinary Eclogue," might almost have been borrowed from Gay's burlesque pastorals. The more serious poems show that Shenstone had been studying the heroic couplets of his favorite poet, Pope. And "The Schoolmistress," although it is called "a Poem in Imitation of Spencer's Stile," is closer to Pope's burlesque, "The Alley," than to Spenser.

"The Alley" is an undistinguished piece of burlesque, even though it is, according to Spence, the joint product of Pope and Gay; but it has qualities that would have appealed to an undergraduate admirer of Pope, and it clearly influenced Shenstone's poem in several respects. In the first place, it treats a "low" scene in an "elevated" style, and the verses are not narrative but pictorial, with a wealth of sensory detail. Impressed by Spenser's boldness in treating matters unpleasant but necessary to his purpose, the authors introduced a good deal of gratuitous obscenity, and the picture of the squalid, filthy alley and its rowdy inhabitants is less like Spenser's work than like Gay's in some of the less savory parts of *Trivia.* At best, however, the piece has a graphic, Hogarthian quality. Secondly, "The Alley" set an example for Shenstone in the matter of stylistic detail. Pope used the regular Spenserian stanza. He ignored the frequent alliteration which is so striking to a new reader of the poet, and satisfied himself with several inverted sentences and a very few archaic words.

That Shenstone undertook his parody with Pope's example in mind is indicated by a letter of June, 1742, in which he related to Richard Graves the history of his changing attitude toward Spenser. "When I bought him first," he remarked, "I read a page or two of the Fairy Queen, and cared not to proceed. After that, Pope's Alley made me consider him ludicrously; and in that light, I think, one may read him with pleasure."

Shenstone's parody, like Pope's, is pictorial and rich in detail,

and like Pope Shenstone chose a "low" scene to describe in elevated language. But by happy accident his scene was "low" in quite
a different way. The fact that he chose to picture the humble dame
school of his own childhood made the poem an essay in recollection and ensured a tone not of mockery but of indulgent and affectionate amusement. The descriptions in "The Schoolmistress"
manage to suggest at once the naïve impressions of a child and the
gentle humor of an adult who remembers well his own childish
thoughts. Only in one stanza did Shenstone indulge in the coarseness that is found throughout "The Alley."

In the matter of style Shenstone seems to have imitated both
Spenser and Pope. His sentences are more distorted by inversions
and oddities of phrasing than Pope's are. He used far more archaic
words, and scattered archaic spellings liberally. He also used the *y*-
prefix freely, even with present participles and adjectives, as in
y-gazing and *y-rare*. But like Pope Shenstone ignored Spenser's
alliteration, though Gay had burlesqued it in "The Shepherd's
Week."

In short, the 1737 version of "The Schoolmistress" owes much
to Pope, both in conception and in execution, and the real excellence of the poem is rather the result of happy accident in the
choice of a subject than of a close imitation of Spenser. But upon
rereading Spenser in 1741 Shenstone revised his poem under the
direct influence of the original, and he declared to Graves that the
new stanzas had more of Spenser's manner than the old. In a
letter to Richard Jago, written on Christmas Eve of that year,
he showed that he had gained new insight into Spenser and had
thought much upon the nature of the various types of burlesque.
The characteristics in Spenser most suitable for humorous imitation, he felt, were "simplicity and obsolete phrase." "And yet," he
continued, "these are what give one a very singular pleasure in the
perusal. The burlesque which they occasion is of quite a different
kind to that of Philips's Shilling, Cotton's Travestie, Hudibras, or
Swift's works." To Richard Graves, who, not knowing Spenser,
preferred the first version of "The Schoolmistress" to the second,
Shenstone defended his revisions, declaring: "The true burlesque
of Spenser (whose characteristic is simplicity) seems to consist in

a *simple* representation of such things as one laughs to *see* or to *observe* one's self, rather than in any monstrous contrast between the thoughts and words. I cannot help thinking that my added stanzas have more of his manner than what you saw before." Shenstone had come to realize that the humor of "The Alley" depended largely upon "monstrous contrast" and that Spenser's "simplicity" was there made the butt of scornful laughter. To him, however, that simplicity, or naïveté, was as charming as it was laughable, and it was allied to another trait which delighted him— Spenser's tenderness of feeling. In the second edition of "The Schoolmistress," a handsome six-penny pamphlet published by Dodsley in 1742, he paid tribute to this quality in the Advertisement: "What Particulars in SPENSER were imagin'd most proper for the Author's Imitation on *this Occasion,* are his *Language,* his *Simplicity,* his Manner of *Description,* and a peculiar *Tenderness* of *Sentiment,* visible throughout his Works." The revised "Schoolmistress" is a more carefully planned mock-heroic poem than the original. Its burlesque nature is emphasized by the addition of an index and of learned footnotes—quotations from Horace and Virgil, which furnish classical parallels to the episodes. There is an invocation of the Muse. The descriptions and episodes are expanded, and there are epic similes and apostrophes. But Shenstone preserved a careful balance between the mock-heroic and the natural elements. The subject matter of course lent itself admirably to such a balance, for the old dame was indeed an epic figure to the urchins in the school and to the former pupil who had preserved something of the naïveté of his childish point of view.

As might be expected, there is a pronounced vein of sentiment in the new version. The old schoolmistress is described with real affection. The boy who is birched is given a little sister who melts in pity at his plight. There are sympathetic references to *"Learning's* Imps . . . who cheerless o'er her darkling region stray." And the revision of the hexameter line of stanza xxvi is a key to the poet's altered mood. In the first version, after describing the "Cath'rine Pear" in the huckster's stall, Shenstone exclaims:

> O! may no Wight e'er pennyless come there,
> Lest led by thee astray, he shameful theft prepare.

In the second version the hexameter line reads: "Lest smit with ardent Love he pine with hopeless Care!"

The second version of "The Schoolmistress" is a more euphonious poem than the first. Freed from his original dependence upon "obsolete phrase" as the chief source of humor, Shenstone labored to improve lines that were at first rough with inversions and archaisms. That the music of Spenser's verse had come to delight him he confessed to Richard Graves.

I am now . . . from trifling and laughing at him, really in love with him. I think even the metre pretty (though I shall never use it in earnest); and that the last Alexandrine has an extreme majesty.—Does not this line strike you . . .
      'Brave thoughts and noble deeds did *evermore* inspire.'
Perhaps it is my fancy only that is enchanted with the running of it.

For no other poet did Shenstone express such warmth of feeling. It must be remembered, however, that there were reservations in his regard for the poet ("His plan is detestable, and his invention less wonderful than most people imagine.") and that his poem is not straightforward imitation. At this time Shenstone nervously feared that readers might overlook the humor of the poem and accuse him of the "simplicity" which he had set out to burlesque. The "ludicrous Index" of the second version and the Latin motto were added to show the public that he was writing in jest!

Shenstone continued to read Spenser and to alter "The School-mistress" in accordance with his increasing understanding of the poet. In November, 1745 he wrote to Graves: "I have read Spenser once again: and I have added full as much more to my *Schoolmistress,* in regard to *number of lines; something* in point of *matter* (or *manner* rather) which does not displease me." The addition of some twenty-eight stanzas evidently seemed excessive to Graves, who complained that the new verses were "excrescences" rather than integral parts and that they made the poem "too diffuse and flimzy." Shenstone deferred to his friend's judgment, promising to sacrifice some of the added portions if he should publish the poem again but declaring that he would "read and shew it" with the new parts intact. "I own," he confessed, "I have a fondness for several, imagining them to be more in Spenser's way, yet more independent on the antique phrase, than any part of the poem."

Early in 1748, however, he was called upon to make the difficult sacrifice. Dodsley's *Collection of Poems by Several Hands,* which was issued in January of that year, reproduced "The Schoolmistress" in its 1742 version, without Shenstone's permission and with the poet's name, which had not hitherto appeared with the poem. Hearing that the *Collection* was so popular as to require a second edition within the year, Shenstone suppressed his annoyance and offered to revise "The Schoolmistress" for Dodsley. The second edition of the *Collection* therefore contains a new version of the poem—that which is now usually reproduced as the standard text.

In its new form "The Schoolmistress" contained only thirty-five stanzas, instead of the fifty-odd that the poet must have shown in manuscript to his friends, for Shenstone did abide by Graves's decision, *multa gemens,* as he declared. Of the original twenty-eight stanzas two were discarded and the others were carefully revised. Convinced that the poem should be "agreeable in itself" and that the humor should appear rather in the scenes and sentiments portrayed than in the burlesque manner of expression, Shenstone discarded many of the archaic words and most of the "antique" spelling. The evolution of one quatrain will illustrate the modification of the burlesque tone, the heightening of the pictorial quality, and the increasing ease in the movement of the verse. In the earliest version the poem begins:

> In evrich Mart that stands on *British* Ground,
> In evrich Village less y-known to Fame,
> Dwells there, in Cot uncouth, a far renown'd,
> A Matron old, whom we *School-Mistress* name;

In the version of 1742 (stanza ii) the lines read:

> In ev'ry Mart that stands on *Britain's* Isle,
> In ev'ry Village less reveal'd to Fame,
> Dwells there, in Cottage known about a Mile,
> A Matron old, whom we *School-Mistress* name;

The third version is:

> In ev'ry village mark'd with little spire,
> Embow'r'd in trees, and hardly known to Fame,
> There dwells in lowly shed, and mean attire,
> A matron old, whom we school-mistress name;

The modification of the burlesque effect was furthered by the omission of the "ludicrous Index" and the Latin footnotes. A comparison of stanza xxi of the third version and its original, stanza xv of the second, reveals Shenstone's increasing tact in the handling of burlesque. In the revision the pompous speech of the little girl disappears, along with the Virgilian quotation (in the footnote) which had suggested it; and the simple representation of childish woe which Shenstone substituted in its place is a particularly happy addition to the poem. Stanza ii underwent a similar revision, slighter but no less effective. In describing the children kept in from play, the version of 1742 reads "They grieven sore in Durance vile y-pent," while the later version has "in piteous durance pent." It is this delicate balance between mock-heroic convention and a "simple representation of such things as one laughs to see" which gives the final version a peculiar charm; and the author's unobtrusive but telling revision of words and phrases toward this end may be seen throughout the poem.

Of the new stanzas which Shenstone discarded there remains not a trace; but the ones he refused to part with provide a clue to their nature, for these have a quality quite distinctive, however well they fit into the original body of the poem. They are predominantly pictorial, and are indeed, as the author protested, "more in Spenser's way, yet more independent on the antique phrase, than any part of the poem."

Two of these stanzas, which describe the devout nature of the schoolmistress, show Shenstone to be so perfectly in control of the idiom and tone of his poem that he could fuse thereby elements as disparate as his visual memories of old Sarah Lloyd and his current uneasiness about the political situation. Stanza xiv shows the dame in her garden, singing Sternhold's version of Psalm CXXXVII. The second stanza gives further evidence of her staunchly Protestant faith:

> For she was just, and friend to virtuous lore,
> And pass'd much time in truly pious deed;
> And, in those Elfins's ears, would oft deplore
> The times, when truth by Popish rage did bleed;
> And tortious death was true devotion's meed;

And simple faith in iron chains did mourn,
That nould on wooden image place her creed;
And lawny saints in smould'ring flames did burn:
Ah! dearest Lord, forfend, thilk days should e'er return!

These lines clearly reflect Shenstone's concern about the outcome of the great rebellion of '45, for in the very letter which announced the composition of the new stanzas (November 22, 1745) the poet wrote apprehensively to Graves of the threat of popery that would accompany a restoration of the Stuarts. And he expressed a hope that the common people would make a firm stand against any change in government or religion. The old dame's attitude is a reflection of the poet's. Or perhaps, so real does she become, his is a reflection of old Sarah Lloyd's. Her picture of popery seems to have been gleaned from John Foxe's *Actes and Monuments of These Latter and Perilous Days;* and it may be that one of her "lawny saints" is Thomas Cranmer, who is pictured therein in the full lawn sleeves of a bishop, being burned at the stake.

Three other new stanzas of the third version are of special interest, for they offer a clue to the particular parts of Spenser which impressed Shenstone as he reread the poet in 1745. The first two describe the schoolmistress' herb garden. Catalogues of flowers are, of course, common in poetry, and there is a well-known catalogue of trees in the first book of *The Faerie Queene.* But it seems probable that Shenstone's catalogue of herbs was suggested by a similar passage in Spenser's "Muiopotmos, or the Fate of the Butterfly." In that poem Clarion, the butterfly prince, tastes the pleasures of an Elizabethan garden (stanzas xxiv and xxv):

And then againe he turneth to his play,
To spoyle the pleasures of that paradise:
The wholesome saulge, and lavender still gray,
Ranke smelling rue, and cummin good for eyes,
The roses raigning in the pride of May,
Sharp isope, good for greene wounds remedies,
Fair marigoldes, and bees-alluring thime,
Sweet marjoram, and daisies decking prime:

Coole violets, and orpine growing still,
Embathed balme, and cheerful galingale,
Fresh costmarie, and breathfull camomill,

> Dull poppie, and drink-quickning setuale,
> Veyne-healing verven, and hed-purging dill,
> Sound savorie, and bazill hartie-hale,
> Fat colworts, and comforting perseline,
> Cold lettuce, and refreshing rosmarine.

The schoolmistress' garden offers a less brilliant array, for its plants are strictly "for use and physick":

> Herbs too she knew, and well of each could speak
> That in her garden sip'd the silv'ry dew;
> Where no vain flow'r disclos'd a gawdy streak;
> But herbs for use, and physick, not a few,
> Of grey renown, within those borders grew;
> The tufted Basil, pun-provoking Tyme,
> Fresh Baum, and Marygold of chearful hue;
> The lowly Gill, that never dares to climb;
> And more I fain would sing, disdaining here to rhime.
>
> Yet Euphrasy may not be left unsung,
> That gives dim eyes to wander leagues around;
> And pungent Radish, biting infant's tongue;
> And Plantain ribb'd, that heals the reaper's wound;
> And Marj'ram sweet, in shepherd's posie found;
> And lavender, whose spikes of azure bloom
> Shall be, ere-while, in arid bundles bound,
> To lurk amidst the labours of her loom,
> And crown her kerchiefs clean, with mickle rare perfume.

A third stanza names one more herb mentioned by Spenser, Rosmarine. The similarity between the passages lies deeper than the mere listing of herbs, however. The description of useful properties, the choice of epithet, and even the movement of the verse seem in Shenstone's poem to reflect a Spenserian quality. "Pun-provoking Tyme" is like a humorous echo.

Stanza xix of "The Schoolmistress" is also reminiscent of "Muiopotmos." In beginning a description of the urchin about to be caned Shenstone writes:

> Ah luckless he, and born beneath the beam
> Of evil star! it irks me whilst I write!
> As erst the bard by Mulla's silver stream,
> Oft, as he told of deadly dolorous plight,
> Sigh'd as he sung, and did in tears indite.

> For brandishing the rod, she doth begin
> To loose the brogues, the stripling's late delight!
> And down they drop; appears his dainty skin,
> Fair as the furry coat of whitest Ermilin.

"Deadly dolorous plight" brings to mind the first line of "Muiopot-mos": "I sing of deadly dolorous debate." (The phrase "deadly dolorous" occurs nowhere else in Spenser.) And the poet's grief for the ill-starred pupil is amusingly like that of Spenser for ill-fated Clarion:

> Who now shall give unto my heavie eyes
> A well of teares, that all may overflow?
> Or where shall I find lamentable cryes,
> And mournful Tunes enough my griefe to show?

The latter part of Shenstone's stanza xix might be a comic reversal of the arming of young Clarion, whose retainers spread over his back the tawny fur "of some wild Beast" which he had slain. There is another trace of evidence in the first stanza of "The Schoolmistress." Where the edition of 1742 reads "Lend me thy Trumpet, Goddess," the later one has, like an echo from "Muiopotmos": "Lend me thy *clarion,* goddess!"

There is no reference to "Muiopotmos" in Shenstone's letters, and no external evidence that Shenstone read the poem at all. But the quality of these added stanzas in "The Schoolmistress" is per-haps the more remarkable if he was *not* influenced by the tale of the butterfly—if through understanding of Spenser's serious manner in *The Faerie Queene* he was able to divine and share the mood, at once sportive and tender, in which the Elizabethan poet would treat the lightest of mock-epics.

Each version of "The Schoolmistress" is rewarding to the reader who is interested in imitations of Spenser. And the three together show clearly how a young poet, growing to maturity at the height of Pope's fame, first adopted the fashionable attitude toward Spenser, then gradually developed an independent taste for that most Elizabethan of poets.

Under Spenser's influence Shenstone wrote his best poem. But "The Schoolmistress" is as far from slavish imitation as it is from outright caricature. In reading and rereading Spenser Shenstone was moved to write in a way that combined most happily his own best gifts—his eye for detail at once clear-cut and suggestive, his fresh and yet gentle humor, his warmth of feeling for and keen insight into the great and small concerns of children and simple folk. These several qualities have been differently rated by different readers. The early romantic poets valued the tenderness of sentiment which pervades the poem and ignored the burlesque element, while certain present-day critics feel with Richard Graves that the mock-heroic element is the poem's chief distinction and that the purely descriptive later stanzas might be spared for the sake of the "ludicrous Index" of the second version. But Shenstone was never successful when he indulged in sentiment without humor, and his attempts at unrelieved wit are always dull. The excellence of "The Schoolmistress" rests upon the delicate balance of humor and sentiment.

The poem has weathered two hundred years remarkably well. In the first century of its existence it inspired a dozen or more imitations, by poets as well as by poetasters, and won the approval of critics of such dissimilar tastes as Dr. Johnson and Horace Walpole, Thomas Gray, Charles Lamb, Robert Burns, and William Wordsworth. And it still finds admirers among those who come upon it in anthologies of eighteenth-century verse. Rewritten many times over a period of twelve years, compounded of recollections of childhood and echoes from Spenser, of reflections of religious and political opinion, of everyday observation and playful fancy, it yet retains a spontaneity and a charm which have endeared it alike to lovers of Spenser and to those who enjoy the special quality of eighteenth-century poetry.

THOMAS CHATTERTON

Bertrand H. Bronson

EVERYONE at all familiar with Chatterton's story knows that he was a posthumous child. Yet it is doubtful if the fact has ever been given its due weight as a conditioning factor in not so much his physical as his psychic environment. For consider: Chatterton found his ideal father-substitute in William Canynge, the lavish and loving giver of all good things; he found his own deepest identity in Rowley, fifteenth-century poet and historian, receiver of benefits spiritual and material which he repaid with testimonial honor and devotion to the giver; he preferred death to the further chances of life on earth before he had completed his seventeenth year. In a profound sense, the past was Chatterton's future. This precocious and irresistible urge backward was the most vital impulse in his short existence. Its abnormality, we may reasonably believe, finds its wellspring in the equal abnormality of his father's death before the child was born. By this simple fact, an indissoluble bond was dramatically established in Chatterton's infant mind between his father, the past, and death. The father belonged wholly to the past by virtue of the fact that he had ceased to draw breath before ever the son drew the first gasp of life. He had never touched the present: there was a breach of continuity between generation and generation.

The past to a very young child is all one time, just as the present is one, distinct from all that lies back of one's own physical awareness. There is then and now. The summer of 1752, when his father died, was as far away from the boy as any other part of the past. His father was buried, like his other forebears, in St. Mary's across the way, a family mansion where you went to live when you were dead. That was home, a palatial residence more fitting than the temporary lodging to which his mother had transferred her little family after his father's death. St. Mary's was a fine place, spacious, full of fascination. Famous people lived in it, invisibly—"The

Parlyament of Sprytes" would one day testify to this assurance—
and their names were recorded on the monuments there. It would
be natural for his father to have an impressive tomb. Very early
the boy picked his favorite one, and we know in part what use
his imagination was to make of it, his frustrated filial needs swarm-
ing about the Canynge memorials in unrestrained, fantastic self-
fulfillment. By the time he was able to puzzle out the words on
tablet and tomb his emotional life, as the Canynge legend proves,
was too deeply involved here to be dissociated by clearer notions
and distinctions of persons. Rather, it took over the historical record
and fed upon it, transmuting it by a subtle alchemy of which he
alone possessed the secret—bones to coral—into the record of that
imaginary fifteenth-century society of whose doings Chatterton
later made such breathtaking and startlingly full report.

Other significant hints of the associative and affective power of
the child's filial hunger may be collected from the second
"Eclogue," where artistic unity has all but collapsed under the
pressure of unconscious emotional compulsions. The body of the
poem paints with amazing brilliance and speed the pageantry of
the Third Crusade. But this bold and assured canvas has been
enclosed and divided into panels by a weak and unsuitable cheese-
cloth frame. The descriptive narration is assigned entire to the
"pious Nygelle," who, as we learn at the end, has been awaiting
his father's return from some undesignated voyage, and who tags
most stanzas with the sentimental prayer:

> Sprytes of the bleste, and everyche Seyncte ydedde,
> Poure owte youre pleasaunce on mie fadres hedde.

The filial reunion is indicated with a helpless, anticlimactic appeal
to the reader to imagine it for himself. There is pathos here in plenty
but it lies beyond the margin. The mere abstract idea of a meeting
between father and son has served as adequate climax for the
starved psyche of the poet, even where it is an irrelevant intrusion.

We have no direct evidence on the point, but it is a safe inference
that the memory of the elder Chatterton was not denigrated by
his widow. Not herself a strong character, she had married at
eighteen a man twice her own age; and therefore even if she feared

more than loved him, she must have felt, when left at the age of twenty-one with two babies to provide for—a third had died—that times were better when there was a man at the helm. The hard present and the gloomy prospect would not make for a light-hearted home atmosphere, and all references must have pointed the contrast with the past and have exalted the father's stature in his son's imagination. The neighbors would be commiserating ("So young to be left a widow," etc. "Poor child, he never even saw his father," etc.). To a child's mind the inferences would be inescapable. His father, it was plain, was all-important to his family and to him; his father lived in that golden age, the past; his father was dead; and in that case, surely, death (conceived by child and savage as the obverse of life, but yet a conscious state) must be good. By some such associational train of ideas the child's emotional orientations were set in reverse, and the negatives of others became his psychic positives. There was always, moreover, the splendor of St. Mary's at hand to prove that he was right. For St. Mary's was the visible symbol of the difference between the past and the present . . . Whether or not there are errors in the particulars of our hypothesis, it yields conclusions which accord with all the facts presented by Chatterton's life and work.

It is highly indicative, in the light of his subsequent precocity, that the boy was dismissed from his first school as stupidly impervious to knowledge. His mind at that age was too busy with its own inner activity to submit to be distracted. Absorbed by his teeming fantasies, he was as yet insulated against any realization that the drab symbols of modern print could contain value for him, could provide a bridge to parts of his private world that he had not explored. They were associated instead with things that were repellent or at least indifferent to him. The august personages of his fancy would write and express their thoughts in other terms altogether, just as they had dressed more magnificently and built more grandly and lived more dramatically. But when his eye was caught by the old manuscript in his mother's hands, he saw the connection between that mysterious beauty and his other world. His mother perceived her opportunity in his interest—it was her one recorded moment of insight—and found him eager to learn the black letter and read big old books. The road was now open; he quickly entered and took possession of his kingdom.

Grotesquely unsuited to Chatterton's needs as was the so-called "education" provided by Colston's Hospital, and incarcerated as his body was by the strict regulations of the place, he found it by no means intolerable, and the seven years he spent there were probably the happiest of his life. Since the school taught nothing but writing and accounting, there was the utmost freedom to pursue the wayward bent of his own intellectual interests; and the very paucity of subject matter for scholastic instruction could not but have left more time for reading, even if sub rosa in school hours. Besides, as his sister was later to report on the authority of his schoolfellows, "he retired to read at the hours allotted for play." The school's attention to penmanship—for the boys were to be put apprentices and in them it would by no means be held "a baseness to write fair"—could only reinforce that interest which bookish adolescents usually take in their own chirography, and perhaps even encourage the experimental practice of different styles of handwriting. In fact, we know that it was to the verse-minded Phillips, his older schoolfellow and subsequently the junior master at Colston's, that Chatterton brought his first imitation of antique writing on parchment. Luckier for him, perhaps, had he been less expert or his senior better informed! The fact of his attempting this mischief, however, shows that the early fantasies were proceeding apace and beginning to insist on tangible expression. His trying it on the one person of his acquaintance whom he genuinely admired may tell much or little about his motives. Doubtless these were mixed; but the words of Falstaff have a grotesque relevance in this connection: "To counterfeit death when a man thereby liveth is to be no counterfeit." Judged by the measure of vital energy expended, the boy's outer existence, we may readily allow, was the counterfeit, his Rowleian existence was "the true and perfect image of life indeed."

During these years his expanding mind was God's theater. He became a *helluo librorum*. He spent his little allowance on the circulating libraries, and borrowed elsewhere. Between his eleventh and twelfth years, his sister said, he catalogued the books he had read to the number of seventy, mostly in history and divinity. He lived with monastic asceticism, refusing meat and drinking only water, "because he had a work in hand, and would not make himself more stupid than God had made him." Medical research has latterly brought us the assurance that serious deficiencies of certain kinds in the diet can produce extreme psychosomatic excitement, and it seems clear that Chatterton deliberately kept himself in such a state by denying his body the nourishment it needed. Of artificial stimulants such as Barrett, for reasons best known to himself, tried to coax him into taking he had no need: he had already discovered a far cheaper and more efficient mode of inebriation. He saw the matter in a different light; but the Church could have given Rowley some useful hints.[1]

Be that as it may, Chatterton discovered the condition in which he could work most effectively, wherein ideas "streamed into his mind, as it were, most divinely." His nerves exacerbated by spare diet and moonlight, he became more and more intoxicated with the past, and before he left Colston's he had acquired a deal of out-of-the-way learning, in local history, architecture, heraldry, chivalry, paleography, and the elder poets of England. He re-created fourteenth-century Bristol in his imagination, seizing on the pageantry, the chivalry, and those picturesque aspects of it which appealed especially to a boy. He became at home in that society, and shared with surprising particularity in its community life. He would walk out into Redcliffe meadows with his schoolboy friend, William Smith, and in a particular spot "would frequently lay himself down, fix his eyes upon the church, and seem as if he were in a kind of extasy or trance." By this time, apparently, or very little later, Rowley and his fellows had acquired their full proportions in his imagination. It was himself at about this period that he was idealizing when, through the mouth of Rowley, now conceived as an old man, he described the youth of Canynge:

> I saw hym eager gaspynge after lyghte.
> In all hys shepen gambols and chyldes plaie . . .
> I kenn'd a perpled lyghte of Wysdom's raie;

---

1. Fifty years later another poet was recovered from hallucinations by Peacock's timely prescription of mutton chops, well seasoned.

He eate downe learnynge wyth the wastle cake. . . .
Greete yn hys councel for the daies he bore.
All tongues, all carrols dyd unto hym synge,
Wondryng at one soe wyse, and yet soe yinge.

There is no doubt that the examples of Macpherson, whose current fortunes put rash ideas into his head, and Percy's *Reliques,* which Meyerstein calls "almost the efficient poetical cause of Rowley" and "a model to anyone who wished to produce antique verse, and appeal to his century at one and the same time," were a most exciting stimulus to Chatterton's budding creative impulses. Ossian he imitated in a number of pieces which he readily acknowledged upon challenge; and "The Bristowe Tragedy" may rightly be regarded, as Meyerstein says, as his attempt to match the *Reliques.* Sooner or later, however, he came upon a book which has never received its due as Rowley's inspiration, and which has perhaps an even better claim than the other two names to be considered a formative influence on the actual poetry, if not the ambition, of Rowley's creator. This was Elizabeth Cooper's *The Muses' Library,* 1737 (reissued with new title pages, 1738, 1741), a work which deserves to be better known. In this chronologically arranged anthology, extending from Edward the Confessor to Samuel Daniel, and in its readable notes of introduction, Chatterton found abundant encouragement, a variety of poetic types, metrical patterns, stylistic models, which he copied—it would be easy to document the assertion did space permit—now closely, now distantly; a notable example of a poet-monk, Alexander Barclay, praised editorially for his eminence and merit as the improver of our language and for his elegancy of manners (whilst Lydgate is disparaged); and in general a poetic tone and temper highly congenial to his own inclinations at this impressionable moment. In spite of the ostensible historic range of the collection, its whole content, after the first thirty pages, is really sixteenth-century verse. By plan and editorial handling the book suggests a homogeneity among the elder poets in which distinctions of style and language are relatively insignificant. An untutored reader would naturally collect the impression from its pages that the differences of a hundred and fifty years were quite negligible, a matter rather of individuals than of times. Thus it came about that a fifteenth-century Rowley could write as if he lived in the full tide of the sixteenth century.

But the present point is that *The Muses' Library,* by and large, in tone and temper, in metrics and subjects, is at the very heart of the Rowleian afflatus. Of no other single work accessible to Chatterton can such an assertion be made. The pieces in the *Reliques* are for the most part much lower than Rowley's emotional and rhetorical pitch, the temporal range scattered and late. Variety of interest is the key to Percy's effort and method. By comparison *The Muses' Library* is naïve in the extreme; but it communicates the strong impact of those brave translunary things that were most congenial to Rowley's genius. His works belong beside it on the shelf. Spenser's influence it is possible to overemphasize: he is too patient, too leisurely, too involved with ideas to accord with Rowley's impetuous, dramatic, essentially unintellectual temper. Dixon is right in saying that Marlowe is Chatterton's nearest spiritual kinsman.[2] But this avatar of that fiery spirit canceled an old debt by learning most of all from the younger Shakespeare. There is hardly a scene in his masterpiece, "Ælla," that does not owe thanks to some similar scene or passage in comedy, history, or tragedy.[3]

It is well known that, to aid him in his composition, Chatterton drew up alphabetical lists of old words, one ancient-modern, the other modern-ancient, mostly compiled from John Kersey's revision of Phillips' dictionary, *The New World of Words* (1706, *sic*), supplemented from Speght's Chaucer glossary and Bailey's later work. These lists were obviously for the purpose of building up his vocabulary, so that he could think and write in his chosen language, just as anyone would acquire the vocabulary of a foreign tongue. Chatterton often lamented that he knew no tongue but his own; yet he might have comforted himself with the thought that in that he was actually bilingual. It is scarcely to the point that Rowley's language, strictly speaking, had no existence else-

2. W. Macneile Dixon, *Chatterton* (1930), p. 13.

3. *The Two Gentlemen of Verona, Midsummer Night's Dream, The Merchant of Venice, Henry IV, V, VI, Romeo and Juliet, Julius Caesar, Hamlet, Othello, Lear, Macbeth, The Tempest* were all obviously laid under contribution, though Rowley well knew how to subdue them to his own needs.

where than in his own mind and work. The same thing may be said, and truly, of Spenser's language, and Burns's and Hopkins'— and even Shakespeare's! Rowley's language is distilled from the poets, and the glossarists, with whom he was intimately conversant; and he uses it with perfect mastery and sensitive awareness of its capabilities.

> The water slughornes wythe a swotye cleme
> Conteke the dynnynge ayre, and reche the skies . . .
> The gule depeyncted oares from the black tyde,
> Decorn wyth fonnes rare, doe shemrynge ryse;
> Upswalynge doe heie shewe ynne drierie pryde,
> Lyche gore-red estells in the eve-merk skyes;
> The nome-depeyncted shields, the speres aryse,
> Alyche talle roshes on the water side;
> Alenge from bark to bark the bryghte sheene flyes;
> Sweft-kerv'd delyghtes doe on the water glyde.

What antiquating recipe will turn the eighteenth-century music into such as this? On the contrary, this was Chatterton's genuine voice; this was his native speech; in these cadences his thought moved freely, and in them he was most truly at home. The same falling-off in assurance and inspiration occurs when he leaves them for modern speech as when Burns leaves his Ayrshire idiom for contemporary English.

It is natural to suppose that he did not acquire this mastery all at once, however swiftly. And a careful statistical analysis might very probably show an incidence of favorite words, and a varying range of vocabulary, which, together with particular preoccupations of subject and characteristic variations of spelling, would provide clues to the relative order of composition. He may, of course, have worked his poems over as his growing maturity prompted.[4] We have the two versions of the "Battle of Hastings" to show us how rapid this growth was. It is altogether probable that when he told Barrett he himself had written the first version, he was already deep in the composition of the second, and was

4. He must have done so for "Elinoure and Juga" if, as was claimed by his schoolfellow years later, some form of that piece was in existence as early as 1764. For it is highly unlikely that he would have chosen, as the first piece to exhibit Rowley's powers in public print, an early poem which had been laid aside untouched for four years while the genius proceeded on its impetuous course.

confident of its superiority, which he could attribute to the "genuine" Rowley without fear that it would be beneath that level. Similarly, when he told his mother that he had written the "Bristowe Tragedie," the confession was no doubt a private piece of self-criticism, an acknowledgment that Rowley's pinion was for a loftier flight:

> Cannynge & I from common course dyssente;
> Wee ryde the stede, botte yeve to hym the reene;
> Ne wylle betweene crased molterynge bookes be pente,
> Botte soare on hyghe, & yn the sonne-bemes sheene.

A better way than acknowledgment, he soon discovered, was attribution to lesser talents, Iscam, Gorges, or Canynge. Such attributions were critical judgments much less dangerous than confessing oneself an imitator; and they saved Rowley's name just as well for excellence. But, in any case, it is much more probable that so impatient a spirit usually tried a new flight than that he reverted to labor with hammer and file on his earlier things. So that we might put some reliance upon the casual evidences of developmental change.

Now, having achieved poetry of such assured authenticity, what was to be done about it? Here we come face to face with the crucial dilemma of Chatterton's life. It involves us in questions of time and place as well as private psychological problems. There is, of course, no doubt that Chatterton's age felt a strong and steadily increasing interest in the past. Itself one of the most complacent of times, its self-confident expectations of further advance were nourished not only by the current scientific progress but by a vivid conviction of the distance it had already traveled toward rational enlightenment out of ignorance and superstition. The more barbarous the past, the brighter the present. "Let us therefore inspect that obscurity!"

There was little in this impulse that stemmed from respect or veneration. The abstract idea of age, to be sure, was impressive to contemplate; the past was picturesque and romantic, interesting, even awful; but these were the qualities of distance and depended on the point of view of the beholder: they were not values which the past had possessed when it was the present. True value still lay in standards accepted by today, in "those rules of old discovered not devised" which were still current, and in the universal laws which were being established by the new science. Since the value of antiquity was thus for this age almost entirely subjective, imitations, no matter how genuinely and deeply re-creative, could earn no higher credit than that of ingenuity or cleverness—*unless* they were downright successful deceptions. Bring to light genuine relics, or supposed relics, and fame and fortune might follow. Bring forth excellent imitations and nothing followed but mild applause. Hence the way of the literary transgressor never looked more tempting, nor, indeed, at its commencement more innocent; and we are treated in consequence with that curious parade of hoaxes, from Ossian to Ireland, that is so marked a feature of later eighteenth-century literary history. Hence, likewise, the acrimony of the controversies which accompanied the procession: since, for defenders as well as opponents, values were almost entirely conditional upon the bare fact of antiquity, not upon qualities inherent in the documents themselves.

Now Chatterton, it is clear, wrote his Rowleian poetry not to deceive but in response to the deepest promptings of his being. For him the true had no value beyond the sham; in fact, the sham could not be called so without violence to the truth. His emotional maturity, his finest aesthetic perceptions, his deepest inspiration, lay in Rowley. The question of deception was fundamentally irrelevant: Rowley was genuine. But the only way he could win a fair hearing in that time and that place was through deceit.

Yet, making equally for concealment, one can hardly doubt that there were also at work up until the very end obscure but deep-lying compulsions of a private nature in Chatterton's predicament. Names, in their subconscious implications and operations, are curious things to contemplate. "Though my blood run red," warns Ribold in the ballad,

> "My name must not be said.
> Yea, though thou see me fall,
> My name thou must not call!" . . .
> E'en as she spake the fatal word
> Wounded was he with many a sword.

Now Rowley had this primitive significance for Chatterton. He was a projected embodiment of the child's innermost life, an essential personification, emerging from the earliest years, of the dreams and wishes of his secret being. The idea of the first person singular is vague and of late development in comparison with such third-personal projections of identity. When Chatterton began to write poetry, he was Rowley; only by this imaginary identification could he write with confidence and conviction. Rowley's integrity and actuality, the very continuance of that inspiration, depended on such imaginative faith. Had he acknowledged, upon the challenge of outsiders, that he was merely "pretending," and that Rowley was really himself, himself as defined by his social context and others' ideas of him as well as his own, it is hardly possible that he could have continued his make-believe. Rowley in the charity school daylight would have evaporated, leaving only the absurd mockery of this Bristol apprentice seriously trying to write poetry like a medieval monk. So long as Chatterton continued to write poetry under the Rowleian inspiration, so long, it appears to me, would he be committed to the vital necessity of preserving his secret. Artistic self-preservation depended on his persistence in the Great Lie. To confess was to have done, once and for all. As to morals, therefore, Coleridge, Keats, Rossetti, and every other admirer of the poetry is guilty of complicity with Chatterton.

Indeed, even if he kept his secret, it became every day more doubtful that he would be heard. When Chatterton turned for encouragement to the only persons within reach who had an interest in antiquity, he found them cold to poetry. What Barrett wanted was illustrations for his history of Bristol: only on that basis was he willing to entertain verse. Burgum and Catcott had a still more restricted view. Thus, to private necessity and the general pressures of the age were added peculiar limitations of place; and Chatterton, eager for fame, acceded without question to these conditions of Rowley's survival. So long as he could stave off the demand for the production of the documents themselves, he found it easy to feed these local antiquaries the kind of draff and husks for which they clamored: pedigrees, deeds of gift, architectural notes. Never was there a more willing suspension of disbelief than theirs. There might be a certain amount of fraud somewhere, they saw; but it was preposterous to suppose that the boy should have invented everything. Encouragement was their cue: and when they had won his confidence, he might provide them with the originals which he was holding back, and they could judge for themselves and dispense with his services. But he had his own reasons for remaining indispensable. The few "originals" which he produced, with an almost contemptuous lack of due precaution, seemed to pass well enough; but if he was to be condemned to copying off on parchment all Rowley's works, present and to come, the prospect was gloomy and the chances of detection enormously increased. Before long it became clear to him that these owls would never understand that Rowley's poetry was the Thing, and that he must find other foster fathers if his ambitions were to be realized. He must try elsewhere; and who so likely to listen as Dodsley, the publisher of Percy's *Reliques?* So he wrote Dodsley, offering "Ælla" in a letter of incredible naïveté; and was of course completely ignored. When a second letter, hardly so wise as the first, elicited no response, he turned to Horace Walpole, this time having the sense to enclose specimens of Rowley's wares. Here his success was immediate and overwhelming: this must have been the golden moment of his earthly life. Walpole not only found his communication "very valuable" and his notes "learned," but went on: "Give me leave to ask you where Rowley's poems are to be found. I should not be sorry to print them, or at least a specimen of them, if they have never been printed." At last Chatterton had found his own Canynge, the patron who would open all the doors to fortune and fame; and Rowley would come forth from the most distinguished press in England, that which had but a decade before ushered out the lofty odes of Gray!

The sequel is well known. Further inquiry convinced Walpole that the pieces were spurious. He thereupon recommended to Chatterton to be a diligent attorney's apprentice, and told him "that when he should have made a fortune he might unbend himself with the studies consonant to his inclinations." So, in an instant, all the high hopes were dashed to the ground.

In the first bitterness of disappointment, Chatterton started a poem of hate to Walpole, which is important to us for three reasons: (1) its self-pity contains an overt avowal of his abiding filial need, now frustrated anew by Walpole's refusal to fill the vacancy; (2) it is a tacit acknowledgment of his authorship of Rowley; (3) it expresses a defiant faith in Rowley's ultimate survival.

> Walpole, I thought not I should ever see
> So mean a heart as thine has proved to be.
> Thou who, in luxury nurst, behold'st with scorn
> The boy, who friendless, fatherless, forlorn,
> Asks thy high favour—thou mayst call me cheat.
> Say, didst thou never practise such deceit?
> Who wrote Otranto? . . .
>   But I shall live and stand
> By Rowley's side, when thou art dead and damned.

The poem was never finished.

The same tide of effort to burst the Bristol dam which carried the appeals to Dodsley and Walpole seems to have prompted him to send "Elinoure and Juga" to the newly established *Town and Country Magazine*. The poem, "Written three hundred Years ago by T. Rowley, a Secular Priest," was dated "Bristol, May, 1769." If the date is correct—the poem appeared in the May number of the magazine—it may be that Chatterton was encouraged to send it by Walpole's being so completely deceived by his first communications in the preceding March.[5] After the shock of Walpole's considered negative judgment, Chatterton seems to have tried nowhere else with Rowley until July of the following year, when he sent the "Charitie" ballade to the same magazine. The publisher did not print it that month, and inside the August title page Chatterton would have read: "The Pastoral from Bristol, signed D.D., has some share of merit: but the author [*sic*] will, doubtless, discover upon another perusal of it, many exceptional passages." But by the time this number appeared Chatterton was dead.

In the meantime Chatterton had been growing up. He still be-

---

5. It is surely one of the most wryly comic events of Chatterton's career that this poem, sent at the age of sixteen but possibly written several years earlier, had the fortune to be modernized the following month, in the pages of the same magazine, by a Westminster scholar (Robert Nares), signing "S.W.A., aged 16," clearly a boy of forward parts!

lieved in Rowley; but it was becoming all too plain that Rowley could do nothing for him in his present need. To find his account with his own age he would have to turn to other courses. He would have to learn another language, less native to him but better understood by the public he had to address. He had already been feeling out these possibilities for some time. With his negative orientation toward the present, it was inevitable that he should turn to satire. This was the obverse of the shield. Everything positive that as yet he had to say lay in Rowley. The first pieces in modern English to reveal any individuality, therefore, were satirical attacks: "Sly Dick" and "Apostate Will." It is of some psychological significance that the first deals with filched treasure, the second with dissembling. It is also no accident that one of the most affective concepts in all Chatterton's work is that of secret, uphoarded wealth, its discovery and safeguarding, the miser's chest, the "gouler's" (usurer's) gold, the treasure chest, the cave or cavern, the casket, or coffin, the murky wood, the underground well.

Disregarding his journalistic prose, which signifies nothing but a *cacoethes scribendi,* and the urge to see his own words—any words of his—in print, we watch him now attempting occasional verse on various subjects and in various kinds—'prentice work, in large part empty of emotional content. Amongst it are several poems addressed to "the fair." In all these his emotional immaturity is painfully evident. He borrows the attitude of conventional gallantry, or the cynical one of the circle of young apprentices among whom he was picking up a knowledge of life and manners, and by overemphasis compensates for extreme youth at every turn.

Churchill's recent satires now provided him with congenial models for violent personal invective; and he adopted the "patriotic," anti-authoritarian point of view with the same facility that he had applied to other kinds of journalism. The outcry and noise and ill manners all suited his exacerbated spirit, and he aped the conventional attitudes of party with perfect mimicry. But apart from a pervasive animosity, a general hostility which flared to a brighter intensity when its fuel was some known personality, he had no convictions. Clever, even talented, though it was, this sort of work grew on the topsoil of his mind: it was rootless. Intellectually and emotionally he was a mere child in the political sphere, as he had been in the amatory one: as yet he was not within possible reach of any deep and genuine experience in these directions. And unfortunately he had met no one, man or woman, who could or would teach him, or with sympathetic understanding advise patience at this crucial period.

But in Rowley he had already grown up. In Rowley he had achieved a rich and deep experience. Its authenticity was a touchstone which only served to reveal the shallowness of his other attitudes.[6] And what, and who, was Rowley? *Vox et praeterea nihil!* A bodiless ghost, addressing an audience that except for one solitary soul had died about the year 1600. To the interests of today, even to the valid and insistent interests of maturing youth, Rowley was dead. Already receding into the distance, in face of the hurry and stress of Chatterton's life in London, he could hardly be resurrected. There was nothing in that life to fill his place. Yet he was Chatterton himself: the embodiment, the articulate record of the most intense life Chatterton had ever known. The dichotomy was too poignant to be endured. At last, the poet and his age were of one opinion. If the age was unable to accept Rowley as Chatterton, there was yet an opposite way out, satisfactory to all concerned. On the night of August 24, 1770, Chatterton took it, shut the doors of the present, and became Rowley forever. The world has been content to remember him so.

When he decided to go home to the past, Chatterton did not know what the world might conclude. The chances are that he thought he and Rowley would both be forgotten. Nothing that he had written had reached print over his own signature. Nothing— not even the "African Eclogues"—had been adjudged by that objectively critical intelligence to be as good as Rowley's poetry, or good enough, therefore, to deserve his name. And, except for

---

6. With strictest accuracy he gauged that impact in his fantastic "will":
   "Rowley . . . my first, chief curse!
   For had I never known the antique lore,
   I ne'er had ventured from my peaceful shore
   To be the wreck of promises and hopes,
   A Boy of Learning, and a Bard of Tropes;
   But happy in my humble sphere had moved,
   Untroubled, unrespected, unbeloved."

"Elinoure and Juga," which had caused no perceptible stir of excitement, all Rowley's poetry lay still in manuscript, in the hands of dolts who did not appreciate it, and with slight chance of being printed. These facts have a bearing on the question of his persistence in a lie, and his determination to take his secret with him to the grave. What were the profit of announcing to the world that he had written what no man regarded, when until now his record of denial was consistent and literally perfect? Why idly brand oneself a liar, as the last act of one's life, when nothing was to be gained except obloquy? And if, by a stroke of luck, Rowley should be printed and appreciated, his best chances for survival, and for Chatterton as his discoverer, lay, as experience seemed to prove, in his being taken for a genuine ancient. Why, then, destroy that slender hope?

It is perhaps useless to surmise what Chatterton might have done had he chosen to live; but we may be fairly certain that of Rowley, even under the most favorable circumstances, we should have had little more. The better informed he became, the less confident he would be of his ability to write fifteenth-century English good enough to fool the experts, and concomitantly the harder it would prove to lose himself in his fantasy. But even more important, there were too many interests in the maturing mind which would be pressing for expression, and to which Rowley, with his special handicaps, could not possibly give voice. There is some evidence that Chatterton was trying latterly to widen the Rowleian base and range, and we may perhaps regard the japes and fragments appearing only in the collected remains as tentative experiments toward compromise between Rowley and Chatterton, the past and the present. For this reason, it is probable that the best of Rowley is not the very last, but was done in the long solitary hours of freedom in that first year or so in Lambert's office, in the full flood of the early adolescent tide of hope and belief. Rowley was a true Bristolian and one can hardly believe that he ever visited London, in spite of the date, July 4, 1770, on the "Excellent Ballade of Charitie." It is significant that in sending that lovely poem to the magazine from London Chatterton marked it as from Bristol.

What he would have done in other kinds is probably still more idle to conjecture. His natural bent was clearly toward drama. But if he was going to write a first-class satirical comedy of manners, with his handicaps in social background and education he had a long, hard road ahead of him. To suppose that he could ever have achieved a first-rate tragedy, with the contemporary influences and examples at work upon him, is to suppose that he could have done more in that age than anyone else was able to do with whatever advantage. And for great verse satire or a great novel his knowledge of life and reflection upon it would long be insufficient. All in all, he may have rung down the curtain at the climax of the play.

WILLIAM COWPER

Kenneth MacLean

E VERYONE knows Cowper's poems and letters, but how many have seen that small volume, the *Memoir of the Early Life of William Cowper, Esq. Written by Himself?* Beginning ominously, this little piece of psychic Hogarth achieves the ultimate in terror. We see a young man, thirty-two years old, unnerved by the prospect of a public examination for a parliamentary clerkship, for which he had been studying a half year without any perception. He takes a vacation at Margate, but returns little improved for the final push. The day preceding the public examination was one of confused suicidal purposes. No one intent on destroying himself ever turned so quickly from poison to pond to knife to halter. That wayward mind, so evident in Cowper's writings where it assumes runaway symbols, was never more shifting than on this semifatal day. The morning of the examinations found Cowper in a swoon on his chamber floor, the much too elegant garter with which he had attempted to hang himself having broken. Now follow days of paralyzing religious thoughts. The sinner eats alone in the dark. Dreams terrify him at night.

Satan plied me closely with horrible visions, and more horrible voices. My ears rang with the sound of torments, that seemed to await me. Then did the pains of hell get hold of me, and, before daybreak, the very sorrows of death encompassed me. A numbness seized upon the extremities of my body, and life seemed to retreat before it; my hands and feet became cold and stiff; a cold sweat stood upon my forehead; my heart seemed at every pulse to beat its last, and my soul to cling to my lips, as if on the very brink of departure.

At this moment of final terror madness came upon Cowper with a darkness. He was taken to Dr. Cotton's College for the Insane at St. Albans. Here we will not so much say that his mind was restored as that his sins were forgiven under the care of the pious little physician. He left St. Albans in a state of religious euphoria. Nothing is more terrible than neurotic ecstasy. At Huntingdon, where his brother had found him rooms, we see him praying deliriously in the fields and weeping in church for the love he felt for the faces there. On November 11, 1765, a rather manic Cowper sank down into the comfort of the home of Mrs. Unwin whom hereafter we shall come to associate with mother and chickens, but who will remain for us very much of a quiet mystery.

Cowper's *Memoir* is a document in neurotic terror, and the terror it directly describes is, we feel, central to all his writings. True, he expresses many feelings that seem conventionally and pleasantly romantic—a love of the country, a liking for simplicity, a sentimental taste for tear-stained faces. But such sentiments cannot be understood in reference to a romantic movement: they can be seen properly only in reference to the Cowper whose nerves needed the isolation of Olney, whose neurotic rigor asked for a severe puritan plainness in speech, whose instability expected tears. Neurosis and not the romantic movement was responsible for everything that he was as a writer—the very need itself to write and enshrine the dying life, the tone of sincerity which cannot still tell quite all the truth, the limited symbolism from the garden of Orchardside. Needless to say, Cowper interests our times greatly, hardly less than Byron whom he so much resembles in their common sense of injury and damnation.

> The world and I fortuitously met;
> I ow'd a trifle, and have paid the debt;
> She did me wrong, I recompens'd the deed . . .

We wonder particularly about his devastating modern nihilism which allowed for daily walks and daily letters and a daily number of verses but left the whole great course of things to a ruining providence.

His early poetry, much of it, was a kind of shiny pastoral addressed to a dazzling Delia, a star seen through that remarkable instrument, "passion's optic." Daydreams, parting, absence, curl-saving—and then this course of true love was suddenly interrupted by illness, and the poetry to Delia becomes something else. Now in a poem Cowper records a dream in which the beloved appears as he is trying to drink from a stream that at once flies and thickens into mud. She gives him water in a goblet, and then takes him strangely into a flight from which he falls with dreamlike gravity. The poem ends with the waking hope that the real Delia will come to him when health, in the unreasonable way of Cowper's causeless world, will suddenly return. This poem of terror is followed by related poems in the next few years, in some of them those painful images of shipwreck which Cowper's imperial English imagination fully explored. Then in his own "storm of '63" which took him to Dr. Cotton's, we come to a poem which, for language and image, could hardly be surpassed in the presentation of terror.

> Man disavows, and Deity disowns me:
> Hell might afford my miseries a shelter;
> Therefore hell keeps her ever hungry mouths all
>   Bolted against me.
>
> Hard lot! encompass'd with a thousand dangers;
> Weary, faint, trembling with a thousand terrors;
> I'm called, if vanquish'd, to receive a sentence
>   Worse than Abiram's.
>
> *Him* the vindictive rod of angry justice
> Sent quick and howling to the centre headlong;
> *I,* fed with judgment, in a fleshly tomb, am
>   Buried above ground.

This has the accent of Hopkins, of the last "terrible sonnets." We suspect that Hopkins knew Cowper, who like himself felt at times that rather sadistic bursting of colored beauty on the senses which excites to divine love. Such affinities might give hints to Cowper's biographers, who as yet have said nothing about the psychology of this poet who has left such a complete account of himself.

Cowper, as we have seen, interpreted his emotional variations in the language of the rising evangelicalism of his day. Elation was a sign of grace and faith, depression of guilt and rejection. It was in a state of elation that he had left Dr. Cotton's to enter the pious Unwin home, and grace still continued with him when, after Mr. Unwin's death, he and Mary left the blue willows of Huntingdon for Olney, a center of experiential religion with the presence of John Newton. He lived closely in the first years in Olney: the ego was hardly ever exposed. He did however attend

Newton's prayer meetings, begun in 1769, where with some embarrassment he told the story of his own religious experience, a
story that attains the status of a fixed idea in his writings. When
after the first years in Olney faith began to give way to depression,
Newton urged Cowper to interest himself in the composition of
hymns for their prayer meetings. Thus his hymns were composed
for the little saints of Olney, who, we trust, were not among those
who gossiped to Newton when in later years the poet was seen
entering a lady's carriage to visit a charming Catholic family, the
Throckmortons, often called in the letters "the Throcks"! The
basic imagery of the Olney hymns is, I believe, the country village.
We hear indeed as so frequently in Protestant religious writings
the language of landholding and property. To speak of the religious
experience in the language of the village was to speak closely to the
parishes of England, and of New England as well, where the spirit
of Cowper, its healthier part so largely exploited by Emerson, has
been particularly at home. In these country hymns we feel little of
that sense of innocence which Blake is shortly to associate with the
village symbol. The Olney hymns are poems in religious, in primitive fear, and emotions of fear, let us remember, were little considered by poets in Cowper's time. Part of the fear stems from a
feeling of hatred for God, imaged in materials we think of especially as Emily Dickinson's, steel and stone. The art of these
hymns in all ways suggests this New England poet, who perhaps
did not overlook one title, "The Narrow Way." Cowper has her
same restricting wit which will call the Lord's Supper a "treat."
He has too some of her expanding imaginative phrasing. And in
both poets agony is lyrical. These careful hymns are reassuring
to anyone anxious about Cowper's art. He was not above allowing
his publisher to emend his poems. Nonetheless, he knew the business of poet.

The writing of the Olney hymns preceded another period of
insanity, in 1773 and 1774, accompanied by the "fatal dream"
which left with Cowper the lasting impression that he was damned.
Hereafter he was never without depression. All religious exercises
ended, even grace and private prayer. The withdrawal from church
developed into a distaste for the cloth, whom he was known to

avoid in his walks. Alone now with Mrs. Unwin at Orchardside, he sought distraction in simple human activities: in gardening, in keeping his pet hares—Tiney, Puss, and Bess—in making furniture for the house. But carpentry was hard on the eyes, and so was sketching, he discovered. The search for proper distraction led Cowper again to poetry, and the greenhouse in the narrow walled garden at Olney, lined with mats and fragrant with flowers, became a poet's room. Poetry was not only easy on the eyes. It becomes clear as one examines Cowper's life that terror took a vocal form for him. He heard voices, as in that "fatal dream" when he heard the word of despair. From his account of his early troubles in the *Memoir* it is evident that he tried to drive out such voices by quoting reassuring Bible sentences to himself. Hereabouts lies the reason for his life-long battle with the Deists who would destroy the essential, truly saving word of God. In time Cowper discovered that the poetic creation of language was very helpful in drowning out inner voices of despair.

> There is a pleasure in poetic pains
> Which only poets know.

And as he wrote to save his own soul, he developed with his longer poems an aesthetic which had something to do with the saving of the soul of poetry in his day. Before Wordsworth he was spokesman for a prose-like speech in poetry, and though there is much of the homely elegance of a Hitchcock chair in his verse, he sometimes achieved Wordsworthian naturalness, in the blank verse of "The Task" most frequently. He also practiced and preached in his longer poems that free-running, digressive manner which Wordsworth, Keats, and Byron were to exploit in a poetry of association. The winged fancy, the runaway horse, the grasshopper —these varied symbols preside over Cowper's new achievement in free form.

In a period of eleven excited months he wrote the eight long poems comprising the volume of 1782, which we may especially admire for its splendid picture of the England of that day. It is an England that has in a way ceased to be England. The international flavor is everywhere, in tea, in silks, in Negro servants, in Chinese fans and Indian cane. Emporium of this England is London, its wharves fragrant with the spices of ships harbored from India. Here are the merchants investing in foreign trade, and their lawyers. Some merchants are bankrupt and in prison, and their attorney now is the poet Cowper, himself always hard up and ready to plead that "insolvent innocence go free." Behind this London lies the sea, and Cowper who devoured all the voyage literature he could borrow is not deficient in giving us a sense of the sea—its flags and guns and canvas and wind. These poems exhibit that power prized by the modern poet of seeing a society standing on its economic foundations. Cowper could see England as "commercial England." He can give us that whole blue period, of blue sea and blue naval uniforms and Lowestoft china and blue pipe smoke. He pictures commercial England, and then proceeds to draw up a moral balance sheet for a commercial society where luxury has brought weakness. Men are collecting antiques, listening to music, honoring Handel on Sunday, and dancing on softest nights to sweetest music. "Hark! how it floats upon the dewy air!" Cowper's social poems bespeak a horror of effeminacy, a horror felt by his age but felt particularly strongly by this poet who deeply sensed his own personal weakness. Out of this weakness came the strength, comparable to Wordsworth's, with which he spoke for a more masculine England, a more English England, the England of the oak.

The poems of 1782 set some of the themes for "The Task," an important national poem. But "The Task" is more than just a social poem. Its chief theme is surely nature and the soul. Of all things in nature, air and wind seemed to have interested Cowper most. He was allergic to the bad air of London. The air at Olney he found healthful in summer but in the winter damp and aguish, especially at Orchardside where the rooms were filled with melancholy vapors rising from a water-filled cellar. This circumstance, in part, prompted Cowper and Mrs. Unwin to move from Olney to Weston-Underwood, leaving a home of twenty years, the house associated with nearly all the poetry. Empty, this old home looked like a little House of Usher—"no inapt resemblance of a soul that

God has forsaken." Cowper's attention to air is reflected in his interest in flowers and flowering shrubbery. He loved the air of flowers—in the garden, carnation, mignonette, canary lavender—by the summerhouse, pinks and roses—in the Wilderness, honeysuckle and lilac. No one was more sensitive than this poet to the fragrance of England's disappearing commons. It was perhaps Cowper's interest in air which drew him to the Throckmortons' lawn many a time to see a balloon go up in the year after Montgolfier's experiment. Cowper the correspondent always assured his confiding friends that he was "hermetically sealed." But it was the wind moving through the air that the poet was most conscious of, the wind that in the first splendid descriptions in "The Task" sweeps the skirts of the woods, making the sound of waves on a shore. It was Cowper's Leibnizian notion that nature, the dancing girl, is never at rest; and he supposed that the wind was the primary element at the center of this motion. These thoughts are expressed in a passage in the excellent first book of "The Task," beginning "By ceaseless action all that is subsists." But there is no Leibnizian harmony for Cowper, for like Hopkins he felt God beating in the wind, the God of his own damnation—"He who has commanded me to wither,"—He by whose will "the flow'rs of Eden felt the blast,"—He by whose pleasure still the fiend of famine "blows mildew from between his shrivel'd lips." This presence makes the final experience of nature a fearful one. And so, while there are many rhythmical moments in "The Task," its essential mood is fear. Aren't we always retreating from the fresh open scene where Wordsworth keeps us into weather-houses, greenhouses, alcoves, colonnades? Aren't we clinging beside garden walls? Isn't the huge Russian ice palace pictured in the opening of the fifth book simply the greatest and biggest shelter of all? Aren't we shutting shutters on winter evenings, giving ourselves occupational therapy with our books, our weaving of nets for fruit, our twining of silken threads on ivory reels? Peeping at the world through the "loop-holes of retreat"—the newspapers! The stricken deer is hiding in the shade.

But comedy always stands closely beside fear in Cowper's pages. Shy in any company, Cowper found relief for his embarrassment in watching people's motions and gestures. Sterne would call this "translating." Imprisoned in his Olney house, he was devoted to the street window. Obviously a peace treaty had been signed: "Every man's posture bespoke a pacific turn of mind." He saw the surface of human life, and this surface is essentially comic. His delightful poem, "Conversation," is full of the comedy lying before an eye which would see a person conversing with his face too close to the other person's. In his very first poem we are amused simply in watching the walk of a peasant who is missing one heel. "The Task" is rich in comic observation. Indeed, it begins with all the comedy that can slide, twitch, sprawl, or doze on the seat of a chair. Cowper especially loved the comedy that lies in shadows.

With the writing of "The Task" much of his creative work as poet was done. "The mind of man is not a fountain, but a cistern." Poetry had something of a period in his life, but not the letter which he always wrote. He was an authority on the letter, who knew among other things that the "epistolary race" is "always won by him that comes in last." His letters have often been called the finest in English. One claim surely might well be made for them—that they contain as much of the myth of England as any piece of English literature. Here is the English character fully represented in the writings of one whom we should think incapacitated to the point of being unable to represent anything. This may be a commentary at once upon psychological disturbance and upon the suitability of English culture to a human soul. The Cowper of the letters is the complete Englishman—liking a well-cocked hat —taking his exercise—medicating shamelessly—very timid about bathing machines—feminine in his humor—liking privacy—defending the home against polygamous relations—relishing "fine" food, even as much as Hazlitt—like Lamb, deaf to music—gentlemanly but not lordly—charitable—patriotic—independent—bold enough to be ready to thresh Dr. Johnson's old jacket till the pension jingled in his pocket! These letters are an intimate picture of an Englishman. And since they are letters they particularly exhibit an English trait without which there would be no letters—a deep sense of friendship, not unlike a Prospero's.

So much health combined with such weakness, the very health growing out of the disease—this essential but much forgotten irony lies in Cowper's letters. While his despondency, he thought, would not be suspected by a visitor, it is apparent enough in his letters where we hear a good deal, but not too much, about this illness which crippled him in his morning writing hours, allowing him a certain alertness only toward the later afternoon when, as we remember, the pet hares too were more lively. The neurotic death-sense moves all through these letters, growing more intense rather than less with age. Against the stream of time (and Cowper remembered Shakespeare's thought that no man bathes twice in the same stream) we see him and Mary Unwin, who surely shared his terrors, setting up a kind of still life for themselves which a vivacious Lady Austen was not allowed to disrupt. We sense terror as well as melancholy in these letters when Cowper takes us inside his mind where thoughts stand in sober livery, the tallest and loudest among them calling, "It is all over with thee; thou hast perished." We partly see the dreams of this mind, and we hear Cowper express his disturbing and very modern opinion that dreams are true.

The tone of despondency and terror is just as it should be in the letters. Cowper has subdued the direct statement into quiet phrases and sentences. Some of these we shall never forget: "On this very day twenty-two years ago left I London." "Yesterday was one of my terrible seasons . . ." "Nature revives again; but a soul once slain lives no more." "There is a mystery in my destruction . . ." One sentence we shall remember because it puzzles: "Mine is merely a case of relaxation." The sense of terror is restrained in the letters. It is also, we note, most skillfully transferred into the symbols of those excellent poems frequently enclosed in a letter. In some of these Cowper has drawn upon his beloved sea imagery as in "The Castaway," his last poem and an ultimate image in lonely terror. One sea poem in the letters is the splendid Horatian piece on the halibut which survived as an egg in the great immensity of the ocean, only to be devoured by the poet. To swim the wide dangerous seas

> Where flat Batavia just emerging peeps
> Above the brine,

only to lie dead on a poet's plate—this thing was always happening in this Humian world of no proper cause and effect. Out of his deep conviction about such matters Cowper wrote for enclosure in another letter the verses, "On the Loss of the Royal George." Eight hundred men on a stout oaken ship safely in harbor, and then a little land breeze shook the shrouds, and not a life was saved! No world is more terrible than one where this kind of thing can happen. And Cowper saw this happening every day. Most of these poems, which are surely Cowper's greatest achievement, draw their imagery from the garden at Orchardside and near by. And this is what we see about this garden. We see the head of a rose snapped off as one is shaking raindrops from it. We see kittens hypnotized by a snake's forked tongue, and we see a large man killing the small snake. We see a pet rabbit going to his last long home. Tiney had been safe in the garden walls from the pursuit of greyhounds. He had known the security of russet apple peels and Turkey carpets. But the protected life had no security from death. We see birds about this garden. There are two goldfinches in separate cages: one works his way out of his cage, but unable perhaps because of his own deep experience of terror to seek his own freedom, he clings to the cage of the other bird. Mirror everywhere for Cowper and Mary Unwin. We see in one of the best of these poems a raven nesting in a neighbor's elm. Ravens may have the gift of prophecy, but this bird has no idea what is going to happen to her, nor does she know the map of danger. Cowper observed her anxiety during an April storm lest the bough break and her eggs be lost. The eggs went not to the storm but to Hodge who climbed the tree to get them as a present for his pregnant wife. Hardy must have loved Cowper.

> An earthquake may be bid to spare
> The man that's strangled by a hair.
> Fate steals along with silent tread,
> Found oft'nest in what least we dread,
> Frowns in the storm with angry brow,
> But in the sunshine strikes the blow.

Cowper's poems and letters are a record of a terror which must interest the modern reader. What is particularly remarkable about this record is its mark, often painful, of sincerity and simple truth. Nothing has been faked. This is human terror. This is terror in a garden.

BURNS AND "GUID BLACK PRENT"

J. W. Egerer

MY Proposals for publishing I am just going to send to the Press," Burns wrote his friend Robert Aiken on April 3, 1786. Eleven days later these proposals were ready for distribution, and the work of compiling, printing, and paying for the Kilmarnock edition was under way. Could Burns clear nine guineas—"the price of wafting me to the torrid zone"— his sole reason for publishing would be realized; even before this goal was reached, however, we sense in the poet's correspondence an excitement which was to drive from his mind all thoughts of migrating to Jamaica, an excitement which was to carry him to the peak of literary and social fame in Edinburgh within a few months. This experience was also to be fatal, for once Burns felt the exhilaration of knowing that he had a reading public, he was a marked man. The effect that this knowledge was to have on him and on his future work is the subject of this essay.

Burns began his composing spontaneously and for a rustic and friendly audience. Like the bards—and he was often fond of comparing himself to a bard—he first composed primarily for listeners rather than readers. Had he not thought it expedient to leave Scotland and, in order to do so, to raise the money necessary for the ocean voyage to the West Indies, it is quite possible that the world would never have seen his poems. This initial enlargement of his audience through the 612 copies of the Kilmarnock edition opened up the vista of an even larger group of readers could he but push his efforts beyond the borders of Ayrshire.

From Burns's first biographer, Heron, we learn of the enthusiasm with which the first edition of *Poems, Chiefly in the Scottish Dialect* was received.

Old and Young, high and low, grave and gay, learned or ignorant, all were alike delighted, agitated, transported. I was at that time resident in *Galloway*, contiguous to *Ayrshire:* and I can well remember, how that even plough-boys and maid-servants would have gladly bestowed the wages which they earned the most hardly, and which they wanted to purchase necessary clothing, if they might but procure the works of BURNS.

Purchasers of this volume probably provided a good cross section of Ayrshire society, from the humblest scullery maid up through the gentlemen of the county to the lairds, and even to the peerage. With such startling success behind him it is little wonder that Burns could set his sights on vaster prospects.

John Wilson, the printer of the Kilmarnock edition, refused to print a second edition unless he had £27 to hand, perhaps, as Franklyn Bliss Snyder thinks, because he felt that the market was satiated and he was unwilling to risk another venture. At all events, Wilson's refusal to cooperate was not such a blow to the poet, for at this point he was willing to try a larger gamble. The October issue of *The Edinburgh Magazine, or Literary Miscellany,* published November 3, 1786, had carried a review of the Kilmarnock edition. Was not this enough to whet the appetite which was beginning to crave more readers? Burns was still speaking of the projected trip to Jamaica in September and excusing himself to his friend John Richmond for not being on his way because "The Nancy, in which I was to have gone, did not give me warning enough." He had had money when the Nancy sailed but, it seems to me quite obvious, he was purposely delaying because of the lure of more poems to appear in "guid, black prent." A month and a half later enough printer's ink had seeped into his veins to cause him to write to his friend and patroness, Mrs. Dunlop, assuming as he did so the technical jargon of the professional author, "I am thinking to go to Edinburgh . . . to throw off a second Impression of my book." On November 28, 1786, he rode into the capital.

The effect of Burns's arrival on Edinburgh society was immediate and spontaneous. In little more than a week after his coming he was writing to Gavin Hamilton that plans were already well under way for the publication of a second edition (the subscription bills for it were to appear the day after the letter was penned), and such worthies as the Earl of Glencairn and Henry David Erskine, as well as the members of the fashionable Caledonian Hunt, to which organization Burns dedicated the Edinburgh edition, had already taken him under their collective wing. Here at last was fame in her most intoxicating form! An audience of discriminating gentlefolk and an edition of poems which was to run to some three thousand copies.

But Burns was not long in realizing that these new-found friends were little more than a claque. "The novelty of a Poet in my obscure situation . . . has raised a partial tide of public notice which has borne me to a height, where I am absolutely, feelingly certain my abilities are inadequate to support me," he writes Mrs. Dunlop in the middle of January, 1787. What does he mean when he uses the word "abilities"? Surely he does not doubt his poetical abilities; he must refer to what he considers his lack of the social graces or the ability to keep up with the gay whirl. Other letters during this period are bristling with remarks such as, "I know very well, the novelty of my character has by far the greatest share in the learned and polite notice I have lately got." "Novelty may attract the attention of mankind a while; to it I owe my present eclat." "To the rich, the great, the fashionable, the polite, I have no equivalent to offer." "I am afraid my numerous Edin^r friendships are of so tender a construction that they will not bear carriage with me," etc., etc. And in the *Journal of the Border Tour,* he writes, ". . . the Greenland bay of Indifference amid the noise and nonsense of Edin^r." What Burns did realize, then, and realize thoroughly, was that he had acquired an audience that was ephemeral. He was still seeking an outlet for his talents, and, in spite of the numerous gibes at the brittle and transient qualities of city life and the yearnings to get back to the farm which appear over and over again in the letters written during the first few months of 1787, he was already thoroughly infected by the virus of publication. That his fashionable readers would pass with the season was a fact which, luckily, he knew (did not Lady Christian Graham write to her niece of the Edinburgh edition that she was "tea'zd to subscribe to it"?). But where could he find an audience that would appreciate his real, his poetical talents? It was for this audience that he left Ayrshire, but as yet he had not found it.

Let us return for a moment to a phrase quoted above: "my abilities are inadequate to support me." If there ever was a poet who was sure of his poetical abilities, it was Burns. He writes to Dr. John Moore in February, 1787: "I am very willing to admit that I have some poetical abilities." Throughout this same period in his life, when he was so vitriolic about the reception of himself as a curiosity, one comes across such sentences in the letters as the following: "The appellation of, a Scotch Bard, is by far my highest pride; to continue to deserve it is my most exalted ambition.— Scottish scenes, and Scottish stories are the themes I could wish to sing." His scorn for the Edinburgh gentry and their opinion of him, as well as a definite feeling of hurt pride because the élite did not really appreciate his poetry, is amply revealed when he writes, again to Mrs. Dunlop, "I set as little by kings, lords, clergy, critics, &c. as all these respectable Gentry do by my Bardship," and he is not using the word "Bardship" facetiously. What then was his attitude toward his future literary work in the spring of 1787? He was still looking for a sympathetic and understanding reading public and, of course, a medium by which his talents could be exhibited to that public. He found that medium in James Johnson.

This Edinburgh music engraver published the first volume of *The Scots Musical Museum* in May, 1787, and in it appeared two of Burns's songs—an inauspicious beginning indeed for one who was to contribute over two hundred more to the five volumes that comprise the set. Johnson offered the opportunity for further publication as well as for changing the entire course of Burns's poetical activity. From then on he was to be primarily a song writer. During the last eight years of his life most of his talents were turned in this direction. Had it not been for Johnson, the "Songs of Burns," which as Carlyle writes, "we reckon by far the best that Britain has yet produced," might, in large part, never have been composed. Thus, in a few short months, most of that vivid and exciting gift of lyricism and satire was turned to writing, rewriting, and editing for the *Museum* and, later, for George Thomson's *Scottish Airs*. He had, it is true, composed songs before the publication of his first volume, but it is to be doubted that he ever thought seriously of devoting himself entirely to the production of song literature. Very few songs appear in the Kilmarnock and Edinburgh editions, and these are rather lost among the other poems in those volumes. Not only did Burns furnish the *Museum* with songs; he was also its virtual editor until his death. Internal evidence points to his authorship of the prefaces in Volumes II and IV. When he writes Johnson, "I am preparing a flaming Preface for your third Volume," we can certainly assume that the prose introduction to Volume III was written by his Bardship. And for this, as well as for the threescore songs he did for Thomson, he asked nothing but the privilege of publication. Thomson, it is true, attempted to make a business arrangement with Burns, but he would have none of it.

The songs certainly kept the poet's poetical imagination from atrophying; on the other hand, had any encouragement come from publishers other than Thomson or Johnson, I feel certain that we would have had more "Twa Dogs" and "Holy Willie's," for whenever the poet did receive encouragement the results were notable and sometimes miraculous. There were, it is true, many friends who attempted to feed the fires of his inspiration, and seldom did they go unrewarded when they asked him for some of his poetical productions.

"It eases my heart a good de [al, as R] hyme is the coin with which a Poet pays his debts of honor or gratitude," he writes Josiah Walker in 1787, enclosing "The Humble Petition of Bruar Water."

". . . the inclosed poem," this to Charles Hay later in the same year, and enclosing "On the Death of the Late Lord President," "was in consequence of your suggestion, last time I had the pleasure of seeing you."

"Wherever I am, allow me, Sir, to claim it as my privilege, to acquaint you with my progress in the trade of rhymes," he writes Dugald Stewart the year following.

Some months later he writes to William Dunbar, "I enclose you a Poem I have just finished.—It is my first Essay in that kind of Poetry, & I ask your Criticism on it."

These few extracts give only a hint of what Burns was doing to maintain an audience; even if that audience were confined to his correspondents, it mattered not so long as he was being heard. Mrs. Dunlop, who encouraged him more than any other of his friends, and to whom Burns wrote more letters than to anyone else, hardly received a letter from him without some verses in it.

The farm at Ellisland and the five years' residence at Dumfries offered him nothing, or certainly very little, in the way of appreciative listeners or readers. True, Ellisland kept him painfully close to the soil, and his work with the Excise, after he had given up farming, was exacting enough, but hard work had never kept him from his poetry before. I am convinced, therefore, that, could he have found congenial listeners, as of the old days in Mauchline, or a publisher who realized his worth, the world would be richer by many poems. As an example let us look at the result of his friendship with Francis Grose, the poem "Tam o'Shanter."

Grose, an English antiquary, was traveling through Scotland gathering material for his two-volume work, *The Antiquities of Scotland*. Robert Riddell, a neighbor of Burns's at Ellisland, introduced the two men and they were immediately congenial. Grose was interested in the folklore of Ayrshire, which the poet had at his finger tips. When Burns suggested that the old haunted church at Alloway be included in the forthcoming *Antiquities,* Grose complied immediately but with the stipulation that the poet furnish him some verses to go with the text and the engraving. The "verses" furnished were "Tam o'Shanter," which, ironically, appeared in a footnote in the second volume of the publication. It is somewhat frightening to think how much chance had to do with the production of one of the great narratives in the language. At the same time, we may contemplate with sorrow the fact that chance had not intervened oftener.

The second volume of the *Antiquities* was published in 1791. This, with the exception of the songs in the *Musical Museum* and the appearance of the poem to Thomson in the Earl of Buchan's *Essays* (1792), was to be Burns's last association with a formally published book for two years. Creech, who had managed the printing and sale of the first Edinburgh edition—he was not its formal publisher—had realized a goodly sum on that volume. The time now seemed ripe for another Edinburgh edition and, of course, further profits. He wrote Burns in the early spring of 1792, asking him if he had any material he would like to add to a new edition and also what price he was asking for such material. The poet replied: "I suppose, at a gross guess that I could add of new materials to your two volumes, about fifty pages. . . . A few Books which I very much want, are all the recompence I crave, together with as many copies of this new edition of my own works as Friendship or Gratitude shall prompt me to *present*."

The earlier warm association with Creech had cooled rapidly in the atmosphere of a monetary disagreement, so Burns asks for no money; but he was still anxious to get his poems before the public eye. On February 16, 1793, the two volumes were advertised for sale. Two weeks later Burns was writing Creech: "I understand that my Book is published.—I beg that you will, *as soon as possible,* send me twenty copies of it.—As I mean to present them among a few Great Folks whom I respect, & a few Little folks whom I love, these twenty will not interfere with your sale.—If you have not twenty copies ready, send me any number you can." It is painful to think that Creech did not have the grace to inform Burns of the publication of the edition and, further, that the poet had to *beg* for some copies of it. Obviously, this man could or would do him little good. Burns had not yet found his understanding and sympathetic publisher.

The 1793 edition, which probably numbered not over a thousand copies, and is, oddly enough, a fairly scarce item today, must have sold very well indeed, for it was followed by another edition in the next year. Burns may not have known of or cared about the existence of the new edition. His letter to Creech in May, 1795, "Send me . . . three copies of the last edition of my Poems; which place to my account," is not too clear an indication that he is referring to the 1794 edition. At all events, this is the last appearance of *Poems, Chiefly in the Scottish Dialect.* These two editions and the first volume of Thomson's *Scottish Airs* were to comprise the last outlet Burns had, so that his publishing career was over almost two years before his death. And what had it really amounted to? Monetarily certainly very little: about £20, after expenses, for the Kilmarnock edition, and about £450 for the Edinburgh edition, most of which went to his brother Gilbert, in the form of a loan that was never repaid during Robert's lifetime, or into the unfortunate purchase of the farm at Ellisland. And that is all the money that Burns ever received for his published works! "Pride and Passion," Burns's own phrase and the title DeLancey Ferguson uses for his admirable study of the poet, kept him from accepting any remuneration from either Johnson or Thomson and from entering into another disagreeable relationship with Creech. The association with Johnson and Thomson also changed the character of his compositions. Most of his talent, after 1787, was turned to the writing of songs. In that occupation he was at least achieving his ideal of being a Scottish bard and, at the same time, attracting the attention of two sympathetic publishers as well as some sort of audience.

The bibliographer is often in a position to see farther beneath the surface than the outside appearances of his trade might seem to indicate. In this instance, bibliography brings an ironic piece of news to light—Burns had a large, appreciative, and ever-growing audience during his lifetime of which he was completely unaware. Over and over again the poems appeared in formally published editions, in broadsides, in chapbooks, in anthologies, and in newspapers, but of most of these the poet seems to have been ignorant.

And what of the editions that were unknown to him? There was, in the first place, the "third," or London edition published by Strahan and Cadell "in the Strand; and *W. Creech, Edinburgh*" (I italicize purposely), probably late in the year 1787. Did Creech ever inform Burns that a London edition had appeared? There is no indication that he did, and the natural assumption to make is that Burns remained ignorant of his popularity south of the Border. He was attracting a reading public not only in England but also in Ireland. James Magee, a prominent publisher of Belfast, had his pirated edition of the *Poems* in the booksellers' shops of that city on September 24, 1787, some weeks before the London edition was out. This edition was published both in Belfast and in Dublin with the name of that city and the copublisher, William Gilbert, in the imprint.

The year 1788 was to see two more editions and these in America. The first appeared in Philadelphia on July 2, published by Peter Stewart and George Hyde; the second was published sometime around the middle of December in New York under the auspices of two brothers, J. and A. M'Lean, natives of Glasgow. These editions were advertised in newspapers from Massachusetts to North Carolina, but I doubt if Burns ever dreamed of their existence.

The poet's popularity waxed in Ireland, for Magee and Gilbert issued a Belfast-Dublin edition once more in 1789 and again in 1790. A third Irish edition was ready for publication three years later when news of the appearance of another Edinburgh edition was received. Nothing daunted, William Magee, a nephew of the now deceased James, extracted all the new material from the Edinburgh edition, stole a few of Burns's songs from the *Musical Museum,* added some poems by other authors, and came out triumphantly with two volumes, the first a reprint of the 1790 edition, the second the pastiche described above. With these, and the Edinburgh editions of 1793 and 1794, we see the last of the editions of Burns's poems published while he was yet alive—thirteen in all, if we count the Belfast-Dublin editions as two. Three he saw through the press. Ten were most probably unknown to him.

All was fish that came to the net of the editor of an eighteenth-century newspaper, and it is little wonder that the "Address to a Haggis" appeared in *The Caledonian Mercury* on December 19, 1786, some months before the formal publication of the poem in the first Edinburgh edition. Creech may have been responsible for the insertion of the poem in the *Mercury* as Burns scorned to put his name to a poem in a newspaper, even though he did, on occasion, submit to such publication over a nom de plume. The "Prologue" for Mr. Woods appeared in the same paper in April, 1787, and the verses written at Taymouth were in the *Edinburgh Courant* on September 6 of that year. These were all first appearances, "first editions" in a newspaper, if such they can be called. There are, to the best of my knowledge, twenty-two of Burns's poems which were first published during his lifetime in newspapers in Scotland, England, and Ireland; most of them do not seem to have been sent in by Burns himself. Other than these first appearances, reprints of the poems appeared in droves between 1786 and 1796. It is almost impossible, for example, to estimate the many times the "Mouse," or the "Daisy," or the "Cotter's Saturday

Night" were printed in newspapers and periodicals during the time the poet was alive, but the number must be in the hundreds. Even in far-off Philadelphia the *Pennsylvania Packet* reprinted practically the entire Edinburgh edition in twenty-five installments between July, 1787, and June, 1788, and other reprints throughout the United States were legion. Considering the inadequacy of eighteenth-century communications and the fact that Burns was, after all, an obscure person during the last eight years of his life, it is safe to say that he was totally unaware of the spread of his poems through newspapers and periodicals alone.

Pamphlets, broadsides, chapbooks, and anthologies containing Burns's poems are reasonably numerous as well. James Maxwell, a poetaster of Paisley who hated Burns, first published the lines beginning "Here Stewarts once in triumph reigned," in a scurrilous pamphlet entitled *Animadversions*. This appeared in 1788, and during the following year "Holy Willie's Prayer" was issued in a surreptitious little pamphlet with no author, publisher, or place appearing on the title page. Burns was well aware that the Presbyterian "auld lichts" knew of the existence and authorship of the satire, so it is quite possible that he had nothing to do with its appearance even though the strictest anonymity was maintained. "The Ayrshire Garland," a broadside, came out with "The Kirk's Alarm" in 1789, and a series of broadsides was issued with "Wham will we send to London Town," "Fy, let us a' to Kirkudbright," "Twas in the Seventeen Hunder Year," and "Wha will buy my troggin," during 1795–96. It is possible that Burns had a hand in these himself; they were another opportunity to appear in print. The "Address to the Deil," reprinted from the Kilmarnock edition, came out in a chapbook in 1795, and the next year Stewart and Meikle began their now famous series of tracts with the first appearance of the "Twa Herds" and "An Unco Mournfu' Tale." And, finally, the anthologies. It is difficult to know how often Burns's poems were printed in these publications, but beginning with *The English Parnassus* (London, 1789), and running through to *Roach's Beauties of the Poets* (London, 1795), I have seen some five anthologies with his productions in them. There are probably more.

There were other appearances which I have not listed, but these will do. The picture, I believe, is clear enough: the poet wanting passionately to be read and, when he discovered that his public had reached the saturation point, seeking other means of expressing himself. Indeed, we are richer by having the songs—one could really ask for no more—but we might have had other lyrics and satires and narratives if Burns had only realized that his dream of a large and appreciative audience was a reality.

BLAKE AND THE FLAXMANS

Margaret Ruth Lowery

THE publication of William Blake's private notebook gave wide circulation to his caustic judgments of many of his acquaintances. These remarks, recorded privately for emotional relief, have helped create the impression that Blake had few friends. His circle of friends was always somewhat narrow for several reasons. He chose to live to himself, to do his work in his own highly individualistic way. Engraving in itself was not a profession inviting sociability. Temperament—and perhaps temper—made him wish to be independent of other people. His early repudiation of the smart society which scorned Mrs. Blake and patronized him, as reported in *An Island in the Moon,* excluded him from circles which other artists would have made profitable to themselves. The reputations of certain radical leaders like Joseph Priestley, Thomas Holcroft, Joseph Johnson, Gilbert Wakefield, Thomas Paine, and William Godwin were not exactly favorable for the extension of his friendships and may even have increased his sense of isolation. At least, he was enough aware of the unpopularity of these associations to regard them as having some danger to himself. Professionally Blake quarreled with several people, among whom were Cromek and Stothard. His stubborn adherence to his own convictions and ideas, as amply shown in the many allusions to himself in his poetry, has made the picture of him so forbidding that it has become easy to assume that Blake was perhaps incapable of friendship. Such an assumption, however much these miscellaneous circumstances seem to establish it, would not be just to Blake.

When Blake said that he "never made friends but by spiritual gifts," he spoke truly, and it is on such a basis that one must understand the warmth, the strength, and the long continuance of the friendship that Blake had with John Flaxman and his wife Ann. New light on this friendship comes from one of Blake's poems which has received little consideration since its first publication in 1919.

In the London *Times* of November 4, 1919, in a letter from Professor Grierson, there appeared in print for the first time a ten-line poem by William Blake, entitled "To Mrs Ann Flaxman":

> A little Flower grew in a lonely Vale
> Its form was lovely but its colours pale
> One standing in the Porches of the Sun
> When his Meridian Glories were begun
> Leapd from the steps of fire & on the grass
> Alighted where this little flower was
> With hands divine he movd the gentle Sod
> And took the Flower up in its native Clod
> Then planting it upon a Mountains brow
> 'Tis your own fault if you dont flourish now.
>
> *William Blake*

Originally this poem was written on the last page of the illustrations for Gray's poems which Blake executed in 114 designs, upon the wide margins of large folio drawing paper, 16.5 by 12.5 inches, around the text-inset of the poems. A pencil drawing of Blake by John Flaxman, in striking resemblance to a drawing made in 1804, was pasted at some time on the flyleaf, giving one indication of the personal association the book had. Blake's poem occupies a space the same size as that used by the text of the poems. The design of this page, listed in the table of illustrations as No. 12 of the designs for "The Elegy" and named by Blake "A Spirit Conducted to Paradise," is not really an illustration of any passage in Gray's "Elegy." It seems clearly an additional item. The illustration is an individual and especially delicate one, composed of two figures and no other design, against a misty background of clouds. One figure in gracefully flowing garments is poised at the left of the inset, with the right arm stretched above the head, the right finger pointing upward, and with the left arm extended appealingly toward the lower figure. The latter, similarly attired but more masculine, floats horizontally beneath the inset, with face upturned and hands widely spread as if in surprise or indecision. Both faces are delicately drawn, and the figures are unlike those used in the other illustrations. Their individuality sets them apart.

Blake's acquaintance with John Flaxman began previous to 1780, very likely as early as 1775, and continued with only one serious lapse for the remainder of their lives. When Flaxman married, he lived near Blake at 27 Wardou.˙ Street. The two men were closely associated in the early days of the New Jerusalem Church, John Flaxman being one of the original members. Among several benevolent actions of Flaxman in Blake's behalf was his recommendation of Blake to William Hayley to engrave plates for Hayley's poems and draw portraits for his library. On Hayley's invitation William and Catherine Blake went in September, 1800, to Felpham, to a cottage by the sea, where they lived until September, 1803, when Hayley's plans so restricted Blake, "the enthusiastic hope-fostered visionary," that he could no longer meet Hayley's demands. Serious as this break was, as shown in *Milton,* Blake succeeded in preserving a friendly correspondence with Hayley after his return to London. "It is easier to forgive an enemy than to forgive a friend," he once said, and forgiveness to him meant love and brotherhood. He attained thus a selflessness, he believed, that gave his imagination true scope.

These years at Felpham were happy ones in many respects, and there is abundant evidence in Blake's correspondence to show that he was deeply grateful to Flaxman for the experience. September 12, 1800, he wrote Flaxman that he owed to him the principal happiness of his life, and in an enclosed poem he thanked God that he ever saw Flaxman's face. He wrote:

> And My Angels have told me that seeing such visions
> I could not subsist on the Earth,
> But by my conjunction with Flaxman, who knows to
> forgive Nervous Fear.

Blake recognized Flaxman as one friend who understood him and had patience with him. With Flaxman he had spiritual kinship. Flaxman's tolerance, his even temperament, his purity and simplicity of character endeared him to Blake. The same month Blake wrote another appreciative letter, expressing his ardent wish to entertain Mr. and Mrs. Flaxman beneath "his thatched roof of rusted gold." Writing to Hayley in 1804, Blake said: "Gratitude is heaven itself; there could be no heaven without gratitude." It is highly probable that, when Blake finished the designs for Gray's poems, he gave the folio as a gift of gratitude to the Flaxmans. As Professor Grierson has said, the date of executing the designs "cannot be more closely ascertained than . . . probably 1800." Since the folio was addressed directly to Ann Flaxman, as it clearly was, the gift was doubly complimentary to Flaxman whose domestic happiness was noteworthy. A new interpretation of the poem, however, enables one to see how truly complimentary Blake was to Flaxman, and causes one to think that the poem could have been composed earlier than is generally conceded.

Professor Grierson suggested in the London *Times,* November 4, 1919, that Blake meant to tell in this poem what his inspired art had done for the refined academic poetry of Gray. Two days later, however, confessing that this explanation was his first impression, he interpreted it to mean Blake's gratitude for Flaxman's planting him at Felpham, Blake being the flower in the poem. Another explanation seems more consistent with the information at hand. The poem was written to Mrs. Flaxman. Blake must have meant her for the "flower." This was an expression he seemed to keep in mind for he used it in another poem, "To My Dear Friend, Mrs. Anna Flaxman," included in a letter of Catherine Blake to Mrs. Flaxman (in Blake's hand, however), September 14, 1800, which began:

> This Song to the flower of Flaxman's joy,
> To the blossom of hope, for a sweet decoy:
> Do all that you can or all that you may,
> To entice him to Felpham & far away: . . .

"One standing in the Porches of the Sun" could be no other than Flaxman, who, by the time of his marriage in 1782, had attained sufficient reputation and employment for Blake to feel that his "Meridian Glories had begun." The latter phrase is echoed from the poem, "The Distracted Lover" in Percy's *Reliques,* a copy of which Blake owned. This is a neat and generous compliment to a friend on a success which he himself had been denied. By Blake's use of "Porches of the Sun" he may have had some symbolism in mind not now apparent, for he later used the phrase in the symbolical *Vala;* and in *The French Revolution* he wrote, ". . . like spirits of fire in the beautiful Porches of the Sun, . . ."

"Its form was lovely but its colours pale" is but the poet's way of describing the maidenly appearance of Ann Denman, who, as the daughter of a tradesman, a gunmaker in Whitechapel, held an unpretentious social position such as could have been described by the "lonely Vale" and the "native Clod." The altered position to which her marriage with John Flaxman brought her could have been, in comparison, fittingly described as the "Mountains brow." Blake's appreciation of her new position was rendered beautiful and poetic when he used "hands divine" to refer to the hands of a sculptor, whom he once addressed as "Dear Sculptor of Eternity." Flaxman's vigorous, positive nature is reflected in Blake's description of his manner of action:

> Leapd from the steps of fire & on the grass
> Alighted where this little flower was . . .

That Blake's conception of the "flower" is related to happiness is apparent if one recalls an earlier use of the phrase. In "Contemplation" he wrote: "Those who want Happiness must stoop to find it; it is a flower that grows in every vale." If the poem "To Mrs Ann Flaxman" belongs as early as 1782, it is even possible that Blake had the Flaxmans in mind in this passage.

The last line, " 'Tis your own fault if you dont flourish now," shifts to the second person as if addressing Flaxman. This is another reason for dating the poem nearer the time of Flaxman's marriage, for it stands in such pleasing antithesis to the dismal prophecy of Sir Joshua Reynolds, who said when he learned that Flaxman had married: "Then your improvement is at an end." Mrs. Flaxman's sister, Maria, who made her home with Mrs. Flaxman and was in reality adopted by her, said: "Courtship and matrimony rather doubled his diligence than retarded it." There is a legend that it was Reynolds' remark that spurred Flaxman to sacrifice everything to study in Italy for a period of seven years. If the closing line of the poem takes cognizance of Reynolds' remark, it points to one reason why Blake disliked Sir Joshua Reynolds, the man "Hired to Depress Art," as Blake said in his annotations. Reynolds had already "humbled Flaxman's conceit" when he refused to give Flaxman a Royal Academy award.

Since Blake's poem thus gives prominence to Mrs. Flaxman, it is interesting to inquire what manner of person she was. Once in 1808, Blake wrote an epigram, "To Nancy":

> How can I help thy Husband's copying me?
> Should that make difference 'twixt me and Thee?

This shows that whatever the cause was of the estrangement between Blake and Flaxman that came to a climax in 1808 and may have gone on to 1810, as the "Public Address" would indicate, Blake felt that he did not wish on account of it to give up the friendship with Mrs. Flaxman. This one time Blake used the name Nancy, which was Flaxman's own familiar name for Mrs. Flaxman, used before their marriage and the only one by which he ever addressed her. Again, if one may discount the extravagances of expression to which Hayley was much given in his poetic effusions, one can still see in the long poem which Hayley wrote to Mrs. Flaxman, June 7, 1798, a tribute he paid to a high-minded, gifted, and charming woman. Such is also the impression of her given in the picture of her reproduced by H. N. Morris in *Men of Genius*. Samuel Smiles in his *Life of Wedgwood* says that Mrs. Flaxman had a true taste for art and literature, understood French and Italian and acquired some knowledge of Greek, and was besides a good domestic manager and constant cheer to her husband. In a letter she wrote to Hayley in 1797, she spoke of reading Enfield's *History of Philosophy,* a translation in two quarto volumes. Crabb Robinson once recorded in his diary that she accompanied him on December 12, 1811, to hear Coleridge lecture. On an earlier occasion he read to her part of "Schlegel's Critique on the Designs of Dante which of course gratified her." Perhaps it was a compliment that the garrulous Crabb Robinson described her as a "shrewd, lively, talkative woman." When young Hayley lived in Flaxman's home, he wrote to his father, December 6, 1795, that Mrs. Flaxman was so kind and attentive to him that he had a high regard for her. She evidently entered into the youth's interests, for her playful letters signed Titania, written after the youthful

Thomas had returned home, tell of her fanciful and entertaining behavior. She had a lively epistolary style and outdid her husband in quaint mannerisms. In a letter that Flaxman wrote her before their marriage, he described her epistle as "dictated with the greatest good sense, and . . . terms of affectionate sensibility," and he also spoke of her "lovely disposition." Soon after Mr. and Mrs. Flaxman returned from Italy, Flaxman composed, as a birthday gift to his wife, a poetical allegory, *The Knight of the Burning Cross,* with forty illustrations, some of which clearly reflect the influence of Blake's visionary style. One wonders if this kind of gift set an example for Blake in his own gift of Gray's *Illustrations.*

Sir Richard Westmacott, who succeeded Flaxman as Professor of Sculpture at the Royal Academy, told Allan Cunningham: "Flaxman, sir, lived as if he did not belong to this world; his ways were not our ways . . . he dined at one, wrought after dinner, which no other artist does; drank tea at six; and then, sir, no one ever found him in the evening parties of the rich or the noble: he was happy at home, and so he kept himself." This reveals again something of the character of Ann Flaxman, and illustrates why, when she died, her sister should speak of Flaxman's loss of "this most inestimable wife."

These scattered bits of evidence suffice to show why Mrs. Flaxman was so highly regarded by Blake and help one to understand why it was gratifying to Blake that she should approve of his engravings for *The Shipwreck.* He called her in a letter to Hayley, December 18, 1804, a "connoisseur of engraving." Blake evidently did not think of Flaxman without Mrs. Flaxman. Flaxman wrote Hayley, August 12, 1805: "Blake brought a present of two copies of the *Songs,* it is beautiful work, Nancy and I are equally delighted with your bounty to the poet-artist." Writing to his brother James in 1803, from Felpham, Blake said he was sending five copies of "N 4 of the Ballads of Hayley for Mrs. Flaxman." It must be remembered that both John and Ann Flaxman had a copy of the *Poetical Sketches.* In making gifts, then, Blake showed Mrs. Flaxman individual consideration.

The Illustrations to Gray's Poems, ably edited by Professor Grierson, was reproduced by the Oxford University Press in 1922 from the unique copy in possession of the present Duke of Hamilton. The bibliographical story involved is of much interest not only for the further light on Blake's friendship with the Flaxmans but for his interest in Gray.

The original book remained in the Flaxman library until July 1, 1828, when Flaxman's effects, after his death in 1826, were sold. William Clarke, a bookseller in New Bond Street, purchased the book. Apart from the following mention of it in William Rossetti's "Descriptive List," published in 1863 in Gilchrist's *Life of Blake:* "One hundred and fourteen Designs to Gray's Poems [Duke of Hamilton]. Reputed to be among the very finest works executed by Blake," the book was unrecorded and seemingly unknown until the Hamilton Palace was dismantled. Gilchrist made no mention of it in the *Life* itself, and the unpublished correspondence of Flaxman in the Fitzwilliam Museum contains no reference to it. There is no allusion to it in Blake's letters unless one considers the volume to have been one "of the many formidable works" which he had "finished and ready," as he stated to his brother, January 30, 1803. "I am now labouring in my thoughts Designs for this & other works equally creditable," he said. It could have been one of the "giant forms" to which he alluded in the prefatory address to *Jerusalem*.

Rossetti rightly assigned the book to the possession of the Duke of Hamilton. Susanna Euphemia Beckford, the daughter of the eminent bibliophile William Beckford, married her cousin, the tenth Duke of Hamilton. Upon her father's death she inherited his library, the catalogue of which listed twelve works of Blake, all described as "excessively rare." *The Illustrations to Gray's Poems* was not one of the twelve although it was obviously a part of the library. One cannot know what chance oversight or interest withheld it from the sale. Furthermore, no Blake items appeared in the catalogue of the Hamilton library, where it remains today.

Only one copy of the *Illustrations* to Gray is known. The close association of that copy with the friendship existing between Flaxman and Blake and the motive behind the gift of the folio are given fitting emphasis by the application of one of the passages in Gray's "Ode to Music":

"What is Grandeur? What is Power?
"Heavier toil, superior pain.
"What the brief reward we gain?
"The grateful mem'ry of the Good.
"Sweet is the breath of vernal shower,
"The bee's collected treasures sweet,
"Sweet music's melting fall, but sweeter yet
"The still small voice of Gratitude."

The poem addressed to Mrs. Ann Flaxman expressed Blake's gratitude as nothing else could have done. It was especially fitting to the happy friendship which Blake treasured.

THE STRUCTURE OF ROMANTIC
NATURE IMAGERY

W. K. Wimsatt, Jr.

STUDENTS of romantic nature poetry have recently had a great deal to tell us about the philosophic components of this poetry: the specific blend of deistic theology, Newtonian physics, and pantheistic naturalism which pervades the Wordsworthian landscape in the period of "Tintern Abbey," the theism which sounds in the "Eolian Harp" of Coleridge, the conflict between French atheism and Platonic idealism which even in "Prometheus Unbound" Shelley was not able to resolve. We have at the same time been instructed in some of the more purely scientific coloring of the poetry—the images derived from geology, astronomy, and magnetism, and the coruscant green mystery which the electricians contributed to such phenomena as Shelley's Spirit of Earth. We have considered also the "sensibility" of romantic readers, distinct, according to one persuasive interpretation, from that of neoclassic readers. What was exciting to the age of Pope, "Puffs, Powders, Patches, Bibles, Billet-doux" (even about these the age might be loath to admit its excitement), was not, we are told, what was so manifestly exciting to the age of Wordsworth. "High mountains are a feeling, but the hum of cities torture." Lastly, a recent difference of critical opinion has reinvited attention to the romantic theory of imagination. One influential critic has described the "imagination" of Coleridge and Wordsworth as a form of sentimental high seriousness, chiefly notable for its failure to comprehend the witty tension—the "fancy"—which characterizes the poetry of the metaphysicals. Another, in a handsome study of Coleridge, analyzing the *esemplastic* imagination or power of verbal coadunation in the light of Coleridge's comment on certain intense lines of Shakespeare, has gone far to place Coleridge at the very heart of all past and any future theories of imagination.[1]

1. This paragraph alludes especially to Joseph Warren Beach, *The Concept of Nature in Nineteenth-century English Poetry* (New York, 1936), chaps. ii–viii; Newton P. Stall-

We have, in short, a *subject*—simply considered, the nature of birds and trees and streams—a *metaphysics* of an animating principle, a special *sensibility,* and a *theory* of poetic imagination—the value of the last a matter of debate. Romantic poetry itself has recently suffered some disfavor among advanced critics. One interesting question, however, seems still to want discussion: that is, whether romantic poetry (or more specifically romantic nature poetry) exhibits any imaginative *structure* which may be considered a special counterpart of the subject, the philosophy, the sensibility, and the theory—and hence perhaps an explanation of the last. Something like an answer to such a question is what I would sketch.

For the purpose of providing an antithetic point of departure, I quote here a part of one of the best known and most toughly reasonable of all metaphysical images:

> If they be two, they are two so
>   As stiff twin compasses are two,
> Thy soul the fixed foot, makes no show
>   To move, but doth, if th'other do.

It will be relevant if we remark that this similitude, rather farfetched as some might think, is yet unmistakable to interpretation because quite overtly stated, but again is not, by being stated, precisely defined or limited in its poetic value. The kind of similarity and the kind of disparity that ordinarily obtain between a drawing compass and a pair of parting lovers are things to be attentively considered in reading this image. And the disparity between living lovers and stiff metal is not least important to the tone of precision, restraint, and conviction which it is the triumph of the poem to convey. Though the similitude is cast in the form of statement, its mood is actually a kind of subimperative. In the next age the tension of such a severe disparity was relaxed, yet the overtness and crispness of statement remained, and a wit of its own sort.

knecht, *Strange Seas of Thought* (Durham, 1945), chaps. ii–iii; Carl H. Grabo, *A Newton among Poets* (Chapel Hill, 1930), chaps. vi–vii; and *Prometheus Unbound: an Interpretation* (Chapel Hill, 1935), pp. 142–143, 151; Frederick A. Pottle, *The Idiom of Poetry* (Ithaca, 1941), chap. i; Cleanth Brooks, *Modern Poetry and the Tradition* (Chapel Hill, 1939), chaps. i and ii; I. A. Richards, *Principles of Literary Criticism* (New York, 1934), chap. xxxii; and *Coleridge on Imagination* (New York, 1935), chap. iv.

> 'Tis with our judgments as our watches, none
> Go just alike, yet each believes his own.

We may take this as typical, I believe, of the metaphoric structure in which Pope achieves perfection and which survives a few years later in the couplets of Samuel Johnson or the more agile Churchill. The difference between our judgments and our watches, if noted at all, may be a pleasant epistemological joke for a person who questions the existence of a judgment which is taken out like a watch and consulted by another judgment.

But the "sensibility," as we know, had begun to shift even in the age of Pope. Examples of a new sensibility, and of a different structure, having something to do with Miltonic verse and a "physico-theological nomenclature," are to be found in Thomson's *Seasons*. Both a new sensibility and a new structure appear in the "hamlets brown and dim-discovered spires" of Collins' very early example of the full romantic dream. In several poets of the mid-century, in the Wartons or in William Stanley Roscoe, one may feel, or rather see stated, a new sensibility, but at the same time one may lament an absence of poetic quality—that is, of a poetic structure adequate to embody or objectify the new feeling. It is as if these harbingers of another era had felt but had not felt strongly enough to work upon the objects of their feelings a pattern of meaning which would speak for itself—and which would hence endure as a poetic monument.

As a central exhibit I shall take two sonnets, that of William Lisle Bowles "To the River Itchin" (1789) [2] and for contrast that of Coleridge "To the River Otter" (1796)—written in confessed imitation of Bowles.[3] Coleridge owed his first poetic inspiration to Bowles (the "father" of English romantic poetry) and continued to express unlimited admiration for him as late as 1796. That is, they shared the same sensibility—as for that matter did Wordsworth and Southey, who too were deeply impressed by the sonnets of

2. The sonnet "To the River Lodon" (1777), by Bowles's Oxford senior, Thomas Warton, shows sensibility with even less structural support.

3. Coleridge's sonnet first appears in its entirety and as a separate poem in the pamphlet collection which he published privately in 1796 (cf. n. 7); the sonnet reappears in the 1797 *Poems* of Coleridge under the half-title "Sonnets attempted in the manner of the Rev. W. L. Bowles."

Bowles. As a schoolboy Coleridge read eagerly in Bowles's second edition of 1789 [4] (among other sonnets not much superior):

> Itchin, when I behold thy banks again,
> Thy crumbling margin, and thy silver breast,
> On which the self-same tints still seem to rest,
> Why feels my heart the shiv'ring sense of pain?
> Is it—that many a summer's day has past
> Since, in life's morn, I carol'd on thy side?
> Is it—that oft, since then, my heart has sigh'd,
> As Youth, and Hope's delusive gleams, flew fast?
> Is it—that those, who circled on thy shore,
> Companions of my youth, now meet no more?
> Whate'er the cause, upon thy banks I bend
> Sorrowing, yet feel such solace at my heart,
> As at the meeting of some long-lost friend,
> From whom, in happier hours, we wept to part.

Here is an emotive expression which once appealed to the sensibility of its author and of his more cultivated contemporaries, but which has with the lapse of time gone flat. The speaker was happy as a boy by the banks of the river. Age has brought disillusion and the dispersal of his friends. So a return to the river, in reminding him of the past, brings both sorrow and consolation. The facts are stated in four rhetorical questions and a concluding declaration. There is also something about how the river looks and how its looks might contribute to his feelings—in the metaphoric suggestion of the "crumbling" margin and in the almost illusory tints on the surface of the stream which surprisingly have outlasted the "delusive gleams" of his own hopes. Yet the total impression is one of simple association (by contiguity in time) simply asserted— what might be described in the theory of Hume or Hartley or what Hazlitt talks about in his essay "On the Love of the Country." "It is because natural objects have been associated with the sports of our childhood, . . . with our feelings in solitude . . . that we love them as we do ourselves."

Coleridge himself in his "Lines Written at Elbingerode in 1799"

---

4. "I made, within less than a year and a half, more than forty transcriptions, as the best presents I could offer" (*Biographia Literaria*, chap. i).

was to speak of a "spot with which the heart associates Holy remembrances of child or friend." His enthusiasm for Hartley in this period is well known. But later, in the *Biographia Literaria* and in the third of his essays on "Genial Criticism," he was to repudiate explicitly the Hartleian and mechanistic way of shifting back burdens of meaning. And already, in 1796, Coleridge as poet was concerned with the more complex ontological grounds of association (the various levels of sameness, of correspondence and analogy), where mental activity transcends mere "associative response"—where it is in fact the unifying activity known both to later eighteenth-century associationists [5] and to romantic poets as "imagination." The "sweet and indissoluble union between the intellectual and the material world" of which Coleridge speaks in the introduction to his pamphlet anthology of sonnets in 1796 must be applied by us in one sense to the sonnets of Bowles, but in another to the best romantic poetry and even to Coleridge's imitation of Bowles. There is an important difference between the kinds of unity. In a letter to Sotheby of 1802 Coleridge was to say more emphatically: "The poet's heart and intellect should be *combined,* intimately combined and unified with the great appearances of nature, and not merely held in solution and loose mixture with them." [6] In the same paragraph he says of Bowles's later poetry: "Bowles has indeed the *sensibility* of a poet, but he has not the *passion* of a great poet . . . he has no native passion because he is not a thinker."

The sententious melancholy of Bowles's sonnets and the asserted connection between this mood and the appearances of nature are enough to explain the hold of the sonnets upon Coleridge. Doubtless the metaphoric coloring, faint but nonetheless real, which we have remarked in Bowles's descriptive details had also something to do with it. What is of great importance to note is that Coleridge's

5. Cf. Walter Jackson Bate, *From Classic to Romantic* (Cambridge, Mass., 1946), chap. iv, ". . . The Premise of the Association of Ideas."

6. Coleridge has in mind such loose resemblances as need to be stated "in the shape of formal similes" (*Letters* [1895], I, 404). Cf. Bowles, *Sonnets* (2d ed. 1789), Sonnet V, "To the River Wenbeck," "I listen to the wind, And think I hear meek sorrow's plaint"; Sonnet VI, "To the River Tweed," "The murmurs of thy wand'ring wave below Seem to his ear the pity of a friend."

own sonnet "To the River Otter" (while not a completely successful poem) shows a remarkable intensification of such color.

> Dear native Brook! wild Streamlet of the West!
> How many various-fated years have past,
> What happy and what mournful hours, since last
> I skimmed the smooth thin stone along thy breast,
> Numbering its light leaps! yet so deep imprest
> Sink the sweet scenes of childhood, that mine eyes
> I never shut amid the sunny ray,
> But straight with all their tints thy waters rise,
> Thy crossing plank, thy marge with willows grey,
> And bedded sand that veined with various dyes
> Gleamed through thy bright transparence! On my way,
> Visions of Childhood! oft have ye beguiled
> Lone manhood's cares, yet waking fondest sighs:
> Ah! that once more I were a careless Child!

Almost the same statement as that of Bowles's sonnet—the sweet
scenes of childhood by the river have only to be remembered to
bring both beguilement and melancholy. One notices immediately,
however, that the speaker has kept his eye more closely on the object. There are more details. The picture is more vivid, a fact which
according to one school of poetics would in itself make the sonnet
superior. But a more analytic theory will find it worth remarking
also that certain ideas, latent or involved in the description, have
much to do with its vividness. As a child, careless and free, wild like
the streamlet, the speaker amused himself with one of the most
carefree motions of youth—skimming smooth thin stones which
leapt lightly on the breast of the water. One might have thought
such experiences would sink no deeper in the child's breast than
the stones in the water—"yet so deep imprest"—the very antithesis
(though it refers overtly only to the many hours which have intervened) defines imaginatively the depth of the impressions. When
he closes his eyes, they *rise* again (the word *rise* may be taken as
a trope which hints the whole unstated similitude); they rise like
the tinted waters of the stream; they gleam up through the depths
of memory—the "various-fated years"—like the "various dyes"
which vein the sand of the river bed. In short, there is a rich ground
of meaning in Coleridge's sonnet beyond what is overtly stated. The

descriptive details of his sonnet gleam brightly because (consciously or unconsciously—it would be fruitless to inquire how deliberately he wrote these meanings into his lines) he has invested them with significance. Here is a special perception, "invention" if one prefers, "imagination," or even "wit." It can be explored and tested by the wit of the reader. In this way it differs from the mere flat announcement of a Hartleian association, which is not open to challenge and hence not susceptible of confirmation. If this romantic wit differs from that of the metaphysicals, it differs for one thing in making less use of the central overt statement of similitude which is so important in all rhetoric stemming from Aristotle and the Renaissance. The metaphor in fact is scarcely noticed by the main statement of the poem.[7] Both tenor and vehicle, furthermore, are wrought in a parallel process out of the same material. The river landscape is both the occasion of reminiscence and the source of the metaphors by which reminiscence is described.[8] A poem of this structure is a signal instance of that kind of fallacy (or strategy) by which death in poetry occurs so often in winter or at night, and sweethearts meet in the spring countryside. The tenor of such a similitude is very likely to be subjective—reminiscence or sorrow or beguilement—not an object distinct from the vehicle, as lovers or their souls are distinct from twin compasses. Hence the emphasis of Bowles, Coleridge, and all other romantics on spontaneous feelings and sincerity. Hence the recurrent themes of One Being and Eolian Influence and Wordsworth's "ennobling interchange of action from within and from without." [9] In such a structure again the element of tension in disparity is not so important as for metaphysical wit. The interest derives not from our being aware of disparity where likeness is firmly insisted on, but in an opposite activity of discerning the design which is latent in the multiform sensuous picture.

7. See the more overt connections in the poem "Recollection" (*Watchman* No. V, April 2, 1796) from which lines 2–11 of this sonnet were taken. "Where blameless Pleasures dimpled Quiet's cheek, As water-lilies *ripple* thy slow stream!" "Ah! fair tho' faint those forms of memory seem, Like Heaven's bright bow on thy smooth evening stream."

8. "It is among the chief excellencies of Bowles that his imagery appears almost always prompted by surrounding scenery" (Coleridge to Southey, December 17, 1794, *Letters*, I, 115).

9. Cf. Stallknecht, *op. cit.*, pp. 37, 46–47.

Let us notice for a moment the "crossing plank" of Coleridge's sonnet, a minor symbol in the poem, a sign of shadowy presences, the lads who had once been there. The technique of this symbol is the same as that which Keats was to employ in a far more brilliant romantic instance, the second stanza of his "Ode to Autumn," where the very seasonal spirit is conjured into reality out of such haunted spots—in which a gesture lingers—the half-reaped furrow, the oozing cider press, the brook where the gleaners have crossed with laden heads.[10] To return to our metaphysics—of an animate, plastic Nature, not transcending but immanent in and breathing through all things—and to discount for the moment such differences as may relate to Wordsworth's naturalism, Coleridge's theology, Shelley's Platonism, or Blake's mysticism: we may note that the common feat of the romantic nature poets was to read meanings into the landscape. "The puddle," says Hazlitt, "is filled with preternatural faces."[11] The meaning might be such as we have seen in Coleridge's sonnet, but it might more characteristically be more profound, concerning the spirit or soul of things—"the one life within us and abroad." And that meaning especially was summoned out of the very surface of nature itself. It was embodied imaginatively and without the explicit religious or philosophic statements which one will find in classical or Christian instances—for example in Pope's "Essay on Man":

> Here then we rest: "The Universal Cause
> Acts to one end, but acts by various laws,"

or in the teleological divines, More, Cudworth, Bentley, and others of the seventeenth and eighteenth centuries, or in Paley during the same era as the romantics. The romantic poets want to have it and not have it too—a spirit which the poet himself as superidealist creates by his own higher reason or esemplastic imagination. Here one may recall Ruskin's chapter of *Modern Painters* on the difference between the Greek gods of rivers and trees and the vaguer suffusions of the romantic vista—"the curious web of hesitating sentiment, pathetic fallacy, and wandering fancy, which form a

---

10. Compare the "wooden bridge" in Arnold's Keatsian "Scholar Gipsy."
11. "On Mr. Wordsworth's Excursion."

great part of our modern view of nature." Wordsworth's "Prelude," from the cliff that "upreared its head" in the night above Ullswater to the "blue chasm" that was the "soul" of the moonlit cloudscape beneath his feet on Snowdon, is the archpoet's testament, both theory and demonstration of this way of reading nature. His "Tintern Abbey" is another classic instance, a whole pantheistic poem woven of the landscape, where God is not once mentioned. After the "soft inland murmur," the "one green hue," the "wreaths of smoke . . . as . . . Of vagrant dwellers in the houseless woods" (always something just out of sight or beyond definition), it is an easy leap to the "still, sad music of humanity," and

> a sense sublime
> Of something far more deeply interfused,
> Whose dwelling is the light of setting suns.

This poem, written as Wordsworth revisited the banks of a familiar stream, the "Sylvan Wye," is the full realization of a poem for which Coleridge and Bowles had drawn slight sketches. In Shelley's "Hymn to Intellectual Beauty" the "awful shadow" of the "unseen Power" is substantiated of "moonbeam" showers of light behind the "piny mountain," of "mist o'er mountains driven." On the Lake of Geneva in the summer of 1816 Byron, with Shelley the evangelist of Wordsworth at his side, spoke of "a living fragrance from the shore," a "floating whisper on the hill." We remark in each of these examples a dramatization of the spiritual through the use of the faint, the shifting, the least tangible and most mysterious parts of nature—a poetic counterpart of the several theories of spirit as subtile matter current in the eighteenth century, Newton's "electric and elastic" active principle, Hartley's "infinitesimal elementary body." The application of this philosophy to poetry by way of direct statement had been made as early as 1735 in Henry Brooke's "Universal Beauty," where an "elastick Flue of fluctuating Air" pervades the universe as "animating Soul." [12] In the high romantic period the most scientific version to appear in poetry was the now well-recognized imagery which Shelley drew from the electricians.

12. Joseph Warren Beach, *op. cit.*, pp. 94–99.

In such a view of spirituality the landscape itself is kept in focus
as a literal object of attention. Without it Wordsworth and Byron
in the examples just cited would not get a start. And one effect of
such a use of natural imagery—an effect implicit in the very philosophy of a World Spirit—is a tendency in the landscape imagery to
a curious split. If we have not only the landscape but the spirit
which either informs or visits it, and if both of these must be
rendered for the sensible imagination, a certain parceling of the
landscape may be the result. The most curious illustrations which
I know are in two of Blake's early quartet of poems to the seasons.
Thus, "To Spring":

> O THOU with dewy locks, who lookest down
> Thro' the clear windows of the morning, turn
> Thine angel eyes upon our western isle,
> Which in full choir hails thy approach, O Spring!
>
> The hills tell each other, and the list'ning
> Vallies hear; all our longing eyes are turned
> Up to thy bright pavillions: issue forth,
> And let thy holy feet visit our clime.
>
> Come o'er the eastern hills, and let our winds
> Kiss thy perfumed garments; let us taste
> Thy morn and evening breath; scatter thy pearls
> Upon our love-sick land that mourns for thee.

And "To Summer":

> O THOU, who passest thro' our vallies in
> Thy strength, curb thy fierce steeds, allay the heat
> That flames from their large nostrils! thou, O Summer,
> Oft pitched'st here thy golden tent, and oft
> Beneath our oaks hast slept, while we beheld
> With joy thy ruddy limbs and flourishing hair.
>
> Beneath our thickest shades we oft have heard
> Thy voice, when noon upon his fervid car
> Rode o'er the deep of heaven; beside our springs
> Sit down, and in our mossy vallies, on
> Some bank beside a river clear, throw thy
> Silk draperies off, and rush into the stream: . . .

Blake's starting point, it is true, is the opposite of Wordsworth's or
Byron's, not the landscape but a spirit personified or allegorized.

Nevertheless, this spirit as it approaches the "western isle" takes on certain distinctly terrestrial hues. Spring, an oriental bridegroom, lives behind the "clear windows of the morning" and is invited to issue from "bright pavilions," doubtless the sky at dawn. He has "perfumed garments" which when kissed by the winds will smell much like the flowers and leaves of the season. At the same time, his *own* morn and evening breaths are most convincing in their likeness to morning and evening breezes. The pearls scattered by the hand of Spring are, we must suppose, no other than the flowers and buds which literally appear in the landscape at this season. They function as landscape details and simultaneously as properties of the bridegroom and—we note here a further complication—as properties of the land taken as lovesick maiden. We have in fact a double personification conjured from one nature, one landscape, in a wedding which approximates fusion. Even more curious is the case of King Summer, a divided tyrant and victim, who first appears as the source and spirit of heat, his steeds with flaming nostrils, his limbs ruddy, his tent golden, but who arrives in our valleys only to sleep in the shade of the oaks and be invited to rush into the river for a swim. These early romantic poems are examples of the Biblical, classical, and Renaissance tradition of allegory as it approaches the romantic condition of landscape naturalism—as Spring and Summer descend into the landscape and are fused with it. Shelley's Alastor is a spirit of this kind, making the "wild his home," a spectral "Spirit of wind," expiring "Like some frail exhalation; which the dawn Robes in its golden beams." Byron's Childe Harold desired that he himself might become a "portion" of that around him, of the tempest and the night. "Be thou, Spirit fierce," said Shelley to the West Wind, "My spirit! Be thou me."

An English student of the arts in the Jacobean era, Henry Peacham, wrote a book on painting in which he gave allegorical prescriptions for representing the months, quoted under the names of months by Dr. Johnson in his *Dictionary:*

April is represented by a young man in green, with a garland of myrtle and hawthorn buds; in one hand primroses and violets, in the other the sign Taurus.

July I would have drawn in a jacket of light yellow, eating cherries, with his face and bosom sunburnt.[13]

But that would have been the end of it. April would not have been painted into a landscape puzzle picture where hawthorn buds and primroses were arranged to shadow forth the form of a person.

In his Preface of 1815 Wordsworth spoke of the *abstracting* and *"modifying* powers of the imagination." He gave as example a passage from his own poem, "Resolution and Independence," where an old leech gatherer is likened to a stone which in turn is likened to a sea beast crawled forth to sun itself. The poems which we have just considered, those of Coleridge, Wordsworth, and Blake especially, with their blurring of literal and figurative, might also be taken, I believe, as excellent examples. In another of his best poems Wordsworth produced an image which shows so strange yet artistic a warping, or modification, of vehicle by tenor that, though not strictly a nature image, it may be quoted here with close relevance. In the ode "Intimations of Immortality":

> Hence, in a season of calm weather,
> Though inland far we be,
> Our souls have sight of that immortal sea
> Which brought us hither;
> Can in a moment travel thither—
> And see the children sport upon the shore,
> And hear the mighty waters rolling evermore.

Or, as one might drably paraphrase, our souls in a calm mood look back to the infinity from which they came, as persons inland on clear days can look back to the sea by which they have voyaged to the land. The tenor concerns souls and age and time. The vehicle concerns travelers and space. The question for the analyst of structure is: Why are the children found on the seashore? In what way do they add to the solemnity or mystery of the sea? Or do they at all? The answer is that they are not strictly parts of the traveler-space vehicle, but of the soul-age-time tenor, attracted over, from tenor to vehicle. The travelers looking back in both space and time see themselves as children on the shore, as if just born like Venus

13. With these prescriptions compare the allegorical panels of seasons and months in Spenser's *Cantos of Mutabilitie*, VII, xxviii ff.

from the foam. This is a sleight of words, an imposition of image upon image, by the *modifying* power of imagination.

Poetic structure is always a fusion of ideas with material, a statement in which the solidity of symbol and the sensory verbal qualities are somehow not washed out by the abstraction. For this effect the iconic or directly imitative powers of language are important—and of these the well-known onomatopoeia or imitation of sound is only one, and one of the simplest. The "stiff twin compasses" of Donne have a kind of iconicity in the very stiffness and odd emphasis of the metrical situation. Neoclassic iconicity is on the whole of a highly ordered, formal, or intellectual sort, that of the "figures of speech" such as antithesis, isocolon, homeoteleuton, or chiasmus. But romantic nature poetry tends to achieve iconicity by a more direct sensory imitation of something headlong and impassioned, less ordered, nearer perhaps to the subrational. Thus: in Shelley's "Ode to the West Wind" the shifts in imagery of the second stanza, the pell-mell raggedness and confusion of loose clouds, decaying leaves, angels and Maenads with hair uplifted, the dirge, the dome, the vapors, and the enjambment from tercet to tercet combine to give an impression beyond statement of the very wildness, the breath and power which is the vehicle of the poem's radical metaphor. If we think of a scale of structures having at one end logic, the completely reasoned and abstracted, and at the other some form of madness or surrealism, matter or impression unformed and undisciplined (the imitation of disorder by the idiom of disorder), we may see metaphysical and neoclassical poetry as near the extreme of logic (though by no means reduced to that status) and romantic poetry as a step toward the directness of sensory presentation (though by no means sunk into subrationality). As a structure which favors implication rather than overt statement, the romantic is far closer than the metaphysical to symbolist poetry and the varieties of postsymbolist most in vogue today. Both types of structure, the metaphysical and the romantic, are valid. Each has gorgeously enriched the history of English poetry.

PART IV

OTHER ASPECTS OF THE AGE

DR. JOHNSON, ROUSSEAU, AND REFORM

Richard B. Sewall

WHENEVER Dr. Johnson spoke of Rousseau, he found it impossible to restrain his irritation and contempt. He was a good hater, and here he indulged himself. No epithet was too scurrilous, no charge too fantastic: a dealer in paradoxes, a childish seeker after novelty, a public menace, a bare-faced writer of nonsense, a charlatan who laughed at the world for taking him seriously. Even Boswell was shocked. "Do you really think *him* a bad man?" "Sir, if you are talking jestingly of this, I don't talk with you. If you mean to be serious, I think him one of the worst of men; a rascal who ought to be hunted out of society, as he has been."

So strong an antipathy was more than merely whimsical. It had legitimate philosophical foundations. But Johnson's extreme abuse, like Burke's later attacks on Rousseau and in our own day Irving Babbitt's, arouses our suspicion. We cannot feel that he did justice either to himself or to Rousseau. He behaved like the arch Tory and persecutor he was not, and his version of Rousseau is too iniquitous to be credible. The real and important issues of this troubled affair have been obscured by much name calling; we see it now through a glass, darkly.

To put in a clearer light the opposition between these two pivotal figures requires, first, that we compare them on grounds which each would have considered fair. I assume that the issues of charlatanism or primitivism (Johnson's most frequent charges against Rousseau) may now, in the light of recent research and criticism,[1] be discarded as fanciful, or at most only partially true. Fundamentally, Johnson and Rousseau were getting at much the same thing: the problem of what to do about the ailing society in which

1. e.g., the work on Rousseau by C. W. Hendel, Arthur O. Lovejoy, Albert Schinz, Ernst Cassirer, E. H. Wright, C. E. Vaughan.

they found themselves. Each man assumed constantly throughout his career the role of moralist or spiritual physician to his age, and to compare them on this basis is both legitimate and suggestive. Johnson's abusiveness can be seen for what it is, and Rousseau appears in his proper light.

But first, what was the state of affairs to which, as critics of society, they addressed themselves and how did each interpret and prescribe for it? Though less acute, the moral situation of mid-century England was much the same as that of France. To use Toynbee's terms, a "creative minority" was losing its creativity and its "charm." In all the institutions which reveal the temper of a society there were signs of stagnation. Toryism, one of the substitutes for charm, was all but "cosmic." [2] The optimism of Pope, debased and extended by Soame Jenyns, for instance, justified a status quo very desirable to those on top and made for a dangerous cleavage between the institutions and those whom they were intended to benefit. Laxity among the clergy was scandalous, as the great strides of the Wesleyan movement clearly showed. The universities were languishing. Gibbon found only one professor at Oxford who was earning his hire, and Gray compared Cambridge with the desolation of Babylon. "The learning of this age," said one observer, "seems to be no more than comments on that of the last." Politics was the perquisite of the upper classes. In the world of letters the dominant tone was of the end of an era, urbane and satirical. The rise of skepticism in speculative thought discouraged a positive, hopeful attitude toward social problems; Hume, as he said in a famous passage, was chilled by the implications of his own discoveries. The growing materialism of a prospering country encouraged smugness and conservatism among those in whom the power of change lay. A few isolated and ineffectual moralists warned of a decline and fall.

Perhaps the kindest way of putting it is to say that England was marking time. In 1750 she was in a sort of interregnum, or spiritual dead center, between two eras of achievement—to men of acute social consciousness a very vulnerable time. It happened that in this year, the very dead center, both Johnson and Rousseau spoke to the

2. Cf. Basil Willey, *The Eighteenth-century Background* (London, 1940), chap. iii.

problem, each in his own way, and foreshadowed the two courses which the diverging thought of the age was to follow. Let us see, first, how Rousseau proposed, on this occasion and later, to meet the conditions that distressed him.

The experience which led to Rousseau's publication in 1750 was transcendent and cataclysmic, almost Pauline. He was walking to Vincennes to visit Diderot when he saw in the *Mercure de France* the Dijon prize question for the year on the moral effects of the arts and sciences. In a moment of vision the brooding, scattered thoughts of his years of vagabondage suddenly achieved unity and direction. He saw the whole problem of man and society in a new light. His mind reeled with a multitude of new thoughts; he almost swooned as with vertigo. If, he later wrote, I could have recorded a quarter of what I saw and felt then, "with what clarity should I have revealed all the contradictions of the social system, with what force would I have exposed all the abuses of our institutions." [3]

He conceived a passionate hope and formulated a method. The essence of his vision was creative and dynamic. He saw man as fearful and craven after centuries of living under a doctrine which regarded all human misery as the just and inevitable punishment for innate sin. He realized the sinister uses of such a doctrine to justify tyranny of all sorts, cynicism, do-nothingism. It came to him that what man needed was to be reminded of certain native human goodnesses in terms of which regeneration might be possible. Man, in a sense, had been argued out of his true nature; surely *all* his miseries were not foredoomed. He must learn how they came about and seek their cures in their origins. Later, Archbishop Beaumont accused him of heresy; Rousseau replied: "All you can see is man in the hands of the devil, but I see how he came there. . . . We both agree that man was created good, but *you* say he is wicked because he has been wicked, while *I* demonstrate how he came to be wicked." [4] The task before modern man, then, was to re-examine all those habits, customs, and institutions which have so largely

---

3. Letter to Malesherbes (Jan. 12, 1762), C. W. Hendel's translation in his *Citizen of Geneva* (New York, Oxford University Press, 1937), p. 208.

4. Cf. Lucien Lévy-Bruhl, *History of Modern Philosophy in France* (Chicago, 1899), p. 238. Tr. by Miss G. Coblence.

made him what he is—even those institutions with which authority says we are not to tamper. Even in his moment of vision Rousseau realized that perfect success was impossible; there never can be a painless world. But he saw society as an organic whole, with the health of one part vitally necessary to the health of all the others. The world he saw about him was far from healthy, and the challenge to the leaders was inescapable.

Charged with these convictions, he became an author (as he later wrote of the experience on the way to Vincennes) "almost in spite of myself." He set out to teach the age "how to live."

The essay of 1750 was the opening gun of a twelve-year campaign. Following the suggestion of the Dijon prize question, he aimed first at the top. The men of learning and their patrons, he said, were guilty of a moral failure. There was an ever widening chasm between the world of learning and the needs of the common man. Precarious benefits as they were, the arts and sciences had become the tools of pride and the source of luxury and effeminacy. Learning had declined to pedantry and wisdom to cleverness. The philosophers were lost in bickering and skepticism. He urged upon the academies, the universities, and the heads of states a more responsible concern for general human welfare and the promotion of virtue. Meanwhile he urged "ordinary men" to trust rather to the "voice within" than to the false leadership of the intelligentsia as they then were. In short, he proposed the question, healthy for any society to face, as to whether its boasted refinements were really refinements at all.

Five years later, after much controversy with various defenders of the Enlightenment who charged him with sheer subversiveness, he tried to justify more theoretically his hope for mankind. In the *Discourse on Inequality* he reopened the question of what man by nature really was. He could not accept Hobbes's view that man is wolfish and that a rigid social hierarchy and an authoritarian government are the only guarantees against barbarism. In what may be the first proposal of its kind, he suggested a ten-year expedition by a group of scientists and philosophers to see what light a study of the primitive societies could throw on this problem. Meanwhile, he staked his position on the view that its findings would refute the Hobbesians, and in this belief called in question the current social inequalities. They were not to be justified, he said, by any "law of nature" or theory of divine right. Is it "natural," he concluded in a resounding sentence, that "children should command old men, fools wise men, and that the privileged few should gorge themselves with superfluities, while the starving multitudes are in want of the bare necessities of life?" Again he insisted that an aristocracy must have some other justification than birth or special favor. In a polemical fling which was more misunderstood in England than any other part of the essay and was snatched up by an already emerging cult of the "noble savage," he suggested that in certain ways, such as health, freedom, and animal contentedness, the solitary life of the savage might conceivably be superior to the "petulant activity" of modern egoism. Although he upheld the "primitive" virtues of simplicity and compassion, he nowhere suggested that animal contentedness was superior to the life of reason and in a crucial passage warned against interpreting his doctrine as a call for a return to the woods. He drew a fearful picture, to be sure, of the greed and brutality of civilized men, but there was hope in his insistence that this picture was not the inevitable one.

His more positive suggestions on "how to live" began with the *Nouvelle Héloïse* in 1761. Against the sophisticated, dissolute manners of the aristocracy, he held up the healthy life of the small rural community. Here man is at his best—far from Fleet Street and Charing Cross. But life on the Wolmar estate was hardly that of the savage. Julie's household was a model of piety and good management. Her regard for the welfare of her retainers threw a new light on the master-servant relationship. In the long discursive letters between Julie and her friends, on subjects ranging from the care of vineyards to education and religion, Rousseau showed in detail what he meant by the good life and the principles on which he thought it must be based.

In *Émile* (1762) he described how the child should be reared for the sort of life he envisioned. Here was an "education according to nature" not in the sense that Émile was to be brought up like a young savage but rather as "by nature" a freedom-loving and compassionate individual. The infant—Rousseau was the first to draw attention to the importance of the earliest years—was no lump of sin to be whipped and prodded into shape. The repressive use of swaddling clothes and the fashionable practice of farming out babies to nursing homes were, he suggested, the individual's first legitimate complaint against society, even the seed of future rebellion. In due course should come games and projects that would develop the child's physique and powers of independent observation and judgment. There must be restraint and punishment, but he was to learn the moral lessons as far as possible from experience rather than precept. Books, theory, even religious instruction were to come as his native curiosity demanded them and when he had gained some powers of discrimination. He should eat simple food, live in the country, and learn a trade.

Such an education, thought Rousseau, would prepare a youth to become a citizen in the ideal state which, in rounding out his "grand design" for his age, he described in *The Social Contract* (1762). Here, having willingly renounced natural for civil liberty, the citizen would assemble with his equals to determine "the general will." He would bring to the problems of citizenship an independent and discerning mind. He would be compassionate and devout, with a keen sense of the common good and capable of enjoying liberty under law. This, and not the savage state, Rousseau upheld as the true felicity for mankind. He was aware, as in all his other proposals, of the many practical difficulties in the way, especially in states much larger than his native Switzerland, his model. But (he would agree with a modern theorist) "although it is absurd to expect perfection, it is not absurd to strive for it." Indeed, he would add, in striving for it lay our only hope.

Such in briefest outline was Rousseau's program of reform. I have given, of course, little notion of his wide-ranging and lavish treatment. Before he was through, he had touched upon even the minutest aspects of the life of his time. Of the multitude of fresh ideas, many proved fruitless or, still worse, were so distracting and irritating as to obscure the value of his major insights. Only a few of his contemporaries saw what he was about; for the most part he was cordially hated. Among orthodox and conservative Englishmen the force of tradition and the growing tensions of the age would have required, for any other verdict, almost superhuman detachment and perception. This we must remember as we turn to Dr. Johnson, to his prescription for his age and to what he made of Rousseau's.

In the same year (1750) that Rousseau broached his radical proposals, Johnson took a long, sad look at human affairs and stated the principles from which he never departed:

The cure for the greatest part of human miseries is not radical but palliative. Infelicity is involved in corporeal nature, and interwoven with our being; all attempts therefore to decline it wholly are useless and vain: the armies of pain send their arrows against us on every side, the choice is only between those which are more or less sharp, or tinged with poison of greater or less malignity; and the strongest armour which reason can supply, will only blunt their points, but cannot repel them.[5]

Man, in short, is born to suffer; human happiness does not depend on externals, on institutions; it is rather the product of individual discipline and inner composure, the capacity to enjoy the few delights and to endure the many miseries of life. The only practicable reform is that which is aimed at individual human nature through moral persuasion and encouragement, or at the most a few private charities and the righting of local wrongs. Radical changes, or changes en masse, would very probably make things even worse than they are. "Laws are now made," he wrote later, "and customs are established; these are our rules, and by them we must be guided." [6] The reformers are undermining the precarious structure of civilization and threaten to bring it down on our heads.

This is not to call Dr. Johnson an unmitigated Tory. He himself had suffered, and he was deeply troubled both by the misery he saw about him and by the complacency of those who refused to recognize the evil. In certain moods he came closer to Rousseau than he perhaps realized.[7] He too saw "worth by poverty oppressed" and could address men of rank, like Lord Chesterfield, with Rousseauistic bitterness. When he wrote of Soame Jenyns that "this author and Pope perhaps never saw the miseries which they imagine thus easy to be borne," he echoed Rousseau's verdict upon an irrespon-

5. *Rambler* 32.

6. *The False Alarm* (1770).

7. *Cf.* Albert Schinz, "Les Dangers du cliché littéraire: le Dr. Johnson et J.-J. Rousseau," *M.L.N.* (1942), pp. 573–580.

sible aristocracy. It was not Rousseau but Johnson who wrote, "I am always afraid of determining on the side of envy or cruelty." He spoke out against debtors' prisons and urged better asylums for the aged and outcast.

But these resemblances between the two show merely that neither lacked humanity or a sense of justice. Fundamentally Johnson believed Rousseau's schemes to be tainted at their source, mistaken in principle, and fraught with possibilities for disaster.

It is clear that Johnson lumped Rousseau with all those visionaries who had succumbed to what Imlac called in *Rasselas* "the dangerous prevalence of the imagination." Cutting loose from the "wisdom of the race," they were going it alone, following "sudden irradiations of intelligence" and "immediate intuition." In a *Rambler* article in 1751, perhaps in response to Rousseau's first *Discourse,* he called this intuitionism "the mental disease of the present generation." Later he accused the French writers of proceeding on "the mere power of their own minds"—and (he added) "we see how very little power they have." They were not "scholars."

In their rhapsodies, Johnson believed, they ignored the sober facts and jumped to false conclusions. Every close observer must agree with Hobbes that man is by nature wolfish. Children and savages are always cruel. Man has raised himself from the fearful state of his origins by the painfully acquired social virtues, and has established society on principles learned through sad experience. Inequalities are "very necessary for society," even though they involve some injustice and suffering, because the very existence of society depends upon authority and authority requires "subordination," Rousseau would lead us to a "romantick" morality of anarchic individualism—the surest way to barbarism.

"Human experience," said Johnson in 1763, speaking of the second *Discourse,* "is constantly contradicting theory." From then on, as the tensions of the age grew stronger, his voice became increasingly strident against the "theorists." It was in 1766 that he wished Rousseau at the plantations. "Governments," he wrote in 1770, "are never to be tried by a regular theory. . . . We must be content with them as they are; should we attempt to mend their disproportions, we might easily demolish, and difficultly rebuild them." [8] The social contract theory is but the "unmeaning clamour of the pedants of policy, the delirious dream of republican fanaticism." [9] Every day "we see the towering head of speculation bow down unwillingly to grovelling experience." [10] In the affair of Wilkes he saw nothing but "sedition and obscenity": should the freeholders of Middlesex sink into nonexistence, there would simply be room for a new rabble, with its new "patriotism" and its Bill of Rights. In 1775 he wrote facetiously of the sounds of "noisy triumph" which "the winds are wafting from the Western Continent." [11]

All such vast social problems as faced the mid-eighteenth century desperately need, of course, the qualities of both a Johnson and a Rousseau. If Johnson did not sense the extent to which the age was impoverished, Rousseau, like many writers of emotional genius, overstated the case, asked for too much, and succeeded too often in merely hardening the conservatives in their position or impelling the youthful and enthusiastic to absurd extremes.

But that Rousseau read the times more clearly there can be little doubt. Even in England things developed in his way and not Johnson's. The Wesleyan movement, the growth of philanthropy and of concern for such canker spots as the prisons and the poor laws, the deeper penetration of literature into the lower reaches of society— such stirrings were being felt even before Rousseau came on the scene. England was developing a conscience, for which Rousseau provided both encouragement and method. In Scotland during the third quarter of the century a more concerted movement showed that a new and non-Johnsonian view of man and society could be assimilated into the British tradition with fruitful results. Adam Smith, Adam Ferguson, Hume, Kames, Monboddo (leaders in what has recently been called "The Scottish Inquiry"),[12] all felt his influence in one way or another. Out of their efforts were to come a new economics, the modern study of sociology and anthropology,

8. *The False Alarm.*
9. *Taxation no Tyranny* (1775).
10. *The False Alarm.*
11. *Taxation no Tyranny.*
12. Gladys Bryson, *Man and Society, The Scottish Inquiry of the Eighteenth Century* (Princeton, 1945).

new ideas on education, agriculture, public and personal health, and eventually—and indirectly, through such men as Beattie, Burns, and Wordsworth—a new literature. In many particular ways it can be shown how Rousseau impinged upon this movement, but perhaps he was most useful in helping to create a state of mind in which it was possible. We can scarcely realize, wrote an observer in 1860, how intensely the eighteenth-century conservatives resisted not only innovation but "the mere raising of the faintest question of the necessity of matters being as they are." The Scottish intellectuals were more judicious in their appraisal of Rousseau than were the Londoners. "Even if my own ideas are mistaken," Rousseau had said in *Émile,* "my time will not have been wasted if I stir up others to form right ideas." The Scots were very clear about what they considered his mistakes, but they frequently testified to his constructive and energizing power. They became, in a sense, followers of Rousseau (as the most stimulating figure in the entire French reform movement) without being Rousseauists.

Thus Boswell, a good Scot himself, having just returned (in 1766) from a tour of Europe, was more than personally disturbed at Johnson's sarcastic remark: "It seems, Sir, you have kept very good company abroad, Rousseau and Wilkes!" Boswell had read "many of Rousseau's animated writings with great pleasure, and even edification," and as he had sat with Rousseau at Môtiers he had seen in him many of the same qualities he revered in Dr. Johnson. This violence of Johnson's, he wrote, "seemed very strange to me. . . . Nor can I yet allow that he deserves the very severe censure which Johnson pronounced upon him." But by 1766 Rousseau had become for Johnson a symbol of all evil, as he later was for Burke. Any common meeting ground, either for the good of the age or anything else, was out of the question. Rousseau apparently sensed this sooner than Boswell. In the enthusiasm of his visit, Boswell had proposed a meeting between the two. He enlarged upon the merits of his great friend—but he made the mistake of telling him of Johnson's epigram on Hume as one of "sceptical innovators." Rousseau demurred. "I would like that man," he said to Boswell, "I would respect him. I would refrain from shattering his principles were I to find I could do so; but from far off for fear he might deal me a blow. . . . He would detest me; he would say, 'Here is a Corrupter: a Man who comes here to milk the Bull.' " [13]

13. *Boswell Papers*, IV, 101.

BISHOP BERKELEY,
METAPHYSICIAN AS MORALIST

Ellen Douglass Leyburn

TWO of Boswell's stories concerning Bishop Berkeley display Johnson in his best vein; and since good things bear repeating, there is more than an interested reason for rehearsing them. The more famous one is an episode of the farewell trip to Harwich early in Boswell's friendship with Johnson: "After we came out of the church, we stood talking for some time together of Bishop Berkeley's ingenious sophistry to prove the non-existence of matter, and that every thing in the universe is merely ideal. I observed, that though we are satisfied his doctrine is not true, it is impossible to refute it. I never shall forget the alacrity with which Johnson answered, striking his foot with mighty force against a large stone, till he rebounded from it, 'I refute it *thus.*'" [1] The other of a much later date shows perhaps more wit, if less strength: "Being in company with a gentleman who thought fit to maintain Dr. Berkeley's ingenious philosophy, that nothing exists but as perceived by some mind; when the gentleman was going away, Johnson said to him, 'Pray, Sir, don't leave us; for we may perhaps forget to think of you, and then you will cease to exist.'" [2] There are two references much less commonly quoted which are worth setting beside these. One occurs during a lecture to Boswell against self-absorbed dejection: "It is by contemplating a large mass of human existence, that a man, while he sets a just value on his own life, does not think of his death as annihilating all that is great and pleasing in the world, as if actually *contained in his mind,* according to Berkeley's reverie." [3] The other is simply a recorded judgment: "Talking of the Irish clergy, he said, . . . Berkeley was a profound scholar, as well as a man of fine imagination; . . ." [4]

1. Boswell's *Life,* I, 471.
2. *Ibid.,* IV, 27.
3. *Ibid.,* III, 165.
4. *Ibid.,* II, 132.

At this late date Berkeley's philosophical system needs no defense against the misconception which Johnson seems to have shared with Boswell. Suffice it to say that the false notion that Berkeley preached the nonexistence of matter was common throughout the eighteenth century and had made Berkeley as early as 1710 complain "that men who have never considered my book should confound me with the sceptics, who doubt the existence of sensible things." [5] His protest against the prejudiced and careless misreading of his early work grows still more vehement: "But whoever reads my book with attention will see that there is a direct opposition between the principles that are contained in it and those of the sceptics, and that I question not the existence of anything we perceive by our senses. I do not deny the existence of the sensible things which Moses says were created by God. They existed from all eternity, in the Divine Intellect; and they became perceptible (i.e. were created) in the same manner and order as is described in Genesis." [6] Johnson may have read Berkeley's book with attention and yet have come away with the same prepossession he took to it, failing as other readers did to distinguish Berkeley's effort to make clear in what the reality of the sensible world consists from a denial of that reality. Whatever the degree of his actual understanding of Berkeley, the circumstances must have colored his condemnation of the bishop's supposed "sophistry" in each of the recorded references except that of the sober appreciation of his learning and imagination.

In Harwich the conversation turned to Berkeley in a moment of religious awe when Johnson had just made Boswell perform an act of piety before his setting out. If Berkeley's name was linked in Johnson's mind with skepticism about sensible objects, it might easily have been connected with skepticism concerning God, in spite of the fact that the central object of Berkeley's whole philosophical structure is to prove the existence and providence of God. Something of the violence of Johnson's denunciation of Hume or of any disturbance of his religious belief must have gone into that blow from which he rebounded, something of the feeling with which

5. Letter to Percival quoted in Editor's Preface to the *Dialogues between Hylas and Philonous*, in *The Works of George Berkeley, D.D.*, ed. A. C. Fraser (Oxford, 1901), I, 353.
6. *Ibid*.

he declared, "Every man who attacks my belief, diminishes in some degree my confidence in it, and therefore makes me uneasy; and I am angry with him who makes me uneasy." [7] He is in effect here kicking against his own temptation to skepticism.

The story of the gentleman who was so unfortunate as to "maintain Dr. Berkeley's ingenious philosophy" shows Johnson "in company" and winning a conversational victory by his wit. It must be taken rather as a triumph in Johnson's favorite sport than as a serious judgment on Berkeley. Nevertheless, the basis of the triumph is a disapproval of Berkeley's views which Johnson takes for granted.

The other derogatory reference to Berkeley occurs when Johnson associates him with what he regarded as one of the cardinal sins, the courting of unhappiness by an undue self-regard. The paragraph in which he labels "Berkeley's reverie" the folly of the individual's thinking "of his death as annihilating all that is great and pleasing in the world, as if *actually contained in his mind,"* ends with a most characteristic Johnsonian utterance: "Let us guard against imagining that there is an end of felicity upon earth, when we ourselves grow old, or are unhappy."

Viewed as a condemnation of Berkeley, this pronouncement has an inappropriateness that accentuates the whole irony of Johnson's failure to appreciate Berkeley as a moralist. Indeed we wonder, in spite of the praise of Berkeley's fine imagination and deep learning, if Johnson had read *Alciphron* at all, for we look in vain in Johnson's comments for any praise of Berkeley as a teacher of ethics. Yet the ultimate ethical test of his views is implied even in his earlier works; and the whole purport of *Alciphron* is that the test of his philosophy, his religion (since his philosophy is simply the proof of his religion, it seems legitimate to use the terms interchangeably), is that it works. It produces the sound result of making men better. The fourth dialogue, to be sure, contains the essence of Berkeley's philosophical proof of the being of God: that the perceptible universe is the language through which God communicates to man by sensible signs; but in the negative dialogues which lead up to it and in most of the defense of Christianity which follows it Berkeley

7. Boswell's *Life,* III, 10–11.

is talking about morality, not metaphysics. Indeed he always objected to having the term metaphysics used at all with reference to his thought, the whole test and worth of which he found in its validating Christian ethics. For all the brilliance of his speculative genius, which perhaps seems most un-English, he was a true son of his country and of his age in finding the proof of the soundness of his views in practical morality.

This is the test to which he subjects the false views of Shaftesbury and Mandeville which he is refuting; this is the test to which he likewise submits his own belief in Christianity. The question for them is "whether the notions of your minute philosophy are worth proving; I mean, whether they are of use and service to mankind." [8] The defense of the principles to which he clings is its direct corollary: "Might it not therefore be inferred, that those men are foolish who go about to unhinge such principles as have a necessary connexion with the general good of mankind?" [9] What he undertakes to prove is "that the belief of a God, of a future state, and of moral duties are the only wise, right, and genuine principles of human conduct." [10] The basis of his proof of these principles is that they have "a necessary connexion with the well being of mankind." [11]

Berkeley's battle against the views of Mandeville is half won by his letting the worthless Lysicles be their advocate. He simply displays the young gentleman in all his frivolous insipidity, as much as to say: this is the human product of the paradox, "Private vices, public benefits." Crito's stories introduce much more monstrous demonstrations, such as that of Callicles, who "killed his old covetous father with vexation," [12] or of Cleon, who "dressed well, could cheat at cards, had a nice palate, understood the mystery of the die, was a mighty man in the minute philosophy; and having shined a few years in these accomplishments, he died before thirty, childless and rotten, expressing the utmost indignation that he

8. *Alciphron; or, The Minute Philosopher*, in *The Works of George Berkeley, D.D.*, II, 63.

9. *Ibid.*, p. 65.

10. *Ibid.*, p. 67.

11. *Ibid.*

12. *Ibid.*, p. 75.

could not outlive that old dog his father." [13] Crito says that "the minute philosopher Magirus, being desirous to benefit the public, by circulating an estate possessed by a near relation who had not the heart to spend it, soon convinced himself, upon these principles, that it would be a very worthy action to dispatch out of the way such a useless fellow, to whom he was next heir. But, for this laudable attempt, he had the misfortune to be hanged by an underbred judge and jury." [14] He multiplies his satiric tales of people corrupted by the principles Lysicles espouses. But all the while there is Lysicles himself with his silly answers convincing us more than do all Crito's stories of the hollowness of Mandeville's doctrine.

In this second dialogue Berkeley is no Puritan preaching asceticism. He almost takes Johnson's side in the century-long argument about luxury. He makes Euphranor confound Lysicles' proposition that "vice circulates money and promotes industry" [15] with the comment that "A sober healthy man, . . . in a long life, may circulate more money by eating and drinking, than a glutton or a drunkard in a short one." [16] He is willing to let Lysicles say that "Happiness is the end to which created beings naturally tend," [17] especially since Euphranor himself has asked leave to cite such authorities as Aristotle and Cicero, "such authorities as I know, and have passed for many ages upon the world." [18] Nor does he frown upon a due enjoyment of pleasures of sense. But he shows the folly of considering man's chief happiness to consist in these pleasures by letting Lysicles say that the superiority of brutes in "sensual happiness . . . hath made several gentlemen of our sect envy brutes, and lament the lot of human-kind." [19] Berkeley carries his ridicule of Lysicles to the point of making Crito say, "It was a consideration of this sort which inspired Erotylus with the laudable ambition of wishing himself a snail." [20] But after Crito has

13. *Ibid.*, p. 105.
14. *Ibid.*, p. 79.
15. *Ibid.*, p. 76.
16. *Ibid.*, p. 77.
17. *Ibid.*, p. 90.
18. *Ibid.*, p. 80.
19. *Ibid.*, p. 92.
20. *Ibid.*

had his fun at Lysicles' expense, Euphranor gives impassioned utterance to Berkeley's view:

> Reason, therefore, being the principal part of our nature, whatever is most reasonable should seem most natural to man. Must we not therefore think rational pleasures more agreeable to human-kind than those of sense? . . . A beast, without reflexion or remorse, without foresight, or appetite of immortality, without notion of vice or virtue, or order, or reason, or knowledge! What motive, what grounds, can there be for bringing down man, in whom are all these things, to a level with such a creature? What merit, what ambition, in the minute philosopher to make such an animal a guide or rule for human life? [21]

As it is the public good which has been debated throughout in terms of Mandeville's paradox, Berkeley has started from the question, "whether the public good of a nation doth not imply the particular good of its individuals?" [22] It is by ruining men that vice ruins the public since it doth not "only thin a nation, but also debaseth it by a puny degenerate race." [23] Consequently, it is fitting that Crito should draw this day's conversation toward a close by saying:

> . . . with respect to these great advantages of destroying men and notions, . . . I question whether the public gains as much by the latter as it loseth by the former. . . . Errors and nonsense, as such, are of small concern in the eyes of the public; which considers not the metaphysical truth of notions, so much as the tendency they have to produce good or evil. Truth itself is valued by the public, as it hath an influence and is felt in the course of life . . . this I say must be allowed, supposing, what I by no means grant, your notions to be true. For, to say plainly what I think, the tendency of your opinions is so bad that no good man can endure them, and your arguments for them so weak that no wise man will admit them. [24]

The next day Alciphron takes the field in defense of the views of Shaftesbury. These seem to Berkeley so fantastically at variance with the facts of human nature as he has observed them that he answers more by mockery than by serious refutation. Alciphron is a more absurd figure than Lysicles because his pretensions are greater, being no less than to demolish "the whole fabric of human

21. *Ibid.*, p. 93.
22. *Ibid.*, p. 85.
23. *Ibid.*, p. 88.
24. *Ibid.*, pp. 113–114.

folly and superstition." [25] The self-complacency of the minute philosopher is fully displayed. After one of his periods, "Alciphron having said this made a pause, and looked round on the company." [26] Later, Berkeley says, "Alciphron stood over against us, with his arms folded across, and his head reclined on his left shoulder, in the posture of a man meditating. We sat silent, not to disturb his thoughts; and after two or three minutes he uttered these words—Oh truth! oh liberty! After which he remained musing as before." [27] Throughout the third dialogue, as he retreats from one position after another, Alciphron retains the air that Johnson ascribes to his own Shaftesburian philosopher in *Rasselas* of one who "had co-operated with the present system." [28] The inflated manner of Shaftesbury seems to have been irresistibly funny to Berkeley, for he returns to laughter at it in the fifth dialogue, where he renders one of Shaftesbury's purple passages in blank verse which makes the country-bred Euphranor exclaim, "why should we break off our conference to read a play?" [29] Whatever we think of the fairness of such methods of attack, Shaftesbury had laid himself open by claiming ridicule as the test of truth. Berkeley does not perhaps make a fair representation of either Shaftesbury or Mandeville; but what concerns us here is the basis of his disparagement of each: the pernicious *effect* of doctrines contrary to Christianity.

The real ridiculousness of Shaftesbury's views as Berkeley presents them is the inadequacy of the idea of Beauty, for the relish of which "there must be a delicate and fine taste" [30] and "a certain ardour or enthusiasm that glowed in the breast of a gallant man" [31] to produce virtuous action in the mass of mankind. Euphranor asks, "Doth it not follow . . . that the beauty of virtue, or τὸ καλόν, in either Aristotle's or Plato's sense, is not sufficient principle or ground to engage sensual or worldly-minded men in the practice

25. *Ibid.*, p. 42.
26. *Ibid.*, p. 36.
27. *Ibid.*, p. 40.
28. *The History of Rasselas, Prince of Abissinia*, ed. R. W. Chapman (Oxford, 1927), p. 100.
29. *Alciphron, op. cit.*, II, 221.
30. *Ibid.*, p. 126.
31. *Ibid.*, p. 122.

of it? . . . it will follow that the hope of reward and fear of punishment are highly expedient to cast the balance of pleasant and
profitable on the side of virtue, and thereby very much conduce to
the benefit of human society." [32] Alciphron retreats to the statement:

Moral beauty is of so peculiar and abstracted a nature, something so subtle,
fine, and fugacious, that it will not bear being handled and inspected, like
every gross and common subject. You will, therefore, pardon me if I stand
upon my philosophical liberty; and choose rather to intrench myself within
the general and indefinite sense, rather than, by entering into a precise and
particular explication of this beauty, perchance lose sight of it; or give you
some hold whereon to cavil, and infer, and raise doubts, queries, and difficulties about a point as clear as the sun, when nobody reasons upon it. [33]

Alciphron's ineffectiveness is emphasized by Lysicles' repudiation:

If I must subdue my passions, abstract, contemplate, be enamoured of virtue;
in a word, if I must be an enthusiast, I owe so much deference to the laws of
my country as to choose being an enthusiast in their way. Besides, it is better
being so for some end than for none. This doctrine hath all the solid incon-
veniences, without the amusing hopes and prospects, of the Christian. [34]

Euphranor continues to plague his adversary with the question
which he persistently asks: "What service can it do mankind to
lessen the motives to virtue, or what damage to increase them?" [35]

The fourth dialogue is a masterly presentation of Berkeley's
proofs of the being and nature of God "who speaks every day and
in every place to the eyes of all men." [36] Crito declares that "this
Visual Language proves, not a Creator merely, but a provident
Governor, actually and intimately present, and attentive to all our
interests and motions, who watches over our conduct, and takes
care of our minutest actions and designs throughout the whole
course of our lives, informing, admonishing, and directing inces-
santly, in a most evident and sensible manner." [37] As Crito's speech
plainly shows, this dialogue which argues the epistemological
proofs of a God is no digression from the main ethical course of

32. *Ibid.*, p. 128.
33. *Ibid.*
34. *Ibid.*, pp. 130–131.
35. *Ibid.*, p. 152.
36. *Ibid.*, p. 171.
37. *Ibid.*, p. 175.

the whole. Instead of being a metaphysical interlude, it is an integral step in the discourse on morality. Believing that the consciousness of God holds the sensible world in being and through it speaks to the consciousness of man gives the believer a very potent motive to please the God who "watches over our conduct" as over all his creatures.

This conception forms the basis of the last three dialogues which deal specifically with "the use or benefit of the Christian religion." [38] Berkeley puts into Crito's mouth the point toward which the whole of *Alciphron* has tended: "one great mark of the truth of Christianity is, in my mind, its tendency to do good, which seems the north star to conduct our judgment in moral matters, and in all things of a practical nature; moral or practical truths being ever connected with universal benefit." [39] There is a measure of self-satisfaction in Crito's assurance that the English-speaking world of the eighteenth century is superior in manners and morals to classical civilizations; but the whole use of his praise of his times is to attribute the softening, polishing, and embellishing of the manners [40] of Britons to Christianity. Furthermore, the work would scarcely be that of the author of *An Essay Toward Preventing the Ruin of Great Britain* if it did not contain a warning to prick the boast. And so it does: "Under the Christian religion this nation hath been greatly improved. From a sort of savages, we have grown civil, polite, and learned. We have made a decent and noble figure both at home and abroad. And, as our religion decreaseth, I am afraid we shall be found to have declined. Why then should we persist in the dangerous experiment?" [41]

The sixth and seventh dialogues discuss doctrinal questions such as the inspiration and authority of the Scriptures, man's moral responsibility for his own guilt, immortality, and divine justice and grace, "particularly those articles of our Christian faith, which, in proportion as they are believed, persuade, and, as they persuade, influence the lives and actions of men." [42] To the last, the reason

38. *Ibid.*, p. 198.
39. *Ibid.*
40. *Ibid.*, p. 206.
41. *Ibid.*, p. 240.
42. *Ibid.*, p. 345.

given for faith is the result it produces. Crito, faithful to his function as illustrator, in the final dialogue supposes the case of a
"minute philosopher, prodigal and rapacious," tempted to a vil-
lainous act. Such a man is wholly unaffected by appeals to the
enjoyment of an "interior moral sense," and "strongly affected
with a sense of corporeal pleasures. . . . Whereas that very man,
do but produce in him a sincere belief of a Future State, although
it be a mystery, . . . he shall, nevertheless, by virtue of such belief,
be withheld from executing his wicked project." [43]

It is impossible to read *Alciphron* with Johnson in mind without
finding there sentiments that almost make us forget relations of
time and space and think them echoes of *Rasselas* and the *Rambler*.
The passages of idyllic description of the shores of Rhode Island
or of the country life of church-going and farming and rural
pleasures near the Newport of a simpler day recall to us that Johnson's works could not have been among those with which Berkeley
beguiled his enforced leisure at Whitehall, even though *Alciphron*
begins with the Johnsonian sentiment: "Events are not in our
power; but it always is, to make a good use even of the verv
worst." [44] The impossibility of Berkeley's knowing Johnson makes
it seem all the more a pity that Johnson, who did have access to
Berkeley's book, should not have valued *Alciphron*. For it is easy
in reading the dialogues to let the imagination propel the Doctor
back to 1729-30 and across the ocean to these shores and to hear
Crito speaking in his voice. To be sure, he was not fond of America, and he would have had to walk under the "delicious shade" of
plane trees and "on the smooth sand, with the ocean on one hand,
and on the other wild broken rocks." [45] But the conversation was
good; he could seat himself in the "hollow glade" or over a dish
of tea in the library or in the "summer parlour which looks into
the garden"; he could make his wise pronouncements and illustrate them with stories; and he could have the last recorded word,
for "while Crito was saying this, company came in, which put an
end to our conversation." [46]

43. *Ibid.*, pp. 338–339.
44. *Ibid.*, p. 32.
45. *Ibid.*, p. 70.
46. *Ibid.*, p. 368.

JOHNSON, CHESTERFIELD, AND BOSWELL

Sidney L. Gulick, Jr.

FOR want of keeping a diary, the fourth Earl of Chesterfield lost a bout with history or, more accurately and to his own disadvantage, gave literary historians a blank page. All we know of his opinion of Samuel Johnson is what he wrote in two essays in the *World,* commending the forthcoming dictionary—written, of course, prior to Johnson's angry missive. There is no word in Chesterfield's letters or elsewhere of what he thought of Johnson's reaction to those letters or of the man. But what Johnson wrote and said about Chesterfield fills several pages of Boswell's *Life,* from which generations of readers have taken their opinion of the earl. Yet as one reads and rereads Boswell's pages, including the famous letter by Johnson, inconsistencies appear—not one, but several—so that one feels less and less certain as to what exactly did happen or how the earl did offend the lexicographer, beyond failing to send other gifts to follow the first, of ten pounds.

Perhaps the major loss to Boswell from his not meeting Johnson until 1763 was his having to recount at second hand the events of 1747, when the *Plan* was published and when Chesterfield told Johnson, according to Boswell, that *great* should be pronounced to rhyme with *state,*[1] and those of 1755, when Johnson disburdened himself of the letter. The modern reader, too, will regret that Boswell was not there to shepherd the conversation, if need be, and to remember the flow of it, according to his custom. And if Boswell had been admitted to Chesterfield's drawing room, as Robert Dodsley was, he might have seen for himself the letter lying on the table and heard the earl point out those severe passages which made men of the world such as Horace Walpole smile at the rude

---

1. Boswell, *Life of Johnson,* II, 161.

bear worrying his dancing master. Instead, over a period of years Boswell gathered bits of information about the two events, prodded the Doctor into writing from memory a copy of his letter, pounced upon Langton's copy (Johnson had asked that, if it were printed, Langton's copy be used), and finally wrote a story which has been avidly read through the years. Yet, as already stated, the famous letter committed to print by Boswell in 1790, thirty-five years after Johnson wrote it, fails to explain the cause of the quarrel, and Boswell's account of the affair leaves the reader no better informed, as will be shown below.

Furthermore, when one reads not only this part of the *Life* but the numerous other comments of both Boswell and Johnson on Lord Chesterfield, there comes the impression, difficult to prove but palpable nevertheless, that as the years went by Boswell felt a continued bitterness toward the earl, whereas Johnson mellowed.

Of the two related problems—the discrepancies in the story of the quarrel, for one, and the possibility that Johnson mellowed in his attitude toward the earl whereas Boswell did not, for the other—the first yields more easily to examination.

Indisputable facts are these: in the autumn of 1747 Johnson addressed to Chesterfield a proposal to compile a dictionary of the English language. Chesterfield made some suggestions, gave Johnson £10. Seven years later, hearing that the *Dictionary* would soon appear, Chesterfield wrote two laudatory papers in the *World* (Nos. 100, 101; Nov. 28, Dec. 5, 1754). Johnson replied with the letter in question.

Obviously, these facts do not explain the chain of events. Does Johnson's letter? He wrote of visiting Chesterfield

upon some slight encouragement . . . but I found my attendance so little encouraged, that neither pride nor modesty would suffer me to continue it. When I had once addressed your Lordship in publick, I had exhausted all the art of pleasing which a retired and uncourtly scholar can possess. I had done all that I could; and no man is well pleased to have his all neglected, be it ever so little.

Seven years, my Lord, have now passed, since I waited in your outward rooms, or was repulsed from your door; during which time I have been pushing on my work . . . without one act of assistance, one word of encouragement, or one smile of favour. Such treatment I did not expect, for I never had a Patron before.[2]

Here one reads that his pride and modesty forbade his continuing to attend upon Lord Chesterfield, for when he had *once* addressed his lordship in public, he was done. Seven years had elapsed, he wrote, since he had waited *or* was repulsed—surely a curious alternative, particularly in view of the gift of £10 at that time. To be sure, he later told Langton to gloss the phrase "without one act of assistance" as ignoring Chesterfield's "inconsiderable" gift. In view of these contradictions, exactly what did happen? One may assume that possibly Johnson called several times upon Lord Chesterfield; the address to him "in publick" may have been the dedication of the *Plan,* which, Boswell states,[3] he had already discussed with Chesterfield. From then on, apparently, Johnson expected the earl to take the initiative and to supply his needs. Instead, Johnson had only a bitter memory. But all this explanation is only assumption, not knowledge. No, Johnson's famous letter gives no adequate account of the events which disillusioned him.

Is Boswell more specific? In the twelve pages of text and notes in Hill's edition [4] there is apparently the answer: Boswell takes pains to kill the story, printed in Sir John Hawkins' *Life of Johnson* [London, 1787, p. 189], that Johnson was kept waiting an hour while Chesterfield talked to Colley Cibber, then poet laureate, whom Johnson despised, and that upon discovering for whom he was kept waiting, Johnson rushed from the house. "Johnson himself assured me, that there was not the least foundation for it. He told me, that there never was any particular incident which produced a quarrel between Lord Chesterfield and him; but that his Lordship's continued neglect was the reason why he resolved to have no connection with him." [5]

2. *Ibid.,* I, 261–262.

3. *Ibid.,* I, 184; II, 161. Mr. Herman Liebert has called attention to the fact that Chesterfield read the *Plan* in MS (now in the Adam Collection) and returned it to Johnson with comments in his own hand. This was apparently unknown to Boswell.

4. *Ibid.,* I, 256–267.

5. *Ibid.,* I, 257. Boswell had had, of course, this refutation in his journal since 1773; see *Boswell Papers,* VI, 94.

Continued neglect, then, it is to be. But eight pages below, Boswell tells another story, this time basing the quarrel on a single incident: Dr. William Adams, Johnson's friend, the Master of Pembroke College,

expostulated with Johnson, and suggested, that his not being admitted when he called on him, was, probably, not to be imputed to Lord Chesterfield; for his Lordship had declared to Dodsley, that "he would have turned off the best servant he ever had, if he had known that he denied him to a man who would have been always more than welcome"; and, in confirmation of this, he insisted on Lord Chesterfield's general affability and easiness of access, especially to literary men. "Sir, (said Johnson) that is not Lord Chesterfield; he is the proudest man this day existing." "No, (said Dr. Adams) there is one person, at least, as proud; I think, by your own account, you are the prouder man of the two." "But mine (replied Johnson, instantly) was *defensive* pride."

Inconsistencies can doubtless be explained away. Johnson may have meant that there was no particular incident between him and Lord Chesterfield, lumping into the neglect some footman's denying him entry. That *may* have been the reason for this inconsistency; again, since the accounts do in fact vary, it may not. Boswell obviously tells the first story to deflate Hawkins; the second—belying his refutation of the single incident as setting off the quarrel—seems to be presented for the sake of Johnson's irrelevant repartee. Both reflect on Chesterfield. Boswell's very eagerness to inculpate Chesterfield and exculpate Johnson confuses his story. Again, no one can assert positively what did happen, only that each story has been told with a particular end in view and on that account varnished in Johnson's interest.

One may ask, in passing, what was Chesterfield's defense? Boswell's is the sole contemporary account: "His Lordship endeavoured to justify himself . . . but we may judge the flimsiness of his defence, from his having excused his neglect of Johnson, by saying that 'he had heard he had changed his lodgings, and did not know where he lived.'" [6] Even if that were the entire defense —and apparently it was not—Johnson would be justified in feeling it to be flimsy only if the two men had stood on a roughly comparable footing. But who was Johnson in 1747? Hill writes

6. Boswell, *Life,* I, 265.

that he was known to the public only as the author of *London*,[7] for which Dodsley had paid him 10 guineas—approximately the same as Chesterfield's "inconsiderable" gift of £10. For the anonymous *Life of Savage* he had received 15 guineas; for his translation of Lobo's *Abyssinia,* five. On that scale, the *Plan* rewarded him handsomely, although of course it would not support him very long. Not by these productions, but by writing for the *Gentleman's Magazine,* Johnson had been earning a "tolerable livelihood" for several years.[8] As has been frequently pointed out, by Messrs. Croker, Brougham, and others,[9] in 1747 Johnson was no more than a literary hack. On the other hand, Chesterfield was besieged by applicants for patronage—including a host of nonentities.[10] With increasing unhappiness, he shared with the Duke of Newcastle the Secretaryship of State; he was then building Chesterfield House (only recently torn down), in the intervals of writing a tremendous number of letters, both official and private. During the next seven years Chesterfield resigned from office, moved into his house, went to Bath and elsewhere for his health, suffered from deafness, spoke for the reform of the calendar, wrote a number of essays for the *World,* found himself increasingly burdened with declining health. During these same seven years Johnson wrote *The Vanity of Human Wishes,* some two hundred essays for the *Rambler,* and an undetermined number for the *Adventurer.* Why should Chesterfield worry about the little-known hack

7. *Ibid.,* I, 176, n. 2.

8. *Ibid.,* I, 115.

9. J. W. Croker, *Boswell's Life of Johnson* (1831), I, 245–255, notes; [Lord Brougham], *Quarterly Review,* LXXVI (September, 1845), 476–480; William Ernst, i.e., Ernst-Browning, *Memoirs of the Life of Chesterfield* (1893), pp. 466–469; Charles Strachey, *Letters of . . . Chesterfield* (1901), pp. lix–lxv; W. H. Craig, *Life of Lord Chesterfield* (1907), pp. 320–323; Roger Coxon, *Chesterfield and His Critics* (1925), pp. 22–25.

10. With dedications of printed works such as James Ralph, *Night: a Poem in Four Books* (1728); [A. Hill] *The Art of Acting* (1746); William Dunkin, *Bœotia, a Poem* (1747) and *Epistle to . . . Chesterfield* (1759); Sir Charles Hanbury Williams, *Tar Water, a Ballad* (1747); Henry Jones, *Poems on Several Occasions* (1749) and *The Earl of Essex, a Tragedy* (1753); Thomas Sheridan, *British Education* (1756)—in connection with which Chesterfield wrote, "The truth is, that the several situations which I have been in, having made me long the *plastron* of dedications, I am become as callous to flattery as some people are to abuse"—and even one presumably by one of Johnson's assistants in preparing the *Dictionary:* V. J. Peyton, *The True Principles of the French Language* (1757) [cf. Boswell, *Life,* I, 536, 187 n., ll. 11–12].

writer who, incidentally, was obviously busy doing other things—none of which, one might note, was dedicated to the earl?

Yet when Chesterfield heard from Robert Dodsley that the *Dictionary* was nearly ready to appear, he wrote the two essays for the *World*. Boswell says that these essays were a "courtly device" to "insinuate himself" with Johnson,[11] but there is no other evidence that Chesterfield's friendliness was not genuine; what right had Boswell to impute duplicity to Chesterfield's every word? One may as justifiably question Johnson's veracity from his failure to mention in his letter Chesterfield's gift of £10, or call him unprincipled for seizing on the dedication to the earl as a pretext for delay in writing his *Plan*.

Whatever led up to it, Johnson wrote the letter and sent it to Chesterfield; people heard about it. Johnson, remarks Boswell, had a "remarkable delicacy" about showing his copy of it; on one occasion he refused to do so with the sentence, " 'No, Sir; I have hurt the dog too much already'; or words to that purpose."[12] Yet some years later he dictated a copy to Baretti for Langton and afterward dictated it again to Boswell. And Tom Davies, the publisher, wrote in an anonymous pamphlet four years after Chesterfield's death that this letter "will live for ever in the memory of those who have been favoured with the recital of it."[13] Men of affairs in the eighteenth century, however, minimized it. When Johnson's friend Dr. Adams expressed surprise that Chesterfield showed the letter to Dodsley and others, with comments on its strong phrasing, "Poh! (said Dodsley) do you think a letter from Johnson could hurt Lord Chesterfield?"[14] And in 1798 Horace Walpole agreed: "His papers in recommendation of Johnson's Dictionary were models of that polished elegance which the pedagogue was pretending to ascertain, and which his own style was always heaving to overload with tautology and the most barbarous confusion of tongues. The friendly patronage was returned with ungrateful

11. *Op. cit.,* I, 259, 257.

12. *Ibid.,* I, 260, n. 3.

13. *Lord Chesterfield's Characters . . . Reviewed* (1777), p. 86; John Nichols, *Literary Anecdotes of the Eighteenth Century* (1812–16), VI, 428, identifies Davies as the author as well as publisher of this pamphlet.

14. Boswell, *op. cit.,* I, 264.

rudeness by the proud pedant; and men smiled, without being surprised, at seeing a bear worry his dancing-master." [15]

Chesterfield received the letter; Johnson preserved it; Boswell perpetuated it; anthologists now regularly select this letter of Johnson's, if nothing else from his pen, as perhaps his strongest production. And unfortunately, although we still remain in the dark as to what did actually occur to make Johnson feel and write as he did, Boswell's interpretation, too long taken at face value, has tarnished Chesterfield's reputation.

Having perpetuated Johnson's letter, Boswell presents a second question to the inquiring reader. Can one distinguish, in the references to Chesterfield through the years, any change in attitude on the part of Johnson? Or on the part of Boswell? Admittedly, the materials in the *Life* are not only scanty but unclear: some are dated, to be sure, but others are inserted out of their chronological place; yet with the aid of Boswell's journals one can develop an interesting hypothesis.

Johnson, one may safely say, grew less bitter toward Lord Chesterfield as the years passed. No one will question his anger at the time he wrote his letter; his words then and afterward, in reviewing the occasion, show that. But a study of his later comments, when the earl is mentioned, finds him rarely derogatory, as one would expect had the wound rankled within him. A few days after Chesterfield's death in 1773 Johnson could remark, upon Boswell's raising the subject, "almost all of that celebrated nobleman's witty sayings were puns," but then quote one which was not. Two years later, speaking of Chesterfield's *Letters to His Son,* he said, "It was not to be wondered at that they had so great a sale, considering that they were the letters of a statesman, a wit, one who had been so much in the mouths of mankind." Although, on the one hand, on the publication of those letters Johnson did not refrain from pronouncing his famous though inaccurate epigram, "They teach the morals of a whore, and the manners of a dancing master," yet in May of 1776 he gave them tolerable praise: "Lord Chesterfield's Letters to his son, I think, might be made a very pretty book. Take

15. *Works* (1798), I, 536.

out the immorality, and it should be put into the hands of every young gentleman." [16]

On the whole, Chesterfield's manners came in for praise. At the time of the quarrel, of course, Johnson remarked that Chesterfield was "the proudest man this day existing." Nearly thirty years later he would say that Chesterfield was dignified but insolent; but the following year, the year of Johnson's death, he stated, "His manner was exquisitely elegant, and he had more knowledge than I expected." [17]

As positive evidence, these passages are admittedly inconclusive. Like anyone of independent mind, Johnson gives at different times different aspects of his judgment of a man, depending upon the circumstance. But negatively, in every reference to Chesterfield following the account of the quarrel one can read the story: given the opportunity, Johnson does not let fly the slighting epithet. Most telling of such omissions to take up a cudgel against the earl came in 1779 when

One of the company [not identified, alas, in the journal] mentioned Lord Chesterfield, as a man who had no friend.[18] JOHNSON [turning the subject]. "There were more materials to make friendship in Garrick, had he not been so diffused." BOSWELL. "Garrick was pure gold, but beat out to thin leaf. Lord Chesterfield was tinsel." JOHNSON [again turning away from the earl]. "Garrick was a very good man, the cheerfullest man of his age . . ."

Taken by and large, then, these references (and there are no others of significance) would show that once the ardor of the occasion had passed Johnson was content to speak his mind without rancor and occasionally to praise the earl.[19]

With Boswell, thanks to the journals, one can reach certain conclusions with more ease, but the final answer must nonetheless be guesswork. Those journal passages mentioning Chesterfield which parallel the *Life* show, with one exception only, no adverse

16. Boswell, *op. cit.*, II, 211, 329; I, 266; III, 53.

17. *Ibid.*, I, 265; IV, 174, 333.

18. Bonamy Dobrée makes short work of this assertion, mentioning Lord Scarborough, the Bishop of Waterford, and Solomon Dayrolles. *The Letters of Lord Chesterfield* (1932), I, 41.

19. Boswell, *Life*, III, 387. The quotations from the Reverend John Hussey, given by Mr. Powell in Appendix G (I, 540–541) as notes to I, 264, 265, and 266, substantiate this conclusion.

comment on Boswell's part.[20] All other references, whether paralleled in the *Life* or not, are either noncommittal or actually imply admiration, as when Boswell read some letters in the forthcoming *Miscellaneous Works* of Chesterfield: "I was charmed with those I read . . . to Madame de Boccage and Mr. Dayrolles. . . . I was greatly refreshed."[21] The noncommittal nature of the journals throughout may account for the lack of unfavorable comment, yet it cannot account for the favorable tone of his remarks on reading those letters and later on receiving a copy of the published book.[22] It is only in the *Life* that Boswell vituperates the earl, and that only in the account of Johnson's quarrel with him. Since Boswell presumably wrote his account of this quarrel after 1784—Mr. Geoffrey Scott states, "There is no indication that he began his task [writing the *Life*] till after Johnson's death"[23]—one may interpret it as revealing Boswell's judgment at that time. It comes as a shock, then, to find Boswell's tone so different from the dispassionate recording of the journals. The account of the quarrel exhibits to the most casual reader a kind of venom on the part of the narrator, being filled with words and phrases known in semantics as "loaded" or "affective." The cumulative effect of these is considerable: Chesterfield

had flattered himself . . . attempted, in a courtly manner, to sooth, and insinuate himself with the Sage; . . . some studied compliments, so finely turned, that if there had been no previous offence, it is probable that Johnson would have been highly delighted . . . This courtly device failed of its effect. Johnson . . . despised the honeyed words, . . . indignant . . . that Lord Chesterfield should, for a moment, imagine, that he could be the dupe of such an artifice . . . Chesterfield must have been mortified by the lofty contempt, and polite, yet keen satire . . . He, however, with that glossy duplicity which was his constant study, affected to be quite unconcerned . . . This air of indifference, which imposed upon the worthy Dodsley, was certainly nothing but a specimen of that dissimulation which Lord Chesterfield inculcated as one of the most essential lessons for the conduct of life.[24]

20. "Chesterfield was tinsel." *Boswell Papers*, XIII, 234; *Life*, III, 387. Other parallels [*Boswell Papers* first, *Life* in parentheses]: VI, 86 (II, 211); VI, 94–95 (II, 211; I, 256–257); X, 160–161 (I, 266–267; II, 329); XV, 181 (IV, 174).

21. *Boswell Papers*, XI, 158.

22. *Ibid.*, XII, 159.

23. *Ibid.*, VI, 161.

24. Boswell, *Life*, I, 257–265.

Now Boswell did not hesitate in the *Life* to tell his opinion of those about whom he wrote or freely to characterize them. Minute descriptions of Johnson's failings—which Boswell labels his "particularities"—from external characteristics like the post-touching compulsion and his personal slovenliness to deeper ones like his aggressiveness in conversation, provide a considerable portion of the *Life*. Told with a merciless detail, these highlight Boswell's judgments on Goldsmith ("a fertile but thin soil") and Garrick ("beat out to thin leaf"), as well as the lesser characters crossing the stage, such as Bolingbroke, whose works were "wild and pernicious ravings." (Yet he was not universally the moralist: John Wilkes, who under any dispassionate analysis would deserve moral censure to a far greater degree than Chesterfield, Boswell terms "my gay friend"; the reason, of course, was Wilkes's stand for liberty.) But throughout the *Life,* as the characters pass in review, one finds remarkably little further writing of the same character as that describing Johnson's quarrel with Chesterfield. Boswell expresses his opinions abundantly, but only rarely colors the anecdote so palpably as in his story about Johnson's letter.

The most obvious explanation for such treatment of Chesterfield would be that Boswell wrote in righteous anger at his friend's mistreatment. Although some thirty-five years had elapsed—and indeed Boswell had only secondhand information on the subject—those who assign the heat of Boswell's account to this reason may be right in believing that as the biographer thought of the disparity in the fortunes of the two men and re-created in his mind the long-vanished scenes, he became imbued with a sense of outrage and wrote accordingly. Yet his surviving notes in the journals offer no support for such an interpretation.

An alternative explanation would be that for some reason Boswell himself felt some rancor toward the earl and that when he came to write these pages he charged them with his own feelings. An episode in which the eager young celebrity hunter, in his early years in London, aspired to the company of the celebrated nobleman, only to be repulsed and humiliated, would supply such an explanation if there were the slightest shred of evidence for it. But there is not, not even in the journals, and one must look further for a hint of some other clash between the two men. A clue to such an antagonism occurs in Boswell's long footnote to the passage in question: "I can by no means approve of confounding the distinction between lawful and illicit offspring, which is, in effect, insulting the civil establishment of our country, to look no higher."[25] A cynical modern might comment that Boswell was well equipped to make such a statement, having outdone Chesterfield in the procreation of both. Certainly, the £10 a year which Boswell contributed to the support of his illegitimate son and the subsequent lacunae in that boy's history[26] make a sad contrast to Chesterfield's lifelong care, oversolicitous as it was, for his own son. Boswell himself must have felt this difference, for in the same footnote he continues, "I cannot help thinking it laudable to be kindly attentive to those, of whose existence we have, in any way, been the cause." The contrast should not please honorable men of any generation, but of course, if one flaunts one's love for an illegitimate son even to the extent of giving him one's own name and making him respectable by buying for him a seat in Parliament, as Chesterfield did for Philip Stanhope, tongues will wag. There is less noise from the moralists if the matter is hushed up so that no trace remains of the unfortunate unnamed son—and later of the unfortunate daughter Sally—of the various liaisons. To a lawyer and Scottish laird, however, staunch defender of primogeniture, the distinction between lawful and illicit is a mighty chasm, unbridgeable by paternal affection; to attempt to bridge it is to jeopardize the social structure. Such an interpretation of Boswell's warmth in writing this passage is incapable of proof; further support comes only from the diffuse materials which delineate his character—his deep sense of legal procedures, his reverence for "subordination." Yet it rings truer than the earlier interpretations—the greatest heat comes from the depths. It is not unthinkable that Boswell was antagonized by Chesterfield not because of his failure as a patron, nor for the eight objectionable passages in the *Letters to His Son,* but because those hundreds of letters were a continuous insult to the prerogatives of legitimacy.

25. *Ibid.,* I, 266, n. 1.
26. Chauncey Brewster Tinker, *Young Boswell,* pp. 22, 24-25.

Near the end of the Victorian era, when he came to write the introduction to his edition of Chesterfield's letters to his godson, the Earl of Carnarvon admitted that he had begun his task with great reluctance and distaste, but that as he got well into the work he found himself admiring Chesterfield. Almost all of those who have made a study of that earl have found themselves sharing in that admiration. Perhaps those who in the past have so blindly accepted the adverse criticisms stemming from Boswell's *Life of Johnson,* without realizing that both Johnson and Boswell on occasion tempered that criticism with praise, would modify their judgments and give credit to the admirable qualities of the earl if they learned the facts. Perhaps a new understanding might then help to repair the loss to his reputation which the Earl of Chesterfield sustained because he failed to keep a diary.

HORACE WALPOLE AND TWO
FRENCHWOMEN

Warren Hunting Smith

VISIONS, the only happiness," Walpole wrote in his "Paris Journals." [1] "Poetry, love, ambition, Romans, Delphi's sleep; astronomy, religion, fame, Louis XIV, romance, etc. etc."

"Visions . . ." he wrote to Montagu in a less cryptic passage,[2] "have always been my pasture. . . . Old castles, old pictures, old histories, and the babble of old people make one live back into centuries that cannot disappoint one."

To Mann, February 26, 1781, he wrote: "Yet if one excluded visions, and attended only to the philosophy of reflection; if one always recollected how transitory are all the glories in the imagination; how insipid, how listless would life be!"

"I am outrageous at the destruction of all the visions that make history delectable," he wrote again; [3] "without some romance it is but a register of crimes and calamities. . . ."

Walpole was obviously one of those who enjoy the past only when their imaginations are stirred by the romantic color of particular eras—eras which, for them, are a world where bygone characters are as real as living contemporaries. The age of Louis XIV was thus illuminated for Walpole by the letters of Madame de Sévigné, and it is significant that Louis XIV is mentioned in the passage about visions and romance.

Of all the women who figured in Walpole's life, one of the most important was this Frenchwoman whom he never saw and with whom he never corresponded except in so far as one can correspond vicariously with a lady who has been dead for over half a century. Her grip on his imagination, however, made her a formidable rival

---

1. *Horace Walpole's Correspondence with Madame du Deffand,* ed. W. S. Lewis and W. H. Smith (Yale University Press, 1939), V, 357–358.
2. January 5, 1766.
3. Walpole to Mary Berry, July 10, 1790.

of the Grifoni, the Misses Berry, and the other women who at one time or another came into his life. Living ladies might come and go, but Madame de Sévigné's letters remained on his shelves and deep in his affections. "There is scarce a book in the world I love so much as her letters." [4]

When he made his first visit to France in 1739, he had not yet fallen under the spell of his "saint" as he later called her. France was not yet for him a land of romance, and Louis XIV's constructions at Versailles provoked him to ridicule. [5] His imagination at that time was chiefly captivated by the art of the Italian Renaissance, and Italy was the climax of his grand tour. The reign of Louis Quatorze probably seemed as unromantic then as the Victorian period did to those of us who were born soon after its close —it was a period which was just around the corner, outmoded but not antique, pompous and a bit ridiculous. Its treasures patiently awaited discovery in country houses and châteaux where the gardens were unchanged, the furniture unrenovated, and the libraries full of unpublished manuscripts. "The times immediately preceding their own are what all men are least acquainted with." [6]

Early in the 1740's Walpole apparently read Madame de Sévigné's letters, [7] and France under the Grand Monarque assumed for him a new radiance—"Madame de Sévigné spread her leaf-gold over all her acquaintance, and made them shine." [8] The exact date of his enlightenment is uncertain, but his first reference to Madame de Sévigné is in 1743. [9] Perhaps Montagu or Selwyn, who were also devotees of the "saint," performed the introduction; Gray had known Madame de Sévigné as early as 1738. [10] Henceforth the seventeenth century became a golden period for Walpole; he pub-

4. Walpole to Mann, September 12, 1749, O.S.

5. Walpole to West, ca. May 15, 1739, N.S.

6. Walpole to Mann, November 18, 1771.

7. His copy was in 9 vols. dated 1738 (MS catalogue of his library). He may have met Madame de Sévigné previously in extracts from her letters in Andrew Ramsay's L'Histoire du Vicomte de Turenne (see the World, No. XIV, April 5, 1753, in Walpole's "Works" [1798], I, 165).

8. Walpole to Nuneham, December 6, 1773.

9. Walpole to Mann, August 14, 1743.

10. See Gray to West in Toynbee and Whibley, eds., Correspondence of Thomas Gray (Oxford, 1935), p. 93. The letter is conjecturally dated December, 1738, and the footnote shows that Gray knew Madame de Sévigné's letters in that year.

lished the memoirs of Gramont and the life of Lord Herbert of Cherbury; he admired [11] and collected the letters of Madame de Maintenon (whose retreat at St. Cyr he later visited). A special case at Strawberry Hill was devoted to Madame de Sévigné's letters and to books about her circle.[12] Subsequent editions of her correspondence were eagerly purchased; he even secured a few original letters and manuscript copies. He collected copies of her portraits, and engravings of people mentioned in her letters—these prints were later assembled in a large volume.[13]

It would be surprising to find no traces of "the dear woman" in his own epistolary style. Mr. Ketton-Cremer [14] has concluded that her influence was not so much upon the phraseology of his letters as on the concept of correspondence as illustrative of a society and an era. Her great scenes may have inspired Walpole with the idea of a letter's becoming a vivid fragment of history. It is certainly true that his set pieces such as the trial of the rebel lords or the burial of George II were written after his acquaintance with Madame de Sévigné and are comparable to those passages in her letters which he particularly admired. His accounts of the Conclave at Rome, written back in 1740, show how much he had then to learn as a narrator of history. They are breezy, disconnected anecdotes, witty in places, but lacking the atmosphere, the background, and the dramatic interplay of tragic and comic elements which he displayed in his best letters.

His changed attitude toward country life may be partly due to Madame de Sévigné's idyllic letters from Livry and Les Rochers. As a boy Walpole had been bored by summer sojourns at Houghton, but in the mid-'forties he left London in the summer to rent a "tub" at Windsor and finally to settle among the "enamelled meadows with filigree hedges" of Strawberry Hill where he spent part of every year for the rest of his life, imbuing the scenery with that magic glow which makes it still attractive to literary pilgrims.

A trip to Paris in 1765 therefore offered enticements which it had not presented in 1739. When Walpole made his re-entry into

11. Walpole to Strafford, June 6, 1756.
12. Walpole to Mann, June 12, 1753.
13. Walpole to Mann, September 27, 1783.
14. *Horace Walpole* (1940), pp. 133–134.

France, he stepped into Madame de Sévigné's world at Chantilly, where everything was so unchanged that he felt like asking "Où est Vatel?" [15] At Paris he visited the Hôtel de Carnavalet and the Couvent de Ste. Marie; he made an excursion to Livry where his "saint" had so often stayed with her uncle. "Nothing has interrupted my Sévigné researches but the frost," he wrote.[16] Grignan and Les Rochers were too remote for pilgrimages, though Selwyn, Lord Carlisle, and some of their circle had visited Grignan or had secured introductions to Madame de Sévigné's somewhat disappointing descendants in Provence.[17] The only relative whom Walpole met was her great-granddaughter's husband.[18]

It was Madame du Deffand, however, who became Walpole's living link with Madame de Sévigné. She could remember Madame de Coulanges (so often mentioned in the letters of the "saint"); she could herself write letters comparable to those of her great predecessor; she could in her livelier moments display some of Madame de Sévigné's Gallic wit and gaiety. To be sure, Madame du Deffand had no cherished daughter; in fact she had no children at all. The girl who had attempted this relationship had been chased away after a bitter quarrel; a genuine daughter would have fared no better, but this fact meant nothing to Walpole, who regarded Madame de Sévigné's maternal outpourings as the least attractive part of her letters. He preferred her chronicles of Louis XIV's court—especially such tableaux as the death of Turenne and the arrival of James II.[19] He enjoyed Madame de Sévigné's vivid and witty portraits of her acquaintances—"Tell me whether you do not know their persons as if you had lived at the time." [20] The fact that Madame de Sévigné's passion was the mainspring of her genius seems to have escaped him; he was like the old lady who wanted a love story with no sex in it. He himself could write dazzling descriptions of historic scenes from sheer joy of writing—why shouldn't

15. Walpole to Lady Hervey, September 14, 1765.
16. Walpole to Gray, January 25, 1766.
17. John Heneage Jesse, *George Selwyn and His Contemporaries* (1882), I, 271, II, 206–207, III, 329, 357, IV, 126, 205; S. Parnell Kerr, *George Selwyn and the Wits* (1909), pp. 248–249.
18. Castellane. See Walpole's "Paris Journals," September 14, 1767.
19. Walpole to Pinkerton, June 26, 1785.
20. *Ibid.*

Madame de Sévigné have done the same? And why couldn't Madame du Deffand do it now?

When he left Paris and began his fifteen years' correspondence with Madame du Deffand, these questions were soon raised. Madame du Deffand was quite different from Madame de Sévigné, and she lost no time in saying so. Whereas Madame de Sévigné was interested in everything and everybody, Madame du Deffand was bored, cynical, forgetful, and tired. Blindness was probably the least of her impediments. Instead of sending witty gazettes of Parisian life, she lapsed into laments for Walpole's absence, together with embarrassing expressions of affection for him. This wasn't what he had bargained for. He scolded her severely. She retorted that her endearments were far more restrained than those of Madame de Sévigné, but she found to her surprise that he regarded Madame de Sévigné's outbursts as weaknesses which supreme artistry alone kept from becoming a bore—"There is too much of sorrow for her daughter's absence; yet it is always expressed by new terms, by new images, and often by wit. . . ." [21]

Madame de Sévigné's excessive tenderness was, to Walpole, a regrettable feature of her letters, but at least she had an excuse for it. Madame du Deffand, in his opinion, did not. His attitude toward her was somewhat filial, but her attitude toward him was not maternal, nor could her letters be regarded as solicitude for an adopted son.

His efforts to steer their correspondence into what he considered the proper channels are pathetic but amusing. He sometimes threatened to break it all off, but, just as a rupture appeared inevitable, the unhappy old lady would bow to his stipulations and would try to fill her letters with the proper names which he preferred. He kept all her letters; he annotated them; he considered publishing them, and he finally left them to be published by Miss Berry. Madame du Deffand had bequeathed to him all her papers, which he insisted upon having, though the Prince de Beauvau tried to withhold some of them.

21. *Ibid.* See also the *World,* No. XIV, April 5, 1753: "If this fair one's epistles are liable to any censure, it is for a fault in which she is not likely to be often imitated, the excess of tenderness for her daughter" (Walpole's "Works" [1798], I, 165).

Walpole was undoubtedly fond of the old Marquise, for whom he felt the tenderness which old ladies often aroused in him; [22] he was disgusted at the way in which the heedless Parisians ate her suppers and made fun of her behind her back. He enjoyed her reminiscences of the Regency, and of Voltaire and her other celebrated friends, and especially of Madame de Sévigné's circle. One cannot help feeling, however, that he saw himself corresponding with Madame de Sévigné's modern counterpart. To be sure, when Madame du Deffand wrote him a letter in the name of Madame de Sévigné, he didn't guess who wrote it [23]—so many of the Parisian ladies knew of his Sévigné passion—but he felt that her style was in the tradition of the reign of Louis Quatorze: "the genuine French spoken by the Duc de la Rochefoucauld and Madame de Sévigné, and not the metaphysical galimatias of La Harpe and Thomas, etc., which Madame du Deffand protested she did not understand." [24] In dedicating his edition of Hamilton's memoirs of Gramont to her, he wrote: "L'éditeur vous consacre cette édition, comme un monument de son amitié, de son admiration, et de son respect; à vous, dont les grâces, l'esprit, et le goût retracent au siècle présent le siècle de Louis Quatorze et les agréments de l'auteur de ces mémoires."

The letters between Horace Walpole and Madame du Deffand are a unique example of one great correspondence conducted in the light of another. Both correspondents had already been compared, as letter writers, to Madame de Sévigné. As early as 1749 Horace Mann quoted (in reference to Walpole's letters) some lines from Madame de Sévigné, and was rebuked by Walpole for such sacrilege.[25] Madame du Deffand's old admirer, the President Hénault, had already written [26] in his "portrait" of her that "Il serait bien à souhaiter que ce qu'elle a écrit ne fût pas perdu: Madame de Sévigné ne serait pas la seule à citer." Moreover, Walpole and Madame du Deffand were often comparing each other's letters

22. For Walpole's "mother complex," see W. S. Lewis' introduction to *Horace Walpole's Correspondence with Madame du Deffand*, Yale Edition.

23. See W. S. Lewis, *Horace Walpole's Letter from Madame de Sévigné* (Farmington, Conn., 1933).

24. Walpole to Lady Ossory, September 17, 1785.

25. Walpole to Mann, September 12, 1749, O.S.

26. *Horace Walpole's Correspondence with Madame du Deffand*, Yale Edition, VI, 53

to those of "the dear woman" though Walpole did so only when Madame du Deffand was on her best behavior. Most of his letters do not survive, but her answers show that he must have compared her fairly often with Madame de Sévigné. He once told her [27] not to be discouraged by the comparison; her style was her own, just as Madame de Sévigné's had been, and any direct imitation would have been fatal. To Montagu he wrote: [28] "Affectionate as Madame de Sévigné, she has none of her prejudices, but a more universal taste. . . ." In the preface to his *Description of Strawberry Hill* he said that Madame du Deffand's letter in the name of Madame de Sévigné was "not written in imitation of that model of letter-writers, but composed of more delicacy of thought and more elegance of expression than perhaps Madame de Sévigné herself could have attained. The two ladies ought not to be compared—one was all natural ease and tenderness—the other charms by the graces of the most polished style, which, however, are less beautiful than the graces of the wit they clothe."

Certainly Walpole did not deliberately provoke and prolong his correspondence with Madame du Deffand in order to give to posterity a new Madame de Sévigné—he was far too sensible and too subtle for that—but it must be admitted that Madame du Deffand's link with Madame de Sévigné was one of her great attractions for him. When she told him of her visit to Madame de Coulanges, he himself confesses [29] that he hit her out of sheer ecstasy. Whether he slapped the old lady on the back or thumped her on the knee is uncertain; they were riding in a carriage together. Walpole was not in the habit of giving fillips to elderly marquises (and this action may have been inadvertent), but the revelation that Madame du Deffand had known one of Madame de Sévigné's friends could make him break all rules. His most exuberant gesture to Madame du Deffand, therefore, was really inspired by Madame de Sévigné.

Walpole saved most of the letters which he received, but few of them did he annotate so carefully as he did Madame du Deffand's. Other letters might have been saved because they helped

27. Walpole to Madame du Deffand, September 22, 1768.
28. September 7, 1769.
29. Walpole to Madame du Deffand, January 27, 1775.

to explain his own, but, in the case of Madame du Deffand's, his own were preserved only in footnotes to those of his correspondent. He was quite aware that her letters constituted a valuable literary heritage, and he was probably not without pride that he should have been both their inspiration and their custodian.

It is a tribute to the power of the human spirit that a woman, long after her death, could so charm a talented man by her writings that he was inspired to regard another woman as the living representative of her genius. The eternal triangle assumes a new aspect when one member of the trio is a deceased authoress whom both the other members are thought to resemble. Walpole in this case might well write "Visions the only happiness," for certainly his relations with his deceased "saint" were happier than those with his "dear old blind woman."

NEW LIGHT ON MRS. MONTAGU

Katherine G. Hornbeak

LUCKILY for Mrs. Montagu's peace of mind and prestige, the most unsympathetic account of her by a contemporary was not published until nearly a century after her death. Occasionally during her lifetime some critical comment on the Queen of the Blues struck a discordant note in the chorus of adulation. In 1785 Richard Cumberland's pretentious Vanessa was immediately identified as Mrs. Montagu. In 1794 Mathias in *The Pursuits of Literature* devoted a couplet to her:

> Nor can I pass LYCISCA MONTAGU,
> Her yelp though feeble, and her sandals blue.

These, however, are only pinpricks compared to the cruel portrait finally published in 1896. So far as I know, none of the biographers of Mrs. Montagu has ever looked into two ponderous volumes of verse by James Woodhouse, who spent eighteen years in her service. This neglect is regrettable—though not surprising. Who would expect to find in *The Life and Lucubrations of Crispinus Scriblerus* a wealth of intimate though unflattering detail about the Queen of the Bluestockings? Even if the student of Mrs. Montagu happened to know of this autobiography of James Woodhouse, the poetical shoemaker who became her bailiff and steward, the sheer bulk of the book, nearly thirty thousand lines of plodding couplets, is enough to daunt the hardiest reader. Furthermore, since Mrs. Montagu is never mentioned by name in the book, one might read it to the end without identifying his patroness, whom he calls Vanessa and Scintilla, unless one happened to know much more of the relationship than is to be gleaned from the printed records.

With the details of the connection, which can be filled in from the Montagu correspondence in the Huntington Library, I shall deal elsewhere, for the present suggesting some of the highlights and overtones. Mrs. Montagu first became interested in Woodhouse in 1764 (he was not quite thirty; she was his senior by fifteen years); the final rupture occurred nearly a quarter of a century later, about 1788. After working indefatigably to promote the success of his poems, published by subscription, Mrs. Montagu—in 1767—provided more substantially for him, his wife Daphne, and their ever increasing brood, by employing him as bailiff on her Berkshire estate, Sandleford Priory. As she wrote Lord Lyttelton, "I have taken from Apollo to give him to Ceres, who is a more benignant Deity & feeds her Votaries better." [1] Woodhouse served Ceres and Mrs. Montagu until 1778. In the autumn of that year accumulated stress and strain led to a rupture (which Mrs. Montagu declared should be final), and Woodhouse returned to Rowley, his native village in Staffordshire. Three years later, however, Mrs. Montagu recalled him to be steward of the palace she had built in Portman Square. For the next seven years he served as her major-domo, dividing his time—according to the season—between Portman Square and Sandleford. At last, however, the situation proved intolerable: Woodhouse had become increasingly evangelical and equalitarian (a "methodistical" leveler), and Mrs. Montagu apparently rather imperious and peremptory. The clash of incompatible personalities led to Woodhouse's dismissal.

Such are the bare outlines of the relationship. Its quality can be suggested by a few passages from the unpublished correspondence. In the early stages of the relationship Mrs. Montagu was rapturous. After having worked hard to promote the subscription for his second edition, she first met him during the winter of 1765 when he dined with her several times in Hill Street. She writes her sister a glowing account:

I have not had time to tell you how much I have been charmd with my poetical shoemaker. I never saw so much humility & gentleness. He is perfect simplicity without awkwardness. His voice is remarkably musical, his language unaffected but elegant . . . you will wish to know the figure of this extraordinary man it was remarked that he is very like Raphaels picture of St John. He has an expression of sense sweetness & humility softened by bashfullness.

1. All the excerpts from the letters of Mrs. Montagu and Woodhouse are quoted from unpublished manuscripts in the Huntington Library, except for one passage, the source of which is cited below. I am indebted to the trustees of the Huntington Library for permission to quote from the Montagu MSS.

A few months later she wrote her husband, "Where did he get greatness of mind enough to be above pride?" In September, 1767, while the Woodhouse family was settling in at Sandleford during Mrs. Montagu's absence at the collieries, she wrote her husband praising the new bailiff's sense, sobriety, and steadiness. After the Woodhouses had been at Sandleford several months she wrote Lord Lyttelton: ". . . he exceeds even my hopes & wishes. Integrity, diligence, & sagacity, are by him employ'd for me with unremitting zeal, from the rising to the setting sun. . . . She [Daphne] is an excellent housewife, makes the best butter I ever tasted, & seems indeed not only worthy of Woodhouse the Farmer, but also of Woodhouse the Poet." In Daphne Mrs. Montagu detected "elevation of sentiment, & delicacy of manners." ". . . she is fair, & pretty, & elegant, in her Person. Such a shepherd and shepherdess are worthy of a place in Arcadia. . . . I really think I may say they are very happy."

Unless Woodhouse was a hypocrite and a liar in his letters (and even when most exasperated with him Mrs. Montagu admits his honesty and integrity), he was breathless with adoration in the early stages of the relationship. In May of 1766, after he had met Mrs. Montagu but before he had moved his family to Sandleford, he wrote her: ". . . I found in all my other Friends Fathers & Mothers, but none so truly parental as you. . . . Receive mine & Daphne's Love & good Wishes; for Compliments are a cold Treat from Hearts so dearly loving to One so much beloved." In April, 1768, seven months after he entered her employ, he wrote her: "God bless your good Heart with all those Joys, & Comforts that it bestows upon the Hearts of others; but then you would be too happy for this State of Tryal, as your Life would be one continued Extasy, a Lot reserv'd for you in a better State."

From Mrs. Montagu's comments on Woodhouse it is clear that his devotion and gratitude to his benefactor did not simply evaporate in words. In fact, his zeal as a farmer exceeded Mrs. Montagu's expectations. "Your Steward," she wrote Mr. Montagu, "has been at harvest every day from morning till 10 at night working by artificial light so much without repose or food than [sic] one night he was extreamly ill." Woodhouse's letters to Mrs. Montagu and her letters to her friends give evidence of the bailiff's busy life. They show him valuing timber, overseeing ditching and plowing and planting, supervising improvements in the main house, forwarding hampers of farm produce to the Montagus in Berkeley Square, arbitrating quarrels among the servants, hunting plovers' eggs, dealing with poachers. He appears on horseback as grand marshal of the procession attending the hock cart, the last load of barley adorned with garlands and bows. In the evenings he read to Daphne and blind John, a retainer of the Montagus. On rainy days he taught little Matt, Mrs. Montagu's nephew and heir, to read. He also, in the capacity of domestic laureate or household bard, produced odes for such festal occasions as the Harvest Home feast and Mrs. Montagu's birthday. In his *Life and Lucubrations* Woodhouse gives an account of his work as bailiff. He drained swamps, discovered peat in the bogs, used the peat ashes to fertilize clover and grass. On Sundays he was on watch for poachers; he claims to have extirpated even the gypsies. Sometime or other he managed to read "each Agrarian tract that grac'd the shelf."

No wonder the farm prospered and "ampler barns" had to be built. In 1773 Mrs. Montagu wrote Mrs. Carter: "The Corn fields promise a rich harvest & all things flourish. Our Farm would astonish any one who had visited it in Atkinsons time." In 1774 she wrote her sister: "Our Wheat is all safe in the Ricks. We have barley enough to feed 10,000 Hogs I believe if the weather will let us get it in. Of turnips a vast quantity." In 1777 she wrote, "We finishd our Hay last night, & begin to reap on Monday. Sandleford never was blest with so rich crops of either." Woodhouse sums up his achievement thus:

> When annual produce rose, on wretched grounds,
> From nearly nothing to ten hundred pounds!

Why, then, just a year later—in the autumn of 1778—did Woodhouse "march off in surly dignity" to his own village? Why in November, 1778, did Mrs. Montagu write Mrs. Carter: "He march'd off with his family before day light. . . . It appears by many symptom [*sic*] this family has done as well for itself as ill for me during their abode here, but as they have killd the golden hen they will one day repent." A few days later Mrs. Montagu declared, ". . . if he is in distress at any time I will assist him, but he shall never assist me."

The causes of the rupture were complex, and the blame must be divided between the two parties. In Mrs. Montagu's version of the situation, Woodhouse and Daphne are at fault; Woodhouse naturally holds Mrs. Montagu responsible. As a matter of fact, there had been friction for nearly ten years. The details must be postponed to later publication, but the main causes of the tension, according to Mrs. Montagu, were Woodhouse's pride, arrogance, and impertinence and Daphne's pride and extravagance. In 1774 Mrs. Montagu, after commenting on the high tide of prosperity at Sandleford, adds, "But what pleases me best is to see Woodhouse in his right & sober senses & his Children tame & civil. He seems very happy now but a Proud Man never is so." In 1778, soon after the departure of her bailiff, Mrs. Montagu wrote: "If Mr. Woodhouse had made every grain he sowed increase an hundred fold I would not have endured his pride & impertinence. He is very honest & was careful & well enough as a Baillif but never contented & pleased. . . . His letters are masterpieces . . . as he did amuse him [Mr. Montagu] it was a satisfaction to me & made me amends at that time for much of his impertinence." A few months later Mrs. Montagu admits that she herself was partly responsible for this pride: "I pity in him the pride which my civility & liberality encouraged & I ought therefore to assist him in any distress which that pride has brought upon him." As early as 1769, eighteen months after Woodhouse entered upon his duties at Sandleford, Mrs. Montagu was finding fault with Daphne: "He [Woodhouse] has behaved very well since my return home, & I believe will not let his Wife make a fool of him again. The farm is in great order, & he seems extreamly happy." In the fall of 1771 occurs this comment on Daphne: "She behaves with decency, but is mad with pride & extravagance, & if her Husband did not, by his integrity, check her expence I shd be obliged to send her back to her Village & poverty." Mrs. Montagu also disapproved of the upbringing of the Woodhouse children. In June of 1768 she wrote, "Mr. Woodhouses Children are far from being as well regulated as my Nephew, but their passions will probably be subdued by their situation in life. I tell him sometimes, that if a young Squire was to be so brought up, he would knock out the brains of half his Tenants the first year he came to his estate." Apparently Woodhouse tried to curb the children, for in 1774, Mrs. Montagu is able to report that she is glad to find them "tame & civil." Other causes of the breach, less fundamental but still exasperating, were Woodhouse's failure with the livestock and his carelessness—despite his unquestioned integrity—in keeping accounts.

Although there is, as usual, another side to the story, it is impossible here to do more than suggest the bailiff's grievances. The situation was difficult for Woodhouse. As a young man he had been encouraged by Shenstone and Lyttelton, had—as a nine days' wonder in London—met Dr. Johnson (who gave him a famous bit of advice), had dined at Mrs. Montagu's table with peers and other notables. He had corresponded with Mrs. Montagu on the Sublime and the Beautiful and the authenticity of Ossian. His picture had appeared in a contemporary periodical; his story had been told in the *Gentleman's Magazine* and the *Annual Register*. At this time, before he was employed by Mrs. Montagu, he wrote, "I know you are both [Mrs. Montagu and Lord Lyttelton] so elevated above my Reach that I shall never engross so much of your Attention as I wish." He had hoped that, as bailiff of Sandleford, he would have leisure to read and study, but even while lamenting the lack of time he recognizes with some bitterness the contracted sphere to which circumstance confines him. On an occasion of some tension between him and his employer he declared, ". . . I rejoice & am thankful for an elevated Mind, that sets me upon an Equality with any other human Being." No wonder this proud and sensitive soul, who had been invited "To dine, drink, talk, ride, sup, and lodge, with Lords," did not make the perfect dependent!

He especially resented Mrs. Montagu's tone to Daphne. On June 26, 1769 he wrote Mrs. Montagu: "I have thought, upon some Occasions, that I perceived an Abatement of your Confidence & Esteem towards me; & my Wife has experienc'd frequently, to her Grief, & to the Loss of my Peace, a Sharpness & Harshness in your Conduct towards her, & Conversation with her, that ill agrees with your

Conduct aforetime, & Professions of Regard, as it also oppresses her Sensibility." In his *Life and Lucubrations,* written long afterward, he is still bitter about the anguish Daphne suffered from "proud Employer's keen, sarcastic, tongue," which he compares to the sting of a serpent or hornet. (Daphne spent sleepless nights worrying over Mrs. Montagu's complaints about soggy bread and addled eggs.) His mistress' "snubs and sneers and freezing frowns" rankled for years. Not even the children escaped. In his autobiography he says that Mrs. Montagu decreed their sports, diet, dress, hours of sleep.

No wonder there was an open breach in 1778. The wonder is that three years later Mrs. Montagu invited Woodhouse to become her steward and that he hastened to express "the humblest Acceptation of your kind, your tender, your beneficent Offer," adding that she knew "how to endear a Gift by the Manner of giving." For seven years Woodhouse served as steward or major-domo of the new mansion in Portman Square and the old Gothic pile at Sandleford. In his autobiography he gives an account of his duties: he was in "full command of town, and country, domes"—all the servants, liveries, books, archives, storerooms, silver, linen, fuel. In town he marketed for state banquets; during dinner he stood at attention by the sideboard. On gala evenings, when crowds of guests attended Mrs. Montagu's musicales or dramatic readings, Woodhouse stood near the drafty entrance to oversee the auxiliary footmen—hired or borrowed for the occasion. During the summer months spent at Sandleford, in addition to his routine duties, he directed builders, laborers, gardeners in the execution of improvements planned by "Capability" Brown and Wyatt. According to Woodhouse, however, his most faithful services were rewarded with coldness, neglect, and distrust. Added to these sources of irritation, mistress and man did not see eye to eye on politics and religion. About 1788 they came to the final parting of the ways.

Woodhouse, set adrift at fifty-three, with a frail wife and several children to support (of twenty-seven children, at least fifteen were stillborn), set up a small bookshop in Grosvenor Square, whither he retired to lick his wounds. Here he brooded over his grievances. Out of this bitter resentment came his *Life and Lucubrations,* a catharsis of emotion *not* recollected in tranquillity. Here one would obviously look in vain for balanced, detached judgment. Nevertheless, even while discounting Woodhouse's exaggeration and distortion, one must admit that he has caught certain typical traits and features of Mrs. Montagu.[2]

The reader who is familiar with the superlative praise lavished on Mrs. Montagu by her better known contemporaries will be startled by Woodhouse's indictment. William Pitt pronounced her "the most perfect woman he ever met with." Garrick endorsed a letter from her "Mrs. Montagu, first of women." Mrs. Thrale, in ranking women of her acquaintance, gave Mrs. Montagu a score of 101 out of a possible 120. (The next highest score, Hannah More's, is only 72.) Woodhouse, however, in comparing Mrs. Montagu to his own Daphne ("a spotless lamb"), calls her fox, hyena, harpy, tiger!

The basic charges Woodhouse brings against Mrs. Montagu are pride and vanity, manifested in ostentation. According to Woodhouse, her husband agreed with this view of his wife:

> He so far analiz'd his Consort's heart
> As clearly, to infer Pride fill'd a part;
> That Vanity another part possest,
> And Ostentation occupied the rest. . . .

The mainspring of most of her activities, he claims, is pride and vanity. She was dominated by "thirst for Pomp, and lust for Fame," craving "idol-worship from the Whole." For instance, rooted in her "love of Eulogy" was her patronage of men of letters, especially poets,

> For they could best bestow delightful dow'rs,
> By flattering speech, or fam'd poetic pow'rs.

He is convinced that he would never have been dismissed if—as her household bard—he had been willing "To puff Protectress, in bold birth-day Ode," to draw "A wonderous Woman-Deity," surpassing Minerva, Venus, and Juno.

2. Any reader curious to explore the passages of Woodhouse's autobiography dealing with Mrs. Montagu and his relations to her will find the following references useful: James Woodhouse, *The Life and Lucubrations of Crispinus Scriblerus* in "Works" (1896), I, 67, 76–105, 123–223, 233–237; II, 1–34.

Mrs. Montagu's benevolence and philanthropy are, according to Woodhouse, tainted by these same qualities. He claims that Vanessa's husband

> knew her heart's vain-glorious bent;
> What all her bustle, all her bounties, meant:
> Saw thro' the colouring that the latent Cause
> Was popularity, and Self-applause.

Woodhouse charges that her famous May Day feasts for the chimney sweeps of London were really inspired by "Morning-paper's rapturing paragraph." The annual Sunday school treats at Sandleford, where her thirsty ears, "greedy of puerile applause," drank "Dolts' harsh huzzas," were simply another instance of her pride's assuming "celestial Charity's outside." He imputes an even less attractive motive to her charity than vanity: he claims that she

> Thought Charity, tho' sour'd with selfish leav'n,
> Might purchase some snug settlement in Heav'n.

·   ·   ·   ·   ·

> She fancied Seas of broth might well suffice,
> To swim both Soul, and Body, to the Skies.

He finally sternly bids her not to aim

> to occupy superior Niche
> Among the pious, patronizing Rich!

Mrs. Montagu's keen interest in experimental farming is likewise explained by Woodhouse as dictated by her ambition to shine in yet another sphere. While her agricultural fads were primarily the result of love of praise, she was not, says Woodhouse, averse to profit. In fact, he baldly accuses her of greed in her exploitation of her estates and the mines near Newcastle:

> Racks every tenant, ransacks all her Mines,
> To build her Temples, and adorn her Shrines!

It was, says Woodhouse, ambition—her own and that of her family—which brought about the match between young Elizabeth Robinson, not quite twenty-two, and the elderly Edward Montagu, nearly thirty years her senior. With vindictive relish Woodhouse analyzes what appeared to him a loveless and mercenary marriage.

The disparity of years (" 'Twas Chaucer's January match'd with May") merely aggravated temperamental incompatibility:

> He, unassuming—She, like Satan, proud.
> He lov'd retirement—She, a courtly Crowd.
> He modest—unaffected—studious—plain—
> She, splendid—specious—talkative—and vain.
>
> .   .   .   .   .
>
> A thoughtful Owl, from every eye retir'd,
> And pompous Peacock ne'er enough admir'd.
>
> .   .   .   .   .
>
> Kings, and their Creatures were His warmest hate—
> But She ador'd a Court, and courtly State.

Poor Woodhouse, caught in the crossfire of their disputes about morals, politics, and religion, was—he says—called upon to act as referee. With "One proof of perfect love" Woodhouse does credit her: "She wish'd him, Soul and Body, safe above." But for more than thirty years Heaven frustrated her desire to "Secure the Money, and discard the Man." Woodhouse positively gloats over the fact that her husband had inconsiderately lingered until she was fifty-four, "So sour'd in temper, and so sunk in Age" that she could not hope to marry a title.

According to Woodhouse, Mrs. Montagu welcomed her husband's death, which left her in possession of his substantial estates, enabling her to realize some of her ambitions:

> Death having now Vanessa's knot untied,
> Her soul felt pregnant with full broods of Pride;
> While to exhibit more Wealth, Wit, and Taste,
> Resolv'd to realize vast schemes at last.
>
> .   .   .   .   .
>
> Determin'd much sublimer Domes to build,
> Than those mean Fanes, her Pride, before o'er-fill'd—
> With Altars high'r, and Off'rings richer, stor'd;
> Where she, great Goddess! might be more ador'd,
> By Worshippers well-pick'd, of pompous—proud—
> And rich—and rare—from great Augusta's crowd.

(A fragment of a letter from Mrs. Montagu to one of her brothers, written six weeks after her husband's death, reveals much: "I find

I grow more good humored every day being in my unyoked condition ungalled in any. . . ." The rest of the letter is missing.) The mansion in Portman Square and the handsome new dining room and octagonal drawing room at Sandleford, then, were designed as a background for her ostentatious entertaining. This was repaid by "Flattery's incense, or fresh sprigs of praise." At her dinners

> Flesh—Fish—Fowl—Game, and Fruit, must grace the Treat;
> With large libations of most costly Wine,
> That Scholars—Commons—Lords—and Dukes—might dine—
> Each proud expence tried Taste could then contrive,
> To keep Importance, and loved Fame, alive!

Dazzled by this lavish display of wealth, who would ever have suspected Mrs. Montagu of penny-pinching behind the scenes? Woodhouse, who had to scour the cheapest markets for oysters, ducklings, guinea fowls, fruit, and cheese for these sumptuous feasts, then hired an economical cook, "To dress large dinners at the least expence." But the last straw was being compelled to buy smuggled coffee in violation of his conscience and the law of the land. Armed with a note signed by his mistress, Woodhouse—"His smuggling Patroness's Plenipo"—sought out the shop of a Mrs. Green, where Mrs. Montagu dealt. (There is abundant evidence in Mrs. Montagu's letters of her buying smuggled tea, silks, handkerchiefs, etc. She boasted to her sister-in-law, an invaluable accomplice, of her "good luck in smuggling.") After the banquet it was Woodhouse's duty to lock up any delicacies from the servants, who ate brown bread, lukewarm vegetables, "Fish-bones, heads, tails, with some few fibres, left," rumps and wings of poultry, and rabbits' heads. Any funeral baked meats that escaped a state banquet unscathed furnished forth a lesser feast for less elegant friends. The wax lights that blazed on state occasions gave way in private to smoky tallow ends. Woodhouse explains this apparent contradiction—public extravagance and private parsimony—as a means of "magnifying Fame, yet sparing Pelf."

Closely related to Mrs. Montagu's frugality was her suspicion that her servants were cheating her. She was sure the butler was watering the wine, that her Abigail was pilfering tea, that the laundress was filching indigo, starch, and soap. She even suspected

Woodhouse of purloining food and books! Her accusations, he declared, were couched in foul-mouthed Billingsgate that would degrade a demirep. She also feared attack from without. Every night, before she was undressed, the maid had to look under the bed and chairs lest a burglar be lurking "To pilfer Property, or Life destroy." Over Woodhouse's bed hung a bell, one of an elaborate system of burglar alarms installed to summon aid "When restless Fancy should create a Thief."

Mrs. Montagu's "worldliness" was a thorn in the flesh of Woodhouse, who became increasingly evangelical. He was especially outraged by her Sunday evening parties when from twenty to sixty guests were feasted in Portman Square. This desecration of the Sabbath was aggravated by the fact that bishops led the "Troops of Epicures."

> But how can Sunday-parties Heav'n offend,
> When Priests, so privileg'd the rites attend!
> Blythe Bishops too, sometimes, with smirking face,
> Confirm the Crowd, and consecrate the Place!
> Ev'n Y——k, most reverend, full of Grace, I ween,
> Can, on occasion, sanctify the scene.

With aching conscience Woodhouse had to preside at the sideboard. His heart yearned over the servants thus compelled to break the Sabbath, and he tried to arouse them against this heinous desecration. Woodhouse is especially shocked to see the company—bishops and all—fall upon the feast without a word of thanks to the Almighty. (An entry in William Wilberforce's diary seems to corroborate the omission of grace at Mrs. Montagu's table: "Montagu [Mrs. Montagu's adopted son] took me to task for peculiarities—saying grace, *etc.*") The steward's righteous indignation reaches a crescendo when he flays Mrs. Montagu for turning the ruined chapel of Sandleford Priory into a banquet hall. Although the bones of the monks were exhumed and reburied in Monkey Lane, Woodhouse speaks of Mrs. Montagu's rioting "o'er the tombs." Where Mass had been celebrated (although not for over four centuries), "Now vain Voluptuaries carve and quaff." She dares

> Break down His altars! banish holy rites!
> For festive boards, and Bacchanal delights!

Woodhouse's lurid account of the carousals of Mrs. Montagu's friends—Hannah More, Mrs. Carter, Dr. Beattie, and other eminently decorous guests—in the desecrated "catacombs" (to quote Woodhouse) suggests Walpurgis Night or the orgies at Medmenham Abbey. To purge the polluted place after the Bacchanalian throng had finished their idolatrous devoirs (to quote Woodhouse again), the pious steward would resort thither to pray and sing hymns. Even a less worldly woman than Mrs. Montagu would have found Woodhouse's aggressive piety somewhat oppressive. The reader need not penetrate very far into his autobiography to sympathize with his mistress, who "All moral maxims forcibly forbid!" There is in the self-righteous Woodhouse more than a trace of Malvolio. Many a time Mrs. Montagu must have been sorely tempted to ask, "Dost thou think, because thou are virtuous, there shall be no more cakes and ale?"

Although the Queen of the Blues had been dust and ashes for nearly a century before *The Life and Lucubrations of Crispinus Scriblerus* was printed, we know what she would have thought of Woodhouse's relentless exposé. She was completely out of sympathy with the trend of biography toward realism. In 1754 she lamented Dr. Thomas Birch's treatment of another Queen Elizabeth: "I shall hate these collectors of Anecdotes if they cure one of that Admiration of a great character that Arises from a pleasing deception of sight. . . . I cannot forgive Mr. Birch." More than thirty years later she was indignant at Boswell's exposure of Johnson's "little caprices, his unhappy infirmities, his singularities."

. . . they disgrace a character to a reader as Wens & Warts would do a Statue or Portrait to a spectator. May this new invented mode of disgracing the dead & calumniating the living perish with the short lived work of Master Boswell, but the effect & consequences of such an example of Biography makes one shudder as bitter pens, with still worse intentions, may adopt it, & the Grave be no longer the place where the Wicked cease from troubling.[3]

That shudder was prophetic.

3. Unpublished letter from Mrs. Montagu to Mrs. Thrale in the possession of Prof. James Clifford, by whose kind permission I quote.

BARETTI'S REPUTATION IN ENGLAND

Donald C. Gallup

THE author of *A Journey from London to Genoa* is so little remembered by English-speaking peoples in our day that the position which he occupied in literary circles in England when his principal work was published in 1770 is often forgotten or ignored. It was a source of incredulity to Baretti's enemies, in his own time, that an Italian with no English friends or letters of introduction, small financial means, and almost no knowledge of the language when he arrived in London in 1751 should have been able in a few years' time to ingratiate himself with the foremost figures of his period to the extent which was revealed on the celebrated occasion of his trial for murder.

It will be remembered that Baretti, through no fault of his own, became involved in a street brawl in the Haymarket on the evening of Friday, October 6, 1769, and, in self-defense, stabbed a low character named Evan Morgan with his fruit knife. When Morgan died at the Middlesex Hospital two days later, Baretti was accused of manslaughter and was lodged in prison. The testimony at the coroner's inquest and the subsequent trial, given voluntarily and of course under oath, makes evident the esteem in which Baretti was held by the distinguished persons who chose to appear as his friends.[1]

The first to testify at the inquest on October 11 was Sir Joshua Reynolds, who had then, he said, known Baretti between fifteen and sixteen years. He stated that Baretti was a gentleman "of the best Character & of Great Humanity & of a peaceable quiet Disposition." At the trial nine days later he added that Baretti was "very active in endeavouring to help his friends. I have known many instances of it. He is a gentleman of a good temper; I never knew him quarreling in my life; he is of a sober disposition."

1. The quotations which follow are taken from the manuscript record of the coroner's inquest (before the war preserved in the London Guildhall) and from the printed account of the trial in *Old Bailey Trials* (London, 1769), XIV, 431–432.

Second at the inquest was Dr. Johnson, who said that he "began to know Mr. Baretti in 1753 or 1754. He is a very studious Man of great Peaceableness of Manners." At the trial he added, "I have been intimate with him. He is a man of literature . . . a man of great diligence. He gets his living by study. . . . A man that I never knew to be otherwise than peaceable, and a man that I take to be rather timorous. . . . I do not believe he could be capable of assaulting any body in the street, without great provocation."

William Fitzherbert had known Baretti for about fourteen years and stated that "He has as good & irreproachable a Character as any he knows . . . that he had so good an Opinion of & so great an Affection for him that he has prevailed on him to spend a Summer with him & his Family in the Country." At the trial he described Baretti as "a man that I always chose to have in my family."

Edmund Burke had, at that time, known Baretti for about three years. "He is a Man of very great Humanity, & of the best of Characters . . . & has known many instances of great Tenderness & Humanity in him—& that he is of the most peaceable Disposition." At the trial he further described Baretti as "an ingenious . . . thorough good-natured man."

William Burke had known Baretti also for about three years with great intimacy and stated that "if he was to chose [sic] a person for Humanity & Tenderness he would chuse Mr. Barretti [sic] in preference to or as soon as any Man he knows."

David Garrick said that he had known Baretti intimately since 1764 when he saw him at Venice, "& has great obligations to him . . . & [he, Baretti] would at any time go over the Alps to serve an Englishman. Always keeps the best Company, & the Witness thinks him incapable of doing what he is charged with on this Inquest without sufficient provocation." At the trial he said,

I never knew a man of a more active benevolence. He did me all the civility he could do to a stranger, as indeed he did so to every Englishman that came in the course of my acquaintance with him. When I was at Paris [i.e. Padua], I was very inquisitive about men of literature. I asked who they thought was the best writer in their language; they told me Mr. Baretti. He is a man of great probity and morals. I have a very particular instance of his great friendship to me. Mrs. Garrick got a lameness, and we tried every method in order for a remedy to no purpose; and Mr. Baretti was the person that restored her.

Joseph Wilton, opposite whose house Baretti was then living, said that he had known Baretti twelve years and that he "Is so remarkable for Goodness & Humanity the Witness has adopted him as a Brother—thinks him incapable of doing a base Action."

Dr. Goldsmith had known Baretti "upwards of 3 years," and believed him "The most human benevolent Man in the World— Has expressed himself often with Tenderness towards the unhappy women of the Town, & been very generous to them." At the trial he added that he had "had the honour of Mr. Baretti's company at my chambers in the Temple."

Bennet Langton had known Baretti fifteen years. "His genl. Character is that of a most human benevolent Man, & . . . he has known many instances of the greatest Tenderness & Generosity in him, & thinks him incapable of stabbing a Man but in his own Defence."

Topham Beauclerk testified at the trial that he had known Baretti ten years and that Baretti had given him, upon his going to Italy, letters of recommendation to "some of the first people there, and to men of learning. . . . Unless Mr. Baretti had been a man of consequence, he could never have recommended me to such people as he did. He is a gentleman of letters, and a studious man."

Dr. Hallifax, the last witness, said that "Mr. Baretti is a man extremely affable in his temper, and quite a good-natured man."

Such were the opinions held of Baretti, some seventeen years after his first arrival in England, by men who knew him well, and there are further indications, later, of the reputation which Baretti had built up for himself in England. The Reverend William Mason, when there was a question about the Italian idiom of a letter of Thomas Gray, wrote to Horace Walpole, asking him to seek Baretti's opinion upon the matter. Walpole did not execute Mason's request,[2] but the correspondence would appear to show that Baretti was regarded at least as one of a few authorities on Italian language and literature then in England.

When Hutchinson of the University of Dublin conceived the idea of adding a school of modern languages to that institution, the position of professor was offered to Baretti at a salary of £100 and

2. *Letters of Horace Walpole*, ed. Toynbee (Oxford, 1904), VIII, 310.

lodging. Baretti refused, telling Campbell that the offer "was by no means worth his acceptance," [3] but this incident also has significance; while another anecdote of Campbell's gives additional indication of Baretti's position. Shortly after having been asked by a member of the nobility if he had seen the lions in the Tower, Campbell happened to quote Johnson. Asked if he knew Johnson, he replied: "Yes my Lord I do & Barretti [sic] & several others whom I have been fortunate enough to find willing to extend my acquaintance among their friends—for these my Lord were the Lions I came to see in London. Aye, says he, these indeed are lions worth seeing & the sight of them may be of use to you." [4]

If in his own day people were inclined to wonder how Baretti had managed to achieve the position he had, his success at first appears even more remarkable today. Baretti had faults, and it is quite understandable in view of Boswell's attitude toward him that when he is mentioned at all in the *Life* the faults often loom large. It is the case with Baretti, as with many of the lesser figures of the Johnson entourage, that the twentieth-century reader seldom seeks their acquaintance further than in the pages of Boswell's account.

It is true that Baretti had a frequently irritating amount of self-confidence and a very lively temper. But these were combined with a generally pleasing personality and an extremely impressive appearance which helped him immeasurably in his associations with people. He could be utterly charming when he wished, and certainly in the early part of his career in England, when he was a stranger in a foreign country, he did his best to make himself agreeable. That he was considered a man not only of character but also of considerable talent and great charm is evident from contemporary references to him, and it is apparent that he was admired and esteemed for what he was and not primarily for the work he published. When Johnson praised the *Account of the Manners and Customs of Italy,* he went on to pay more lengthy tribute to Baretti's powers of conversation; [5] and when Baretti was preparing a

3. *Dr. Campbell's Diary,* ed. J. L. Clifford (Cambridge, 1947), p. 53.
4. *Ibid.,* p. 82.
5. Boswell, *Life,* II, 57.

narrative of his travels, Johnson wrote him that "your friends here expect such a book of travels as has not often been seen." [6]

As important as his personality, however, was the surprising command of the language of his adopted country which he gained through years of dogged persistence. He had been working at it in Italy and immediately upon his arrival in London set about a really intensive study. In his *Lettere familiari* (1762–63) he described the method he used in learning the language:

For the first two months I could not understand a single syllable; but when I had succeeded in fixing in my head a few hundred words by continually working at nouns, verbs, and other parts of speech, I made every one I came across read me out these words not once only, but ten times and more, and tried all the while to pronounce the most difficult; and thus, by gradually accustoming my ears to the sound, I made what was considered extraordinary progress in that strange and most irregular tongue. It is true that nature has given me some facility in learning languages, and that my frequent changes from place to place in early life have increased this facility, for I have always tried to speak the dialect of every place where I have ever made a short stay.[7]

Thirty-four years later, writing to his fellow countryman Gambarelli who was finding it hard to get along in London, Baretti described his own difficulties during those first months of 1751:

. . . applying myself in the Coffee-House and at the round table, hiding my infinite troubles in the bottom of my heart and recommending myself with honest frankness to this one and the other, who appeared to have the faces of worthy men, and always studying day and night the language and customs of this race, I came little by little to better my poor situation. Why don't you do the same? . . . The world belongs to the active, not to the faint of heart. Work hard at learning to pronounce the little English you know; do what you can with that, and don't expect people to speak to you, but talk to everyone, and to all kinds of people, for of action is born action, and with the smallest taper one may light a thousand candles and torches . . . England is a large country, full of riches, and full of people willing to share them with those who are wise and wish to do something; and the proverb says that the Lord helps him who helps himself.[8]

No one could have accused Baretti of inactivity in 1751, and his willingness to seize any opportunity indirectly aided him to meet

6. June 10, 1761; quoted in *Life*, I, 365.
7. Lacy Collison-Morley, *Giuseppe Baretti* (London, 1909), pp. 62–63.
8. August 25, 1785; *Epistolario*, ed. Piccioni (Bari, 1936), II, 287–289.

the literary figures of the London of that time. When Mr. Lennox asked, in the Prince of Orange Coffee House, for an Italian to help his wife in translating Shakespeare's sources in return for instruction in English, Baretti was quick to volunteer. He thus met Charlotte Lennox, the woman who introduced him to Samuel Johnson.

Dr. Johnson himself was an important factor in Baretti's mastering of the language. In an often-quoted passage from the letter already mentioned, written to Baretti at Milan on June 10, 1761, Johnson thanked him for the three letters he was then answering, and wrote: "Your English style still continues in its purity and vigour. With vigour your genius will supply it; but its purity must be continued by close attention. To use two languages familiarly, and without contaminating one by the other, is very difficult; and to use more than two, is hardly to be hoped. The praises which some have received for their multiplicity of languages, may be sufficient to excite industry, but can hardly generate confidence." [9]

Gradually Baretti's reputation for skill in the use of English became established, and we find Malone writing of him that "He was certainly a man of extraordinary talents, and perhaps no one ever made himself so completely master of a foreign language as he did of English." [10] Twiss said that he thought he never knew a foreigner who spoke English so well as Baretti, [11] and Mrs. Thrale, who knew whereof she spoke, offered her testimony:

Baretti could not endure to be called or scarcely thought, a foreigner, and indeed it did not often occur to his company that he was one; for his accent was wonderfully proper, and his language always copious, always nervous, always full of various allusions, flowing too with a rapidity worthy of admiration, and far beyond the power of nineteen in twenty natives. He had also a knowledge of the solemn language and the gay, could be sublime with Johnson, or blackguard with the groom; could dispute, could rally, could quibble, in our language. [12]

At his death, Baretti's command of English was the achievement of his most widely commented upon. *The Diary; or, Woodfall's*

9. Boswell, *op. cit.*, I, 362.

10. Sir James Prior, *Life of Edmond Malone* (London, 1860), p. 392.

11. *Early Diary of Frances Burney*, ed. Ellis (London, G. Bell and Sons, 1913), I, 296.

12. *Autobiography, Letters and Literary Remains of Mrs. Piozzi (Thrale)*, ed. Hayward (2d ed. London, 1861), I, 93.

Register observed: "35 years he lived in a foreign country, in whose language he was such a master, that he would wield it in attack on its inhabitants, sometimes better than they could in their defence." [13]

Almost as helpful to Baretti as his knowledge of the tongue, and of course dependent upon it, was his talent as conversationalist. In the London of his time wit was a quality much sought after. Johnson towered head and shoulders above his friends, but he had many competitors. This aspect of Baretti's popularity is indicated by Fanny Burney in her description of her first visit with the Thrales at Streatham: "About noon, when I went into the library, book hunting, Mrs. Thrale came to me. We had a very nice confab about various books, and exchanged opinions and imitations of Baretti; she told me many excellent tales of him, and I, in return, related my stories." [14]

Baretti's behavior in conversation appears to have been modeled somewhat on Johnson's, if we are to judge it by an example which Mrs. Thrale gives: "Will. Burke was tart upon Mr. Baretti for being too dogmatical in his talk about politics. 'You have,' says he, 'no business to be investigating the characters of Lord Falkland or Mr. Hampden. You cannot judge of their merits, they are no countrymen of yours.' 'True,' replied Baretti, 'and you should learn by the same rule to speak very cautiously about Brutus and Mark Antony; they are my countrymen, and I must have their characters tenderly treated by foreigners.'" [15] Many people were insulted by Johnson's remarks, and not a few were displeased with Baretti's. Cornelia Knight was "disgusted by his satirical madness of manner," although she admitted him to be a man of great learning and information; [16] and Goldsmith, according to Davies (who had reason to be prejudiced against the Italian), "least of all mankind, approved Baretti's conversation; he considered him as an insolent, over-bearing foreigner." [17]

13. May 12, 1789, [3]. Adapted however from Mrs. Piozzi's communication to the *World,* May 10, 1789, for which see Piozzi, *op. cit.,* I, 317.

14. *Diary & Letters of Madame d'Arblay,* ed. Dobson (London, 1904), I, 76.

15. Piozzi, *op. cit.,* I, 93.

16. *Ibid.,* I, 92.

17. Thomas Davies, *Memoirs of the Life of David Garrick, Esq.* (3d ed. London, 1781), II, 168.

Certainly Baretti was able to meet the members of the literary circle on their own ground and ask no quarter; and that he occasionally made a definite effort to please is shown in a letter which he wrote to a friend in Italy: "The houses I frequent are numerous, and would be more numerous did I wish it. My familiarity with English ways and my Italian gaiety—which is usually, I might almost say always, greater here than in Italy—makes people readily open their doors to me." [18] He was in some ways so oddly naïve that he made many foes. Boswell and he were cordial enemies almost from their first meeting. Goldsmith was jealous of Baretti's social ease; Mrs. Thrale, later on, resented Baretti's interference in her domestic affairs, and Johnson became angry with Baretti as the result of a violent argument. For Baretti was tactful and yet had no tact. He could flatter Mrs. Thrale and yet advance to the fight with her, all banners flying. He was content at times to humble himself before rich friends, expecting that he would be rewarded for his humility, but almost always something happened which he could not stomach, and his carefully laid plans were in a moment of anger destroyed.

Outside the immediate literary group of which he was a member there were more enemies. A furious quarrel with Thomas Davies, who published several of Baretti's books, was apparently caused by a misunderstanding about the financial arrangements for an edition and translation of *Don Quixote* which Baretti never completed. William Kenrick had made Baretti his ill-wisher by an attack, which Baretti felt was unwarranted, in the *London Review;* when Baretti retaliated in kind in his *Easy Phraseology* (1775), Kenrick and he became established foes. Smollett considered Baretti an unworthy opponent, and Baretti returned Smollett's dislike. There were other altercations, major and minor, during Baretti's years in England, and in Italy. In most cases, it may be said that Baretti had grounds for vexation, but he never possessed qualities of a peacemaker, and although he made resolutions at various times not to pay attention to attacks, he forgot them when he became angry. His statement in his account of his quarrel with Mrs. Thale that "my bile suddenly rose to such a degree, that I am sure I uttered

18. Letter to Carcano, April 20, 1770; Collison-Morley, *op. cit.,* p. 231.

my indignation in the most severe terms," [19] is illustrative of his conduct in controversy.

Baretti's life and work in England represent in a way the Italian element in English literature; for his fiery Latin temper was at the root of the trouble. This cost him friends; but the capacity for deep devotion which went along with this temperament brought them around him in time of need. The element is noticeable also in his criticism, for only rarely did he see a book from manuscript to published form without some trivial controversy. He had, in the latter part of his career, the Johnsonian sin of sloth to a Johnsonian degree and, in most cases, it took an outburst of passion to spur him into activity—passion, or dire need. Works which he wrote without these incentives, or with these in the background, are the ones upon which his English literary reputation must be based. It is unfortunate that so large a part of his work was occasional—a momentary flaring of angry passion, as soon forgotten as over. This weakness, inherent in his character, marred his career, social and literary, and continues to mar his reputation in English-speaking countries. In Italy this temperament can be understood and forgiven; but not in England. His best work, from an English point of view, is the sane, controlled portion, that in which he forgot invective and expressed his really profound love of literature and studies. About the Baretti of the controversial books and pamphlets there is a kind of pyrotechnic flash, partly reflected, perhaps, from the great Johnson, and in small measure the Italian's tribute to his master.

Yet Baretti was not a typical Italian of the eighteenth century, and he aptly described himself late in life as "a kind of demi-Englishman." Of him Collison-Morley wrote in *The Athenaeum* on the occasion of the two hundredth anniversary of his birth:

. . . no amount of good advice or careful schooling could possibly have enabled a typical eighteenth-century Italian man of letters . . . to follow in his footsteps. It was because he was not typical of his age that Baretti so readily found himself at home in his new surroundings. He possessed in no small degree those qualities which were supposed to be typical of an Englishman of his time, the foundations upon which that liberty which Italians had been taught to admire by Voltaire himself was based—sound common sense,

19. *European Magazine*, XIII (May, 1788), p. 315.

sturdy independence and an out-spoken frankness which, in Baretti's case, amounted to roughness, and even at times to brutality.[20]

Baretti was in effect a foreign counterpart on a smaller scale of Dr. Johnson; and from Johnson Baretti got a good deal of his critical theory and much of the inspiration for his literary productions. Both were lexicographers, and they seem to have had similar powers of mind; while Johnson, as well as Baretti, had his quarrels and disagreements.

Just as Baretti's relation with the men and women with whom he was associated daily was one of ups and downs, so his reputation with the English public fluctuated violently. His debut had been a fortunate one: he entered under the right auspices, and made the most of this opportunity by working hard on the language and on his early publications. Here was a foundation firm enough for the critical renown which he hoped to gain for himself in England. This reputation mounted slowly but steadily to 1760, and even after his return to Italy in that year the public was made to keep him in mind by the Italian dictionary and the *Grammar* reprinted from it. When he came back to England for good in 1766 his acclaim was approaching its peak. The *Account* (1768) was, in its noninvective sections, his most satisfactory work to date; his exemplary behavior at his trial in 1769, with the commendations he received from the most important people in the literary world, set him higher in the public opinion; and he established his fame at the psychological moment with his longest and most creditable original production, *A Journey from London to Genoa* (1770), which had been some ten years in the making.

From 1770 on, Baretti, I fear, rested too much upon the oars, trusting to the current of his reputation to carry him on. Much of his time during the three years following the publication of the *Journey* was taken up with various projects, few of which saw the light of day, and with Italian editions which did not contribute materially to his English reputation. From 1773 to 1776 the Thrales occupied all his attention, and the *Easy Phraseology* (1775), though entertaining, was not of the solid worth of the *Journey*. The period of the American Revolution saw a desperate but on the whole woe-

20. XCII (April 25, 1919), 244.

fully unproductive activity on his part. His *Discours sur Shakespeare et sur Monsieur Voltaire* (1777) "produced him nothing but a few copies to give to his friends"; his Spanish dictionary was stillborn in 1779; "his *Tolondron* [1786] never sold, [and] his letters in the European Magazine he gave to the printer." [21]

There is unfortunately no impartial contemporary judge to inform us of the actual status at any time of Baretti's critical reputation in England. The reviews are for the most part prejudiced, and their notices are an account of Baretti's hates and quarrels, not of the development of his literary fame; they can be considered as witnesses only when their prejudices are balanced and an average taken.

The truth is probably that Baretti's abilities were esteemed, and his thoughtless tirades regretted, by those whose opinions best merited respect. A fair estimate may perhaps be arrived at from contrasting the comments which appeared in *The Morning Post and Daily Advertiser* shortly after his death. The first was violently antipathetic:

He was a snarling old brute with some literature, but wholly destitute of genius and liberality. His works are poor miserable things, unworthy of critical notice. If this man had not contrived to obtrude himself into an acquaintance with Mr. Johnson, who was very credulous with all his great parts and knowledge, he would have ended his days in a garret. Dr. Johnson, however, detected him in a lie and discarded him, but not till his countenance had given Baretti a passport into the republic of letters.[22]

The second, several months later, was more impartial:

. . . the best answer that can be given to all those accounts which have represented him as a man of a brutal and ferocious temper, is the attachment which many of his young friends felt while he was living, and preserve to his memory now he is no more.

. . . In his general intercourse with the world he was social, easy, and conversible; his talents were neither great nor splendid; but his knowledge of mankind was extensive; and his acquaintance with books in all modern languages which are valuable, except the German, was universal . . .

In point of morals he was irreproachable; with regard to faith, he was rather without religion than irreligious . . . but his scepticism was never

21. *Gentleman's Magazine*, LIX (June, 1789), 570.
22. May 11, 1789, [3], col. 1.

offensive to those who had settled principles, never held out or defended in company, never proposed to mislead or corrupt the minds of young people. . . . If this was the least favourable part of his character, the best was his integrity, which was, in every period of his distresses, constant and unimpeached.[23]

Mrs. Thrale's opinion was probably, all in all, the most nearly just:

. . . I never altered my sentiments concerning him; for his character is easily seen, and his soul above disguise, haughty and insolent, and breathing defiance against all mankind; while his powers of mind exceed most people's, and his powers of purse are so slight that they leave him dependent on all. Baretti is for ever in the state of a stream dammed up: if he could once get loose, he would bear down all before him.[24]

Beyond his personal reputation and the value of his contribution to English literature, Baretti played an important role in the popularization of Italian literature in England at this time. The language had been studied for many years, but the great body of Italian literature was not well known. Baretti wrote much upon Dante; and to some extent as a result of his work, interest in the poet began to grow during these years and continued to increase with rapidity into the nineteenth century. Paget Toynbee, in his *Dante in English Literature from Chaucer to Cary,* writes that "The various works published by Baretti in England on Italian literature no doubt did much to advance the study of Dante in this country in the eighteenth century." [25]

In the same way, Baretti did something toward furthering the already considerable popularity of Ariosto in England, and would have done more had his plans not been interrupted by another of his quarrels. He later concerned himself particularly with modern Italian writers, and the vogue of Metastasio and Gozzi on the continent and in England was due largely to his efforts. Baretti also did much to popularize English literature in Italy—where his reputation has always been high—and in his *Frusta letteraria* brought English critical theory to bear upon Italian writing with salutary effect, making his fellow countrymen aware of the virtues of a more vigorous literature.

Association with an Italian of such wide interests and on the

23. September 3, 1789, [3], col. 1.
24. Piozzi, *op. cit.,* I, 103.
25. London, [1909], I, 257.

whole praiseworthy character could be only beneficial to the English of the Age of Johnson, who were all too prone to regard anything foreign as suspect per se. Johnson himself was no exception, for he was as Baretti observed, "a real *true-born Englishman*. He hated the Scotch, the French, the Dutch, the Hannoverians [*sic*], and had the greatest contempt for all other European Nations: such were his early prejudices, which he never attempted to conquer." [26] The furor caused by such exotic exhibits as Omai, Paoli, the publications of George Psalmanazar, and Bruce's lectures on Abyssinia was but one aspect of this eighteenth-century provincialism. There was, at the same time, an active curiosity about all strange things, and early interest in Baretti was to a certain extent this type of curiosity; his slightly different clothes and his manner of wearing his hair in a tail made the lower classes at least set him down as a "Frenchman" to be made fun of. But Baretti, after he had attracted attention with the *Account,* his trial, and the *Journey,* made many Englishmen aware that, though Italian, he was not very much different from them, and there came about a gradual change in their attitude toward him.

The part Baretti played in bringing about a better understanding of the Italian people by the English was especially important. Particularly with the *Account,* and also with other books, Baretti demonstrated to the English that their Italian neighbors, though papists, were not entirely unlike them, and did much to promote good feeling between the nations. He was peculiarly fitted for this missionary role, not being a typical Italian, and having come to England an exile from his native land, with a penchant toward English ways of thinking. His extraordinary power over the language and his charm, which made people forget his nationality, helped him to overcome prejudice and broaden the outlook of the English. It is probable that no one else could have done exactly what he did, and that it could have happened in no other age. Baretti and his work assume, therefore, in the literary history of his period, an especial significance which should be obscured neither by the prejudices of Boswell nor the ill-advised vituperations of Baretti himself.

26. Manuscript note in his copy of *Letters to and from the Late Samuel Johnson, LL.D.,* ed. Hester Lynch Piozzi (London, 1788), I, 121. This copy is in the British Museum.

GILBERT WHITE, POETIZER OF THE COMMONPLACE

Lansing V. Hammond

"Happy the man! who knows . . . how to keep himself innocently and usefully employed; especially where his studies tend to the advancement of knowledge, and the benefit of Society."
—Gilbert White, Letter to Thomas Pennant, November 28, 1768.

THE devotion of English writers to the beauty and charm of their countryside, and the resulting nature motif with which English literature is permeated, has often been commented upon. Whether it was a semiclassical Arcadian landscape, a generalized "pleasing prospect," or a homely primrose hedge that attracted the writer, the rural scene has never failed to exercise a profound influence upon English men of letters. The amount and quality of this homage have, of course, varied from time to time; but even in the midst of periods when it seemed as though, for a while at least, the countryside had been forgotten, there arose prophets to testify that in the breasts of trueborn Englishmen "the poetry of earth is never dead." Such a prophet was "Robin" Herrick; such a one was Izaak Walton; and such a one was the Reverend Gilbert White, antiquary and natural historian of Selborne, in Hampshire.

A country parson of comfortable means, who was not immoderately constrained by his parish duties, Gilbert White passed the greater part of his mature life in the village of his birth. Here he cultivated his garden and planted his trees, corresponded with and received visits from his friends and, above all, learned to "watch intently Nature's gentle doings." He was interested in everything that surrounded him. He noted temperatures and rainfalls, the dates when flowers first blossomed in spring and birds disappeared in autumn; he inquired into the habits of otters and rabbits, the rate of growth of trees, the appearance of fossils, and the activities of earthworms. He speculated about the migration of swallows

and the cause of leprosy; he noted the survival of village superstitions and was much concerned with the excavation of Roman
remains. And in these investigations he was scrupulously painstaking; for though he welcomed the birds and eggs and nests
which sympathetic neighbors brought him, he was enough of a
skeptic to reject mere hearsay evidence until he had had an opportunity to verify phenomena for himself. This cautiousness in procedure not only saved Gilbert White from falling into many of the
vulgar errors entertained in his day but also made it possible for
him to advance the boundaries of natural science. It is true that he
shared, in part, the popular superstition concerning the hibernation
of swallows. "Swallows certainly sleep all winter," Dr. Johnson told
Boswell. "A number of them conglobulate together, by flying round
and round, and then all in a heap throw themselves under water,
and lye in the bed of a river." Gilbert White, convinced that he had
seen these birds, "about the time of departure," congregating in
osier beds by the rivers, concluded that "this . . . seems to give
some countenance to the northern opinion (strange as it is) of their
retiring under water." But against this amusing misconception may
be set his discoveries that the harvest mouse was a British species;
that there were three distinct types of willow-wren; and, most
important of all, his anticipation of Darwin's theories of the usefulness of earthworms and the importance of love and hunger as
factors in what later came to be called "the struggle for existence."

Like so many of his contemporaries, Gilbert White commenced
keeping a sort of diary or journal during his undergraduate days.
Given a man with his temperament and interests, the transition
from this college diary, through a *Garden Kalendar* (1751–68), to
a *Naturalist's Journal* was inevitable. At about the same time that
this transition was taking place he was forming friendships with
several well-known naturalists who did much to stimulate him into
further activity. Of these, the two who exercised most influence
were Thomas Pennant, with whom he began corresponding in
1767, and the Honorable Daines Barrington, whom he first met in
London two years later. To these men the nucleus of *The Natural
History of Selborne* was addressed in the form of private correspondence, largely drawn from the daily observations recorded in

the *Journal* and not originally intended for publication. Yielding to the importunities of these friends, Gilbert White later selected 110 of the letters, subjected them to a certain amount of editing, and had them printed in 1789. They were favorably reviewed in the *Gentleman's Magazine* and during the ensuing years *The Natural History of Selborne* has become a classic; more than one hundred separate editions have since been printed.

One of the features of this book which the *Gentleman's Magazine* especially praised was Gilbert White's success in breaking away from "the custom which has too long and too generally prevailed of compiling books from books." The commendation was deserved; for what impresses a twentieth-century reader is the freshness and independence of the writer's observations; the entries and descriptions have all the sparkle and, if you will, monotony of Nature herself. "Open the book anywhere," said Lowell, "and it takes you out of doors." Appropriate as this comment is to the *Natural History,* it is even more applicable to the *Naturalist's Journal.* Never has there been a more poetic cataloguing of facts in prose, or a simple record of the revolving seasons more permeated with the spirit of the English countryside:

Larks frolick much in the air . . . Crocus's in high glory . . . Hedge sparrows sing vehemently . . . Tom-tit attempts it's spring note. . . . Green wood-pecker laughs at all the world . . . . rooks have finished their nests, . . . cocks begin to feed the hens, who receive their bounty with a fondling tremulous voice & fluttering wings, & all the little bandishments that are expressed by the young while in a helpless state. . . . The . . . dripping days have done infinite service to the grass, & spring-corn . . . . most delicate ripening weather. . . . Wheatears peep . . . . grass long enough to wave before the wind. . . . Honeysuckles very fragrant, & most beautiful objects! Columbines make a figure . . . Field-crickets *crink;* their note is very summer-like, & chearful. . . . No dew . . . rusty sunshine. . . . Clouds put up their heads. . . . Sky thickens with flisky clouds. . . . Stormy winds and gluts of rain. . . . Sweet moonshine. . . . Sweet hay-making weather . . . golden horizon, red horizon. . . . The whole country is one rich prospect of harvest scenery!! . . . The cat frolicks & plays with the falling leaves. . . . Warm fog . . . walls sweat. . . . Frost begins to come in a door. . . . Ice bears; boys slide on Wollmer pond. . . . Deep snow covers the ground. Beautiful winter-pieces. . . . Vast frost-work on the windows. . . . The air is soft. Violets blow. Snow lies under hedges. Men plow.

Who having read it can ever forget the description of a yellow willow-wren that "haunts only the tops of trees in high beechen woods, and makes a sibilous grasshopper-like noise, now and then, at short intervals, shivering a little with its wings when it sings"?

Part of Gilbert White's magic lies in his ability to endow with charm and novelty what many would consider commonplace. Not until one pauses to reflect does one realize that it is not so much the intrinsic merit of the things being described as Gilbert White's transmutation of them that brings us pleasure. And nowhere is this power more clearly revealed than in his accounts of Timothy, the tortoise. The compiled letters to Pennant and Barrington, in the *Natural History,* summarize the story conveniently enough; but to know of Timothy only through the more formalized account is to lose the enthusiasm and excitement attending each day-by-day discovery. The first reference to the tortoise, in the *Journal,* comes in November, 1771. The naturalist was visiting his Aunt, Mrs. Snooke, at Ringmer; and his attention seems to have been directed toward Timothy from the very start: "M$^{rs.}$ Snooke's tortoise begins to scrape a hole in the ground in order for laying up" (Nov. 1). "Tortoise comes out in the sun about noon, but soon returns to his work of digging a hole to retire into" (Nov. 10). "Tortoise . . . not finish'd his hybernaculum, being interrupted by the sunny weather, which tempted him out" (Nov. 15). The visits to Mrs. Snooke were semi-annual; and entries concerning the doings of Timothy increase in length and intimacy as Gilbert White's understanding of the pet deepened: "The Ringmer-tortoise came forth from it's hybernaculum on the 6th of April, but did not appear to eat 'til May the 5th: it does not eat but on hot days. As far as I could find it had no perceptible pulse" (May 23, 1772). "Timothy, Mrs. Snooke's old tortoise, has been kept full thirty years in her courtyard . . . He weighs six pounds three quarters and one ounce. It was never weighed before, but seems to have grown much since it came." Then, in March, 1780, three exciting entries appear in rapid succession: "Mrs. Snooke dyed, aged 86" (March 8); "Mrs. Snooke was buried" (March 15); "Brought away Mrs. Snooke's old tortoise, Timothy, which she valued much & treated kindly for near 40 years. When dug out of it's hybernaculum, it resented the

Insult by hissing" (March 17). "As the tortoise will now be under my eye"—one can feel the quiver of excitement in the naturalist's breast—"I shall have an opportunity of enlarging my observations on it's mode of life and propensities," Gilbert White wrote; and there follow nearly 150 entries and observations, cumulatively delightful in themselves and charmingly summarized in Letter 50 of the *Natural History.*

The factual notes are interesting; but the writer's speculations and enthusiasm are the thing! "17 April 1780. On this day Sir G:B:Rodney defeated the French fleet off Martinique. . . . 21 April 1780. The tortoise heaves up the earth, and puts out it's head." Again: "When one reflects on the state of this strange being, it is a matter of wonder to find that Providence should bestow such a profusion of days, such a seeming waste of longevity, on a reptile that appears to relish it so little as to squander more than two-thirds of it's existence in a joyless stupor, and be lost to all sensation for months together in the profoundest of slumbers." In an insert from the *Antiquities of Selborne,* however, the really admiring owner of Timothy says what can be said for tortoises:

Because we call this creature an abject reptile, we are too apt to undervalue his abilities, and deprecate his powers of instinct. Yet he is, as Mr. Pope says of his lord, "—Much too wise to walk into a well:" —and has so much discernment as not to fall down an haha . . . Though he loves warm weather, he avoids the hot sun . . . and spends the more sultry hours under the umbrella of a large cabbage leaf, or amidst the waving forests of an asparagus bed.

As he avoids the heat in the summer, so, in the declining of the year, he improves the faint autumnal beams by getting within the reflection of a fruit wall: and, though he never has read that planes inclining to the horizon receive a greater share of warmth, he inclines his shell, by tilting it against the wall, to collect and admit every feeble ray . . .

There is a season of the year (usually the beginning of June) when his exertions are remarkable. He then walks on tiptoe, and is stirring by five in the morning; and, traversing the garden, examines every wicket . . . through which he will escape if possible. . . . The motives that impell him to take these rambles seem to be of the amorous kind; his fancy then becomes intent on sexual attachments, which transport him beyond his usual gravity, and induce him to forget for a time his ordinary solemn deportment.

The tone of this extract, and the obvious prejudice for his pampered pet, suggest Dr. Johnson's better-known defense of Hodge. "I recollect him [Hodge] one day," Boswell tells us, "scrambling up Dr. Johnson's breast, apparently with much satisfaction, while my friend, smiling and half-whistling, rubbed down his back, and pulled him by the tail; and when I observed he was a fine cat, saying, 'Why yes, Sir, but I have had cats whom I liked better than this'; and then, as if perceiving Hodge to be out of countenance, adding, 'but he is a very fine cat, a very fine cat indeed.' "

From the entries in the *Journal* we can watch Gilbert White as he weighs Timothy, experiments with different kinds of vegetables to discover Timothy's gastronomic preferences, or immerses Timothy in a tub of water, finding that "he sunk gradually & walked on the bottom of the tub. He seemed quite out of his element and was much dismayed. This species seems not at all amphibious." It was no cold, unfeeling scientist, though, who conducted these investigations and subjected Timothy to such indignities; nor did Gilbert White permit the account between them to remain one-sided. In a letter (taken, one assumes, from dictation) addressed to Miss Hecky Mulso and dated "From the border under the fruit wall, August 31, 1784," Timothy was permitted to submit his *Apologia pro vita sua*. After describing his early days in America, his kidnaping, and the kind mistress who had given him shelter for so many years, he turned to his latest owner:

. . . you must know [it is Timothy who is speaking] that my master is what they call a *naturalist* & much visited by people of that turn, who often put him on whimsical experiments, such as feeling my pulse, putting me in a tub of water to try if I can swim, etc; and twice in the year I am carried to the grocer's to be weighed, . . . These matters displease me; but there is another that much hurts my pride: I mean, that contempt shown for my understanding which these *Lords* of the *Creation* are very apt to discover, thinking that nobody knows anything but themselves. I heard my master say that he expected I should some day tumble down the haha; whereas I would have him to know that I can discern a precipice from plain ground as well as himself. Sometimes my master repeats with much seeming triumph the following lines, which occasion a loud laugh:

'Timotheus placed on high
Amidst the tuneful choir,
With flying fingers touched the lyre.'

For my part, I see no wit in the application; nor know whence the verses are quoted; perhaps from some prophet of his own who, if he penned them for the sake of ridiculing tortoises, bestowed his pains, I think, to poor purposes.

In this ability to project his imagination into whatever interested him—even at the risk of being declared an "enthusiast"—quite as much as in his close attention to detail, lies the secret of Gilbert White's appeal. The man who could observe and record that "The water wagtail seems to be the smallest English bird that walks with one leg at a time; the rest of that size . . . all hop two legs together" will never be lacking in readers. Neither so general in appeal as to lose "that intimacy of tone which is the familiar letter's peculiar charm" nor yet so intimate that they disturb one with a guilty feeling of "listening at key holes," [1] his writings are nonetheless of the essence of real letters. Without waste of time they admit one into companionship with a man whom we quickly learn to admire and love. Like Boswell, Gilbert White raised "an art to such perfection that it became, in effect, a new thing"; [2] and like the others in that select group of immortals among the English writers with whom he deserves to stand, he has left an inheritance which has increased the sum total of human happiness and permanently enriched mankind.

1. Chauncey Brewster Tinker, *The Salon and English Letters* (Macmillan, 1915), pp. 242–244.
2. *Ibid.,* p. 268.

WILLIAM HOGARTH: THE GOLDEN MEAN

Robert E. Moore

PAINTERS and critics of painting usually deplore any discussion in which a painter is considered for his literary parts. It is legitimate, they say, to judge design, color, form, texture, or other purely aesthetic qualities, but not subject matter. Yet to neglect the literary side of Hogarth is hardly intelligent, for in his memoirs he has given an account of his method of work which emphasizes this very side: "I have endeavoured to treat my subject as a dramatic writer; my picture is my stage, and men and women my players, who by means of certain actions and gestures, are to exhibit *a dumb show.*" In the advertisements of *A Harlot's Progress* he calls himself not the "artist" but the "author," for his most characteristic work is concerned with narrative subjects which he considers in a literary sense. Furthermore, even though his medium is incapable of the elaboration available to the novelist, he exerted a strong influence on the literature of his time.

One of the literary questions he and his friend Fielding were intensely interested in was a favorite one in the eighteenth century, the distinction between character and caricature. Their interest was natural, for a significant aspect of their genius is that in an age in which caricature reigned they were able to discern its faults and to begin the creation of realistic characters. That Fielding was thoroughly aware and proud of this accomplishment is proved by the celebrated preface to *Joseph Andrews* where he points out that to speak of his characters as mere burlesques would be as mistaken as to call the works of a great comic painter mere caricatures. The comic painter is Hogarth; Fielding calls him by name. Hogarth endorsed Fielding's discussion the next year in the subscription ticket to the *Marriage à la Mode,* a little drawing of heads entitled "Characters and Caricaturas" where the spectator is urged to consult the preface to *Joseph Andrews* for a further elucidation of the distinction between these two modes of composition.

At the time Fielding wrote his preface Hogarth had already been called a caricaturist, as today he still is, but such an estimate is false. The caricaturist discloses the secret of his subject's individuality by exaggerating the most characteristic feature of the subject beyond the bounds of realism. He discovers the disproportions which in nature appear only as inclinations and brings them to a sharp focus in his caricature. The resulting figure is usually a type, an abstraction made concrete—in other words, an idea. The exaggeration of caricature, its subjugation of everything to the ruling passion, often gives it a merciless and even inhuman spirit. This very quality helps to explain why the caricaturist Cruikshank was such an excellent illustrator of the works of Smollett. But this is not Hogarth's way.

In his preface Fielding made clear that Hogarth was not a cartoonist but a creator of character; his figures appear not only to breathe, says Fielding, but also to think. Indeed Hogarth in his pictures had been creating character ten years before Fielding published *Joseph Andrews,* and exerted no small formative influence on the novelist. "His faces go to the very verge of caricature," says Hazlitt, "yet never (I believe in any single instance) go beyond it; they take the very widest latitude, and yet we always see the links which bind them to nature." Thus Hogarth differs from Rowlandson, Cruikshank, and the mass of caricaturists who followed in his wake, by picturing not abstractions but human beings. Like Fielding he often accentuates particular characteristics—what true artist does not?—but he knows there is such a thing as truthful accentuation—that is, accentuation within the bounds of realism.

Examples are at every hand. One of the best is the central figure in the print "Morning" from the *Four Times of the Day,* the old maid whom Fielding, by his own admission, converted into Bridget Allworthy. Hogarth's figure is more subtle than Fielding's, for the novelist has made her into a blatant hypocrite not far from actual caricature. But in Hogarth she is not so obvious. As this evergreen of the sex stands in the middle of Covent Garden at seven in the morning gazing in astonishment at the licentious revelers pouring out of Tom King's Tavern, we cannot supply her thoughts, though her expression clearly invites speculation. Is her obvious virtue really outraged at the freedoms these wenches are publicly inviting, or is she a hypocrite fairly aching to indulge these same caresses herself? We cannot tell, nor can we ever fail to wonder. In other words she is a real character, and Hogarth's refusal to make her an obvious type is the essence of her richness.

If the artist can create the illusion of character in a single picture it is obvious that he can do even more in his several narrative series running to a half dozen or more scenes, for here there is a "literary" structure, a temporal sequence with a beginning, a middle, and an end. Hogarth's greatest achievement of this kind, the *Marriage à la Mode*, contains a heroine of almost tragic proportions. Forced into a marriage with a dandy who cares nothing for her, she displays embarrassment and misery in the very first picture, where she wretchedly dangles her wedding ring on a handkerchief and tries to take comfort from the attentions of the young lawyer at her side. As the tragedy progresses she changes from the soft young girl to the sophisticated paramour of the lawyer, and finally, after the murder of her husband and execution of her lover, to a conscience-crazed being who takes her own life. She is no mere conventional sketch of a time-worn type, the unfaithful wife, but is a thoroughly believable woman trapped in a situation she has been too frail to avoid.

This woman's story invites sentimentality. Not even Fielding and Smollett have avoided it in relating the woes of their fallen women, like Mrs. Bennet in *Amelia,* Miss Williams in *Roderick Random,* or the girl Count Fathom eventually marries. But with one exception, the betrayed seamstress in *A Rake's Progress,* Hogarth's figures are never sentimental. Even when regarding the plight of the pathetic countess in the *Marriage* he remains the comic painter, the satirist whose head is not led astray by his heart. The countess' suicide is a stark enough scene, and Hogarth painting her taut, suffering face obviously feels compassion for her; but even here he finds time to mock her father's stinginess, the physician's impotent rage, and the servant's stupidity, all ironic accouterments of a tragedy. Life does not change much because a woman feels she must take her own life. This attitude gives Hogarth even in his most touching scenes a sobriety and balance unusual for his age. It does not mean that he is the cold, inhuman prosecutor which so many people mistakenly consider him; even in a somewhat inferior work like *Industry and Idleness* his large humanity, untinged with mawkishness, reaches out to embrace the worthless Tom Idle as he stands cowering before his judge. It means rather that his keen pity for suffering is mingled with an unsentimental judgment upon the victim. Mercy tempers justice, yet justice is never obscured.

It is this that I consider Hogarth's heavenly mingle, his golden mean. He speaks in terms not of caricature but of realistic characters, so that his world is the actual world; and he is as free from the bitterness of the misanthropic satirist as he is from the all-forgiving softness of the sentimentalist. In this consists the supreme greatness of Hogarthian comedy. His comic view of the universe, a view containing a fine vein of sympathy, is the sanest, most completely balanced of his century.

The significance of this golden mean to a rightful appreciation of Hogarth may be felt at once when we contrast it with the method of other great comic artists of the age. With two notable exceptions, Hogarth and (in a different way) Fielding, what eighteenth-century comedy in large part lacks is the fine vein of sympathy. The most brilliant of the Augustan satirists, Pope, is as hard as he is amusing. To Pope comedy knows not compassion. In his warmest poem, *The Rape of the Lock,* whatever sympathy he feels for the frivolous society is not nearly so remarkable as the merciless stripping of its faults. The destruction Belinda wields with her eyes is small indeed to what Pope wields with his pen. In the *Epistle to Dr. Arbuthnot* his kindest portrait, that of Addison, is successful largely because he *pretends* to sympathy, to a sincere grief that so great a man could be marred by such petty faults; but such pretense does not hide Pope's jealousy of a successful rival, a man who, he was convinced, had in a number of instances done him injury. *The Dunciad* is today a monument to two things, Pope's wit and Pope's detested rivals whom, no matter how small, he never forgave. Even those critics who regard the poem as an indirect glorification of true learning and the best civilized values must admit that it is the very ecstasy of indirectness. Pope's wit is from first to last merciless.

I do not wish to be misunderstood: all this is not to belittle Pope or to deny the genius of malice; we readily admit with Dr. Johnson that "it was worth while being a dunce then." Yet the splendor of *The Dunciad* is a frightening splendor.

Even more than Pope, the humor of Sheridan is without sympathy. The names of his dramatis personae are a testament of his debt to the clever caricatures of Restoration drama; and caricatures are not human beings. The most famous of them all, Mrs. Malaprop, would in real life have died of mortification at her treatment in the denouement. But Sheridan is never concerned with sympathy and dismisses her with the rest of his gulls amid the gayest laughter. Bob Acres is a rather lovable dunce, but his cowardice is cruelly exposed; Lydia is merrily married off to the young scamp who has from first to last played her for a fool. The *School for Scandal* is composed of Lady Sneerwell, Mrs. Candour, Sir Benjamin Backbite, Mr. Snake. It is not Sheridan's brilliance alone which dazzles but also his hard mockery.

All this comedy has a great lack: we are delighted by its wit but not very genuinely informed by its truth. It is only a partial picture of experience, and its genius consists largely in polishing up that part to a dazzling brightness and pretending that it is the whole. In the final analysis this literature must suffer because of the side that it ignores, the side of the heart. It lacks the balance of Hogarth.

An artist may fall short of what I have called Hogarth's golden mean on either of two sides: the one side is the brittle coldness of Pope and Sheridan; to see the other at its clearest we may turn to the richest comic genius of the next century, Dickens. It seems undeniable to the present writer that Dickens is a greater humorist than Pope and Sheridan as well as their natural descendants, Wilde and Shaw, because his range is so much wider than theirs. Subject matter must be considered in aesthetic judgments. Dickens realizes that the highest humor, as opposed to mere impersonal wit, must include the fine vein of sympathy. Laughter need not necessarily be a part of it. We are more disposed to weep than to laugh at Joe Gargery in *Great Expectations;* yet he is at once recognizable as an excellent comic character. His humor, like that of so many characters in Dickens, is the greater for being in large part wistfulness.

Dickens proves the alliance of laughter and tears. We resist the softer emotions, for they are altruistic, but for the egoistical emotions of comedy we are eager. By making his audience laugh, the author destroys their emotional equilibrium, and while they are without their poise he can switch them into unrepressed pity. This subtle combination of opposites, known best today in the comedy of Charlie Chaplin, is at the root of Dickens' comic genius. It is comedy distinguished by a warmth unknown to any eighteenth-century wit, Hogarth and Fielding not excepted.

But Dickens has to pay the price of this warmth, and it is just here that Hogarth is superior to him. He does not achieve the balance of Hogarth for the opposite reason that Pope and Sheridan do not—sentimentality. *The Old Curiosity Shop* should have been one of the world's best comic novels, but unhappily such masterpieces as Dick Swiveller, the Marchioness, Sampson and Sally Brass, and Mrs. Jarley are dimmed by the ubiquitous presence of two of the most mawkish bores ever created, Little Nell and her grandfather. A comparison with Hogarth is illuminating, for Nell's grandfather meets the same end as Hogarth's Tom Rakewell—they both dissipate their wealth in gambling and come to almost immediate catastrophe because of it. The contrasting judgments which the two artists pass upon the catastrophe mark the difference between the most tasteless sort of Victorian sentimentality and gloriously solid eighteenth-century sobriety. Indeed Dickens shuts the door against judgment altogether and drowns his ending in tears. Although he does not condone the old man's folly, he completely forgives it and attempts to obscure all our other sentiments by means of pathos. Dickens' reason for pardoning him (I imagine) is the very reason that most modern readers would consign him to perdition: he is the grandfather of Little Nell. In too much human sympathy Dickens not only gets farther away from a true judgment than Hogarth but, ironically, farther away from the reader's sympathy also. The author's excess produces a dearth in the reader.

Hogarth is altogether different. He looks at the rake's progress with compassion, but with sobriety too. In the sixth picture Rakewell squanders his fortune in a gambler's den, in the seventh he is incarcerated without hope in a debtor's prison, and in the final scene he is a lunatic chained to the floor in Bedlam. Though it is a terrible ending, Hogarth will not be sentimental, for Rakewell's own stupidity has brought him to this pass. It is folly, not tragedy. Yet the artist sympathizes even as he condemns. Regarding Rakewell's hopeless stare in the seventh painting (Hogarth's fine delineation of countenance is largely lost in the engravings), Charles Lamb could very justly say: "The long history of a misspent life is compressed into the countenance as plainly as the series of plates before had told it; here is . . . grief kept to a man's self, a face retiring from notice with the shame which great anguish sometimes brings with it,—a final leave taken of hope,—the coming-on of vacancy and stupefaction,—a beginning alienation of the mind, looking like tranquility." Rakewell's end is thus much more agonizing than that of the Dickens character, because, far from sacrificing our standards of judgment, we are instead forced to keep them sharply intact. The denouement of *A Rake's Progress* is comic in the highest sense, for the catastrophe is deserved; and it is tragic for the same reason. Dickens' tragic scenes fail; Oscar Wilde indicated the reason when he remarked that no sensitive man could read the death of Little Nell without laughing.

Hogarth's comic view of the universe, a view as alive to the pathetic as to the laughable, puts him in the line of comic geniuses begun by Chaucer and continued by Shakespeare. We surely cannot say that he appreciates the warm and lovable qualities of his sinners to the same degree that the two earlier and greater geniuses do, but he is surely the outstanding example in the eighteenth century of the combination of attitudes that make Chaucer and Shakespeare our first comic geniuses—broad compassion mingled with unerring justice.

Thus far Fielding has been coupled with Hogarth as also possessing this mingle to a very high degree. Quite obviously the creator of Tom Jones and Mrs. Waters and Captain Booth can produce characters compounded of many faults but deserving of sympathy for all that. There is, however, one important respect in which he is not Hogarth's equal: he refuses to be serious. Flippancy is Fielding's most characteristic attitude. *Tom Jones* has been justly called the greatest entertainment of the century, if not of English literature, but the *Marriage à la Mode* is more serious, more searching. This is not to deny the familiar assertions that Fielding's masterpiece is a comic epic and he a Homer in prose, that the continual play of irony gives the book a solid weight of intellect and eminently practical morality. But when we consider what in the final analysis the book has to teach us, especially as regards the conduct of its hero, we must feel that there is a whole range of feeling outside Fielding's reach. Dr. Johnson's comparison of Fielding and Richardson, if blind to Fielding's superior merits, has at least the kernel of truth in it: "Sir, there is more knowledge of the heart in one letter of Richardson's than in all of *Tom Jones.*" The *Marriage à la Mode,* consisting of only six pictures of highly concentrated activity, makes no pretensions to the enormous panorama of *Tom Jones;* but that segment of London civilization which both artists criticize Hogarth treats with a good deal more depth than Fielding. His characters belong to Lady Bellaston's set, and are wrecked because of their indulgence in Lady Bellaston's favorite activity. In the novel, on the other hand, no one suffers much from his licentious folly—Tom is considerably embarrassed, Lady Bellaston merely piqued—and the trick by which Tom extricates himself from the snare is one of the funniest and most ironical strokes in the book, and one that Fielding is not above admiring. Hogarth could not be content with the gaiety of such a solution, for something too fundamental is at stake. Whereas even in *Amelia,* a novel in which adultery looms large, Fielding's characters are hardly scorched, Hogarth's are burned to destruction. Analyzing the corruption of fashionable marriage at its source, Hogarth sees that though the principals may be the dupes of avaricious parents they cannot escape responsibility for their subsequent actions; nor, even if their hearts—like Jones's or Booth's—are in the right place, is the last chapter likely to be written off amid general happiness. When Fielding attempts Hogarthian seriousness, as in much of *Amelia,* he does not succeed; he cannot explore the darker regions of Hogarth with the sovereign ease he exhibits in lighter spheres. The *Marriage* is a serious and penetrating analysis of cause and effect, yet it is conducted with all the ironical commentary of a masterly comic author. It is the subject of a famous essay by Hazlitt in which he ranks the painter among the great English comic *writers*. Hazlitt has scrutinized the pictures much more closely than most spectators, and has been rewarded by an awareness of what they miss—Hogarth's remarkable subtlety and enormous suggestiveness.

The eighteenth century was not an age of tragedy because it was too moral. Overwhelming chance, undeserved fate the age could not accept. A Shakespeare or a Wordsworth could become reconciled to the unjust aspects of this world, but the eighteenth century demanded poetic justice. That stigma, if stigma it be, has fallen upon Hogarth. But the age's strong morality is responsible for most of our finest comedy, especially satirical comedy. And, in one instance particularly, an artist combined the rigorous justice of satire with the fine compassion of divine comedy. He was William Hogarth.

THE SMITHS OF CHICHESTER
Elizabeth W. Manwaring

William, born in Guildford, 1707; died near Chichester, September 27, 1764.
George, born in Chichester, 1713; died in Chichester, September 7, 1776.
John, born in Chichester, 1717; died in Chichester, July 29, 1764.

A LONG warfare with the forces of oblivion"; so to a class of graduate students twenty-five years ago Mr. Tinker described literary scholarship. In that warfare against time and accident, ignorance and prejudice, this minute skirmish attempts to set before literary scholars three briefly famous and after ten years almost forgotten painters of landscape, one of them also a poet: the Smiths of Chichester. The brothers deserve on several counts to be recalled: they represent particularly well that frequent phenomenon of the eighteenth century, the humble artisan-artist, usually self-taught. They deserve to be recalled for their own histories, slight as are the traces to be found in magazines, on gravestones, in parish registers, in their works, and in the affectionate memoir prefixed to the second edition of George's *Pastorals* (1811). For the student of the period in general, the value of the Smiths may lie chiefly in their striking representation of that pervading confusion between respect for the ideal past and interest in the actual present, to be found in literature but more conspicuously in the graphic arts, which accepted as models the landscapes of Claude, Salvator Rosa, and the Poussins but held in affection British scenes which could only by great exercise of fancy be made to resemble the Campagna and the Apennines. Finally, the Smiths are one more warning against accepting the critical judgments of compilers of works of reference and of histories of the arts.

Over such humble literary artists as Stephen Duck and James Woodhouse the Smiths had some great advantages. Their father, though following the trades first of cooper and later of baker, was a general Baptist minister, as his father had been, and therefore gave to the sons whom his and his wife's premature deaths early or-

phaned the benefits of literacy and principles. William, the eldest
brother, was like a father to his younger brothers. The three found,
moreover, in their neighboring patron, the second Duke of Richmond, kind and generous assistance and advice. At the first exhibition of painting held in 1760 by the Society for the Encouragement
of Art, Manufactures and Commerce, George and John won respectively the first and second premiums for landscape, and again
in the following year, when the *London Chronicle* reports, "the
merits of the two candidates were so equal, that it was for some
time debated in the Committee to divide the premium equally between them." In the exhibition of 1762, to which George sent eleven
pictures but did not compete for the premium, the first premium
was awarded to John. In 1763 George for the third time won the
first premium. The April number of the *Universal Magazine,* which
Arthur Young had persisted in starting against the advice of Dr.
Johnson,[1] in a detailed report of the Exhibition (apparently adapted
from a pamphlet) makes this comment: "The superiority of the
Smiths as landscape painters is so incontestably visible . . . that to
declare my opinion in this matter is quite unnecessary. Their pieces,
in general, are finely imagined, accurately drawn, and chastely
coloured."

William, according to Pilkington's *Dictionary,* was deformed,
and the triple portrait of the brothers by their fellow townsman
Pether seems to bear this out, as also the observation that he looked
like John Locke. George's protective attitude toward John, who
had been his pupil, suggests that John lacked the robustness which
characterized George. In 1764 William and John died; George out-
lived them by twelve years. In 1766, aged fifty-three, George married
"Ruth Souther, of St. Pancras, maiden," by whom he had three
daughters. He seems to have settled down quietly in Chichester,
keeping his connection with the larger world of art only by sending annually to the exhibitions of the Society of Free Artists; for
it was with that smaller and less distinguished of the two groups of
artists who abandoned connection with the Society for the Encouragement of Arts, Manufactures and Commerce that he was
identified after 1763. Just once, in 1774, he was represented at the

1. See article on Young in the *Dictionary of National Biography.*

exhibition of the Royal Academy, by four pictures. While some of his pictures, like the prize piece of his brother John in 1762, were of the classical taste in composition, the greater number of the total of 109 exhibited by him were in his pastoral manner. Of those copied by Woollett, Vivares, Peake, and other well-known engravers, and listed by Colonel Grant, at least six are of this kind. Such is "The Hop Pickers," "a gem of grouping, both floral and human." [2] If the folio volume of etchings published by John Boydell in 1770 as by Messrs. George and John Smith of Chichester "after their own Paintings, and other Masters" shows compositions less animated and intimate, this may be due to the artists' lack of ability in the craft of etching. Certainly the lines are heavy and there is too great uniformity of shade, though many of the designs are skillful. The most interesting feature of this work is the credit given to John, dead six years before its publication, for both paintings and etchings. The best of the etching is shown in the copies of Rembrandt, du Jardin, and Waterlo.

More successful in a modest way were George's *Six Pastorals* (Dodsley, 1770) which he prefaced thus:

It is with the greatest diffidence that the Authour has ventured to lay the following pieces before the public. His profession as a landscape painter induced him to study nature very attentively, and the beautiful scenes he often examined, furnished him with a great variety of ideas, many of which, he flatters himself, are new; at least, he has not been happy enough to find them in any authour he has perused. But as he never made the art of writing his particular study, he has not always been able to convey his ideas to the Reader with the same force that he received them from the Book of Nature. Whatever defects, therefore, may be found in the language, he hopes they will be forgiven.

The titles are engaging: "The Country Lovers," "The Contest," "Winter," "Two Boys," "The Complaint of Daphnis," "The Happy Meeting." To the modern reader the first and third are the most original and fresh; but in reviews in the *Monthly* and *Critical,* both very favorable and of considerable length (less, naturally, than the reviews of *The Deserted Village,* which appeared at almost the same date), "The Complaint" seems to be most admired. It has,

2. M. H. Grant, *Old English Landscape Painters* (privately printed, London, 1926), p. 47.

indeed, a musical refrain. "The Country Lovers" shows a genuine rustic pair going to market. Isaac calls for Marget at sunrise and to her protests that he is too early points to the sunbeams on the kitchen wall which have already left the ballads of Rosamond and Chevy-Chace—

> 'Tis five exactly when they gild the tack
> That holds this corner of the Almanack.

The poem abounds in specific homely touches—pinks and tulips, elms and pippin trees, ducks "decking with silver streaks" the pool beside Isaac's cottage. "Two Boys" shows two lads on a summer day, out with their dog, tending the cows, when they think of them, running from one sport to another, reminding each other of all sorts of country pleasures and notions, as natural and unpredictable as two real small boys.

It is to George Smith's credit that he did not himself include the romance "Pastorella" which appeared with the pastorals in the second edition published after his death, in 1811, by the affectionate concern of his three daughters. Some passages, to be sure, seem straight out of his pictures—the children playing with a stubborn pet lamb or running to their mother at a stranger's appearance, the father returning to the cottage after his day's labors,

> . . . whistling to his dog
> That frisking play'd in wanton rings before, . . .
> Now takes a little race, now circling wide,
> Then, turning, leaps against his master's side, . . .

But most of the romance is unreal and the characters vague and incredible.

This second edition was prepared under the guidance of the Reverend John Evans, a Baptist minister and the head for some thirty years of a school in Islington. He is of interest in his own right, as recipient of a degree from Brown University in 1819. The list of subscribers begins with the Duke of Richmond, the Earl of Chichester, and Lord and Lady George Cavendish, and goes on to include, one surmises, parishioners and former pupils of the Reverend Mr. Evans in St. Mary Axe, Camberwell, Whitechapel, and Rotherhithe as well as old friends in Chichester, Portsea, Portsmouth, and Horsham. William Hayley is down for three copies, the Bishop of Exeter for two. Such range of readers would have pleased the author, who had, however, been in his grave since 1776, beside his two brothers and his wife, in the cemetery named "Lightning." [3]

The swift passage of the Smiths from fame to forgetting has a number of likely causes, some of which derive from the anomalous position of their branch of art in their lifetimes and, indeed, until almost the middle of the next century. It must be recalled that landscape, after being considered, along with costume and furniture, a mere accessory to history and portrait, became accessory also to architecture in those baroque palaces which multiplied in Rome from the end of the sixteenth through the seventeenth century. Adornment of these gave to Claude his chance for that popularity which, from about 1635, was a powerful influence in establishing landscape, eventually, as a recognized independent branch of painting; though Claude, the Poussins, and Salvator Rosa usually dignified their compositions by titles as of histories. History occupies the chief position in that *Essay on the Theory of Painting* by Jonathan Richardson which, first published in 1715, reached its elegant final form at Strawberry Hill in 1792, dedicated to Sir Joshua Reynolds "by permission." That book, Sir Joshua said, made him a painter. Almost certainly it was earnestly studied by George Smith when he sought instruction. Richardson gave little encouragement to a young landscape painter; he relegated that art to such inferior status as is implied in "other Branches of Painting: as Landskip, Battels, Fruit, &c." [4] If George Smith read, as is likely, the younger Richardson's *Account* (a standard guide book to British travelers throughout the century) he found such cursory treatment of his idol Claude as "The Chigi is full of Pictures of Claude Lorrain, the Bourgognonne, and Salvator Rosa, and very fine of them," "Several other Pictures of Good Masters" (at the Colonna Palace) with the gloss "Claude Lorranese. Gaspar Poussin, &c." [5]

In the few pages which he does devote to landscape Richardson

3. From Lower's *Worthies of Sussex* (1765), according to a note from Mrs. Woods, wife of the agent of the Duke of Richmond. For this and many other items I am indebted greatly to her kindness, and also to that of the Rector of St. Olave's, the Reverend A. F. Young, for copies of notices in the parish registers.

4. *Op. cit.*, p. 40.

5. *An Account of Some Statues . . . and Pictures in Italy . . .* (1722), pp. 282, 189.

thinks a definition needed: "Landskips are in Imitation of Rural Nature, of which therefore there may be as many Kinds, as there are Appearances of this Sort of nature . . . with Figures or without; but if there are Any, as 'tis necessary there should be, Generally speaking, they must be Suitable, and only Subservient to the Landskip . . . Otherwise the Picture . . . becomes a History, a Battelpiece, &c." [6] But Richardson at least justifies Smith's choice of a model by praising Claude as having, of all who paint landscapes, "the most Beautiful, and pleasing Ideas; the most Rural, and of our own Times"—whatever that last may mean.

It was another misfortune to which these later artists were not at first immune that the landscape painter was expected, under English skies and on English turf, to follow Italian predecessors rather than trust his own eyes. Richardson warned his countrymen, even though he expressed hope for an English School of painting, that as to landscape as well as to histories, "The Italians and their Masters the Ancients . . . have not Servilely follow'd Common Nature, but Rais'd, and Improv'd, or at least have always made a Best Choice of it. This gives a Dignity to a Low Subject, and is the Reason for the Esteem we have for the Landskips of Salvator Rosa, Filippo Laura, Claude Lorrain and the Poussins." [7] Even Hazlitt pronounced Richard Wilson's "imitations in the manner of Claude" to be much the best of his pictures and deplored his choice of subject for the "views of home scenery" which now provide Wilson's claim to greatness.[8] Recalling Sir George Beaumont's endeavor to cast a Poussinish hue over Constable's pictures, we are more surprised that the Smiths dared at all to portray Sussex cottages and farmyards than that George provided his native views with Claudian horizons and that John arranged Chichester Cathedral to resemble one of Gaspar's palaces in middle distance.

The Smiths, like the Sandbys,[9] as well as scores, even hundreds, of other British painters of landscape interest, received encouragement and stimulus from the pastoral and local poetry which, begin-

6. *Essay*, pp. 186, 188.

7. *Ibid.*, p. 161.

8. *Criticisms of Art*, . . . , ed. by his son (1843), p. 184.

9. The more successful Sandbys offer an interesting parallel to the Smiths. See A. P. Oppé, *The Drawings of Paul and Thomas Sandby* . . . (Phaedon Press, 1947).

ning with "Windsor Forest"—indeed, with "Cooper's Hill"—was so marked a development of the eighteenth century in Great Britain.[10] Not until late in the century were these works illustrated, to be sure; but attempts to characterize specific localities, together with attempts to enhance the beauty of parks and houses, must have turned attention of both proprietors and painters to the arts by which the reality out-of-doors could be preserved withindoors to minister to the owners' pride both of possessing and of embellishing "grounds."

Finally, a reason why the Smiths have been disregarded, until Colonel M. H. Grant's spirited and substantial appreciation of them in his *Chronicle History of the Old English Landscape Painters,*[11] is the scarcity of their work in public collections. The Victoria and Albert has one excellent example. Those at the National Gallery are of slight importance. The walls of one room at Goodwood House, seat of the Smiths' generous patron, the Duke of Richmond—it is the sitting room attached to the principal suite for guests at race time—are almost entirely given over to the work of George and John: the very large—78 by 54 inch—premium pictures of 1760, George's having "the colouring warm and harmonious" and "a rich Claude-like far distance." Very occasionally their pictures appear at auctions.[12] The best place in which to see examples of the "potboilers" which, as Colonel Grant says, are the best work by the Smiths, is the Colonel's own collection, which has eight or nine of their pictures; he has recently added a "magnificent" picture by William, "as good as Wilson, and better than anything by George."

This scarcity has helped to keep the Smiths in obscurity and to

10. Robert Arnold Aubin, in *Topographical Poetry in XVIII-century England* (M.L.A., 1936) lists 175 such poems published before 1800.

11. Two vols. folio, privately published, London, 1926; Vol. III, 1948. The first two volumes of this important work, invaluable for the student of both graphic and literary art in eighteenth-century Engand, are out of print, the few copies which had remained unsold having been destroyed by enemy action. Fortunately copies are in almost all libraries of importance, particularly of art museums, and are in the hands of many dealers. Colonel Grant's collection of over 700 paintings was only slightly damaged.

12. Miss Ethelwyn Manning of the Frick Art Reference Library kindly informs me of two sales at Christie's and one at Sotheby's within the last 25 years. One was "Gathering Apples," presumably the rustic scene which was engraved by Woollett. The prices reported indicate that the purchasers got bargains.

allow such misguided and erroneous judgments as those of the Redgraves and (borrowed from them) the cursory estimate in Bryan's *Dictionary* to go unchallenged until Colonel Grant's refutation. The large and handsome engravings after George by Woollett, Vivares, and others are not hard to come by but cannot convey the harmony of color which is one of his great attractions. Fragments of Colonel Grant's description must be quoted:

Wherein George Smith actually excelled was in his capacity to give to the common scenes of rustic life the charm of a work of art . . . His mere craftsmanship, his handling and technique, if not precisely "fine" are exceedingly accomplished. No man could touch in foliage better than he . . . or better cause the sunlight to filter through the greeny gauze upon his delightful little figures and garden blooms . . . Together with his pure, rather "hot" blue skies, in which the clouds are formed by driving a brushful of Chinese white into filmy and ragged edges of paint, they provide an excellent touchstone of genuineness . . . Rarely has gay colour been handled in such profusion yet with more subordination. Smith indeed was not far from being a master of tone, and that in its most difficult exposition, the harmonisation of many tints in a single work . . .

Neither in touch, nor tone, does he, it is true, possess the very highest kind of "quality," the quality of Crome or Wilson, for instance, or even of George Morland. But . . . none before him, and few since, have caught more perfectly than he the subtle aroma of the depths of our English country.

If *Anecdotes of Painting in England* had appeared three years sooner we might, Colonel Grant suggests, have supposed George Smith to be asserting in his "Hop-Pickers" the beauty of Sussex against that of Kent as Horace Walpole described it in the little idyll under the account of George Lambert [13] which so pleased its author. What a pity that Horace Walpole did not take time from the trials of Lord George Sackville and Earl Ferrers, in April, 1760, to visit, or if he did visit it as seems almost inevitable, to inspect more closely the Exhibition of the Society for the Encouragement of Arts! A few sentences from his pen might have preserved one who "has his merit from his very unconsciousness, and from the humility both of his art and his technique." [14]

13. *Anecdotes of Painting* (2d ed. 1782), IV, 140–141.
14. Grant, *op. cit.,* p. 47.

NEW STYLES IN TYPOGRAPHY

Allen T. Hazen

P RINTERS are perhaps as conservative and unchanging as any craftsmen, and the printing of 1700 does not look radically unlike that of 1600; but during Johnson's later life new styles were steadily blossoming forth. Had Johnson's eyes been better, I think he might have blasted away at this typographic contraband somewhat as he did at neologism in language and at strange themes in poetry. For more than most men he liked the style familiarized to him in his youth, and he might have been expected to side vigorously with the many stand-patters who attacked Baskerville's slender types in 1757. It is pleasant to remember, however, that instead of decrying Baskerville, Johnson presented a copy of Baskerville's Virgil in 1769 to Trinity College, Oxford, in recompense for reading privileges extended to him there. His generosity was certainly not stirred by the importance of the text, since Baskerville's text has no independent value whatsoever; and he must therefore have presented the book because of its typographic excellence. But for the most part typographic change was unregarded by Johnson, and I shall refer to books not as printing specimens inspired by Johnson or treasured by him but as specimens of the changes taking place within the span of Johnson's life.

It is instructive to look at the *Miscellany* of John Husbands in 1731, in which Johnson first appeared in print, and to compare that with such sober later printing as the *Lives of the Poets*. The title page of Husbands, with its large type, might easily be mistaken for something printed in 1700, such as a tract by Defoe. The text of the volume, too, is in the older style, with its heavy types that belong artistically in a folio instead of in the cramped Oxford octavo. Old-fashioned, also, are the capitals for all nouns and the italics for all proper names, a style that was to give way within a generation (at least among progressive London printers) to the new style of capital letters for proper names only. Husbands' *Miscellany* is also printed in an older type, just when the more adaptable Caslon is superseding all other types.

Father Lobo's *Voyage to Abyssinia,* printed in Birmingham but published in London in 1735, is somewhat old-fashioned provincial printing and not otherwise notable.

The break from the older style is not precise in books written by Johnson. Dodsley published *London* in 1738 in a format much like the Pope folios of the same time or a little earlier. But by 1749 the *Vanity of Human Wishes* is essentially a modern (i. e., mid-eighteenth century) book: the title page looks like those of the next twenty years, the type is Caslon, and the poem is printed in quarto, the size that replaced the earlier poetical folio. Quarto was to remain until 1800 the normal size for a small poetical pamphlet, and while the general trend to smaller sizes is easily understood, I am always a little startled at the suddenness with which folios dropped out after 1740. Up to 1740 the folio is normal; after 1740 it grows uncommon, and after 1750 it is scarcely used again for short poems.

The *Rambler* in 1750 is perhaps not a fair test, because Johnson and John Payne planned it to look like the *Spectator;* but the handsome *Rambler* in its pot folio looks in fact more like the printing of 1750 than of 1712. The folio keeps the older style of italics for all proper names and initial capitals for all nouns, but the pretty little reprint of 1752 in duodecimo adopts the new style which uses only initial capitals with roman letters for proper names and reduces nouns to lower case. The miscellaneous prose published by Johnson between 1740 and 1750 is of comparatively little typographic interest, although we may like to compare the title page of the *Drury-Lane Prologue,* printed by Cave in 1747, with the handsome Caslon title page of the *Plan of a Dictionary,* also printed in 1747. Cave clung to his old types, either from conservatism or inertia, and his long-time associate Johnson seems to have been well enough satisfied with the *Drury-Lane Prologue.*

Of the great *Dictionary* I scarcely know what to say. Finally published in 1755, it comes just at the middle of Johnson's literary career, a quarter century after Husbands' *Miscellany* and a quarter century before the *Lives of the Poets.* I do not know that its typographic excellence has ever been singled out for praise, and yet the pages of text filled with definitions and illustrations serve the reader well. There seems to me something almost Johnsonian in the sturdy independent way the folio columns present themselves, doing their duty without ostentation; and Strahan's title page with its solid refusal to be clever seems (perhaps by familiarity) to be well fitted to the text it describes.

The next major landmark in Johnson's publishing career, the edition of Shakespeare in 1765, is perhaps disappointing typographically. I have a sentimental fondness for that edition, and yet I confess that it always seems a dull piece of printing. The title pages are flat, the type of Johnson's famous Preface is too widely spaced for the type page, the paper is too thin, and the crowded pages of text and notes seem unsuccessful. Perhaps the octavo format is more to blame than the type or layout: the lines run over very frequently, especially in the notes, to produce a scattered look, Johnson's irregular annotation runs over to another page often enough to confuse us when we read, and a long note is often found to be a mere quotation from Warburton that pushes Johnson's comment far away from the passage he is annotating. Possibly only the majestic quartos that Pope used could have fused Johnson's notes and Shakespeare's text into an attractive page. The *Journey to the Western Islands,* written and printed somewhat hurriedly in 1775, makes a better impression on the reader than does the Shakespeare, probably because the pages are less crowded. It is good sturdy work, satisfactory but not glamorous.

Johnson's last major work, the *Lives of the Poets,* is perhaps not a fair test because the publication was even more than usually a booksellers' venture. It would have been possible for Johnson to advise about format and typography on any other book, but the *Poets* had been planned specifically as a competitive reply to Bell's Edinburgh-printed collection, and Johnson was engaged only to write some "little prefaces," one to be prefixed to each poet. That Johnson's liking for his task led him to write major critical essays does not affect the presumption that the format was determined in advance. But if the format of the *Poets* shows nothing of Johnson's typographic tastes, the little volumes are not unpleasing in themselves: the small format, pot octavo, is unusual and seems somewhat wasteful, but the well-spaced type makes judicious use of the small page and the careful presswork does honor to the fine letter paper that was used. The volumes are attractive if not revolutionary, and Johnson had every right to be pleased when he saw his little prefaces in print. The separate reprint of the *Lives* in 1781, four volumes in medium octavo, was planned more for compact utility than beauty, and it adds nothing to our estimate of Johnson's typographic enthusiasm.

Now if such a survey of the typography of Johnson's books shows chiefly that he paid no attention whatever to the type but merely allowed the stylistic changes of the time to be reflected in his books, one might fairly ask what Johnson's significance is in the matter. The correct answer seems to me to be that Johnson's very imperviousness to typography makes his books a better guide to what was happening between 1730 and 1780. Despite his indifference, his own books illustrate perfectly the change in average commercial printing from the older style (heavy angular continental types, crowded titles, and steady use of italics) to the newer style (the rounder Caslon that is now denominated Old Style, titles with homogeneous type, and italics severely restricted), a change that came just at that time with no assistance from Johnson.

Besides the general change in printing style during his life, Johnson lived through an era of important experimentation. In 1757, after long experimenting with type design, ink, and presswork, and with hot-pressed paper, Baskerville published his edition of Virgil. Two hundred years later, when the various eighteenth-century Old Style type faces have tended to fuse in our consciousness, we may find it hard to comprehend what caused all the excitement. Although the slender and pointed Baskerville letters are very different from the rounded Caslon, perhaps only a book designer would even think of saying today that one type is better (or worse) than the other. But in 1757 feelings ran high; men complained that the narrow Baskerville letters hurt their eyes and that the black ink and shiny paper reflected the glare. Benjamin Franklin proved by a pleasant trick that such people were merely unhappy because of the change from familiar to strange, and that they could not in fact differentiate the two types. I was amused by a similar experience a few years ago when a friend who aspired to some modicum of typographical understanding complained that Horace Walpole was ill-advised to use that horrid Baskerville type, and I could scarcely convince him that Walpole's type was actually not a horrid Baskerville but a dependable Caslon; his dislike of Walpole was genuine enough, but his disapproval of Walpole's choice of types was merely uninformed prejudice.

Baskerville's new type began to influence all type design: Moore and Fry in Bristol and Wilson in Glasgow soon began to offer types that were modified from Caslon in the direction of Baskerville. By the end of the century even the Caslon firm was offering a new font that was as close to Baskerville as it was to the earlier Caslon.

Boswell records that Johnson disapproved of Robert and Andrew Foulis when he met them in Glasgow, but Johnson was enough of a book collector to ask Boswell two years later to send him two books printed by the Foulis brothers. It would be pleasant if we could say that Johnson had requested a copy of the Foulis edition of Gray's *Poems*. The Foulis books were not directly influenced by Baskerville, but they established their own tradition of well-designed book production and careful presswork, to become notable as "trade" publishers who were fine printers.

Perhaps the most important of all fine printers during Johnson's lifetime was Bodoni of Parma, whose handsome editions of the classics began to appear shortly before Johnson died. Had Johnson been able to make his projected Italian journey, I think he would have thought Bodoni worth meeting; but he was unable to go, and I do not know that he was ever aware of Bodoni's work.

Meanwhile, a different manifestation of printing enthusiasm, the private press, was appearing in 1757 at Strawberry Hill. Both Baskerville and the Foulis brothers were commercial printers, important ones if not always entirely prudent. But although Walpole's first venture, Gray's *Odes,* can be called commercial since the edition was printed for Dodsley, Walpole's press was always a private one, presided over by one man—and a boy—and not run for profit. We know that Johnson read Gray's *Odes,* very probably in the Strawberry Hill edition, but we can suspect that his disapproval of the poetry was great enough to blind his eyes to the merits of the printing. There was little enough in Walpole, as a man or as an author, to appeal to Johnson; the rather foppish young man who in 1745 sat in Parliament out of a sense of duty but who preferred to dabble in society verse or to play whist with titled ladies would have seemed a useless dilettante to Johnson, who had learned by years of literary drudgery for Cave that worth rises with painful slowness when weighted down by poverty. Walpole's most important literary friends, besides, were Gray and Mason, almost the only literary men of the middle of the century to remain entirely outside of Johnson's orbit. And then when Walpole established his press he elected to print as his first offering Gray's two obscure odes. One would like to see Johnson's copy of this first Strawberry Hill book, perhaps underscored heavily and angrily at the line, "Give ample room and verge enough," underscored with what dark mutterings as he read. All in all, it is little to be wondered at that Johnson should have failed to praise the typography. Later books printed by Walpole were not written by Gray, at any rate, but one would not expect Johnson to be attracted by Vertue's collections dealing with the lives of the old painters, or by the *Mémoires du Comte de Grammont*. One volume, the handsomest product of the Strawberry Hill Press, might have been expected in Johnson's library. This was the fine Lucan in quarto, with notes by Grotius and by Dr. Bentley. Such a book might well have seemed important to Johnson the classicist, whether or not he approved of Bentley as an editor of Milton. Two other editions of Lucan were in Johnson's library when he died, but not the Strawberry Hill edition. Perhaps it was too expensive, perhaps he had lost it; but I fear the simple truth was that he did not care about it.

An oddly attractive fact in bibliographical history is that Johnson's own publications, so unimpressive in format and typography, should now be the most eagerly collected of books from his century. Johnson was so regardless of printing style that he permitted and expected the printer to alter and regularize his own eccentric spelling, unlike Boswell who implored the printer to preserve his special orthography. Johnson was so regardless of the physical condition of his books that Garrick is said to have been unwilling to let him borrow any of his rare Shakespearean quartos. Perhaps it was not

inappropriate, therefore, that Johnson's own writings were published in the normal range of formats during his lifetime, without
ostentation or eccentric prettiness, as sturdy as his own notes on
Shakespeare or his "Life of Dryden," and that they shared in the
development of commercial printing during his lifetime, even if
they lacked the special graces of the private press or of the new
type designs. And today many a collector treasures the *Vanity of
Human Wishes* or *Rasselas* more highly than Gray's *Odes* or Baskerville's Virgil.

MUSIC IN JOHNSON'S LONDON
Bruce Simonds

IN the nineteenth century, by common consent, the English were considered unmusical. German musicians asserted that they were, and in the nineteenth century it was understood that German musicians were always right. Even today this opinion has not entirely disappeared, if the material of concert programs in America and on the continent of Europe is any criterion. Efforts of conductors and performers to interest the public in English music are met with some reserve (contrast our knowledge of the symphonies of Bax and Vaughan Williams with that of the symphonies of Shostakovich), and there are not a few who still subscribe to Schumann's pronouncement, "English composer, no composer."

The English themselves, throughout the nineteenth century, accepted the fact that they were essentially unmusical with some complacency. Were not their gods Händel and Mendelssohn—two German composers who had stirred them as no English composer had ever done? Everybody conceded that there had been no really great English composer since Henry Purcell. His life had been too short to produce a very impressive body of work; nevertheless he was England's greatest composer; William Byrd and the other illustrious Elizabethans were forgotten. The English bowed to the dictum that they would always be amateurs in music, pursuing it with an athletic ardor, singing in oratorios with zest, even producing catchy tunes in Savoy operas, but incapable of the professional thoroughness which would place them on a level with German or Italian musicians.

This attitude does not appear in Elizabethan times, when the English seized on Italian models with the confidence of being able to equal them, and succeeded; nor in the seventeenth century when both French and Italian ideas were swallowed and completely digested and turned into English flesh and blood by Purcell. In the eighteenth century however occurred a struggle between English and foreign musicians which had devastating results on English morale. It happened that the climax and ultimate decision in this struggle came while Samuel Johnson was alive.

The two chief antagonists in the contest were Thomas Arne and Händel, both of whom were living in London when Johnson arrived there in 1737. At that time it might have been difficult to select them from among all the musicians in London as being of special importance. The craze for Italian music had been fostered by two gifted and temperamental violinists, Geminiani and Veracini, and by the composers Bononcini and Porpora, both of whom had been Händel's active rivals in the field of opera. The city was full of Italian singers; the names of Farinelli, Senesino, Cuzzoni, and Faustina Bordoni come instantly to mind. Each singer had fanatical admirers; witness the lady who cried from her box "One God, one Farinelli!"—while the Cuzzoni and Bordoni factions hissed the rival *prima donna* when she appeared on the stage. But there were signs that the Italians could be dethroned; both the personally popular Bononcini and the thoroughly disliked Porpora (he spoke too familiarly to the Prince of Wales) had failed, confessed themselves vanquished, as Händel never did, and retired from the scene. Porpora had the satisfaction of taking Farinelli with him. Even Castrucci, the "enraged musician" of Hogarth's spirited print, had been obliged in 1737 to yield his post as leader of the opera orchestra to Festing, a "languid" amateurish player whose very name was enough to send Castrucci into a fit of jealous temper.

Of native Englishmen there were plenty. Old Dr. William Turner, who like Purcell himself had studied with John Blow, was now eighty-six, but his son-in-law John Robinson was organist of Westminster Abbey and attracting crowds of people with his brilliant playing. Poor Thomas Roseingrave, who had come into contact with Domenico Scarlatti at Venice and found himself hopelessly second-rate, was retiring at the age of forty-seven from St. George's, Hanover Square, on account of what he called his *crepation,* the "cracking" of his intellect, referred to succinctly by Mrs. Delany as his "mad fits," the result of his having been crossed in love. Henry Carey had just published two folio volumes of songs written and composed by himself, *The Musical Century, in 100*

English Ballads on various subjects and occasions . . . However, he was a tunemaker rather than an accomplished composer and when he wanted professional assistance in the writing of music for his opera, *The Dragon of Wantley,* he turned to a German expatriate, John Frederic Lampe. The result, produced in October of this same year, was most amusing, and the fact that Lampe set the words "after the Italian manner" suggests that at this time the extravagant style of the Italians seemed to be not inappropriate for parody; though perhaps not too much importance should be placed on this since Lampe's serious opera, *Amelia,* produced five years before, had also been "set in the Italian manner." Burney approved of *The Dragon of Wantley* as a worthy successor to *The Beggar's Opera* but far more effective and at the same time more innocent. Probably Johnson never saw the opera and perhaps he would not have been amused by it if he had; though doubtless he would have acquitted it of that "labefactation of all principles as may be injurious to morality" that he found in Gay's production.

A little younger than Carey were Edward Purcell, the son of Henry, and organist of St. Margaret's, Westminster; and Maurice Greene, organist at St. Paul's and composer to the Chapel Royal, for which he wrote anthems in a certain elegant, rather Italian fashion. Still younger were William Boyce, his pupil, and at the age of twenty-one a composer to the Chapel Royal and master of a sturdy English style; and that talented youth John Stanley, the blind organist of the Temple Church, and the favorite among the younger organists.

Händel had been in England since 1711. In the course of twenty-six years he had had one ephemeral success after another and more than one period of apparently utter failure. In June of this very year he retired bankrupt from Covent Garden and went to Aix-la-Chapelle; but there was a fascination for him in the London scene; and he returned in November to take up the battle again. In no sense was he fighting for German music or Italian music or anything save his own music. It was difficult; not that the English were hostile; his few good friends were English: Mrs. Delany, Mrs. Cibber, and Maurice Greene—until that gentleman, having been proved to have hoodwinked the Academy of Ancient Music by presenting Bononcini to that august body as the composer of a madrigal which had been written by Lotti, withdrew from the assemblies at the Crown and Anchor Tavern and "went to the devil" —at Temple Bar. Even Sir Hans Sloane was a friend until Händel inadvertently closed that buttered muffin in the pages of a precious book. It was rather that the English seemed indifferent to his qualities and suspicious of his extraordinary fecundity. His *concerti grossi* appeared in 1739; and of these works which seem today so majestic, so fertile in invention, Hawkins remarks that they are wanting in the elements of "harmony and fine modulation" and "in these respects . . . will stand no comparison with the concertos of Corelli, Geminiani and Martini"; apparently a typical eighteenth-century opinion, and amazingly blind to the fact that the influence of Corelli on Händel had been peculiarly strong ever since the two had met at the beginning of the century. Nor could Händel, like Geminiani or Veracini, appear at Hickford's Room and dazzle the public with his playing. He did play at Vauxhall on the organ so frequently and so beautifully that Tyers commissioned Roubillac to make his statue for the gardens; but everybody knew that Tyers was queer. Händel stood alone; other foreigners kept aloof, like old Dr. Pepusch who had helped Gay in selecting and harmonizing the tunes for *The Beggar's Opera* (in which incidentally a tune of Händel's was taken for unworthy purposes) and who had in 1737 retired to Charterhouse and to his study of Greek music. The unpopular Royal Family had no influence on London taste; so far as they were concerned, Händel was only a focal point for the eternal quarrels between the King and the Prince of Wales. There was no such thing as a foreign claque for Händel in London.

Nor was there a very strong circle of supporters around Arne. His sister Susanna, whom he had trained to sing in Lampe's *Amelia* in 1732, was highly esteemed for her plaintive contralto voice, her powers as a tragic actress (and famous for her unhappy marriage to Theophilus Cibber); but she sang Händel's music quite as much as his own. His wife Cecilia, one of the celebrated Young sisters, had a beautiful, high, birdlike voice and great devotion to her husband until he left her; and his son Michael was later to carry on both good and bad family traditions, and as it happened to add to his father's posthumous fame by writing a song which some have supposed to be the work of the elder Arne, "The Lass with the Delicate Air." But one cannot say that Thomas Arne had numerous enthusiastic followers.

During the first twenty years of Johnson's life in London the two composers were constant rivals for public favor, Händel concentrating on his own affairs and giving no attention to Arne, and Arne highly conscious and jealous of Händel. Fortune seemed to smile first on one, then on the other. In 1738 Händel's *Farimondo, Alessandro Severo,* and *Serse* were all failures (the beautiful Largo "Ombra mai fù" in the last opera was apparently not noticed), but society came to his benefit concert; while Arne's music for Dr. Dalton's adaptation of *Comus,* performed at Drury Lane with the new tenor John Beard, showed, as Burney wrote some years later, a new style of melody different from Purcell's or Händel's—"light, airy, original and pleasing." In 1739 Händel produced *Saul* and *Israel in Egypt,* but no one except Mrs. Delany cared for either, nor can we wonder when we learn that at this time Händel had no more than thirty singers in his chorus and the same number in his orchestra. Imagine the vast choruses of *Israel in Egypt* with only thirty singers! February, 1740, saw the performance of his charming *L'Allegro* which failed partly because the intense cold kept everyone at home; and *Imeneo* in October had only two performances. On the other hand, Arne not only reset Congreve's *Judgment of Paris* but really stirred the public with "Rule Britannia," which appeared in his masque of *Alfred;* and not content with that wrote new settings for the songs in *As You Like It,* songs enhanced as "Rule Britannia" had been by the singing of Thomas Lowe, the latest discovery in voices. Though as a singer Lowe was inferior to Beard and hardly able to read music, his voice was the finest tenor that Burney, writing in 1789, had ever heard.

The year 1741 was a period of eclipse for both composers, but Händel was writing *The Messiah* in his seclusion. He adjourned to Ireland and it chanced that the Arnes followed him a few months later. One wonders whether it was at the first performance of *The Messiah* in Dublin that Mrs. Cibber sang "He was despised" in such a manner as to make Dr. Delany rise from his seat exclaiming "Woman, for this day thy sins be forgiven thee!" When Händel produced *Samson* in London the next year there was a subtle change in the attitude of the English toward him, possibly the effect of Pope's praise in the fourth book of the *Dunciad;* and though *The Messiah* fell flat, that shrewd observer Walpole remarked that Händel seemed to be succeeding better in oratorio than in opera. Characteristically he seized the opportunity afforded by the battle of Dettingen; only twenty days after the battle itself he began the Dettingen Te Deum. It was sung at the Chapel Royal in November, and the King was greatly moved. *Semele,* written during the same summer without having been inspired by any event but merely containing such pearls as "O sleep, why dost thou leave me" and "Where'er you walk," was received quite coolly with "no disturbance at the Playhouse," as Mrs. Delany regretfully noted. She herself heard it again, being a devout Händelian; and it was about this time that she bent herself to the task of making a libretto from *Paradise Lost* for her favorite composer, but history does not tell us how he received it.

In August, 1744, Arne returned to London with eighteen-year-old Charles Burney whom he had met probably at Chester, and proposed to teach. The teaching seems to have degenerated into giving the pupil music to copy and using him as a violinist in the Drury Lane orchestra, of which Arne was the conductor. But Mrs. Cibber, who was in England again, was interested in the young man, and at her house in Scotland Yard he met Händel and other musicians; so even Arne's pupils were drawn into Händel's circle partly through Arne's indifference. It is impossible to be unconscious of Arne's defects of character. A glance at Bartolozzi's famous drawing shows the composer standing at the organ playing "Rule Britannia." In full dress, with sword at his side, the long-jawed face tilted appraisingly, the eyelids drooping and the eyebrows arched, he presents a picture of superciliousness and vanity; and one can imagine Johnson thundering "Sir, the man's a fop, a rake, and there's an end on't." Such an estimate of Arne would in fact have been quite close to the truth; as Fanny Burney remarked, he "took pride . . . in being publicly classed . . . as a man of pleasure." But he was still very active. At this time he became composer to Vauxhall, which needed new blood since (as Walpole declared) Ranelagh had totally beaten it, and nobody went anywhere save to Ranelagh. The orchestra at Vauxhall was enlarged and vocal music by Mrs. Arne, Lowe, and the elder Rheinhold, a German singer, was introduced. And in 1745 Arne had an inspiration. It was the time of the Jacobite uprising; he arranged a new patriotic song, "God save our noble King," using the music of an old minuet; this was sung on September 28 at Drury Lane by Mrs. Cibber, Beard, and Rheinhold with such success that Burney arranged it for Covent Garden and it was heard at both places every night till the end of the crisis. For the second time, then, Arne had furnished the English with a national anthem. It was the time of his greatest reputation, and coincided as his bright periods usually did with a period of eclipse on Händel's part. But Händel was also able, somewhat later, to take advantage of Prince Charlie's revolt. He came before the public with the *Occasional Oratorio* in February, 1746, followed it up with *Judas Maccabaeus* the next year and scored two successes which made his fame at last secure. Arne's new music for *The Tempest,* delicious in its bubbling gaiety, was yet no match for the German's depth, solidity, and tenderness. *Judas Maccabaeus* was revived in 1748 to crowded houses, as were *Samson,* the *Occasional Oratorio,* and *Herakles* in 1749. Händel's *Firework Music* was rehearsed at Vauxhall before twelve thousand people on March 21, with an ear-splitting orchestra of forty trumpets, twenty horns, sixteen oboes, sixteen bassoons, eight pairs of kettledrums, twelve side drums, flutes and fifes. Traffic over London Bridge (there was no Westminster Bridge till the next year) was held up over three hours. When the piece received its official performance six days later at the celebration of the Peace of Aix-la-Chapelle in Green Park, the building erected for the occasion was set on fire by the fireworks (one would like to think by the music) and burned down. The next year on May 1 *The Messiah* was revived and enjoyed a belated but emphatic and lasting triumph. This was the climax to the rivalry between Händel and Arne.

There are no references in Boswell to Händel's *Messiah*. Presumably Johnson did not attend. But four days later the performance of *Comus* for the benefit of Milton's granddaughter took place; for this Johnson wrote a prologue spoken by Garrick; and he must have heard Arne's music at that time though we know nothing of his reaction to it. It is not to be supposed that Arne realized that the turning point of his career had been reached. He may even have renewed his hope of triumphing over Händel, for the next year it was known that his great rival had been attacked with blindness. *Jephtha* was written with great difficulty; by January, 1753, after an unsuccessful operation, Händel was completely blind and quite dependent on his devoted pupil, amanuensis, and manager, John Christopher Smith. He still improvised at concerts and his works were given with increasing frequency; but in 1759 he passed from the scene. Now came Arne's opportunity, but he could not take advantage of it. He tried imitating Händel in his oratorio *Judith;* but the solos were full of trivial ornamentation. In *Artaxerxes,* which appeared in 1762, he succumbed even further to the florid, superficial Italian manner, and won a passing success. In *Thomas and Sally* he still showed command of a light, pleasing style; but more and more he turned to ballad operas and farcical comedies. With the exception of *The Fairy Prince,* produced in 1771, almost all his later work is disappointing. At his death in 1778 he had no disciples; and as Dibdin remarked, "Scarcely had we lost Arne when Irish jigs usurped the musical domain."

There seemed to be no English composer to capture the imagination of the public. Since the death of Händel, John Stanley and Händel's protégé John Christopher Smith had written operas, some of which enjoyed transient success, but much of their time was occupied in producing Händel's oratorios. From 1763 on the Noblemen's and Gentlemen's Catch Club offered prizes for glees, catches, and canons with praiseworthy persistence, and James Hook with equal persistence wrote over two thousand catches and songs. Michael Arne had one real success with *Cymon* in 1767 and then devoted himself to discovering the philosopher's stone, thereby, it was said, starving his second wife to death. William Boyce, who had developed a natural, simple style untainted by Italian exaggeration, had been deaf for years and died the year after Arne. The comic operas of Dibdin, Bickerstaffe, and Shield proved to be of temporary appeal. On the other hand there were enough German musicians in London to keep alive the English respect for foreign music. Karl Friedrich Abel, who made his first appearance there in the very year of Händel's death, was a highly versatile player and composer and became according to Burney the "umpire in all musical controversy"; he had been thoroughly trained at Leipzig by John Sebastian Bach. He was joined by John Christian Bach, whose music, unlike that of his father, adhered scrupulously to the taste of the time. And while English singers and performers were not lacking (one thinks of Arne's pupil Charlotte Brent, Anne Catley, who giggled her way through oratorios, and lovely, short-lived Elizabeth Linley) a single visit by the eight-year-old Mozart and his sister in 1764 was sufficient to show the English that such gifts had not appeared in their own children.

Even the purveyors of concerts were foreign. Hickford's Room near Golden Square was not used for music after 1779, though the room itself, an excellent one for music, was in existence up to 1939. Abel, Gallini, and Bach opened the Hanover Square Rooms in 1775, and concerts were held there into the nineteenth century. Mrs. Cornelys, certainly not an Englishwoman though no one knew exactly what she was (except Casanova perhaps), had started her famous morning musicales in Soho Square as early as 1764 and drew all the high society until 1772, when the cost of keeping three secretaries, thirty-two domestics, six horses, and a pack of hounds (let us hope not in Soho Square) proved too much for her. An exception to the foreign domination of the concert field may be found in the Concert of Antient Music established in 1776 by a committee of Englishmen, including the notorious Earl of Sandwich. The plan of these concerts, which banned all music written in the last twenty years, was conceived by a Yorkshireman, Joah Bates, the earl's private secretary, and he conducted them as well.

In 1783 Bates had the idea of holding a great Commemoration in honor of Händel, and his scheme was carried into execution the following year in Westminster Abbey. Boswell was anxious not to miss this event, and a little concerned when Johnson expressed a wish to go to Oxford that same week. He solved the situation by going to Oxford with Johnson on Thursday, June 3, and returning at once to London for the occasion on Saturday. At this celebration there were 275 singers and 250 in the orchestra, quite a contrast to the modest thirty in each which had been all Händel could muster when he produced *Israel in Egypt;* it led to an annual festival which in 1787 employed over eight hundred musicians. It is an interesting coincidence that the Commemoration came in the year of Johnson's death. He had lived to see the complete triumph of the German musician whose career had in some respects corresponded to his own and whose fame was destined to shine as brightly in the realm of music as Johnson's in literature.

Though Händel had been born in Saxony and remained German to the end in certain superficial characteristics such as speech, there are signs that he was willing to learn from the English. In this his career presents a curious parallel to that of Arne, who was quite willing to learn from the Italians. But while Arne in writing more and more Italianate music was following the taste of the time and losing his own individuality by doing so, Händel's assimilation of English elements is more subtle. It is not that his music sounds like Purcell's, certainly not like that of the great Elizabethans; only in a turn of phrase here and there does one get the impression that it has been influenced by the English scene. One of the most pronounced examples of this is the chorus "Or let the merry bells ring round" from *L'Allegro,* with its imitation of English change ringing; but the same subtle inflection is heard in the E major Variations, in "Where'er you walk," in "Lift up your heads, O ye gates," and in many of his final cadences with their scale-like progressions descending through the octave. The simplicity and directness of his choral writing is English. Far more sensitive as a musician than many have supposed, he could not remain so long in the English environment without being affected by it. Not without reason then did the English accept him as a favorite composer; but unfortunately perhaps they did not realize how English he had become. His music appealed to them, but they could not forget that he had been born in Germany and was ostensibly a German composer. The conviction originating at this period that English composers were no match for German composers remained with the English for over a hundred years.

INDEX

THE YALE PAPERBOUNDS

THE YALE WESTERN AMERICANA PAPERBOUNDS